MW01274152

Canadian Sociology

Edited by

Mahfooz A. Kanwar
Don Swenson

Mount Royal College

KENDALL/HUNT PUBLISHING COMPANY
4050 Westmark Drive   Dubuque, Iowa 52002

Copyright © 2000 by Mahfooz Kanwar and Don Swenson

ISBN 0-7575-0008-0

Kendall/Hunt Publishing Company has the exclusive rights to reproduce this work,
to prepare derivative works from this work, to publicly distribute this work,
to publicly perform this work and to publicly display this work.

All rights reserved. No part of this publication may be reproduced,
stored in a retrieval system, or transmitted, in any form or by any
means, electronic, mechanical, photocopying, recording, or otherwise,
without the prior written permission of Kendall/Hunt Publishing Company.

Printed in the United States of America
10 9 8 7 6 5 4 3 2

To

Our Children

Contents

Mahfooz Kanwar

Dr. Mahfooz Kanwar is a tenured faculty member in the Department of Behavioral Sciences, Mount Royal College (Calgary, Alberta, Canada). He holds a B.A. degree in Political Science, an M.A. degree in Sociology, another M.A. degree in Sociology/Criminology, and a Ph.D. degree in Criminology.

He has conducted research and published extensively in the sociological fields of marriage and the family, religion, crime and social problems. He has authored seven books, five monographs, and a large number of academic and non-academic articles.

Dr. Kanwar has served for three consecutive terms as the chairman of the Department of Behavioral Sciences that includes the disciplines of Sociology, Psychology, Anthropology, Archaeology and Education.

He has extensive teaching experience at various universities and colleges, including the University of Waterloo, Wilfred Laurier University, the University of Calgary, South Waterloo Memorial Hospital, Drumheller Federal Penitentiary, Military Police Platoon (Canadian Forces Base in Calgary), and Mount Royal College (all in Canada); Valencia Community College in Orlando (Florida); and he has guest lectured at the University of Karachi, the Quaid-e-Azam University, the University of Punjab, and the National Police Academy, Islamabad (all four in Pakistan). Over the years Dr. Kanwar has been nominated eight times for excellence in teaching and leadership. He has received three distinguished teaching awards.

Dr. Kanwar resides in Calgary and is actively involved in research in both Canada and Pakistan. He is also active in the community by participating in, and presiding over, the community and government appointed boards and committees. As well, he has responded to issues brought forth in the media, including newspapers, radio, and television.

Don Swenson

Dr. Don Swenson has been on the faculty of Mount Royal College since the fall of 1992. He teaches the sociology of families and the sociology of religion. From the University of Notre Dame, Indiana, he received his PhD degree, which was preceded by his Master's from the University of Calgary and a degree in theology from the University of Ottawa. He has taught at various universities in Saskatchewan, British Columbia, Alberta and Indiana.

His publications include topics on divorce, remarriage, marital quality, celibacy, and a theory of the linkage between religion and the family. His new book entitled *Society, Spirituality, and the Sacred: A Social Scientific Study of Religion*, is being published by Broadview Press and will be available in the summer of 1999. Lastly, he has been active in the National Council of Family Relations since 1987 and has served on the board of that association.

About the Book

Canada is officially recognized as a bilingual and multicultural society. In this multicultural society, there are four major segments of the population: the Aboriginal Canadians, the French Canadians, the English Canadians, and those of all other heritages. The first three groups of Canadians represent their cohesive cultural background respectively.

The fourth category of people represents a variety of cultural backgrounds. When compared with one another, they are drastically different. For instance, the East Indian-Canadians and the German-Canadians represent totally different cultural and ethnic backgrounds. They all share one thing in common: they are distinct from the three pioneer groups. Regardless of their different backgrounds, however, all four groups share the Canadian culture, and that is what the Canadian flag on the front cover symbolizes.

We have tried to make this a concise book of readings by including as much material as is deemed necessary for an introductory sociology course. We have, therefore, avoided some of the sociological jargon that normally appears in large textbooks which, in our experience, go unread by students and undiscussed by instructors.

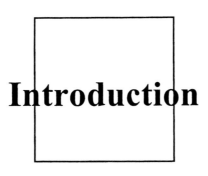

Introduction

Mahfooz Kanwar and Don Swenson

Sociology grew out of major changes in Western Europe during the late eighteenth century and throughout the nineteenth century. The reflections of Auguste Comte, Karl Marx, Herbert Spencer, Emile Durkheim, Georg Simmel, and Max Weber form what we know today as classical sociology. Each of them, in one way or another, constructed theories of modern societies in response to two major revolutions: the industrial in England and the French revolution (see Nisbet, 1966). The industrial revolution radicalized traditional economies while the French Revolution negated the *ancient régime* (the old political order of France).

Note that these sociologists responded to major social issues that were far reaching in their consequences. In this volume, we have undertaken to provide to the reader sociological reflections on important social issues that are important to many Canadians.

Until the 1960s, sociology in Canada was a kind of *branch plant* of its American counterpart. Since the late 1960s, sociology has grown from a marginal discipline to being part of the curriculum of nearly all universities and colleges. It has done so in the light of reflections upon current social issues in Canada that include such processes as the Quebec separatist movement, the growth of the Aboriginal Rights campaign, the codification of multiculturalism and bilingualism, and the feminist movement (Forcese and Richer, 1988).

We have constructed the text about five themes: the theoretical and methodological basis of sociology, issues in culture and socialization, social stratification, deviance and social control, and social institutions.

One way to look at the development of theory is to consider it to be a response to social issues. A second way is to look at it as creating a perspective to enable the sociologist to understand and to interpret modern societies. In pre and post World War II America, in a society that was industrializing rapidly, Talcott Parsons, considered to be a classical theorist by Alexander (1983), endeavored to construct a theory of society that was all comprehensive. It came to be known, against the desires of Parsons (1977), as structural functionalism. Its strength consisted in synthesizing a wide range of social issues and topics. Its weakness is that it could not provide an adequate interpretive framework for all the social issues and topics and it failed to take into account severe social inequalities, African American oppression, gender inequalities and the like.

Being cognizant of this, many mid-century Canadian sociologists utilized a political economy approach that was more kin to Karl Marx than to any of the other classical founders. This framework did and continues to provide an interpretive vehicle in understanding such current issues as health care problems, conflict between Francophone and Anglophone Canada, gender inequality, Native Rights versus other Canadians, regional disparity, American versus Canadian culture, and the Canadian economic system linked to the global system. Many Canadians are suffering today because of the inability of influencing the bourgeoisie that has increasingly becoming a *global bourgeoisie.*

One thing that is in a significant contrast to the United States is that many Canadians are recipients of a wide range of social programs such as state funded health care programs, unemployment insurance, student assistance policies, social assistance, regional disparity programs, and pension funds. These function as safety nets to many needy Canadians. In the recent turn of events, to pay down the debt, there is a real concern that these nets are being eroded by state policy. It is of great importance to the Canadian people that sociological research be conducted to address these issues.

A concern that the editors have in this text is to present an approach that is multidimensional. This means that a framework in sociology should take into account and present equal weight to social action and social structure or order. Alexander (1982) provides insights from which the diagram (Figure 1) was constructed to illustrate multidimensionality.

Figure 1. Social Action and Social Structure

The diagram attempts to capture that social life and institutions are understood both to be created by individuals (from the individualist end of the social structure) and are a result of social structure (the collectivist pole). The figure also intends to convey that social action is both rational and nonrational. Social phenomena, both in their social action and structural dimensions, consist both of rational and nonrational elements as well as being created by individuals and as a source of constraint (and enablement) to individuals.

Before each chapter, the editors have attempted to see how these two dimensions inform each of the issues that are being discussed. In this way, it is hoped that the student would be able to get a fuller appreciation of the topic reflected upon.

References

Alexander, J.
1982

Theoretical Logic in Sociology. Volume I: Positivism, Presuppositions, and Current Controversies. Berkeley, CA: University of California Press.

Alexander, J.
1983   *Theoretical Logic in Sociology. Volume Four: The Modern Reconstruction of Classical Thought:* Talcott Parsons. Berkeley: University of California Press.

Forcese, D. and S. Richer
1988   "Introduction: Social Issues and Canadian Society." In D. Forcese and S. Richer (Eds.). *Social Issues: Sociological Views of Canada.* Pp. 1-9. Scarborough, ON: Prentice-Hall.

Nisbet, R.
1966   *The Sociological Tradition.* New York: Basic Books.

Parsons, T.
1977   *Social Systems and the Evolution of Action Theory.* New York: The Free Press.

SECTION 1

Basic Issues in Sociology

Introduction

Mahfooz Kanwar and Don Swenson

This section continues the classical tradition in sociology in asking the question how the discipline addresses social issues important to Canadians today. In the first chapter, Don Swenson argues that in order to understand Canadian social issues, it is important to outline the basic concepts in sociology, its origins before and during the 19th century, and the current perspectives. He continues with a discussion of the sociological imagination and the birth of the discipline in Canada

In Chapter Two, Kanwar and Swenson outline how sociologists approach their subject matter as social scientists. They summerize important features of research through defining basic concepts, presenting the research process, ethical issues, and the difficulties of doing this kind of research.

Bruce Ravelli, in Chapter Three, argues that most Canadians consciously distinguish themselves from Americans in terms of their cultural and social values. Particularly, the Canadian policy of multiculturalism and bilingualism are examples of Canadian cultural and social diversity, that, according to Ravelli, promote living in harmony with diversity. Quebec separatism and regionalism operate differently to Canadians than Americans. The topic of Quebec separatism is still very much relevant. In spite of the Quebec election of late November of 1998 and the fact that more and more Francophones seem to be distancing themselves from Quebec sovereignty, separatism still is a very important social issues that sociology can shed some light on.

In Chapter Four, Paul Divers attempts to locate these cultural values in the context of socialization. He defines socialization as the process by which an individual acquires a sense of self, knowledge, skills, attitudes, motivations, and behaviors in order to participate in a given society such as Canada. He notes that although many Canadians adhere to national values and norms, the ethnic cultural characteristics in Canada, as subcultures, influence the process of socialization. This cultural diversity, however, may lead to a tension among different ethnic groups. Nevertheless, cultural pluralism itself, Divers notes, is a gift to Canadian society.

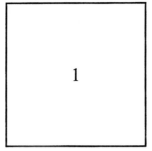

The Theoretical Basis to Sociology: An Introduction

Don Swenson

Overview

We commence our introduction to sociology by outlining the theoretical basis to the discipline. The goal here is to introduce the neophyte of sociology to its central concepts, its social and intellectual tradition, its classical founders and the current perspectives. We shall conclude with a discussion of what is known as the sociological imagination and the birth of the discipline in Canada. The goal of this chapter is to acquaint the student with the focus as well as with the breadth of sociology.

Key Concepts

Sociologists vary considerably in how they study the social world. They agree, however, on two central concepts that capture the heart of the discipline: *social action* and *social structure*. For an understanding of these concepts, we look to a classical founder, Weber (1978) and a current theorist, Alexander (1982) for a definition of social action. For an interpretation of social structure, we look to three other classical founders, Auguste Comte (in Coser, 1977), Karl Marx (1977) and Emile Durkheim (1938) as well as another current sociologist, Anthony Giddens (1984).

Weber (1978:4) presents a definition of social action as: "*action* insofar as the acting individual attaches a subjective meaning to his behaviour; be it overt or covert, omission or acquiescence. Action is *social* insofar as its subjective meaning takes account of the behaviour of others and is thereby oriented in its course." Basic to this definition is freedom: an assumption that humans are substantially free in their personal lives and in their relationships with others and larger social arrangements (social institutions, social organizations and whole societies). Weber adds the insight that because humans are considered to be inherently rational (although they do not act so all the time!) and free when people

3

interact with one another, they do not do so passively. There is an interpretive process occurring within the consciousness of each social actor that endeavours to interpret what the other person is thinking. It is on this basis of interpretation that people respond and act accordingly.

Alexander (1982a) argues that the vital presence of the human actor is fundamental to the understanding of social phenomena. In addition, he accents the importance of the human actor attaching subjective meaning in his or her relationships with others.

From these two sources, we can construct the following definition: "Social action is human action that assumes that persons are free agents who, in their relationships with others, attach a subjective meaning to their behaviour and take into account the behaviour of others."

The second central concept of sociology is social structure. Comte (in Coser, 1977) focussed his attention on the patterns of social action and used the concept to explain how social order was possible in human societies.

Marx (1977) follows with a further insight to this concept. He frames his interpretation of the concept in the development of capitalism in the western world, particularly in England. According to him, the working person for a wage (in contrast to previous workers who were more likely to share in the fruit of their labour) is an effect of the emergence of industrial capitalism commencing with significant changes in England about 1775 (we will detail this in the section on the emergence of the discipline). The behaviour of this person (joined together by many others in the same situation) was significantly restricted by the behaviours of the capitalists who controlled their actions and even exploited them. The relationships between the workers and the capitalists are structured at the expense of the workers and the benefit of the capitalists.

Durkheim (1947) expands the meaning of the concept beyond working relationships between people. His insights inform us that social structure is endemic to all social relationships. However, he does not use this term but calls it "social morphology" or "morphology." Turner, Beechley, and Powers (1995) describe it as the "nature," "arrangement," and "interrelations" among parts. These parts could be individuals or collective units like groups or organizations. They go on to explain that nature refers to the kinds of social arrangements and their functions like economic, political, or familial. Arrangement captures the distribution of parts in relationship to each other and interrelations focus on the modes of communication, motion, and mutual obligations among parts. Turner, Beechley, and Powers (1995) add that Durkheim devoted a major part of his academic career to argue how social morphology (really social structure) impacted culture, individual consciousness, and social action.

A further insight offered by Giddens (1984) is that not only does social structure inhibit the social action of individuals but also enables it. He considers social structure to be similar to a channel, a framework of social action that both inhibits or restricts and facilitates it.

From these impressions, a definition of social structure is: "a pattern or framework of social action that is general throughout a whole society that both functions as an external constraint, sometimes from powerful social groups, and as a facilitator."

4

The Development of the Discipline

The roots of sociology are in the 19th century in Europe. To understand the wider picture, however, it is important to look briefly at the development of Western civilization and the concomitant history of ideas that correspond to this social development. This is done by looking at the commonly accepted division of the western history into three eras, Classical, Medieval and Modern and to add a forth era that reflects our current world or Post-Modern.

Western civilization commences (with Mesopotamian and Egyptian roots) in the emergence of Greece (c. 500 B.C.) and Rome (c. 200 B.C.). Historians agree that this period continued to the collapse of the Western Roman Empire about 400 A.D. (the Eastern one continued through the 9th century). It is from the Greeks and the Romans that reason was attached not only to social relationships but to the interpretation of what it meant to be human and what the universe stood for. Historians of intellectual history call this the Classical Paradigm.[1] The focus was rational: by using empirical observation and logical deduction, the intellectuals of this time sought to understand society, nature, the cosmos, and the human person with the light of reason.

Boorstin (1998) notes that during the sixth century B.C., there occurred what he calls the "Ionian Enlightenment" that questioned the religious, mythological view of the Greeks. It was Herodotus (c. 484–420 B.C.) who was interested in human societies, past and present and who became known as the "Father of History." Like sociology, history is the human investigation wherein the subject and the audience are one. His method was scientific—by inquiry. He asked people, noted their ways, and examined their monuments and thus could learn their present and their past. After Herodotus, Thucydides (c. 460–400 B.C.) established the first "political science" and consigns supernatural causes to political processes and events to death and constructs a method of studying ancient societies. He offers a way to interpret social, political and economic events in the light of lessons of the past and predicts future events if present conditions are met.

In the further study of society, Nisbet (1982) informs us that Plato (427 to 347 B.C.), in his Republic, presented state based on ideal political ideals. Plato argued that political power—the political bond—is the most distinctive and most influential types of all kinds of societies. This perspective, Nisbet notes, leads to a totalitarianism that does not allow for differences. In contrast, Aristotle (384 to 322 B.C.), using study, analysis, and observation of relevant facts about society, argues that the best outcomes for people is to have a pluralist-decentralized political, social community. We owe to these classical social philosophers the importance of ideals in society as well as the task to study and observe the social order to try to understand its inner workings.

A shift occurs with the emergence of Christianity as the dominant interpretive vehicle. With the collapse of the Western Roman Empire (400 A.D.), there was created a vacuum of leadership. In time, this was taken over by the Christian church which eventually became the central institution of the Medieval period and was instrumental in the emergence of Christendom. A common characterization of the relationship between religion and society was the joining of the church and secular society or a wedding of crown and altar. The central social issue was one of political power: who has social authority, the church or the secular state? When the church held political authority over the nobles and princes, we have what may be called the "hierocratic" political paradigm. If, however, the secular prince (emperor, king, queen or prince) held the central power, we had what Weber (1978) called Caesaropapism. At several times in the Medieval period, the secular authority (particularly by Constantine [272 to 337 A.D.]) had greater social authority than did the church leaders.

The central intellectual struggle was between faith and reason. The model which could be termed the Medieval-Intellectual paradigm posited a position that faith was greater than reason and that humans were not the centre of the earth or the universe but a benevolent deity to whom people owed honour and allegiance in matters of reason and morality.

The third period in Western history is the modern one. It begins with the Protestant Reformation of the 16th century and continues through until about the middle of this century. The major social events and intellectual changes of this era formed the basis for sociology as a discipline. It is during this period that we have what may be called the modern paradigm or the positivist paradigm wherein reason combined with empirical observation of the natural and social world become central.

Five major historical events and one intellectual process account for this shift that became, upon reflection, the interpretive framework for the founders of sociology. The five historical events are: the Protestant Reformation, the Age of Discovery and colonization of non-Western societies, the English Great Rebellion of 1642 to 1651, the French Revolution of 1789, and the Industrial Revolution beginning in England about 1775. The shift in the history of ideas occurs with what is known as the Enlightenment from about 1650 to 1800.

The Protestant Reformation

The Reformation is critical in the development of the West. Even though it did not shift the focus from faith to reason, it did introduce a new way of looking at the person and the realignment of Europe according to religious-political regions. Weber (1958) is well known in his analysis of the Protestant ethic and the development of capitalism. He argues that with the coming of Protestantism (through Martin Luther [1483–1546 A.D.] and John Calvin [1509–1564 A.D.]), the Christian stands alone before his or her God without the mediation of community, symbol or sacrament. Thus, the believer becomes more self-reliant in his religion and, in turn, more self-reliant in her or his work. The Protestant ethic was one of religious individualism, frugality, hard work and serious moral effort to know if he or she was one of the chosen ones. A sign of salvation, particularly for the Calvinists, was that of worldly success: if one gained from such hard work, it was a sign that one is saved for eternal glory. The spirit of capitalism emerges from Weber's analysis of Benjamin Franklin who argued that hard work, saving, efficient use of time, and rational thinking was the way one could succeed financially. Weber used the term *elective affinity* to describe the unity of these two ways of thinking and acting to account for the growth of capitalism in the Protestant European and American societies.

As Weber linked the emergence of capitalism to Protestantism, Boorstin (1998) links the genesis of democracy to the Calvinistic Reformation. Calvin introduced democracy into ecclesial government by noting that the only head of the Church was Jesus Christ and that the ministry belongs to every church member. All who were to hold office in the congregation and the presbytery (the regional association of congregations) were to be elected by all members. The church was governed not by a hierarchy (as priests, bishops or popes in Roman Catholicism) but by persons.

The Age of Discovery and Colonization

About the same time as the Protestant Reformation, Europeans began to explore and to colonize the world. This eventually lead to the control of hundreds of societies in the Near and Far East, Africa, the Oceanic islands and North and South America. The economic effect of this was phenomenal. Wealth poured into Europe in the form of precious metals and huge profits made from agricultural products and manufactured goods produced in Europe. Marx (1977) considers this to be the reason for the emergence of a new class in Europe: the merchant class. Many of them made huge profits on the purchasing and selling of trade items. It was this class that Marx further understood to be the predecessors of the capitalists of the late 18th century and 19th century.

The Enlightenment

According to the Canadian sociologist, Zeitlin (1990), the Enlightenment takes centre place in the emergence of sociology. It was part of what is know as a paradigm shift from faith and reason of the Medieval era to reason based on human experience. It includes such elements as the self-sufficiency of human experience, human freedom, social equality, the ability of humans to control their own destiny and the imperative to build a human society built on natural science, reason, democracy and the separation of the state from religion. This was a great impetus to the creation and growth of sociology as it gave it its empirical and rational basis. Zeitlin writes:

> In contrast to the Medieval era, the men of the Enlightenment regarded all aspects of human life and works as subject to critical examination—the various sciences, religious beliefs, metaphysics, aesthetics, education, and so on. Self-examination, a scrutiny of their own actions and their own society, was a essential function of thought. By gaining an understanding of the main forces and tendencies of their epoch, human beings could determine their direction and control their consequences. Through reason and science, humanity could attain ever greater degrees of freedom, an idea permeating the thinking of that era, would serve to further humanity's general progress (1990:2).

The English Great Rebellion

Another major historical series of events was the English Great Rebellion of 1642–1651. The English social historian Stone (1972) informs us that a combination of changes in ideals, shifts in who controlled political power, and spontaneous events resulted in the transference of English political authority from a monarchial system to a parliamentary one that was to shape English society in fundamental ways. The series of events during this period resulted in what the American social historian Tilly (1981) terms *State Building* that has become a hallmark of the modern world that later sociologists would reflect on.

The French Revolution

A more radical political change occurred in France in 1789 when there was a permanent eradication of the monarchial system and the genesis of a more democratic political system. Some of the major changes included: the secularization of French society which removed social and political authority from the church to the secular leaders; the temporary expansion of divorce legislation from 1790 to 1803; the replacement of the regal nobility by the revolutionary leaders; the granting of the franchise to more and more French citizens; and the decline of the power of local community political institutions and the incline of the national state. Again, later sociologists reflected on these series of events as another example of State Building and the emergence of modernity.

The Industrial Revolution

Besides the French Revolution, Robert Nisbet (1966) considers the Industrial Revolution of Great Britain to be the second most critical event that permanently changed the economy of the Occidental world and, eventually, most of the globe. According to the historian Toynbee (1956), economic processes happening for many years culminated in major economic changes in the latter part of the 18th century and the first part of the 19th. As we saw above, with the Age of Discovery and Colonization, a new class of people emerged: the merchant class.

After the Great Rebellion, these persons achieved more and more political power and influence. They were able to convince the British Parliament during the 18th century to privatize common land (publicly owned) in the rural regions of England. For many years before that, most of the English in the rural areas made their living on small land holdings and cottage industries managed by women. In addition to these small private holding owned by who were known as the "yeomen," these small land owners used common lands that could be publicly used for cattle grazing and cropping. With the privatization of these lands, the wealthy merchants purchased these lands and transferred them into sheep grazing holdings for wool production.

Concomitantly, technical advances (like the invention of the steam engine and the Spinning Jenny used to manufacture bolts of cloth from cotton and wool) and the mining of coal for energy made it possible for the creation of the factory system in urban areas like Preston and Lancaster. Many yeomen and their families began to migrate to these urban areas to become the English working class. Thus, according to Marx (1977), a new social-class relationship was created: the capitalists and the workers or the bourgeoisie and the proletariat.

In addition to these changes, ideological changes were occurring as well. The Scottish economist, Adam Smith (1952), published his famous book the Wealth of Nations in 1790 that became the handbook of capitalism. Thus, a combination of agricultural, technological, economic, and ideological changes occurred to result in what came to be known as the Industrial Revolution. The changes that occurred during this period were sources for further reflections by the classical sociologists on the coming of the modern world.

The Post-Industrial Revolution

As the classical foundation of sociology was laid because of these major historical and ideological processes, so also are current sociological reflections based upon what has come to be known as the post-industrial society of the West from the end of the Second World War to the present time. A combination of economic, technological, political, and ideological processes have occurred to initiate these changes.

Economically, more and more workers are being employed in service-information industries than in industrial ones. By industrial we mean the goods manufacturing sector of an economy. By service and information, we mean all those persons working in retail, sales, human services, health care, education, and finances. In Canada (1996), 73% of workers are employed in these kind of occupations. To work here, more and more education is required which accounts for the expansion of the many post-secondary educational institutions. Another major economic change is the decline of the national economic borders. Sociologists and others call this the globalization of the economy which means that raw materials, goods and services are both purchased and sold on a world market rather than a national one.[2]

Technologically, the micro-computer has revolutionized the way we now do business, deliver human services, and educate the population. A more recent update is the Internet system which has the potential of linking millions of computer users (both at the home and in the education-work place) to information useful for a wide variety of purposes.

A combination of political and ideological changes have occurred in the former Soviet Union and Eastern Europe. Left-wing Communism is in decline except for a few strongholds in China. The "buzz-words" in many of these countries are capitalism and democracy. As yet, visible positive effects of these changes have not been witnessed.

In sociology, these changes have produced what we call paradigm shifts. Four shifts have occurred: post-positivism, feminism, post-secularism, and the inclusion of the marginalised. Post-positivist thinking in sociology refers to an alternative to using the empirical-rational method of investigation of the social world by accenting the experience of the subjects of investigation more and more. This is what the philosopher of science, Radnitzky (1973), refers to as the hermeneutic school. The argument here is that human social experience cannot be captured well using questionnaires and surveys that lend themselves to statistical analysis. Using a case study approach and personal interviews, the life experience of the people studied can be much more rooted in their own stories.

Feminism, or "Honouring the Feminine," is a major paradigm shift. The Canadian sociologist, Dorothy Smith (1990), argues for a "standpoint theory." She means that sociology needs to recognize that women have a unique experience in contrast to men and that their voice should be heard from their own standpoint. In essence, this approach in sociology is to both make relevant the unique experience of women in society as well as to critique male power which dominates much of the familial, economic, educational, and political life of people.

A third paradigm shift that has not received much reflection by current sociological thinking is the re-emergence of the experience of the sacred. An assumption of the modern world is that as science and technology grew, the belief systems of people would decline.

This has not occurred even though there are signs of increased secularization in educational and political systems in the Western world.

A fourth paradigm shift for sociologists comes from a sister discipline, anthropology. These researchers have long been doing research on marginalised peoples both in Western and non-Western societies. One might call this approach the "Post Caucasian" one which includes the experience of vast numbers of people who are not Caucasian. One may use the term "Pedagogy of the Oppressed" that reflects how we need to honour the social experience of those who have been oppressed by political, economic and religious institutions.

We thus conclude our discussion on the background to sociology or the social world that led to its emergence. We now will give a brief introduction to the classical founders of the discipline, Auguste Comte, Karl Marx, Emile Durkheim and Max Weber.[3] The sources for this investigation are Lewis Coser (1977) and Anthony Giddens (1971).

The Classical Foundation

August Comte

The French philosopher turned sociologist, August Comte (1798–1857), was the first of the classical founders to reflect on 18th and 19th century historical and social events in the Western World. The impetus to his work was what he perceived to be the major social problems that occurred in the wake of the industrial and French revolutions. He thought that if one applied the method of the natural sciences (observation, experimentation, comparison, and historical research) to the social world, one would be able to discover not only the causes to the social problems but also the solutions.

To him we owe the term sociology which means the study (the Greek *logos*) of the social (the Latin *socio*). In addition, he gave to us as an inheritance in the discipline that the true unit of investigation is not the individual but the social or, at least, the dyad. He believed that the individual person was too much subject to individualism and egoism and that these propensities needed to be curbed by social processes in social groups. For social order to be possible, there needs to be some mechanisms that bind people together: language, religion (for him, this was a secular religion), and occupational groups.

Finally, we also owe to Comte a vision of society that is like a living organism: the division of several parts that form a system of interrelated parts that function for the whole. This came to be known later as structural functionalism.

Karl Marx

Although Karl Marx (1818–1883) is known as a philosopher, an historian and a revolutionary, he is best known as a sociologist who, like Comte, and as we shall see with Durkheim, believed that the basic unit of study is not the individual but the social group. For Comte, the primary social group was the family but for Marx, it was the working social group. It is from work that humans find not only subsistence but also the potential to create ideas and to find meaning to life. The relations of production (relations that people establish with each other when they utilize existing raw materials) constitute the real foundation upon which the whole society, including culture, is erected. Marx, together with Engels (1947:47) writes: "It is not the consciousness of men that determines their being, but, on the contrary, their social being that determines their consciousness."

His focus of investigation was on the modern world of capitalism, particularly in England, where he lived out his last days studying in the London Museum. He argues that the relationships between people are shaped by their relative positions in regard to the means of production and their differential access to the scarce resources and scarce power. Human life is struggle—struggle to access these resources and power. In pre-capitalist times, this access was shared more by all members of a society. In capitalism, these resources and power have become concentrated into the hands of a few who were known as the bourgeoisie and exploited those, the proletarians, who had less access. The latter experienced alienation and suffered from this alienation.

It was difficult for these proletarians. This class was something they were born into and they had little control over their lives. What was needed was a change. Marx's view of humanity was not a passive view. He believed that humans are essentially creative beings whose "natural" propensities are denied by the restrictive character of capitalism. Even though he knew that capitalism was an economic structure of control, it is still the human agent who is the focus of change and he believed that humans make their own history. It is here where we meet Marx the revolutionary. He called, with Engels (1932), to have the proletarians unite in one major revolution against the bourgeoisie and take control of the means of production from them. Thereafter, all citizens and workers would, together, own the means of production and there would be equality and justice for all.

According to the sociological theorist, Jeffrey Alexander (1982b) Marx did not leave to students of society a multidimensional vision of social life. In his first volume of this series, Alexander (1982a:122–126) argues for the importance of fundamental, presuppositional statements that undergird social life and the theories that interpret that social life. Two scientific problems seem to be at the heart of the sociological enterprise: the problem of social action and the problem of social order. The problem of social action is if it is rational (calculating the best means to achieve an end) or is it normative (based on norms or ethics)? On the other hand, is social order produced by individuals or is it constructed by the collective such as social groups, institutions, or whole societies? (Figure 1:1 on the next page provides us with a visual image).

Alexander makes the point that an objective and multidimensional approach to sociological theory is that it needs to include dimensions both of social action and collective order. In addition, both types of social action are to be included: rational or instrumental social action (action motivated by reason) and normative (action inspired by values, norms and morals). On the other hand, the collective order is not established by individuals only or the collective but by both. This is what multi-dimensionality is all about. If any theory accents any one of these alternatives (or only two or three), then it is not multidimensional. If it includes all of these four dimensions, then it is multidimensional.

From this perspective, Marx's sociology is not multidimensional. In his work on Marx and Durkheim, Alexander (1982b) notes that Marx tends to exclusively focus on instrumental social action to the detriment of normative social action. In addition, he concentrates on the plight of the proletariat as being at the mercy of the bourgeoisie who have been those

11

Figure 1.1 Social Action and Social Structure

SOCIAL ORDER
COLLECTIVE

S O C I A L   A C T I O N

R A T I O N A L

N O N R A T I O N A L

INDIVIDUALIST

in power to create the collective order from their privileged position and the proletariat have no power at all. This, Alexander considers, occurs in Marx's later writings, for in his earlier writings, Marx utilized active social action even though he does not ever consider the importance of culture and independent normative action and consistently gives material sources precedence.

Marx's views are central to sociology. Particularly in Canada, we owe to Marx the seeds of what is known as the political economic approach to the study of the modern world that focuses on the economic system, the work environment and the political mechanisms of social control.

Emile Durkheim

Although we do not have any indication that Emile Durkheim (1858–1917) read Marx, we do know that he read Comte. With Comte and Marx, he considers that the basic unit of society is not the individual person but the social group. In fact, Durkheim spent much of his time arguing for this position against a reductionism that took the position that what really matters in social life is individual consciousness. Durkheim is also remembered in the discipline to have become the first professional sociologist at Sorbonne University in Paris.

He believed that the key social problem that the modern age faced was to reconcile individual freedom, which sprung from the dissolution of traditional society, with the maintenance of moral control upon which the very existence of society depended. He applauds this new freedom and does not look with nostalgia to the past. However, this new freedom can easily lead to what he calls *egoistical individualism*. There needs to be some sort of external control that curbs this kind of egoism. This control is what he refers to as the social fact which has coercive power that imposes itself on the individual independent of personal will. In this way, the individual person becomes integrated into society and regulated by society. If this does not happen, an individual may experience what he calls *anomie* which is a social state of normlessness wherein the individual is cast on a sea of humanity with no moorings or direction.

Durkheim is a functionalist. The goal of the modern society is social order that is achieved by a delicate balance of individual freedom and control through mechanisms of cohesion, solidarity, integration, the proper use of authority (that was just) and ritual. Primarily, by ritual he means for it is in religion that is found the par excellence source against egotistical individualism.

These functions are fulfilled not through nebulous forces in society but through social institutions which are sets of beliefs and practices that have become normative and that were focussed on a recurrent and continuing social concern. The central institutions to achieve this are work occupations and the state. He is the first to give us a generic definition of sociology and to paraphrase, sociology is the science of institutions, of their genesis and of their functioning (Durkheim, 1938).

A final major contribution Durkheim made to the discipline was to take Comte's desire to make sociology a science. In his work *The Rules of Sociological Methods*, he said that one needs to consider social facts in the same way as one would consider natural facts and to observe them, describe them, to classify them and, finally, to explain them. He was the first to do an empirical study in the field when he analysed census data to test a theory of suicide. His key theory and finding was that suicide is rooted not so much in individual sources but in social factors (Durkheim, 1951).

Alexander (1982b) believes that Durkheim focussed only on some dimensions of social life and leaving others out. Durkheim reverses Marx and considers that normative social action is the only viable kind of social action. For Durkheim, it is culture that is all important and economic conditions do not matter at all. In addition, even though individuals are free (as acknowledged by Turner, Beechley, and Powers, 1995), it is the collective that orders human life. Thus, like Marx, Durkheim fails in providing a theory that is fully multidimensional.

Max Weber

The last classical founder of the discipline that we investigate here is the German, Max Weber (1864–1920). While Comte, Durkheim and Marx considered that the unit of study of sociology was the social group, Weber argued that the unit of study was the social actor.[4] In fact, for him, sociology is a comprehensive science of social action. In addition, unlike these co-founders who all accented social structure, his work focused on social action (see the section, above, on basic concepts).

Another important feature distinguishes Weber from his predecessors. Comte, Marx, and Durkheim all agreed that social phenomena were similar to natural phenomena and that they could be observed, analysed and explained just as were natural events. Weber disagrees. He believed that the human agent was unique and that because of his or her consciousness, one needs to *enter into* the mind of the social actor to try to understand (*versthen*) what the actor is thinking. He, like Durkheim, offers us a definition of sociology: "...that science which concerns itself with the interpretive understanding (read *versthen*) of social action and thereby with a causal explanation of its course and consequences" (Weber, 1978:4).

Even though his focus was on the individual social actor, he did not spend time in investigating the micro nature of society but was much more concerned with the larger picture. Coser (1977:218), quoting Mannheim (1951:52), notes: "Max Weber's whole work is in the last analysis directed toward the question: 'Which social factors have brought about the rationalization of the Western civilization?'" His work was voluminous and comprehensive. He studied such topics and subjects as the city, the Roman Empire, law, art, the state and major religions like Catholicism, Protestantism, Judaism, and Islam in the West and Hinduism, Buddhism and Taoism in the East. The overall attempt of this investigation was to try to understand why capitalism and the modern state occurred in Western Europe and not in other parts of the world.

His work was more comprehensive than that of Marx in that he looked for factors besides economic to account for the growth of Western modernity: religion, politics, technology, and ideologies. Even though his focus was on the social actor, he did acknowledge the importance of social structures especially when he investigated social class, statuses, bureaucracy and religion. In fact, he considered that the single most important problem of modernity was not social disorder (Comte), alienation (Marx), or anomie (Durkheim) but the imprisonment of the individual in social structures so powerful (as reflected in political and economic bureaucracies) that they would lead the social actor to depression and disillusionment. In this way, Weber is more like a post-modern sociologist than a modernist thinker. His predecessors were all optimistic about the ability of science to solve the social problems of modernity, but Weber put little hope in the sciences. He, in fact, looks to the future with little hope. He writes:

> No one knows who will live in this cage (bureaucracy) in the future, or whether at the end of this tremendous development entirely new prophets will arise, or there will be a great rebirth of old ideas and ideals, or, if neither, mechanized, petrification, embellished with a sort of convulsive self-importance. For of the last stage of this cultural development, it might well be truly said: "Specialists without spirit, sensualists without heart; this nullity imagines that it has attained a level of civilization never before achieved" (1958:182).

Alexander (1982c) credits Weber with recognizing the unidimensional thinking of both Marx and Durkheim. He tried to steer a path between idealist thinking (from Durkheim) and materialist (Marx). Weber begins his sociology with an emphasis on social action that is multidimensional (action is both rational and normative as well as affective and traditional). Indeed, in his early writings, he also acknowledges that the collective order is both constructed by individuals as well as being present and made by collective institutions. This is especially evident in his work on the Protestant Ethic. In this work, he includes all the dimensions of social action as well as the collective order. It is in Weber's later work, as noted by Alexander (1982c), that he shifts to unidimensionality. In his mature studies, as indicated by the above quote from *The Protestant Ethic and the Spirit of Capitalism,* Weber loses heart in the normative part of social action and argues that in the modern world, only rational social action is operative. In addition, the collective order is only established by bureaucracies, and individual social action has lost its potency to change human institutions.

Summary

From our outline of the central concepts of sociology and a look at the classical founders, we are now in a position to compose a definition of sociology. In a word, "sociology is the science of the social group that ranges from a dyad of two persons to whole societies and accents understanding social action, social structure and the collective order."

The Current Main Perspectives

With some variation, most sociologists consider four main perspectives to be the central ones in interpreting the modern world: structural functionalism, symbolic interactionism, conflict theory or the political economic perspective, and feminism.[5] As Figures 1.2 and 1.3 illustrate, all are linked to the classical founders: structural functionalism to Comte, Durkheim and Weber, conflict theory and feminism to Marx, and symbolic interactionism to Weber. A new perspective which is not usually profiled in introductory text is neo-functionalism. I shall address this when we survey the main four. We begin with outlining structural functionalism.

Figure 1.2. Classical Founders

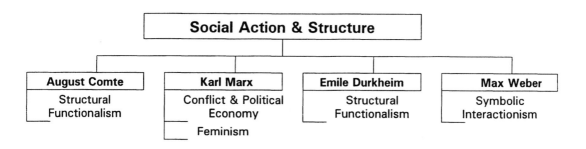

15

Figure 1.3. Key Concepts and Perspectives

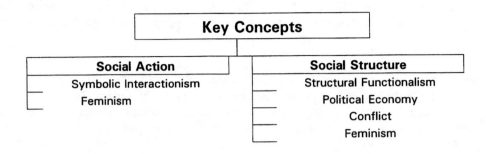

Structural Functionalism

Relying on the Enlightenment philosopher, Thomas Hobbes (1952), Comte and Durkheim laid the foundation of this perspective. Using a biological analogy, the modern society is like a living organism that is a system of structures (like the respiratory, digestive, reproduction structures) which all have functions to fulfill. Each of these structures have a specific function and working together in unison, function for the good of the whole. Biologists and structural functionalists would all say that the "whole is greater than the sum of its parts."

In sociology, the various structures of a society have a unique function to perform and together, as a system, function to supply social order to all members of that particular society. For example, the political structure is present to provide a just social system for all members, or the family is to provide for the socialization needs of societal members. In a vital, interconnecting linkage with all other structures, order is achieved and individuals, in connection to others, can live relatively peaceful lives.

This perspective was augmented by several American sociologists who researched and worked in the first to middle part of the 20th century: Talcott Parsons (1937), Robert Merton (1949), Kingsley Davis (1949). To outline this perspective and the subsequent ones, I am again, relying on Coser (1977).

Structural functionalism rests on an understanding of functional analysis which refers to the interpretation of the interrelationships between social phenomena and the effects of given items for the larger structures in which they are embedded. Functions are seen as effects that make for the adaptation of given structures and dysfunctions that lessen or eliminate adaptation. Parsons' (1937) contribution is his understanding that human actors have a potential to make choices of courses of action (thus the view is voluntaristic) but these choices are constrained by biological and social environmental conditions. It was his hope to provide a comprehensive and complete picture of the modern society that would compare to the attempts made by Newton in physics. Alexander (1983) adds that it is only

Parsons who understood the problems and dilemmas of classical thought and attempted to synthesize their work, adjust their insights to mid-century modern societies, and provide a multidimensional approach to sociological theory. All the other current perspectives (symbolic interactionism, conflict, and feminism) lacked this multidimensionality.

Alexander (1983) considers Parsons' attempt to be bold and courageous. His work sparked so much interest that all the alternative perspectives emerged as a response to and a reaction to Parsons. In an in depth analysis of the man, Alexander (1983) concludes that Parsons was only partially successful. Even though he talked the language of multidimensionality, he tended, like Durkheim, to accent the normative dimension of social action and to disregard the rational aspect as well as the material condition thought to be so important by Marx, conflict and feminist thinkers. Also, he reduced the voluntary part of collective order (order being created by individuals), in his more mature work, to be order created only by the collective institutions which he thought to be embedded in norms, values and mores.

Merton takes off where Parsons left. He termed his theoretical outlook as Middle Range, meaning that theory needs to be abstract enough to cover several social types but concrete enough that it could be testable with specific hypotheses.

Like Parsons, Merton considers the human actor to be free but restrained by social structures and institutions. In this light, he studied crime, the current sources of anomie, the sociology of science, political institutions, and reference groups. He, unlike Parsons, looked at how some social structures did not function well for people. In addition, human actors face many dilemmas and contradictions. Coser (1977:567), relying on Merton's (1976) insights, comments: "...social actors are always faced by sociological ambivalence, ambiguities, conflicting expectations, and dilemmas of choice; and societies, far from being rigidly unified wholes, contain in their structures discrepancies and incongruities that preclude the possibility of treating them as unambiguously unified wholes."

The continuation of a structural functionalist perspective occurs in the work of Davis (1949). In his work, the *Human Society*, he outlines a thorough and systematic view of social structure and social functions in the light both of Parsons and Merton.

Symbolic Interactionism

Emerging from the theoretical positions of George H. Mead and Charles Cooley (who we shall meet in the chapter on socialization) and more currently from Herbert Blumer (1969), who gave this perspective its name, symbolic interactionism focuses on social action and not on social structure. Johnathan Turner writes:

> individuals...are considered to be players in a 'game.' When conceptualized as a game, interaction is more likely to be seen as unstructured and as influenced by the wide range of tactics available to participants....symbolic interactions tend to conceptualize human interaction and society in terms of the strategic adjustments and readjustments of players in a game (1974:177).

Some of the assumptions of the theory are that social actors are relatively independent and that they act in response to stimuli from others and do so by interpreting these stimuli according to their own meanings. In addition, the social world is constructed from interpretive processes arising out of interactions between individuals, and the role of social science is less the search for patterns of these interactions but more so for an awareness of the uniqueness of each interaction.

This perspective was later nuanced by the American social psychologists, Sheldon Stryker and Anne Statham (1985). They add role theory to the perspective to include structural elements that account for the organization and continuity found in social life, for a consensus among social action, and for an integration of the various structural elements of a society.

In conclusion, symbolic interaction is unidimensional in that it accents only social action. To its credit, it does address both dimensions of social action: the rational and the normative but does not address the problem or offer a solution to that of collective order.

Conflict Theory or the Political Economic Perspective

Historically, the beginnings of sociology in the United States was dominated by the kind of sociology that emerged from the University of Chicago that later became known as symbolic interactionism. With the work of Parsons and later by Merton, the Chicago school lost its hegemony as the dominant sociological perspective. However, by the 1960s, structural functionalism itself began to lose its hegemony to be challenged, especially, by the conflict perspective. Conflict theory includes several authors ranging from classical Marxism to include such sociologists as Ralf Dahrendorf (1959) and Lewis Coser (1967). Those closest to the Marxist model are termed political economists whereas the term conflict theorists includes those influenced by Dahrendorf and Coser.

Collins (1988) presents us with a summary of the political economic perspective and conflict theory. The political economic perspective is a hybrid of classical Marxist sociology and some current theorists. The classical model is a combination of the relationships between capitalists, workers, technology and the state. It is argued that capitalists use workers for profit from their labour. However, in the never ending quest for profits, technology takes over much of the labour. This is a problem, for if workers do not work there is no one left to purchase the products produced by the capitalists. Thus, we have a crisis of overproduction and frequent downturns of the economy. In addition, the state is supported by the capitalists and it is much more likely to be influenced by them than the workers even though the latter control the votes.[6]

This perspective is augmented with ideas from world system theory which notes that the capitalist system is now a world system and that the bourgeoisie search the world for cheap raw materials and inexpensive labour to increase profit. Additional theorists accent how the capitalist class does not only control the means of production but also the ideological or cultural systems as well. Lastly, the state is seen to be more of an independent actor which is a major employer and economic actor in its own right.

Conflict theory emphasizes that conflict is endemic to social relationships and that even though conflict can never be completely eliminated, it can be controlled. In addition, according to Dharendorf and Coser, there is conflict between a wide number of social groups beyond just the classes as pronounced by the political economists. Coser argues that there is a positive function of conflict that if not pushed to the extreme results in consensus within a social system.

A criticism of this perspective can be made that it is also unidimensional. It accents only rational social action rooted in the material interests of people. Also, the social actor is not given too much freedom in changing his or her social condition. Collective order is assumed to be mostly in the hands of the powerful and the rich. The creation of collective order from the point of view of the actor may be possible but not too likely.

Feminism

The final major perspective to look at here is feminism. Although there have been feminist thinkers for centuries,[7] it was not until about the 1970s that it made significant strides in academic circles, particularly psychology, sociology, philosophy, history and religion.

This perspective has two primary roots: in political economy and cultural analysis. The political economic root is understood to be that women's economic power (their income and possession of property) affects their personal lives. Collins (1988) notes that the more economic power women have, the more freedom do they experience in their personal life.

Those who search to explain gender inequality in the cultural system focus upon patriarchy (men ruling women). Simply put, the majority of known human societies place women in inferior positions of authority both in the private sphere and the public sphere. Patriarchy has been the pattern. Feminists not only try to understand why this is the case but also endeavour to liberate women from this inequality. This will be outlined in much more detail in the chapter on gender.

To the credit of feminism, it does accent both aspects of the question of the collective order (social life being created by individuals and being at the mercy of already constructed social collectives). There is a strong momentum to encourage women to take charge of the collective in order to change social structures that inhibit the interests of women. Also, on the dimension of social action, equal weight is given to rational social action (with a materialist base) and normative social action (with an accent on the norm or equality for women). However, it suffers from multidimensionality in that its focus is only on one type of social actor, the woman. Men are residual (left out) entities.

Summary

It is important to understand that no one theory can account for the wide variety of human social experience. It depends upon what one is trying to understand. If one is searching for causes and effects of micro social phenomena, symbolic interaction can be a useful tool. On the other hand, if you are interested in macro social phenomena, structural functionalism and political economy-conflict perspectives are useful. If, however, your concern is how social systems achieve consensus and equilibrium, then structural functionalism may be the route. And, if your interest is in power, justice, social inequality, the political economy-conflict perspectives are useful. Lastly, if your interest is on female-male relationships (gender), both on a micro level and a macro level, then feminism would be the likely choice. There is one perspective, however, which attempts to synthesize all of these theories. Just as Weber attempted to synthesize his predessors work (Marx and Durkheim), and Parsons tried to synthesize the whole classical tradition, so does neofunctionalism attempt to synthesize current perspectives. I shall offer this as a conclusion to main stream sociological theory.

Neofunctionalism

Neofunctionalism, as described below, is an attempt to be multidimensional and synthetic. Its authors[8] present a perspective that includes central elements from all the other sociological theories and can be seen as offering a unifying approach to the study of modern societies

According to Alexander (1983), the best in Parsons (1951) is his consideration of society as a system wherein all the elements form a pattern that can be differentiated from some other surrounding environment. In addition, Alexander (1985) notes that Parsons concentrates both on action and function. Integration of these functional parts to the whole should not be considered to be an accomplished fact but a possibility. He, especially, considers Parsons' distinctions of the personality system, the cultural system and the social system to be central to any adequate sociological theory. Beyond that, Parson's contribution to social differentiation theory,[9] his attempt to synthesise the 19th century classical traditions of Durkheim and Weber, and the importance of socialization is all part of a lasting legacy. Alexander (1983) continues with several critiques of Parsons and concludes his argument in his article (Alexander, 1985) by including insights from conflict and interactionist theories which become important corner stones to neofunctionalism.

A central goal of neofunctionalism appears to be the continuity of a reconstruction of the Parsonian legacy and to construct a new theory that focuses more on social action that is informed by symbolic interactionism, exchange theory and ethnomethodology[10] (Alexander and Colomy, 1990). Alexander believes that free agency within the action framework of Parsons to be a vitally missing element in his theory. Also, he adds insights from Marx on the salience of a materialist dimension of social action.

Alexander and Colomy (1990) review a wide variety of researchers who have used neofunctionalist insights including social change, cultural sociology, political sociology, mass communication, feminist projects, the professions, and economic sociology.

A mature reading of neofunctionalism reflects the most recent contributions by Alexander (1998) and what I consider to be vital concepts and propositions that flesh out more fully the neofunctionalist perspective. He retains and extends a discussion on the three-system model of Parsons and considers it to be a permanent contribution to sociology. Alexander presents an extended discussion of action (acknowledging but going beyond exchange theory, symbolic interactionism, and ethnomethodology) that situates it within patterned meanings (the cultural system), psychological needs of the person (the personality system) and the interactional and institutional exigencies (the social system, 1998: 211). Under the rubric of culture, Alexander includes insights from Mary Douglas, Clifford Geertz, and the sociologist, Michael Foucault. From the social system, he outlines civil society as the locus of importance by adding what he calls "societal communities" which mediate between the public civil society and the private world of citizens.

It remains to be seen if this new perspective has a possibility of unifying all major perspectives in sociology. It is my contention that it has and may be seen as being both multidimensional and synthetic. It is multidimensional in that it presents equal weight to the two dimensions of social action and the two dimensions of the collective order. All other theories (Parsonian-Mertonian structural functionalism, conflict theory, symbolic interactionism, and feminism) are unidimensional. It is synthetic in that it utilizes the various systems (cultural, personality, and social) to locate all the major sociological theories.

The Emergence of Sociology in Canada

Sociology originated both in Quebec and in English Canada. Forcese and Richer (1982) note that sociology in Quebec began with a merger of Roman Catholic social teaching and practice, European sociology, and American social thinking. Leo Gerin, using the work of the 19th century European sociologist, Frederic LePlay (1982), did research on the changing family in rural and urban Quebec.

Beyond that, the major influence to formal sociology within the universities came from the Catholic social action movement. This movement was a religious response to social problems and to challenge the more radical left-wing movement from Marxism. The focus was to try to understand the social problems which emerged as a result of a transformation of Quebec society from rural to urban.

Sociology in English Canada also had religious roots. However, the impetus did not come from Roman Catholicism but, rather, from the social gospel movement of Protestantism. This movement used sociology and its reformist attitude as an extension of the Christian missionary and social services interests. The most well known was Christopher Dawson from the University of Chicago who originally was a Baptist minister and later became a sociologist. He founded the first Canadian sociology department at McGill University in 1922 (Forcese and Richer, 1982).

Gradually, the religious influence in sociology began to wane as years passed. Macionis, Nancarrow Clark, and Gerber (1994) add that the new emphasis was on social, political and economic history. The most influential sociologist during this period was Harold Innis who developed a theory of the growth of the Canadian economy. Then, in the 1960s, the political economist perspective begins to be dominant with the monumental work of John Porter (1965), the Vertical Mosaic—a study of power, ethnicity, class and economy. More currently, especially through the work of Dorothy Smith (1990), mentioned above, feminism has become increasingly centre-fold in Canadian sociology. Of all the sociological theories, it seems that conflict theory or the political-economic perspective is dominant in Canadian sociology.

Summary

What this chapter has attempted to do is to present to the student what the key concepts of the discipline were: social action and social structure. Thereafter, several historical events, processes and ideologies were presented that provided background for the classical founders to construct the rudiments of sociology. These included the Protestant reformation, the age of discovery and colonization, the Enlightenment, the English Great Rebellion, The French revolution, the industrial revolution, and the post-industrial revolution. The central classical founders included Comte, Marx, Durkheim, and Weber. Thereafter, four current perspectives were presented: structural functionalism, symbolic interactionism, conflict theory or the political economic perspective, and feminism. Neofunctionalism was offered as an attempt to synthesize all the central theories in the discipline and to meet the demands of a call for multidimensionality.

Notes

1. Paradigm refers to a pattern, example or a model (Webster, 1968).

2. The Canadian Review of Sociology has devoted its August 1995 issue to the topic.

3. Other sociologists may add others like Herbert Spencer (1820–1903), Georg Simmel (1858–1918), Thorstein Veblen (1857–1929), Charles Cooley (1864–1924), George H. Mead (1863–1931), and Vilfredo Pareto (1848–1923). We are restricting our study to those who have been known as the major classical founders of the discipline.

4. In this light, Weber is more akin to social psychology than to sociology.

5. Other common ones are exchange theories (or rational choice), ethno methodology, and phenomenology.

6. A recent example of this is the Canadian federal government's decision to radically reduce the deficit at the call of the world dominant capitalists centered in the United States and other more powerful nations.

7. Stone (1979), a social historian of the family, discovered several feminist movements during the English Great Rebellion. Thompson (1980), a social historian of social class, noted a prominent feminist thinker by the name of Mary Wollstonecraft who published a book in the late 18th century entitled *Rights of Women*. She spoke for the need of a female voice in the economy and the state. Feminism, called 'social feminism,' was part of prohibition of the latter part of the 19th century and the first part of the 20th in the United States and Canada.

8. For the sake of parsimony, I shall only refer to Alexander and Colomy and not to another well known European proponent of neofunctionalism, Luhmann (see Turner, 1991).

9. This term is from Durkheim and Parsons and refers to the historical process that as human societies have evolved throughout history, they have differentiated social institutions.

10. Exchange theory is a theory that argues that social action is based on a cost and benefit analysis. Ethnomethology posits a position that social order is maintained by the use of ways or techniques that give actors a sense that they share a common reality and that it is the actors' acceptance of a common set of techniques that is really important (Turner, 1991).

References

Alexander, J.
1982a   *Theoretical Logic in Sociology: Positivism, Presuppositions, and Current Controversies.* Volume I. Berkeley, CA: University of California Press.

Alexander, J.
1982b   *Theoretical Logic in Sociology: Volume II: The Antimonies of Classical Thought: Marx and Durkheim.* Berkeley, CA: University of California Press.

Alexander, J.
1982c   *Theoretical Logic in Sociology:. Volume III: The Classical Attempt at Theoretical Synthesis: Max Weber.* Berkeley, CA: University of California Press.

Alexander, J.
1983   *Theoretical Logic in Sociology: Volume IV: The Modern Reconstruction of Classical Thought: Talcott Parsons.* Berkeley, CA: University of California Press.

Alexander, J.
1985   "Introduction." Pp. 7–18 in J. Alexander (Ed.) *Neofunctionalism.* Beverly Hills: Sage.

Alexander, J.
1998   *Neofunctionalism and After.* Malden, Massachusetts and Oxford, England: Blackwell Publishers Ltd.

Alexander, J. and P. Colomy
1990   "Neofunctionalism Today: Reconstructing a Theoretical Tradition." Pp. 33–67 in G. Ritzer, (Ed,) *Frontiers of Social Theory: A New Synthesis.* New York: Columbia University Press.

Boorstin, D.
1998   *The Seekers: The Story of Man's Continuing Quest to Understand His World.* New York: Random House.

Blumer, H.
1969   *Symbolic Interactionism: Perspectives and Method.* Englewood Cliffs, NJ: Prentice-Hall.

Collins, R.
1988   *Theoretical Sociology.* New York: Harcourt Brace Jovanovich College Publishers.

Comte, A.
1896   *The Positivist Philosophy of Auguste Comte.* London: Bell.

Coser, L.
1967   *Continuities in the Study of Social Conflict.* New York: Free Press.

Coser, L.
1977   *Masters of Sociological Thought: Ideas in Historical and Social Context.* 2nd Edition. New York: Harcourt Brace Jovanovich College Publishers.

Dahrendorf, R.
1959   *Class and Class Conflict in Industrial Society*. Stanford, CA: Stanford University Press.

Davis, K.
1949   *Human Society*. New York: Macmillan.

Durkheim, E.
1938   *The Rules of Sociological Method*. New York: The Free Press.

Durkheim, E.
1947   *The Division of Labour in Society*. New York: The Free Press.

Durkheim, E.
1951   *Suicide: A Study in Sociology*. New York: The Free Press.

Forcese, D. and S. Richer
1982   "Introduction: Social Issues and Canadian Sociology." Pp. 2–14. D. Forcese and S. Richer Eds.. *Social Issues: Sociological Views of Canada*. Scarborough: Prentice-Hall.

Giddens, A.
1971   *Capitalism and Modern Social Theory*. London: Cambridge University Press.

Giddens, A.
1984   *The Constitution of Society*. Cambridge: Polity Press.

Hobbes, T.
1952   *Leviathan, or Matter, Form, and Power of a Commonwealth, Ecclesiastical and Civil*. Chicago: Great Books of the Western World, Britannica Inc.

LePlay, F.
1982   *On Family, Work, and Social Change*. Chicago: The University of Chicago Press.

Macionis, J. J. Nancarrow Clark, and L. Gerber
1994   *Sociology: Canadian Edition*. Scarborough: Prentice-Hall.

Mannheim, K.
1951   *Man and Society in an Age of Reconstruction*. New York: Harcourt Brace Jovanovich College Publishers.

Marx, K. and F. Engels
1932   *The Communist Manifesto and Other Writings*. New York: International Publishers.

Marx, K. and F. Engels
1947   *The German Ideology*. New York: International Publishers.

Marx, K.
1977   *Karl Marx Selected Writings*. Edited by D. McLellan. New York: Oxford University Press.

Merton, R.
1949   *Social Theory and Social Structure.* New York: Free Press.

Merton, R.
1976   *Sociological Ambivalence and Other Essays.* New York: Free Press.

Mills, C. W.
1959   *The Sociological Imagination.* New York: The Oxford University Press.

Nisbet, R.
1966   *The Sociological Tradition.* New York: Basic Books.

Nisbet, R.
1982   *The Social Philosophers.* New York: Pocket Books.

Parsons. T.
1937   *The Structure of Social Action.* New York: Free Press.

Parsons, T.
1951   *The Social System.* New York: The Free Press.

Porter, J.
1965   *The Vertical Mosaic: An Analysis of Social Class and Power in Canada.* Toronto:
            The University of Toronto Press.

Radnitzky, G.
1973   *Contemporary Schools of Metascience.* Chicago: Henry Regnery, Co.

Smith, A.
1952   *An Inquiry into the Nature and Causes of the Wealth of Nations.* Chicago: The
            Great Books, Britannica Inc.

Smith, D.
1990   *Texts, Facts, and the Feminine: Exploring the Relations of Ruling.* New York:
            Routledge.

Stone, L.
1972   *The Causes of the English Revolution, 1524–1642.* New York: Harper and Row.

Stone, L.
1979   *The Family, Sex and Marriage in England 1500–1800.* New York: Harper and
            Row.

Stryker, S. and A. Statham
1985   "Symbolic Interaction and Role Theory." Pp. 311–378. In G. Lindzey and E.
            Aronson Eds. *The Handbook of Social Psychology.* New York: Random House.

Thompson, E. P.
1980   *The Making of the English Working Class.* London: Penguin Books.

Tilly, C.
1981   *As Sociology Meets History.* New York: Academic Press.

Toynbee, A.
1956   *The Industrial Revolution*. Boston: Beacon Press.

Turner, J.
1974   *The Structure of Sociological Theory*. First Edition. Homewood, Ill: The Dorsey Press.

Turner, J.
1991   *The Structure of Sociological Theory*. Fifth Edition. Belmont, CA: Wadsworth Publishing Company.

Turner, J., L. Beeghley, and C. Powers
1995   *The Emergence of Sociological Theory*. Third Edition. Belmont CA: Wadsworth Publishing Co.

Weber, M.
1958   *The Protestant Ethic and the Spirit of Capitalism*. New York: C. Scribner's and Sons.

Weber. M.
1978   *Economy and Society*. Berkeley, CA: University of California Press.

Webster, N.
1968   *Webster's New Twentieth Century Dictionary of the English Language*. Unabridged. New York: The World Publishing Company.

Zeitlin, I.
1990   *Ideology and the Development of Sociological Theory*. Englewood Cliffs, NJ: Prentice-Hall.

2

An Introduction to Sociological Methodology
Mahfooz Kanwar and Don Swenson

Orientation

Like many other social sciences, sociology is based on scientific inquiry that deals with theory and research. No study is considered sociological if it does not result from empirical data gathered through scientific methods. Scientific methodology is, therefore, an integral part of sociology and its domain. All studies in the discipline of sociology are based on what we see or observe and discover; there is no room for assumptions in sociology. Our hypotheses may result from common knowledge or even general assumptions, but they must be verified by our data collected through scientific methods.

Scientific data lead us into building sociological theories. Scientific research is thus used to verify or disprove, confirm or reject an hypothesis as well as theory. Sociological research methods also help us build new theories or modify the existing theories; it is the cumulative aspect of sociology. Assumptions based on general knowledge, guesses based on common sense, and personal opinions based on intuition provide a lead into a sociological research; but in sociology, they are meaningless without empirical evidence collected through scientific methods.

Sociological methodology is based on certain rules and procedures that lead us into sociological investigations. The scientific methodology is used by many disciplines, social and natural sciences, but sociology in particular emphasizes on the question why? Sociological methodology provides an explanation as to what happens and why it happens. The sociologist is supposed to be interested in finding out what happens and what causes it to happen. Therefore, the relationship between cause and effect becomes the main focus of a sociologist.

Sociological methodology is a complex and extensive area in the discipline. However, for students in introductory sociology, it may suffice to introduce some pertinent aspects and terminology. We shall introduce key concepts, then look how sociologists gather data that is both qualitative and quantitative in nature, outline the research process, discuss

27

ethics and research, and, then, conclude by presenting some of the difficulties of doing sociological research.

Terminology

Construct. The most basic term is called a construct. It is defined as "a term that is a theoretical creation based on observations but which cannot be observed directly or indirectly" (Babbie, 1989:109). An example is religion that was used by Max Weber (1958) in his classic book, the *Protestant Ethic and the Spirit of Capitalism*. He divides this construct into two minor constructs or categories, Protestant and traditional (meaning Roman Catholicism, Judaism, and the various Eastern religions). Another example of a construct is the economy that he further subdivides into capitalism and traditional.

Proposition. When one proposes a link between two constructs, a proposition is the result. In the case of the Weberian tradition, religion is connected to the economy in that religion is a factor that proceeds the economy and that the economy is somehow a result of religion.

Variable. A measurement of a construct is called a variable. Dane (1990:339) refers to it as "the extent to which a measurable construct exhibits more than one value." A construct is too abstract and can only be used in a theoretical sense. From Weber, examples of variables include, under Protestant, the Protestant ethic (an internal way of thinking religiously) and under the construct capitalism, the spirit of capitalism.

Hypothesis. As a proposition is a link between two constructs on a theoretical level, so also are hypotheses measurable constructs or variables proposed connections between two or more variables. Within hypotheses, two kinds of variables are common. An independent variable is the characteristic that becomes a cause or is a creation of an effect. The variable that is caused by an independent variable is called a dependent variable.

An example from Weber's work is that the Protestant ethic was a cause of the spirit of capitalism. Other examples include the following real life situations. If one goes to the bar and drinks more than his limit, drives his car and causes an accident, then the extent of his drunkenness is an independent variable and the resulting accident is a dependent variable. Both can be measured (thus they are variables) and one can establish an empirical link between the two. Medical scientists can relate poor diet, lack of exercise, the use of drugs including smoking and the use of alcohol and genetics to some diseases like heart attacks and cancer.

Correlation. If one tests a hypothesis with data and there is a verification of the hypothesis, one has what is called a correlation. A correlation is an ongoing relationship between two variables. If one can establish a consistent relationship between drunk driving and accidents, a sociologist can argue that there is a correlation between the two. Here, the correlation is more than a variation between two variables for one can predict that drunk driving causes (as an independent variable) car accidents. Here, one can generalize that the more one drinks, the more likely one is likely to cause an accident.

Control variables. An additional question can be asked, however. In doing research and analyzing data, one may consider other factors to be the cause of the accident.

Possibly, the accident is caused by poor road conditions, the weather, or someone else in the vehicle. Sociologists use the term control variable to describe those other factors that may be other independent variables which may explain the changes in the dependent variable. In the example of drunk driving, we are interested in knowing that even if one takes into account other reasons for car accidents (lack of training, listening to a cellular phone while driving, having mechanical problems with the car etc.), driving while intoxicated is still the primary cause of accidents.

Sociological theory. Sociologists are not only interested in predicting and testing to see if two variables are linked. They are also interested in developing a theory that includes many other potential reasons or causes of a social phenomena. In the example here of car accidents, to get a fuller picture of what causes car accidents, one may extend the number of propositions and hypotheses to include more than one cause or reason. Or in the case of Weber's theory of the development of capitalism in the early modern period, there would likely be many more reasons for its emergence.

Merton presents us with a definition of theory:

> It is only when such concepts are interrelated in the form of a scheme that a theory begins to emerge. Concepts, then, constitute the definitions (or prescriptions) of what is to be observed; they are the variables between which empirical relationships are to be sought. When propositions are logically interrelated, a theory has been instituted. (1968:89)

In the chapter on theory, three main theories were presented, structural functionalism, conflict and symbolic interactionism. In the chapter in deviance (Schiessel), the author outlines how these theories endeavour to explain deviance. Many articles have used the propositions derived from these three theories, then have been translated into testable hypotheses and, subsequently, tested with data. A notable example is the work of Merton (1968) who, from structural functionalism, developed the strain theory (see the chapter on Deviance by Bernard Schissel) of deviance. His theory has received empirical support by finding that anomie[1] is higher among lower social classes and that members of these classes do have less access to institutionalized means to success (Bell, 1957 and Tumin and Collins, 1959 and cited in Henslin and Nelson, 1996).

How Data Are Gathered

After one creates adequate constructs, propositions, variables, and hypotheses and before one can test them, data necessarily needs to be collected. In the tradition of research in sociology, data are gathered using three main means: historical, qualitative or quantitative. Historical research, as the name implies, reviews historical materials to test hypotheses. Weber's work on the Protestant ethic and the spirit of capitalism is a case in point.

Qualitative research consists in data that are not easily quantifiable or translated into numbers. Findings from this research is more of a generic nature. Quantitative methods are the more common ones used in the discipline. Concepts are operationalized so that they can be measured. These numbers are later analyzed using statistical methodologies.

Westhues (1982) provides us with those methods which are most commonly used by sociologists: the analysis of historical records, the analysis of contemporary records, fieldwork, demographic techniques, and survey research.

Historical Methods

We shall first of all explain what these methods mean and then present, from Westhues, research examples that have tested the Weberian theory of the rise of capitalism in general and its applicability more recently.

Historical records provide an abundance of data from people who lived in the past and have now passed on. The disciplinary domain of this kind of research is social history or the study of common people from the past.[2] Several historical studies give credibility to Weber's contention that Protestantism preceded the emergence of capitalism. Jonassen (1947) found that in the development of modern Norway, late 19th century capitalism succeeded Protestant revivalist movements in earlier decades. In the creation of capitalism in the United States, Tiryakian (1975) traced its development to its Puritan origins which was one of the Protestant groups that Weber originally targeted as being special carriers of the Protestant ethic.

Qualitative Methods

Analysis of Contemporary Records[3]

The range of the kinds of contemporary records is extensive. It includes such documents as: newspapers; news magazines; legislative acts; directories of prominent people; governmental reports on such data as crime, migration, housing, industry, public health, social welfare; and various kinds of media including TV, movies, Internet sources, and radio. Weshues (1982) notes that each source provides diverse, rich, and varied forms of measures of sociological variables that a sociologist could discover patterns of human, social behavior.

Two well known studies, one by the Canadian sociologist Porter (1965) and the American Anderson (1970), were based on these kinds of data. To present evidence for the continual presence of the linkage between Protestantism and capitalism, in the Canadian study, Porter documented that among the 985 economic elites in Canada, only 10% of them were Roman Catholic. In the American counterpart, Anderson discovered that there was systematic evidence pointing to the white Protestant over representation in the political, economic, and scientific elites in the United States.

Fieldwork

Fieldwork is only possible when the sociologist gets his or her "hands dirty." In this method, the researcher becomes acquainted with the people she or he hopes to study. The field worker may interview people, search for non-verbal indicators of group life, and may even take on a role that is acceptable to the community. In this way, the researcher becomes a participant observer.

One of the obligations of the participant observer is not to influence what happens and record objectively what is observed. Although they overlap, psychologists are likely to conduct observational study in a relatively more controlled atmosphere in a laboratory but sociologists and anthropologists are more likely to do so in the field.

The analysis of qualitative data is quite different from quantitative. Typically, the researcher has vast amounts of written documents. To search for patterns and consistencies in these documents prove to be very difficult. However, recent computer programs have been developed to facilitate the process. One such program is called NUDIST (published by Sage Publications) that has been shown to be very useful in this search.

Another term to describe fieldwork is the case study. It is important that the researcher conducts a detached observation so that what is recorded is as close as possible a mirror of the real social life of the people who are subjects.

Unstructured questionnaires are used in this kind of research. They consist of wide open ended questions wherein respondents are encouraged to answer in any way they want.

This research is very costly both in time and money. Yet, it has the potential of revealing many rich details of a people's social life that could not be discovered in any other way.

Two ethnographers,[4] Redfield and Rojas (1953) went to live among descendants of the Mayan people in Mexico's Yucatan peninsula. In their research, they found one village that thrived on industry, hard work, frugality, and productive effort. The researchers discovered that the elite people of the village had earlier become Protestant because of some missionaries' efforts.

Quantitative Research

This kind of research is the closest approximation to the kind of research used by the natural scientists. This was the dream of Comte who hoped to be able to study human societies as well a physicists, for example, studied inorganic matter. Durkheim extended Comte's vision and actually did a study of suicide in Western Europe using census data (Durkheim, 1951).

In the social sciences, the basic kind of research method that is of a quantitative nature is the experiment. The researcher is interested in discovering or testing for causes of social phenomena using very controlled environments. It is typically done in a laboratory or in a natural setting. There are typically two groups of subjects: the experimental group and control group. The experimental group consists of those subjects who are exposed to the independent variable while the control group are subjects not exposed to the independent variable. After subjects have been randomly assigned to the two groups, measurements on the dependent variable is made on both groups. Then, the independent variable is introduced to the experimental group but not to the control group. As second set of measures is applied to the dependent variable. If there are changes in the dependent variable, then one can safely assume that this difference is a result of the independent variable.

In sociology, this method is rarely used because sociologists are more interested in broad issues in society that cannot be discovered or tested in a laboratory. The experiment is outlined here to illustrate that survey methods are an attempt to approximate the experiment in searching for causes of social phenomena.

Demographic Techniques

Demographers are those social scientists who have specialized in the study of whole populations through national census. They frequently investigate fertility rates, marriage rates, migration rates and mortality rates. Their advantage is that the whole of a population is included in the collection of data. In Canada, one is held every ten years.

Porter (1965), in the same study referred to above, found that there was a strong correlation between Protestant affiliates and higher levels of income. This gives further credibility to the linkage between Protestantism and capitalism.

Survey Research

This technique is one that is most commonly used by sociologists. It is similar to demographic research in that a large number of cases can be included in the data as well as a large number of variables. However, if differs on two accounts. First, the sociologist is the designer of the survey (not state officials) and can include many questions that are relevant to her or his research. Secondly, and more importantly, surveys do not ask questions of whole populations but only of a select few of that population. This is done through a technique called random sampling which means that all individuals within a population have an equal chance of being selected. A special feature of this kind of sampling is that one can generalize to the whole population.

The kinds of questions asked can be either a structured interview or an unstructured one. The former involves written questions that require a predefined set of answers to be responded to. Four common ways for this to happen is to mail out questionnaires to the sample, personally interview them, telephone them or tape record their answers for further recording and analysis. This is the kind of questionnaire that is used in either demographic or survey research.

Surveys are like opinion poles that news magazines use frequently. In social sciences, surveys are used to obtain various characteristics of a population (age, sex, income, religious affiliation, attitudes, beliefs, behaviors). In this way, one can obtain numerical measures of variables that can be used later to see if two variable correlate with one another, or one or more can be found to predict (as independent variables) a dependent variable.

A well known survey that tested the Weberian thesis was done by Gerhard Lenski (1963) in the late 1950s. He was well acquainted with Weber's work in that he searched for questions that would measure the spirit of capitalism or capitalistic attitudes and values. The way he measured this was to ask respondents if they are more happy working or taking life easy. The scale he used was one that measured positive, neutral or negative responses. His measure of Protestantism was simply affiliation. His analysis indicated that there were small but relatively consistent differences between white Protestants and Catholics in their economic attitudes.

The Research Process

For students in an introductory course, if will suffice to learn a general guideline of a research model. The researcher begins with a topic that may help us to understand some aspect of our complex society. After this initial stage, one needs to refer to the existing literature to see what has been found out about this topic before. It also provides background information and a clue to a theoretical perspective.

A second stage is to specify the meaning of the constructs and variables that one is to include within the process. From these constructs and variables, propositions and hypotheses are further developed. A third stage is to choose which research method would best be used to measure these variables and hypotheses. From the last section, these include: the analysis of historical records, the analysis of contemporary records, fieldwork, demographic techniques, and survey research.

If the study is a quantitative one using survey methods, a population needs to be specified. Babbie (1989:97) describes it as that group of people about whom we want to be able to draw conclusions. If for example, one is interested in studying divorce in Alberta, the target population would be all adults who are currently married or have been married and are now divorced. One would not include children or anyone who is not married or has never been married.

From that population, a random sample is to be drawn. This means that a method is selected that does not have any bias (like the use of the 20th number in a phone book, having access to SIN's and having a computer program randomly select the sample). The important feature of this is that every kind of person within the population has an equal chance of being included in the sample (on characteristics of gender, age, social class, religion, ethnicity, race, and the like).

This is followed by the construction of a questionnaire (structured as in the case of a survey and unstructured for field work) that focuses on creating questions that reflect the constructs that were originally established. The methodological term used is called "operationalization." Once the data are collected, the researcher begins to analyze them. This analysis of data leads to the interpretations and evaluation which must be as objective as possible. The final stage is the conclusion or application that consists in the reporting of the results and assessing their application.

Ethics in Sociological Research

Ethics in this case refer to professional standards that a sociologist (indeed any scientist) is required to adhere to. Some of these moral codes consist of openness (offer to share findings with colleagues), honesty, truth, refusing to falsify findings and committing plagiarism. Another code includes confidentiality. To encourage subjects in a study to be honest, researchers promise confidentiality. The American Sociological Association Code of Ethics stipulates: "Confidential information provided by research participants must be treated as such by sociologists, even when this information enjoys no legal protection or privilege and legal force is applied" (quoted in Henslin and Nelson, 1996:137).

Further codes include activities that protect the rights of subjects. For example, informing subjects that they are part of a study, making sure that no harm comes to the subjects, and giving them freedom to respond or not. Participants must be free to be part of a study or not to maintain their integrity.

A good example of the integrity of a researcher who refused to divulge information that he had gathered in a research project to state authorities is provided by Henslin and Nelson (1996). This researcher, Rik Scarce, was studying a radical environmental movement. While he was engaged in his research, a group calling itself the Animal Liberation Front broke into the laboratory of a university, did damage to the facility, and freed some of the animals. Police investigators questioned Scare thinking that he might have some information that would lead them to the guilty parties. He cooperated to the extent of providing information of a generic nature but would not violate his agreements of confidentiality to his subjects. He later was subpoenaed but still refused. For his refusal to cooperate with these authorities, he spent 159 days in prison.

Difficulties in Sociological Research

Like in many other disciplines, there are some difficulties in sociological research. Some subjects may provide the wrong information. They may intentionally create their own answer or they may shy away from the real information. Also, they may be intimidated by a researcher or may provide information that they think the investigator wants to hear rather than being honest with what is truthful. This is what is called "social desirability."

In a study by Kanwar (1980) on satisfaction in marriage and the family, one of the questions asked was if the couple were to marry again, would they marry the same person if they had a personal choice in the matter? When together, they all responded in the affirmative. When questioned separately, however, 57% of husbands and 87% of wives said they would not marry the same person. Likely, in each other's presence, they are not being honest for fear of offending their spouse.

One way to reduce socially desirable answers to questions is to include items in a questionnaire that tests for it. If it is found to be present in the answers given from a subject, that subject's answers are eliminated from the project. An example is the research done by Larson and his colleagues (1994). In this study, many questions were asked of evangelical clergy and their spouses across Canada. A social desirability question was included that went something like this: On a scale of 1 to 7 (1 meaning poor and 7, fantastic), how would you rate your marriage? If a subject answered 7, we would realize that no one really has a fantastic marriage. The respondent was answering this question to please the researcher or give to him or her what the subject thought they would like to hear. The subject was eliminated from the other data because if this question was false, then there is a likelihood that other questions could also be wrong.

Another method to protect information from social desirability responses is to have different ways of receiving the information. In a well known study on human sexuality in the United States by Laumann and his colleagues (1994), a question was asked twice as to the number of sexual partners the subject had in past year. The interviewer wrote on the code book the subject's response. Much later in the interview (these interviews lasted about 2 hours), the same question was asked again. This time, however, the subject was asked to write the answer on a piece of paper. This answer was then put into a sealed envelope and handed to the interviewer. Later, in the laboratory, the responses were compared. If there was discrepancy, the case was not included in the study.

In addition, the presence of the researcher, an outsider, may affect how people respond to certain questions or may change certain behaviors just because of the presence of the reseacher. This has become known as the Hawthorne effect. Babbie (1989) explains.

> During the 1920s and 1930s, two researchers, F. J. Roethlisberger and W. J. Dickson studied working conditions in the telephone "bank wiring room" in the Western Electric Works in Chicago. Their intent was to see if an improved work environment would result in higher levels of productivity. Initially, they found that to be the case. In this room, they improved the lighting conditions and productivity increased. However, when they made the lighting conditions even worse than they were before any of the changes, they found that productivity increased again. Their hypotheses were not substantiated by their research. What really increased productivity was not improved working conditions but, rather, the fact that they were being observed by the researchers. The independent variable, then, was not a change in the work conditions but the presence of the researchers! The lesson from this research is that one needs to be careful in not allowing information to be distorted by the visible presence of the researcher.[5]

Summary

This has been a simple introduction to sociological methodology. Its use may not be translated directly into personal research that the student may do. Much more needs to be learnt. However, one important fruit of this chapter could be that the student is in a better position to judge research that she or he reads in articles or books. Also, many agencies use statistics to tell their stories. Knowing good methodology from poor will enable the student to be more critical and more aware of erroneous information in the public domain.

Notes

1. Durkheim's term and used by Merton to describe a condition of society in which individuals become disconnected from others and detached from the norms that ordinarily guide their social action.

2. The social historian Tilly (1981) assists us in understanding what social history is. According to him, the central question asked by social historians is how did the development of the modern world (like democracy, capitalism or socialism) affect the ways that ordinary people act together in their common interests?

3. Another term used to describe this is content analysis.

4. A person who does ethnographic research. Ethnography is a field of anthropological research based on direct observation of and reporting on a people's way of life. As such, ethnography is the core method of cultural anthropology. Ethnographic subjects are usually cultural groups, such as communities, tribes, or dialect groups. However, classes or institutions within complex urban societies are also subjects of study. Ethnography consists of two phases: the process of observing and recording data, usually called fieldwork, followed by the preparation of a written description and analysis of the subject under study (Grolier Multimedia Encyclopedia).

5. In a laboratory setting, in studying the behaviors of subjects, researchers sometimes stand behind one-way windows wherein the observers can see the subjects but not vice versa. This eliminates the probability of the Hawthorne effect.

References

Anderson, C.
1970   *White Protestant Americans*. Englewood Cliffs, NJ: Prentice-Hall.

Babbie, E.
1989   *The Practice of Social Research*. Belmont, CA: Wadsworth Publishing Company.

Bell, W.
1957   "Anomie, Social Isolation, and the Class Structure." *Sociometry* 20:105–116.

Dane, F.
1990   *Research Methods*. Pacific Grove, CA: Brooks/Cole Publishing Company.

Durkheim, E.
1951   *Suicide: A Study in Sociology*. New York: The Free Press.

Grolier
1996   Grolier Mulitmedia Encyclopedia. Grolier Incorporated and Microsoft Corporation.

Henslin, J. and A. Nelson
1996   *Sociology: A Down to Earth Approach. Canadian Edition*. Toronto: Allyn and Bacon.

Kanwar, M.
1980   "Marriage, Family, and the Social System in Pakistan." Research funded by Mount Royal College and conducted in Pakistan in June-December, 1979.

Laumann, E., R. Michael, J. Gagnon and S. Michaels
1994   *The Social Organization of Sexuality: Sexual Practices in the United States*. Chicago: The University of Chicago Press.

Jonassen, C. T.
1947   "The Protestant Ethic and the Spirit of Captialism in Norway." *American Sociological Review* 12:676-686.

Larson, L., J. Goltz, I. Barker, M. Driedger, T. LeBlanc, B. Rennick, and D. Swenson
1994   *Clergy Families in Canada: An Initial Report*. New Market, ON: Evangelical Fellowship of Canada.

Lenski, G.
1963   *The Religious Factor*. New York: Doubleday.

Merton, R.
1968   *Social Theory and Social Structure*. Glencoe, Il.: The Free Press.

Porter, J.
1965   *The Vertical Mosaic*. Toronto: The University of Toronto Press.

Redfield, R. and V. Rojas
1953   A Village That Chose Progress. Chicago: The University of Chicago Press.

Tilly, C.
1981   *When Sociology Meets History*. New York: Academic Press.

Tiryakian, E.
1975   "Neither Marx or Durkheim ... Perhaps Weber." *American Sociological Review* 81:1–33.

Tummin, M. and R. Collins
1959   "Status Mobility and Anomie: A Study in Readiness for Desegration." *British Journal of Sociology* 10:253–267.

Weber, M.
1958   *The Protestant Ethic and the Spirit of Capitalism*. New York: Scribners and Sons.

Westhues, K.
1982   *First Sociology*. New York: McGraw-Hill.

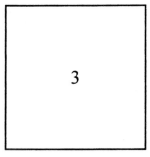

3

Culture

Bruce Ravelli

One of sociology's defining interests is the study of the relationship between the individual and society (Brym with Fox, 1989:4). A critical component of this investigation is attempting to understand the role culture plays in defining one's perception of their social environment. In simple terms, culture can be thought of as the *spice* each society adds to their social world to make their culture different and special.

The first section of this chapter reviews the defining characteristics of culture and many of the concepts sociologists use to analyze and study it. Once you are familiar with these concepts, the second section of the chapter reviews Canadian and American values with the intent to determine if there is a distinctively Canadian culture. The purpose of this chapter, then, is twofold; first, to acquaint you with the sociological analyses of culture, and second, to compare and contrast Canadian and American cultures in the hope of helping you appreciate what it means to be Canadian.

To begin our discussion of culture it is important to review five defining characteristics of culture upon which to build our later discussion and analysis.

Defining Characteristics of Culture

1. **Culture is learned.** Children are not born with culture. Instead, children are immersed in the cultural traditions of their parents, family and peers. Everything from language to attitudes, values to world views, are learned. This does not mean that all your ideas originate in your culture, but it does suggest that your culture modifies and defines your perceptions, values and perspectives. For example, what you define as *food* is a manifestation of what you have been taught. Simply put, your body requires nourishment but it does not care what the source of that nutrition is—be it pot-roast or dried insects. Cultural learning promotes certain foods while degrading others.

2. **Culture is shared.** Culture emerges from people's social interaction and sharing their experiences and meanings with each other. For example, by cheering for Team Canada when they play teams from other countries you are exhibiting a shared cultural experience with other Canadians. Shared collective symbols (e.g., Team Canada, the Maple Leaf, the Royal Canadian Mounted Police, etc.) help create and maintain group solidarity and cohesion. Being a proud fan of Team Canada is only one example of shared cultural values.

3. **Culture is transmitted.** Cultural beliefs and orientations need to be passed from generation to generation if they are to last beyond a single generation. The ability to communicate traditions and orientations to the next generation is one of the defining pursuits of culture. For example, many pre-literate societies have rich oral-traditions by which they communicate the lessons and experiences of their ancestors. By hearing these stories children learn what is important to their culture and what separates them from others.

4. **Culture is cumulative.** As each generation refines and modifies their cultural beliefs to meet their changing needs, they build upon the cultural foundation of their ancestors. Cultures do evolve and change over time and these changes are ideally informed by the lessons and teachings of the past. For example, today's students in Canadian schools are exposed to computers far earlier in their education than they were 10 to 15 years ago. This early experience with computers inspires confidence in students and is translated and built upon in adulthood. Our culture aids this cumulative process by recognizing and supporting the value of early computer training.

5. **Culture is human.** Animals are certainly social (e.g., a lion's pride, or an ant colony) but they are not cultural. Our genetic and physical makeup may give humans the ability to communicate but culture provides the rules for, and the reasons why, we interact. Culture is the product of human interaction and is a distinctly human endeavour. For example, people can gather to share ideas and change their social and cultural relationships (e.g. a marriage ceremony) while animals cannot. Animals may form long-term bonds with their mate but they lack the ability to integrate or modify that relationship beyond the individuals involved.

With these five universal characteristics of culture in mind, a more detailed analysis of how sociologists study culture is necessary.

Sociological Analysis of Culture

The term culture conjures up many images in our mind's eye: art, music, language, religion, holidays, and food. All of these things, and so many more, help a group of people define themselves in a way that sets them apart from others and allows them to feel special and unique.

After waking up in the morning we all perform a series of tasks that are culturally determined. The time we wake up conforms to established rules about when it is appropriate for people to start their day. This guideline for when it is acceptable to wake up varies according to how old you are. Adults generally feel more pressure to *get up* and start their day than do teenagers. Part of the explanation for this difference is that many adults need to get to work on time, but it is also based on our culture's informal rule allowing young people to *sleep in*. Once we are awake, what clothes we decide to wear, what we eat for breakfast, and what we do for the rest of the day are all influenced by culture.

One of the most important issues to consider when discussing culture is that anything we say to try to define what culture is, is a comparative endeavour—what we say about other cultures helps us define our own. When we view the world's diverse cultures, we find very few cultural practices that are identical across human populations.

According to Victor Barnouw, a noted ethnologist, "culture is the way of life of a group of people, the complex of shared concepts and patterns of learned behavior that are handed down from one generation to the next through the means of language and imitation" (Barnouw, 1987:4). However, while Barnouw's definition is helpful, there has been a great deal of academic debate on what culture actually is (see Boesch and Tomasello, 1998:591). Even with a longstanding debate on how to define culture, there is little disagreement on the important role culture plays in defining how a group of people see the world. Generally, social scientists begin their study of culture by looking at material and nonmaterial culture.

Material versus Nonmaterial Culture

Material culture refers to the physical output of human labour and expression. For example, a computer is part of Canada's material culture, as are paintings, novels and popular songs. At the most basic level our material culture helps us adapt to, and prosper in, diverse and often challenging physical environments. For example, the Inuit of Canada's North must endure long, cold, winters and their material culture has responded by developing exceptionally warm clothing and shelters (Balicki, 1970). Conversely, the material culture of the Yanomamo of South America reflects their adaptation to a hot and humid climate by their lack of heavy clothing and their open-walled huts (Chagnon, 1997).

Canadian material culture, like the Inuit or Yanomamo's, is everything we create as a group. For example, Canada's material culture is evident in the university or college you attend, the clothes you wear, and the hockey game you watched on CBC's *Hockey Night in Canada* last Saturday. These institutions and behaviours tell us a great deal about Canadian culture. First, Canadians support a government-sponsored education system as they believe university and college graduates benefit Canadian society. Second, your choice to wear name-brand jeans today demonstrates your desire to belong to, and conform with, cultural standards. Third, your ability to remember the theme song from *Hockey Night in Canada* reinforces that hockey is one of the defining elements of Canadian culture (Trovato,1998).

Material culture helps us adjust to our physical environment, but to truly appreciate culture, one must understand that culture is more than the sum of its material elements. For sociologists, *nonmaterial culture* represents a vast array of values, norms, folkways and mores, that are formed over time and passed on to succeeding generations (Luhman, 1994:65).

41

Values, Norms, Folkways and Mores

Values are general beliefs defining right and wrong or specifying cultural preferences. A belief that sexual harassment is wrong, and a preference for rap-music, are both values. Values provide the members of society with general guidelines on what their society deems important. For example, Canadians believe that the government-sponsored health care system is also one of the defining elements of being Canadian (*Canadian Medical Association News*, 1997: 7; Ravelli, 1994:467).

Norms are more precise than values as they specify what behaviours are acceptable to society and which are not. *Laws* are a particular kind of norm that have been formally defined and enacted. Walking on the left-hand side of a busy hallway is an example of breaking a norm, not a law, but still illicits some kind of sanction. A sanction is anything that communicates a reward for appropriate behaviours or penalties for inappropriate ones. A reward for appropriate behaviour might be getting an "A" in your sociology class, a penalty for inappropriate behaviour might be *glaring* at the person walking on the wrong side of the hall.

Sociologist W.G. Sumner expanded our understanding of norms in his book entitled, *Folkways* (1959[1906]). In *Folkways,* Sumner suggests there were two classes of norms: folkways and mores. *Folkways* are those behaviours that do not inspire severe moral condemnation when violated. For example, walking on the wrong side of the hallway. *Mores*, on the other hand, do inspire strong moral condemnation. For example, extra-marital sexual relations. The important distinction between folkways and mores is not necessarily the act itself, but instead, society's reaction to it. As members of complex societies, values, norms, mores and folkways help society maintain control over behaviours it deems unacceptable.

High versus Popular Culture

The term *culture* is also often associated with a value judgement that to be *cultured* is to be important and special. Cultured people are those who listen to classical music, watch the *A&E* Channel, attend the ballet, and drive $75,000 luxury cars. At times, we feel these people are somehow better than most of us because we listen to country music, watch the World Wrestling Federation, go to hockey games and drive pick-ups. Sociologists refer to the culture of the rich and powerful as *high culture* and the culture of the majority as *popular culture*.

Although, sociologists try to ignore the common value judgements inherent with *high* and *popular* culture, they are interested in understanding why people believe there are differences between the two cultures in the first place. Why is it that we believe that those who go to the ballet are somehow more *cultured* than those who go to hockey games? Could it be because we associate ballet with those who have money and power and hockey with those who don't? If this is true, then we need to emphasize that there is nothing inherently better about ballet than hockey. What is important is that our impressions are often a reflection of the class stratification in society and how it can be used to foster social and cultural fragmentation.

Subculture and Counterculture

A *subculture* is a group of people who promote a set of beliefs, norms and values that are different from those of the larger population. Both panhandlers and media celebrities display certain subcultural behaviours. For example, panhandlers generally congregate in high-traffic areas populated by tourists, while celebrities, don't. Celebrities tend to avoid crowds as they can be unpredictable and dangerous (Meloy and Gothard, 1995: 258). Obviously, there are many other characteristics separating panhandlers from celebrities, but this specific difference should illustrate that both groups operate according to beliefs, norms and values that may not be consistent with those of the larger society.

A *counterculture* is a group of people who form a set of beliefs, norms and values that strongly oppose or contradict those held by the larger society. Counterculture groups are often identified by their outright rejection of contemporary societal standards. For example, *Hippies* of the 1960s were dedicated to demonstrating to the dominant society that they did not adhere to the values of global capitalism and escalating militarism. Conflict often occurred between Hippies and the dominant society and highlighted their different views of the world. Sociologists and anthropologists find that to understand these different worldviews, it is useful to appreciate how ethnocentrism and cultural relativism affects our impressions of others.

Ethnocentrism versus Cultural Relativism

Ethnocentrism is the belief that your cultural practices are superior to all others. To be ethnocentric is to view the actions and attitudes of other cultures as inferior to yours. To some extent, all cultures possess ethnocentric views. For example, in Canada the majority of people observe the practice of gift-giving at Christmas. For these families the tradition of buying gifts at Christmas is important and filled with traditional and emotional significance. However, many Canadian families do not observe Christmas (e.g., Jehovah Witnesses) because they feel it is based on Christian and capitalistic values and beliefs. For either group to believe that their Christmas practices, or lack of them, is *right*, and that others should conform to theirs, is being ethnocentric. The important consideration here is to think about how far you would go to impose your beliefs on another culture. While it is difficult to imagine a person forcing gift-giving on someone else, is the principle any different in believing so strongly in democracy and capitalism that you are willing to go to war over them? For sociologists the differences between the two scenarios are of degree, not of kind.

Cultural relativism is the opposite of ethnocentrism. Cultural relativism is the belief that all cultural practices should be judged in their terms, not yours. To be culturally relativistic is to understand that no individual cultural norm or value is inherently good or bad. As a Canadian, chances are that you would not allow your parents to choose who you marry, however, in many countries arranged marriages are an integral part of their cultural landscape. Being a cultural relativist does not mean you have to agree with arranged marriages per sé, but it does mean that you recognize and support cultural independence and diversity. But, does this mean that all cultural practices are okay? For example, as a cultural relativist, do you have to agree with and support the tradition in many Arab countries where husbands

43

dominate their wives? Although difficult to answer, the short answer is no. Cultural relativism asks you to be conscious of cultural diversity but it does not require you to endorse every behaviour from every culture.

When confronting difficult cultural issues from a culturally relativistic perspective, Macionis and Gerber (1999) offer some useful considerations.

1. Although studying cultural diversity is fascinating, be prepared for emotional reactions when you encounter the unfamiliar.
2. Resist the urge to make snap decisions and try to observe the unfamiliar practice with an open mind.
3. Try to see the issue from their point of view, not yours.
4 After careful consideration, re-evaluate the behaviour/practice and see if your perspective has changed.
5. Use this experience to reflect upon your own beliefs and values and try to understand what they say about you (Adapted from Macionis and Gerber, 1999:77).

Being conscious of ethnocentrism and cultural relativism helps you become a more informed and critical thinker. Issues or behaviours that make you question your own values and beliefs are often the most difficult to confront, but are also the most rewarding. By understanding the dynamic and relative nature of culture, one can better appreciate how cultures change over time.

Culture Change

Cultures change in order to adapt to different pressures and demands. For example, consider how Canadian culture was affected by the implementation of the telephone, affordable air travel, the Cold War, and the Bloc Quebecois. Social scientists generally consider three different factors inspiring or initiating change—discovery, invention/innovation, and diffusion (see Shandro, 1997/98:474; Grubler, 1996).

Discovery occurs when something previously unrecognized or understood is found to have social or cultural applications. Historically, discovery involved findings from the natural world, for example, fire and gravity. Today, discoveries can occur as a result of the scientific process, for example, the discovery of the polio vaccine that virtually eliminated one of the most debilitating childhood diseases (Kendall et al., 1998:56).

Invention/Innovation occurs when existing cultural items are manipulated or modified to produce a new socially valuable outcome. The differences between invention and innovation may appear slight, but the distinction is important. On the one hand, invention refers to manipulating existing ideas and joining them to create something new, for example, synthesizing and/or modifying existing scientific techniques to control nuclear fission. On the other hand, innovation is finding new applications or uses for what is already available, for example, using the steam generated from the nuclear reactor to produce electricity (Grubler, 1996:21).

Diffusion occurs when cultural items or practices are transmitted from one group or society to another (Kendall et al., 1998:57). For example, consider the influence American media has on cultural practices throughout the world. Canadian sociologist Marshall McLuhan understood the power of the media and its ability to transcend geo-political borders when he coined the phrase "Global Village" (McLuhan, 1964). More recently, Katherine McComas and James Shanahan (1999) suggest that *narrative factors* used by the media influence people's reaction to stories. For example, the authours found that the reporting of global climate change by the *Washington Post* and the *New York Times* presented story lines suggesting that global climate change was being "taken care of" and "public attention and concern could move on to other more pressing issues" (1999:51). Presenting global climate change in these terms inoculates the public's reaction to the issue, and by doing so, influences and defines their understanding of the issue. Further, Steven Clayman and Ann Reisner (1998) document how editors *gatekeep* what stories appear on the front page of newspapers. Again, the selection of stories is largely subjective but effectively curtails what information is available to people and how they respond to it. Technological advances like the mass media have challenged and initiated culture change and have often resulted in what sociologists call culture lag and culture shock.

Culture Lag and Culture Shock

William F. Ogburn coined the term culture lag in his book entitled, *Social Change* (1966[1922]). In this work, *culture lag* refers to the situation where the rate of technical change surpasses the culture's ability to develop the moral and legal institutions to accommodate and manage the change. When technological advances occur faster than our culture can keep up with, society suffers social problems and conflict. Culture lag is evident today by Canada's legal system's inability to regulate people's access to questionable material through the World Wide Web (e.g., hate literature and child pornography) (Crawford, 1998:A13). In this situation at least, our technology has surpassed our culture's ability and/or desire to develop more rigorous social control mechanisms.

Culture shock is when a person encounters cultural practices that are vastly different from their own and they become disoriented and bewildered. Often, when traveling a long way from home you may feel uncomfortable by the climate, the different languages being spoken and the myriad of other cultural practices you have never experienced before. This disorientation is a form of culture shock. We generally associate culture shock with people traveling *to* foreign countries, but culture shock can also occur when people return home. A student once told me that he suffered from culture shock when he returned to Canada after living in South Africa for four years. The student said his adjustment to South African society was comparatively easy because he had expected, and prepared for, different cultural practices. However, he did not think he needed the same mental preparation for his return *home*. When he arrived home, however, he suffered from culture shock (e.g., he had difficulty sleeping and nausea). Unfortunately for him, his adjustment to Canada was far more difficult than it was for South Africa.

So far, our discussion has focused on the assumption that human culture is the product of social interaction and social definition. However, there exists a debate over how much human behaviour is defined socially and how much genetically. This debate is commonly referred to as the *nature* (i.e., genetically based behaviour) versus *nurture* (i.e., culturally defined behaviour) debate.

Nature versus Nurture

Sociologists often refer to sociobiology as the clearest example of a science trying to understand nature's role in determining human behaviour. One of sociobiology's leading proponents, Harvard biologist Edward O. Wilson, has built a distinguished career studying ant behaviour. In 1975, Wilson's groundbreaking book, *Sociobiology: The New Synthesis* applied the principles of Darwinian inheritance to explore how human behaviours were selected for and passed on from generation to generation. The core assertion of sociobiology is that social behaviour among humans, like ants, has evolved over time as an adaptation to secure the survival of the species (McGuigan, 1997:44). Although Wilson has been widely criticized over the past thirty years, his efforts in sociobiology has inspired a new field of study to emerge called *Evolutionary Psychology* (see see Barash, 1981; Neimark, 1998).

Like sociobiology, evolutionary psychology argues that Darwinian inheritance can explain contemporary human behaviour (Dijkstra and Buunk, 1998; Neimark, 1998; Roach, 1998). For example, anthropologist John Patton asserts that one can explain why the Achuar Indians of Ecuador have the highest murder rates in the world. His explanation asserts that the act of killing has been selected for and passed on from generation to generation among the Achuar (Roach, 1998). Further, Victor Nell (1998) suggests an evolutionary explanation for why young men drive too fast. Nell argues that when young men reach the "mating and fighting age" (i.e., 16-20 years) their sense of vulnerability is at an all time low while their desire to take risks is at an all time high, an inverse and often lethal relationship (1998:19). Nell states;

> "There is a paradox—some kinds of risk-taking are beautiful or brave, or otherwise socially acceptable, while others are stupid. Our judgements about risky behaviour are often hypocritical. We admire the circus tightrope walker and the young soldier advancing on an enemy position with machine-gun blazing. But when we judge a young driver with his girlfriend snuggled up to him who is driving too fast, or a kid surfing in a violent sea, we say that the soldier and the tightrope walker are brave, but that the surfer and the speeding driver—who are both enjoying the frisson of danger—are stupid. It is important to understand that this mature judgement of risk-taking is irrelevant to injury prevention because it lacks moral weight: the young dismiss these judgements for the hypocrisy they embody, and continue to obey deeper evolutionary urges to take high risks, and thus ensure status and win the most desirable mate (1998:20-21)."

Finally, Pieternal Dijkstra and Bram Buunk (1998) argue that evolution also influences male and female jealousies. They suggest that men are predisposed to value physical attractiveness in women (i.e., a strong indicator of fertility) and women to value social dominance in men (i.e., a strong indicator of his ability to provide resources). If this is true, men should be more jealous of rivals who appear dominant, and women should be more jealous of physically attractive women: which in fact, is what their research found (1998:1164).

46

These avenues of research suggest that there is a relationship between genetics and behaviour but the problem is trying to determine the strength of that relationship.

Socialization

Sociologists and social psychologists generally agree that *socialization* is the lifelong process by which people develop and learn the patterns of their culture. Unlike many other living species whose behaviour may be more influenced by biological forces (e.g., ants), humans rely primarily on social experiences to learn the nuances that are required to survive in contemporary society (Macionis and Gerber, 1999:111). Brian Barber and Joseph Olsen (1997) suggest that early positive socialization is important for children's later social and cultural development and that three factors are particularly important:

1. Children need consistent, positive emotional bonds with significant others.
2. Children need fair and consistent limits placed on their behaviour.
3. Children need to experience, value and express their own thoughts and emotions (1997:287).

In short, the lifelong socialization process allows people to learn about their changing social landscape and to make adjustments as required. One's ability and desire to interact with their social world is defined, in part, by their status and the level of influence they can exert over others.

Ascribed versus Achieved Status

An *ascribed status* is one you are born with. For example, being born the son or daughter of a multi-millionaire or a member of a visible minority. Your ascribed status is defined at birth and has nothing to do with personal abilities or talents. Conversely, *achieved status* is a status you develop. For example, your decision to become a teacher. Your ability to become a teacher is based on your intellectual and scholastic abilities, not who your parents are.

In a complex society like Canada, each person maintains several statuses at the same time by virtue of their membership in various categories, groups or associations. Most of you reading this text are students, but you are also sons or daughters, employees, and perhaps, parents. At any given point in time the combination of these statuses is referred to as your *status set*. Managing different statuses often results in *status conflict* where fulfilling the requirements of one status precludes fulfilling another. For example, you are a student and you need to do well on tomorrow's final examination in sociology. You have set aside all evening to study but, around 3:00 p.m. your boss calls and says you have to work from four to midnight to cover someone's shift. You tell her about your final but she says that if you don't come in she will find someone who will and would "appreciate having a job." On the one hand you have to study, on the other, you have to pay the rent. What do you do? People's resolutions to these types of conflicts are usually resolved by deciding which status is more important to them at that time (i.e., student or employee). Your boss's behaviour raises another interesting discussion when studying culture—the contrast between power and authourity.

Power versus Authourity

Power is the ability to control or determine the behaviour of others. Waving a gun at someone usually means they are going to do what you want because the gun gives you power. *Authourity,* on the other hand, is a special kind of power that applies when others believe you have the right to give orders and have them followed (Luhman, 1994:96). In this situation, you do not need a gun to gain compliance because people want to comply with your wishes. Power, therefore, is the ability to impose one's will on others while authourity relies on the legitimate use of influence through a system of beliefs grounded in culture. Max Weber (1864–1920), one of the most influential early German sociologists, conducted one of the first systematic analyses of power and authourity in his work entitled, *Economy and Society* (1968[1921]). In *Economy and Society*, Weber defined three types of authourity: traditional, charismatic, and legal/rational.

Traditional authourity is present when an individual is granted influence because of their lineage or descent. For example, the social deference many North American First Nations Peoples grant their hereditary leaders. The ability to influence others under traditional authourity is grounded in the cultural belief in the value of age-old rules and powers. Weber found that while traditional forms of authourity were necessary for early societies to guide and manage social action, traditional authourity hindered the development of more complex economic and political systems because of its conservative orientation (Weber, 1968[1921]: 227–228).

Charismatic authourity is present when a person possesses extraordinary powers of persuasion (commonly referred to as *charisma*) that inspires people to obey them. Charisma, as a concept, is difficult to define and quantify since it is so intangible. Perhaps the best way to illustrate what charisma is is to name some people who possess(ed) it: Elvis, Rick Hansen, Hitler, Rene Levesque, Martin Luther King Jr., and Pierre E. Trudeau. All these people influence(d) others, partly at least, through their personal magnetism and charisma. For Weber, charismatic leaders were important for social development because their leadership was inherently revolutionary and anti-conservative (Ritzer, 1996:132).

Legal/rational authourity is present when the mechanism of influence is contained in a position or office. For example, a town's mayor has the authourity granted them by their position as mayor. A mayor's authourity is not grounded in their lineage or their personal charisma, but instead, resides in their position as mayor (although charisma may have been a factor in their winning the mayor's election). Weber argued that the best example of legal/rational authourity was contained within a special social arrangement called the bureaucracy (1968[1921]: 227–220). For Weber, the bureaucracy is defined by five characteristics:

1. Each office within the bureaucratic structure is only responsible for its specified area of competence.
2. The offices are organized into a hierarchical structure.

3. The individuals working in the bureaucracy may require specialized knowledge and training.

4. Positions within the bureaucracy exist independent of the individuals who inhabit them.

5. Administrative acts, decisions and the rules defining the bureaucracy's actions are formulated and recorded in writing (Adapted from Ritzer, 1996:129–130).

Weber believed that although the bureaucracy was very efficient he also saw that it could threaten individual autonomy and liberty. As the dominance of the bureaucracy increases in contemporary society its influence over our lives does as well. The Canadian banking system is one example of how powerful one bureaucratic system can become.

If you have ever negotiated with a bank for a car loan or a mortgage, you may already appreciate Weber's criticisms of the bureaucracy. To qualify for a loan you are required to pass a credit check to document your financial history. Although legislation exists to regulate what may be contained in these files it varies from province to province (Bain, personal communication). However, suffice to say that your ability to secure the loan or mortgage depends on you passing the credit check. This bureaucratic decision may have tremendous impact on your lifestyle. Buying a car or purchasing a house are two of the largest purchases most of us make and the responsibility of the bureaucracy to properly manage and protect this information is critical. The fact that the majority of Canadians (64% in 1993) feel that they have "lost control over how their personal information is used by companies" (Straatsma and Murray, 1996:214) suggests that the bureaucracy remains an alien entity for most people. One factor contributing to this apprehension is our assumption that bureaucracies are controlled by the rich and powerful and are therefore beyond challenge. The old adage, "you can't fight city hall" may be as true today, if not truer, than it was fifty years ago.

Summary of the Sociological Analysis of Culture

The various components of culture we have discussed are the tools sociologists use to investigate, understand, and explain cultural diversity. With these tools in mind, we now move on to the second section of the chapter and the comparison of Canadian and American cultures to determine if there is a distinctly Canadian culture.

Defining Elements of Canadian Culture

Canadian society has been shaped by an intricate and diverse set of physical and social circumstances.

Physically, Canada is the largest country in the world and is blessed with rich and diverse natural resources (Hiller, 1996:258). Noted Canadian writer, Margaret Atwood believes Canada's adaptation to a harsh physical environment has defined Canadian culture, and to some extent, what it means to be Canadian (Atwood, 1972:33 cited in Lipset, 1986:124). Socially, Canadian culture has also been defined by the coexistence of, and conflict between, the English and the French (Hiller, 1996). The fact that 81% of the people living in Quebec identify French as their mother tongue (Statistics Canada, 1996 Census Nation tables) suggests that on this criteria at least, Quebec is certainly *distinct* from the rest of the country. However, Quebec's distinctiveness does not rest solely on language but also on their shared history, symbols, ideas and perceptions of reality (McGuigan, 1997:52). Robert Brym and Celine Saint-Pierre make a convincing argument that Quebec has not only influenced Canadian culture but Canadian sociology as well (1997:543). The importance of Quebec society on Canadian culture is clear, however, given our objectives for this chapter, a more thorough investigation of Canadian and American culture is necessary.[1]

The search for what defines Canadian culture is necessarily a comparative exercise. Studying Canadian-American differences fascinates Canadians (Lipset, 1998:124; 1990:53; 1986:123), and particularly Canadian sociologists (Arnold and Tigert, 1974; Brym and Saint-Pierre, 1997; Brym with Fox, 1989:18,24; Clark, 1942; Clement, 1975; Hull, 1998:4; Porter, 1965; Reitz and Breton, 1994). Indeed, one sociologist, Seymour Martin Lipset has based a career on his study of what makes Canadians and Americans different (Tiryakian, 1991:1040; Waller, 1990:380). Lipset's book, *Continental Divide* (1990) summarizes and consolidates his almost forty-five years of research on Canadian-American differences; in it he justifies his research, arguing that:

> "Knowledge of Canada or the United States is the best way to gain insight into the other North American country. Nations can only be understood in comparative perspective. And the more similar the units being compared, the more possible it should be to isolate the factors responsible for differences between them. Looking intensively at Canada and the United States sheds light on both of them (1990:xiii)."

Canadians, historically at least, defined themselves by what they were not—Americans (Lipset: 1990:53; 1986:123). For Lipset, the primordial event generating the different founding ideologies of Canada and the United States was the American Revolution (Lipset, 1990:8; 1986: 114; 1985:160; 1963:239). The United States emerged from the Revolution as a manifestation of the classic liberal state rejecting all ties to the throne, ascriptive elitism, *noblesse oblige*, and communitarianism (1986:114). On the other hand, English Canada fought to maintain its imperial ties through the explicit rejection of liberal revolutions (Lipset, 1986:115). Canadian identity was not defined by a successful revolution, but instead a successful *counterrevolution* (Lipset, 1993:161; 1990:42). America, conversely, was defined by a rigid and stable ideology Lipset called *Americanism* (1950:181).[2]

Lipset argues (1986:123) that evidence of Canadian and American founding ideologies are present in each country's literature. American literature concentrates on themes of winning, opportunism, and confidence, while Canadian writing focuses on defeat, difficult physical circumstances, and abandonment by Britain (Lipset, 1990:1; 1986:123). Lipset cites well-known Canadian novelist, Margaret Atwood, who suggests national symbols reveal a great deal about the cultural values a nation embraces. For Atwood, the defining symbol for America was "the frontier" that inspired images of vitality and unrealized potential; she stated that the symbol of "survival" summed up Canada's national character: "Canadians are forever taking the national pulse like doctors at a sickbed; the aim is not to see whether the patient will live well but simply whether he will live at all" (Atwood, 1972:33 cited in Lipset, 1986:124). Lipset suggests that the symbols, attitudes, and values of a people do not exist in a vacuum, rather that social and political institutions embody and reinforce them (Lipset, 1990:xiv; 225; 1986:114, 119; Baer et al., 1990a:693). For

Lipset, values were the basis upon which society built its social and political structures, and different value systems would manifest themselves in all social realms, not just literature (Lipset, 1990:xiv).

Lipset argues that social structures reflect a society's values and beliefs (Baer, Grabb and Johnston, 1990a:693; Grabb and Curtis, 1988:129,137; Lipset, 1963:210) and to understand the importance of culture in determining a society's social structure, he incorporated Talcott Parsons' pattern variables typology (Lipset, 1963:210). Parsons' pattern variable typology provided researchers with a method for classifying social values that was more sensitive to cultural variation than the older polar concepts of sociology such as core-periphery, folk-urban, mechanical-organic, and primary-secondary.

Lipset's thesis of cross-national value differences suggests Canadians are more elitist, ascriptive, appreciate racial and ethnic variation, and are more community-oriented than Americans. Although Lipset is a dominant figure in North American sociology,[3] his Canadian-American research has been the subject of much interest and debate. Various researchers (see Baer et al., 1990, 1990b, 1990c, 1993; Curtis et al., 1992; Grabb and Curtis, 1988) have attempted to test Lipset's thesis but have faced several difficulties, the most prominent being:

1. Lipset's research is based on subjective data that are not subject to refutation;
2. Lipset's categories are contradictory and often suggest Canadian-American differences opposite to what his thesis would predict;
3. Lipset fails to recognize the important role social change plays in influencing Canadian and American values;
4. Lipset's approach ignores regional value variation; and,
5. Lipset fails to offer alternative explanations.

In spite of such pointed criticism, sociologists generally agree that Lipset's fundamental proposition that Canadian and American cultural values are different, is sound, but as yet, not clearly defined (see Brym with Fox, 1989:16–18; Clark, 1975:26; Baer et al., 1990a:708; 1990c:276; McGuigan, 1990:127; Ogmundson and Fisher, 1994:196).

To investigate Lipset's assumptions in more detail, I conducted my own research and suggested that one way to evidence Canadian and American cultural differences would be to study a single social phenomenon common to both countries and see if there were differences. For example, investigating how Canadian and American media present a common and familiar issue should illustrate national cultural differences to the extent they are present. After all, media are becoming *the* conduit through which much of the world define and reflect their culture (See Adams, 1978:30; Campbell, 1999; Gamson and Modigliani, 1989:3; Gitlin, 1980; Herman and Chomsky, 1988:2; Parenti, 1993:23; Smith, 1992:210; Tetzlaff, 1992). Further, since both Canada and the United States have a long history of Native-White contact, my own research proposed Native issues as one social phenomenon for study (see Berelson and Salter, 1946; Grenier, 1993; Singer, 1982; Skea, 1993).[4]

To test Lipset's thesis then, I employed a fifty-year longitudinal study of Canadian and American media and how they presented Native issues. The medium I chose for the comparison was newsmagazines, and in particular *Maclean's* in Canada and *Newsweek* in the

United States.[5] These newsmagazines were selected because they are regarded as journalistic leaders (see Roy, 1990:510; van Driel and Richardson, 1988:38) and attract national audiences. To operationalize Lipset's theory (i.e., to make it testable), I formulated seven hypotheses flowing directly out of his four pattern variables (see Table 3.1).

Table 3.1. Testing Lipset's Thesis

Lipset's Pattern Variable		Hypotheses
Elitism-Egalitarianism	1a.	Canadians will view political leaders more positively than Americans
	1b.	Canadians will view minority leaders more critically than Americans
Ascription-Achievement	2a.	Canadians will support government-sponsored redistribution programs more than Americans
	2b.	Canadians will criticize lawlessness more than Americans
Particularism-Universalism	3.	Canadians will support the mosaic perspective more than Americans
Diffuseness-Specificity	4a.	Canadians will support the collectivist perspective more than Americans
	4b.	Canadians will criticize minority challenges to the collective more than Americans

My sampling frame included all articles referring to Natives in *Maclean's* and *Newsweek* from 1943 to 1993.[6] After gathering the articles, I employed a content analysis to determine if there were systematic differences between each magazine and their coverage of Native issues.

My analysis of *Maclean's* and *Newsweek* was from two perspectives, the first a quantitative examination testing whether Lipset's value differences were evident (see Appendix A), the second a qualitative exploration to detect themes speaking to Lipset's thesis (see Appendix B). The quantitative analysis provides a rudimentary statistical assessment of Lipset's thesis while the qualitative allows greater sensitivity to themes appearing in the articles pertaining to cultural differences. By coding the articles from both quantitative and qualitative perspectives I hoped to provide a better appreciation for their portrayals of Native issues than would be possible by using either approach independently.

My results suggest little quantitative or qualitative support for Lipset's thesis of Canadian-American value differences (see Table 3.2).

Table 3.2. Qualitative/Quantitative Results Summary

Pattern Variable	Hypothesis	Quantitative Results	Qualitative Results
Elitism vs. Egalitarianism	1a. Political Leadership	Reject	Reject
	1b. Native Leadership	Reject	Reject
Ascription vs. Achievement	2a. Redistribution Programs	Reject	Support
	2b. Native Lawlessness	Reject	Reject
Particularism vs. Universalism	3. Mosaic Perspective	Support	Support
Diffuseness vs. Specificity	4a. Collectivist Perspective	Reject	Support
	4b. Native Challenge to the Collective	Reject	Reject

Table 3.2 illustrates that six of the seven quantitative results fail to support Lipset's thesis. Statistical differences existed between *Maclean's* and *Newsweek* and their presentation of Native issues, but the differences were often in the opposite direction to what Lipset's thesis would predict. Qualitative results were similar to the quantitative in that four of the seven hypotheses rejected Lipset's thesis.

1. Elitism vs. Egalitarianism—is **not supported** as all four tests reject Lipset's hypothesis.
2. Ascription vs. Achievement—is **not supported** as three of the four tests refute Lipset's hypothesis.
3. Particularism vs. Universalism—**is supported** as both tests support Lipset's hypothesis.
4. Diffuseness vs. Specificity—is **not supported** as three of the four tests reject Lipset's hypothesis.

These findings suggest Canadian and American cultural values do vary, but not in a manner consistent with Lipset's pattern variable thesis. The only pattern variable to be supported was *Particularism vs. Universalism* and suggests Canadians do recognize and encourage racial and ethnic diversity more than Americans. While my research found little support for the three remaining pattern variables, it did find evidence to support the common experience that Canadian and American culture differ (see Reitz and Breton, 1994).

Conclusion

This brings us back to where we began; my attempt to help you appreciate cultural diversity and see if there exists a distinctly Canadian culture. After reading almost 400 magazine articles, on at least three separate occasions, I was struck by how often *Maclean's* presented Native issues with emotion and passion and how rarely any empathy was shown for the plight of American Indians in *Newsweek*. For me, this suggests one of the defining differences between Canadians and Americans—the belief in, and support for, multiculturalism. Granted, Canada's record for dealing with First Nations has often been strained and difficult; however, the dialog between the parties has played a central and defining role in constructing our national consciousness. This level of public debate and discussion between the American Indian and the larger American society has not occurred. Canadians, however, must appreciate that just saying Canada is a multicultural society is not enough. All minorities in Canada need to know, and be shown, that for Canadians multiculturalism is not just an abstract philosophy but one of the defining elements of who we are as a people—multiculturalism means nothing if we don't practice what we preach.

So, is there a distinctly Canadian culture? Absolutely.

Appendix A

My quantitative coding tested Lipset's overall thesis of cross-national value-difference. This was accomplished by comparing how each article portrayed issues that were relevant to Lispet's pattern variables. For example, when an article discussed Political Leaders (pertinent to hypothesis 1a), I noted every reference to political leaders as either positive, negative, or indeterminate on the margins of the article. Positive statements about Political Leaders were coded as PL+, negative as PL-, and indeterminate as PL?. When I completed the coding, I added the number of positive, negative and indeterminate references and determined an overall coding for that article. That is, if the article had 15 positive statements about the political leader, three negative and no indeterminate, I concluded that the article presented a "Supportive" portrayal of political leaders. It is upon these comparisons that the statistical analyses are based. An obvious concern at this point is how confident am I that my coding of the articles was reliable?

Research is deemed reliable when the particular research technique, applied repeatedly to the same phenomenon, yields the same results (Babbie, 1995:124). I am confident my coding was reliable for two reasons. First, there were no instances where totals for the three possible codings (i.e., PL+, PL-, PL?) were within 10% of each other. This indicates that the article's editorial bias (or lack of one) was readily apparent. Second, even though I was the only person coding the articles, I re-coded a ten per cent random sample of the articles (30 articles from *Maclean's*, 10 from *Newsweek*) six months after I completed my initial coding. The coefficient of reliability between the codings was 72% (Coefficient of reliability = number of units in identical category / total number of units). Since coefficient values over 60% are deemed reliable (Jackson, 1995:72), I am confident my coding reliably reflect the article's (and by extension, the newsmagazine's) editorial bias.

Appendix B

Content analysis is a set of procedures to study text (Weber, 1990:9) and is appropriate for most forms of communication (Babbie, 1995:307). Through the use of content analysis I was able to investigate themes in media content that went beyond those explicitly stated. Robert Weber (1990:9) suggests that content analysis of media can reveal international differences and uncover the cultural patterns of groups, institutions, or societies. The ability to look beyond the text makes content analysis well-suited for a cross-national analysis of culture differences in media (Babbie, 1995:315).

Notes

1. The majority of the following analysis is a consolidation of my doctoral dissertation, "Canadian-American Value Differences: Media Portrayals of Native Issues" (1997). Unpublished manuscript, Department of Sociology, University of Victoria.

2. An ideology is a system of beliefs, common ideas, perceptions, and values held in common by members of a collective (Parsons, 1952:349). Ideology can be thought of as the filter through which we interpret our social world.

3. As demonstrated, in part, by his election as *President of the American Sociological Association* for 1993–1994.

4. The term "Native" is used to describe the indigenous populations of North America. This terminology was selected over others (e.g., Aboriginal, First Nations, Amerindian, Indian) as it is the standard in contemporary literature (see Francis, 1992:9).

5. Electronic media is too recent to study over the 50 years and print mediums lend themselves to better contextual analysis (see Neumann et al., 1992:58–59; Vipond, 1992:27, 78, 128).

6. To locate the articles, I first consulted the *Library of Congress* subject heading and found the subject title, Indians of North America. I then manually searched the *Reader's Guide to Periodical Literature* (*Reader's Guide*) and the *Canadian Periodical Index* (*CPI*) for references to the subject title. This sampling strategy located 296 articles in *Maclean's* and 96 in *Newsweek*.

References

Adams, William C.
1978   "Network News research in Perspective: A Bibliographic Essay." In *Television Network News: Issues in Content Research*. Washington, D.C.: George Washington University Press.

Arnold, Stephen J. and Douglas J. Tigert
1974   "Canadians and Americans: A Comparative Analysis." In *International Journal of Comparative Sociology*, (15):68–83.

Atwood, Margaret
1970   *The Journals of Suzanna Moodie: Poems*. Toronto: Oxford University Press.

Babbie, Earl
1995   *The Practice of Social Research* (7th ed.). Belmont, CA: Wadsworth Publishing Company.

Baer, Doug. Edward Grabb and William A. Johnston
1990a   "The Values of Canadians and Americans: A Critical Analysis and Reassessment." *Social Forces*, 68(3):693–713.

1990b   "Reassessing Differences in Canadian and American Values." In *Images of Canada: The Sociological Tradition* by James Curtis and Lorne Tepperman (eds). Scarborough, Ont: Prentice-Hall Canada Inc. Pp.86–97.

1990c   "The Values of Canadians and Americans: A Rejoinder." In *Social Forces*, 69(1):273–277.

1993   "National Character, Regional Culture, and the Values of Canadians and Americans." *Canadian Review of Sociology and Anthropology*, 30(1):13–36.

Bain, Barry
1999   Personal Communication, February 19, 1999. Policy Specialist, Consumer Policy and Program Development Division, BC Ministry of Attorney General.

Balikci, Asen
1970   *The Netsilik Eskimo*. Garden City, New York: The American Museum of Natural History.

Barnouw, Victor
1987   *An Introduction to Anthropology*; Ethnology (Vol. 2, 5th Ed). Chicago: The Dorsey Press.

Barber, Brian K and Joseph A Olsen
1997   "Socialization in context: Connection, regulation, and autonomy in the family, school, and neighborhood, and with peers." *Journal of Adolescent Research*, 12(2):287–315).

Barash, David
1981   *The Whispering Within*. New York: Penguin Books.

Berelson, Bernard and Patricia J. Salter
1946   "Majority and Minority Americans: An Analysis of Magazine Fiction." In *Public Opinion Quarterly*, 10.

Boesch, Christophe and Michael Tomasello
1998   "Chimpanzee and human cultures." In *Current Anthropology*, 39(5)591–614.

Brym, Robert J. with Bonnie J. Fox
1989   From *Culture to Power: The Sociology of English Canada*. Toronto: Oxford University Press.

Brym, Robert and Celine Saint-Pierre
1997   Canada: Canadian Sociology. *Contemporary Sociology*, 26(5):543–546.

Campbell, Kim
1999   "Why We Must Protect Canadian Culture from the U.S. Juggernaut." In *Canadian Communications: Issues in Contemporary Media Culture*, Bohdan Szuchewycz and Jeannette Sloniowski (eds.). Scarborough: Prentice Hall Allyn and Bacon Canada. Pp.214–218.

Canadian Medical Association
1997   "Canada's national health care system?" *Canadian Medical Association News*, 7 (8): 7.

Chagnon, Napolean
1997   *Yanomamo* (5th ed.). Fort Worth, TX: Harcourt Brace College Publishers.

Clayman, Steven and Ann Reisner
1998   "Gatekeeping in Action: Editorial Conferences and Assessments of Newsworthiness." *American Sociological Review*, 63: April 178–199.

Clark, S.D.
1942   *The Social Development of Canada: An Introductory Study with Select Documents*. Toronto: University of Toronto Press.

1975   "The Post Second World War Canadian Society." *The Canadian Review of Sociology and Anthropology*, 12(1).

Clement, Wallace
1975   *The Canadian Corporate Elite: An Analysis of Economic Power*. Toronto: McClelland and Stewart.

Crawford, Blair
1998   "Man gets 10–15 years in Net sex case: Canadian convicted for assault on 13-year-old girl." *Calgary Herald*, November 6, 1998, Final Edition, p.A13.

Curtis, James E., Edward G. Grabb and Douglas E. Baer
1992   "Voluntary Association Membership in Fifteen Countries: A Comparative Analysis." *American Sociological Review*, 57(April):139–152.

Dijkstra, Pieternel and Bram P. Buunk
1998   "Jealousy as a function of rival characteristics: An evolutionary perspective." In *Personality and Social Psychology Bulletin*, 24(11):1158–1166.

Francis, Daniel
1992   *The Imaginary Indian: The Image of the Indian in Canadian Culture*. Vancouver: Arsenal Pulp Press.

Gamson, William A. and Andre Modigliani
1989   "Media Discourse and Public Opinion on Nuclear Power: A Constructionist Approach." *American Journal of Sociology*, 95(1):1–37.

Gitlin, Todd
1980   *The Whole World Is Watching*. Berkeley: University of California Press.

Grabb, Edward G. and James E. Curtis
1988   "English Canadian-American Differences in Orientation Toward Social Control and Individual Rights." *Sociological Focus*, 21(2):127–140.

Grenier, Marc
1993   "Native Indians in the English-Canadian Press: the Case of the Oka Crisis." *Media, Culture and Society*, 16 (April):313–336.

Grubler, Arnulf
1996   "Time for a change: On the patterns of diffusion of innovation." *Daedalus,*
          125(3):19–43.

Herman, Edward S. and Noam Chomsky
1988   *Manufacturing Consent: The Political Economy of the Mass Media.* New York:
          Pantheon Books.

Hiller, Harry
1996   Canadian Society: A Macro Analysis (3rd ed.). Scarborough: Prentice Hall Can-
          ada Inc.

Hull, James P.
1998   From Many, Two: A Bibliographic History of Canadian-American Relations.
          American Studies International, 36(2):4–22.

Jackson, Winston
1995   *Methods: Doing Social Research.* Scarborough: Prentice Hall Canada Inc.

Kendall, Diana., Rick Linden, Jane Lothian Murray
1998   *Sociology in our times: the essentials* (1st Canadian edition). Scarborough, Ont.
          ITP Nelson.

Lipset, Seymour Martin
1950   *Agrarian Socialism: The Cooperative Commonwealth Federation in Saskatche-
          wan.* Berkeley and Los Angeles: University of California Press.

1963   *The First New Nation: The United States in Historical and Comparative Per-
          spective.* New York: Basic Books.

1985   "Canada and the United States: The Cultural Dimension." In *Canada and the
          United States* by C.F. Doran and J.H. Sigler. Englewood Cliffs, NJ: Prentice
          Hall. pp.109–160.

1986   "Historical Traditions and National Characteristics: A Comparative Analysis of
          Canada and the United States." *Canadian Journal of Sociology* 11(2):113–155.

1990   *Continental Divide: The Values and Institutions of the United States and Can-
          ada.* New York: Routledge.

1993   "Revolution and Counterrevolution: The United States and Canada." In *A Pas-
          sion for Identity: An Introduction to Canadian Studies* by David Taras, Beverly
          Rasporich and Eli Mandel (eds). Scarborough: Nelson Canada. Pp. 150–161.

1999   American Union Density in Comparative Perspective. *Contemporary Sociology,*
          27(2):123–125.

Luhman, Reid
1994   *The Sociological Outlook: A Text with Readings,* (4th ed). San Diego, CA: Col-
          legiate Press.

Macionis, John J., and Linda M. Gerber
1999   *Sociology: Third Canadian Edition.* Scarborough, Ont.: Prentice Hall Allyn and
          Bacon Canada.

McComas, Katherine and James Shanahan
1999   Telling Stories about Global Climate Change: Measuring the Impact of Narratives on Issue Cycles. *Communication Research*, 26(1):30–50.

McGuigan, Bruce
1990   *The Comparative Sociology of Seymour Martin Lipset: An Analysis and Critique.* University of Calgary: Unpublished Master's Thesis.

1997   Issues in Canadian Culture. In *Issues in Canadian Sociology* (2nd ed.) by Mahfooz Kanwar and Don Swenson (eds). Dubuque, Iowa: Kendall/Hunt Publishing Co. Pp.35–60.

McLuhan, Marshal
1964   *Understanding Media.* New York: McGraw-Hill.

Meloy, J. Reid and Shayna Gothard
1995   Demographic and clinical comparison of obsessional followers and offenders with mental disorders." *The American Journal of Psychiatry*; 152(2):258.

Neimark, Jill
1998   "E.O. Wilson is on top of the world." *Psychology Today*, 31(5):50–53.

Nell, Victor
1998   "Why young men drive dangerously: an evolutionary perspective." In *The Safety and Health Practitioner*, 16(10):19–23.

Neumann, Russell W., Marion R. Just and Ann N. Crigler
1991   *Common Knowledge: News and the Construction of Political Meaning.* Chicago: University of Chicago Press.

Ogburn, William F.
1922   *Social Change with Respect to Culture and Original Nature.* New York: B.W. Huebsh.

Ogmundson, Richard L. and Lee Fisher
1994   "Beyond Lipset and His Critics: An Initial Reformulation." *The Canadian Review of Sociology and Anthropology*, 31(2):196–199.

Parenti, Michael
1993   *Inventing the Politics of News Media Reality* (2nd ed.): New York: St. Martin's Press.

Parsons, Talcott
1952   *The Social System.* London: Tavistock Publications Ltd.

Porter, John
1965   *The Vertical Mosaic: An Analysis of Social Class and Power in Canada.* Toronto: University of Toronto Press.

Ravelli, Bruce
1994   "Health Care in the United States and Canada." In *The Sociological Outlook: A Text with Readings* (4th ed.) by Reid Luhman (ed.). San Diego: Collegiate Press. Pp.467–468.

Reitz, Jeffrey G., Raymond Breton
1994   *The Illusion of Difference: Realities of Ethnicity in Canada and the United States*. Toronto: C.D. Howe Institute.

Ritzer, George
1996   *Sociological Theory* (4th ed.). New York: The McGraw-Hill Companies, Inc.

Roach, Mary
1998   "Why Men Kill." In *Discover*, 19(12):100–108.

Roy, Denny
1990   "The U.S. Print Media and the Conventional Military Balance in Europe." *Armed Forces & Society*, 16(4):509–528.

Shandro, Alan
1997/98 "Karl Kautsky: On the relation of theory and practice." *Science & Society*, 61(4):474–501.

Singer, Benjamin D.
1982   "Minorities in the Media: A Content Analysis of Native Canadians in the Daily Press." *Canadian Review of Sociology and Anthropology*, 19(3):348–359.

Skea, Warren H.
1993   "The Canadian Newspaper Industry's Portrayal of the Oka Crisis." *Native Studies Review*, 9(1):15–31.

Smith, Ripley L.
1992   "Media Networking: Toward a Model for the Global Management of Sociocultural Change." In *Mass Media Effects across Cultures* by Felipe Korzenny et.al. Newbury Park: Sage. Pp.201–228.

Straatsma, Ray and Catherine Murray
1996   Privacy Potholes on the Information Highway. In *Seeing Ourselves: Media Power and Policy in Canada* (2nd ed) by Helen Homes and David Taras. Toronto: Harcourt Brace Canada. Pp.214–234.

Sumner, W.G.
1959[1906] *Folkways*. New York: Ginn.

Tetzlaff, David
1992   "Popular Culture and Social Control in Late Capitalism." In *Culture and Power: A Media, Culture and Society Reader* by Paddy Scannell, Philip Schlesinger and Colin Sparks (eds.). Sage: London. Pp.48–72.

Tiryakian, Edward A.
1991   Book Review of *Continental Divide: The Values and Institutions of the United States and Canada* by S.M. Lipset. American Journal of Sociology, 96(4):1040–1042.

Trovato, Frank
1998   "The Stanley Cup of hockey and suicide in Quebec, 1951–1992." *Social Forces*, 77(1) 105–126.

van Driel, Barend and James T. Richardson
1988   "Print Media Coverage of New Religious Movements: A Longitudinal Study."
        Journal of Communication, 38(3):37–61.

Vipond, Mary
1992   *The Mass Media in Canada*. Toronto: James Lorimer & Company.

Waller, Harold M.
1990   "Book Review of *Continental Divide: The Values and Institutions of the United
        States and Canada*" by S.M. Lipset. *Canadian Journal of Political Science*,
        23:380–381.

Weber, Max
1968   *Economy and Society* [1921]. Totowa, N.J.: Bedminster Press.

Weber, Robert Philip
1990   *Basic Content Analysis* (2nd edition). Newbury Park: Sage Publications.

Wilson, Edward O.
1975   *Sociobiology: The New Synthesis*. Cambridge, MA: Harvard University Press.

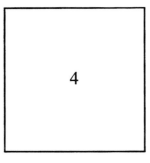

Socialization

Paul P. Divers

In this chapter, the student is to be introduced to the topic of socialization. It is here that sociology meets psychology in what is commonly known as social psychology. Social psychology is "the study of individual behaviour and psychological structures and processes as outcomes of and influences upon interpersonal relationships, the functioning of groups and other collective forms, and culturally defined macrosocial structures and processes" (Borgatta and Borgatta, 1992:1921). It is in socialization that members learn a culture (as described in Chapter Two), become adept in interaction with others, and adapt to social structures such as ethnicity, gender, and social class.

Introduction

> Every year our nation is invaded by several million "things" (one searches for the right word) that are immense, incalculable threats to the social order. They threaten total chaos. They are barbaric. They do not love democracy and suspect communism. They hold no brief for the Judao-Christian tradition. They have no modesty. They do not speak our language, nor our history, nor value our customs. They lack any motive or knowledge that leads them to share, to give and take, to compromise, to accommodate, to cooperate. They are impulsive and demanding. They do not respect authority, show respect to their elders, or express deference.... These invaders are human infants. (Campbell, 1975:1)

In Canada 386,114 infants were born in 1990 (Statistics Canada). We depend on them as much as they depend on us since without them our society would be unable to survive for very long. One central fact about infants is that they are not prepared for the life that lies before them. At birth, infants are unable to cooperate; they have only the potentiality for doing so (Handel, 1988). The process of getting them to cooperate on our terms is called *socialization*. Socialization can be defined as the process by which someone develops a

The author would like to express his appreciation to Paul Zipursky and Elaine Grandin for their suggestions and editorial comments on earlier drafts of this chapter.

63

sense of self and acquires the knowledge, skills, attitudes, motivations, and behaviour required to participate in a given society or social group so they can function within it. Although the socialization process largely takes place through face-to-face interaction in small groups, its purpose is to enlist children into their particular society. Socialization is, then, a process that helps to explain two different types of phenomena: (i) the way that an individual is capable of participating in society; and (ii) how society is possible at all (Elkin and Handel, 1984).

Socialization is not confined to childhood. It is a lifelong cumulative process whereby individuals learn how to adapt existing knowledge, skills, attitudes, motivations, and behaviour to new and changing circumstances. In other words, as individuals move through life they are faced with situations and circumstances that they have not previously experienced. At the beginning of their working lives, the young steel worker, teacher, and secretary soon learn to adapt to the particular circumstances of the occupational role and environment. Should they change jobs in later life, they will join a different occupational group and may have to learn new skills and adopt different mannerisms and styles of dress. The ability to adapt to these changes is based on earlier socialization processes and new ones soon to be acquired. The content of the various forms of socialization are not mutually exclusive, nor are the agents of socialization necessarily working in harmony, so the process actually experienced by individuals is exceedingly complex.

In this chapter we will explore the topic of socialization with emphasis on: (i) the major theories of child development; (ii) the types of socialization experienced over the life course; (iii) the relationship between socialization and society, including the various agencies of socialization that enable us to become part of society; and (iv) subcultural variation in socialization practices. Initially, our attention will focus on childhood socialization since this is the most crucial time period during which individuals learn how to participate in society. Thereafter, we will open our discussion to the complexities of socialization and the social roles adopted by individuals over the life course.

We will begin with a discussion of the theories of child development and socialization to society. In this chapter only five such theories are discussed. You should be aware, however, that there are a myriad of theories dealing with this process in the literature. Nevertheless, the theories presented here should provide you with a general understanding of some of the work that has been done in this area.

Theories of Child Development and Socialization

Cognitive Development Approach

Jean Piaget: Cognitive Development

The cognitive development approach to child development has as its chief spokesperson, Swiss psychologist Jean Piaget (1896–1990), whose general theory is a stage theory focused on the cognitive or intellectual development of children. Piaget's main stages of intellectual development are presented in Table 4:1. You should keep in mind that the age range highlighted in each stage are approximate age ranges. Some children develop intellectually faster and reach each stage sooner than other children of the same age.

Piaget assumes that thinking follows its own developmental style in children, with the development of language usually coming after the attainment of a certain level of thinking. Piaget has provided substantial experimental evidence of some of the intricate ways that thinking and language are interrelated. It seems from Piaget's studies that even though attempts are made to train young children in special ways of language to talk about problem-solving, such training is of very little use to children whose capacity for thinking has not developed to the state, point, or level at which they can meaningfully consider concepts represented in the special language. However, Piaget's work also demonstrates that the capacities for thought and language do begin to interpenetrate one another in very young children, from about eighteen months to two years of age. Subsequently, this process becomes so interwoven that by the age of five to six years it is exceedingly difficult to sort out the primary causal influences of either thought or language.

Table 4:1
Piaget's Stages of Intellectual Development

Stage	Approximate Ages[1]	Characterization
1. Sensorimotor	Birth–2 years	Infants differentiate themselves from objects; gradually become aware of the relationship between their actions and their effects on the environment so that they can act intentionally and make interesting events last longer; learn that objects continue to exist though no longer visible.
2. Preoperational	2–7 years	Uses language and can represent objects by images and words; are still *egocentric*, the world revolves around them and they have difficulty taking the viewpoint of others; classifies objects by single salient: if A is like B in one respect, it must be like B in other respects.
3. Concrete Operational	7–12 years	Become capable of logical thought; achieve conservation concepts in the following order: number (age 6), mass (age 7), weight (age 9); can classify objects, order them in series along a dimension (such as size), and understand relational terms (A is longer than B).
4. Formal Operational	12 and older	Can think in abstract terms, follow logical propositions and reason by hypothesis; isolates the elements of a problem and systematically explores all possible solutions; becomes concerned with the hypothetical, the future, and ideological problems.

1. The ages corresponding to each stage are approximations. Some children develop at different rates, often associated with socioeconomic background and ethnicity. All children pass through each stage in the same sequence according to Piaget.
Source: Adapted from Piaget, Jean (1928). *Judgement and Reasoning in the Child.* New York: Harcourt.

Sensorimotor Stage. Piaget emphasizes the close relationship between motor activity and perception in infants during the first two years. During this period infants are busy discovering the relationship between sensations and motor behaviour. Examples of what infants learn include: how far they have to reach to grasp an object, what happens when they push their food to the edge of a table, and that their hands are a part of themselves while the crib rail is not. Naturally as infants grow older they acquire many new abilities. One important discovery during this stage is the concept of **object permanence**: an awareness that an object continues to exist even when it is not present to the senses. For example, if you were to place a cloth over a toy for which a six-month-old is reaching, they will lose interest and act as if the toy were not there. In contrast, a ten-month-old infant will actively search for the object because they know the object does exist.

Preoperational Stage. The preoperational stage gradually takes place between the ages of two and seven. The key change in the intellectual development of children during this stage is the concept of **conservation**, the ability to understand that objects and quantities remain constant despite changes in their appearance. By the end of this stage children learn that the amount (mass) of a substance is not altered when its shape is changed. For example, if you were to have two identical balls of silly putty, children age four will tell you that they are the same. Now, if you were to roll one ball out into a log, children aged four will tell you that they are different; in fact, the log consists of more silly putty! However, by age six or seven children no longer simply rely on visual impression but have developed greater cognitive ability to know that two items that were identical remain the same in mass, regardless of their different shapes.

Operational Stages. Between the ages of seven and twelve, the *concrete operational stage,* children master various conservation concepts and begin to perform additional logical manipulations. For instance, children in this stage are capable of drawing maps to their friend's house and can provide verbal directions. In contrast, a five year old could not give verbal directions since their ability to do so is based on visual places of reference. Children younger than seven or eight are seldom capable of creating the mental images necessary to draw a map or provide verbal directions to a specific place; although they can physically take you there. Not until the final stage of cognitive development, the *formal operational stage,* which begins around seven or twelve, are children able to reason in purely symbolic terms. During this stage children are able to deal with several alternatives that are not immediately present in a conversation. They are able to reason about the consequences to their behaviour and offer compromises that are reasonably well thought out. In addition, children around age twelve have the capacity to give directions, using abstract terminology such as north, south, east, and west.

Jean Piaget: Moral Reasoning and Judgement

Piaget's work also extended to include the examination of moral reasoning (the sense of what is right and wrong) in child development. According to Piaget (1932) the moral reasoning of children is best exemplified in their response to paired stories illustrating different degrees of responsibility for damage done. For example, in one story a girl named Marie decided that she wanted to surprise her mother by sewing a present for her. Since she did not know how to use the scissors properly she cut a big hole in her dress. In

66

its companion story, a girl named Margaret decided to play with some scissors while her mother was out of the house. She also did not know how to use the scissors properly and made a small hole in her dress. Piaget asked children of various ages which girl was more at fault. In comparing the responses to these paired stories, Piaget found that children under the age of nine tended to measure the gravity of the deed in terms of the amount of damage done. In most cases, children under nine years of age insist that Marie was more wrong because she made a bigger bole in her dress. These children also felt that Marie should be more severely punished than Margaret even though Marie's intent was to surprise her mother, whereas the little hole in Margaret's dress was made because she was playing with the scissors. According to Piaget, young children base their morality on objective standards. Thus, the greater the damage, the greater the guilt. This view Piaget considers a direct outgrowth of what he calls **moral realism,** a view that the severity of punishment should depend on the amount of damage done, regardless of intent. In other words, moral realism demands that "the letter rather than the spirit of the law shall be observed." (Piaget, 1962:207).

At about age nine, however, children gradually lose this sense of objective responsibility and begin to place more emphasis on subjective intentions. These children in response to the same paired stories felt that Margaret was more at fault for the hole in her dress since her accident was due to careless play; whereas, Marie's accident was due to an unintentional act while trying to surprise her mother. Piaget calls this **moral autonomy**, a view that the severity of the punishment should depend on the intent of the act.

According to Piaget, very young children learn from their parents objective responses to situations during the early stage of moral realism. During this time period they learn that parents make the rules and offer few explanations for their decisions (i.e., "Don't touch that Bethany or you'll get a spanking" or "Ryan, you will be grounded if I find you playing with the Stafford boys"). Piaget believes that children tend to learn that broken rules are acts of consequence. It is not until they begin to play more actively with peers that they learn that rules are social constructions and are flexible under certain circumstances. Piaget believes that the development of children's cognitive capacities enables them to reach a level of moral thought that is consistent with society's.

The Psychoanalytic Explanation

Sigmund Freud: Father of Psychoanalysis

Freud (1856–1939) is clearly the founder of psychoanalysis. His theories developed over a forty year period of clinical work culminating in 24 volumes of text. Freud frequently used the analogy that the mind was like an iceberg. The small part above the surface of the sea represents *conscious experience,* while the larger mass—below sea level—represents the *unconscious:* a store of impulses, passions, and primitive instincts that affect our thoughts and behaviour. According to Freud, the roots of human behaviour lie in the unconscious (*instinctive*) aspect of the human mind. Consequently, for the individual to function effectively in society, personality development requires that the unconscious (*instinctive*) aspects of the human mind be tempered and controlled. In Freud's view, the

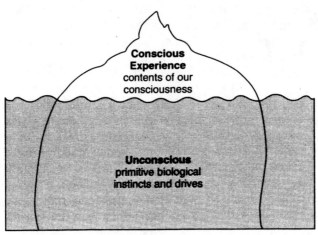

Freud compared the human mind to an iceberg.

individual is mainly governed by irrational instincts where conscious and rational dimensions constitute only a fragment of the total personality.

In this psychoanalytic view, the personality is composed of three major energy systems with each trying to exert itself over the others: the **Id**, the **Ego**, and the **Superego**. The **Id** is the original source of personality, present in the newborn infant, from which the ego and superego later develop. It consists of everything that is inherited, including the reservoir of primitive biological instincts that are continually striving for expression. Thus, the id seeks immediate gratification of primitive, pleasure-seeking impulses. The id, like the newborn infant, operates on the *pleasure principle:* it strives to obtain pleasure and to avoid pain regardless of any external considerations. For example, newborns showing little regard for their sleeping parents, will awaken during the night crying because they are hungry and wet. According to Freud, the id operates in each of us even as adults.

The **Ego** (or *self*), on the other hand, is that aspect of the human personality which is readily available to the individual in their conscious or waking state. It includes the normal functions of memory, perception, and thinking. The ego develops out of the id because of the necessity for dealing with the real world. For example, a hungry college student may not be able to immediately satisfy her hunger pangs until the lecture is over. Thus, the ego obeys the *reality principle,* which requires it to test reality and delay gratification until the appropriate conditions are available. The ego, therefore, takes the real world into consideration; including, what actions are appropriate, which id instincts will be satisfied, and in what way. As such the ego mediates between the demands of the id, the realities of the world, and the demands of the superego. The ego, according to Freud, attempts to reconcile the demands of the id and the superego by means of defense mechanisms (i.e., rationalization, repression, and projection).

The third energy system of the personality, the **Superego** (or *conscience*), represents the internalized values of society which oppose the expression of unacceptable impulses, such as sexual and aggressive drives. The superego judges what is right and wrong according to the standards of society. For example, although you may be very tempted to physically assault your sociology instructor after they give you a lower grade than you had expected, you do not because striking another individual—especially your sociology instructor—is in violation of our societal standards of acceptable conduct.

Often, the distinction made between the three energy systems of the personality can best be thought of as the difference between the child (id), the adult (ego), and the parent (superego). In other words, the child is spontaneous, the adult is responsible, and the parent imparts appropriate morals, values and constraints.

Erik Erickson: Psychosocial Development

Erickson, a trained psychoanalyst from the Viennese Psychoanalytic Institute under Anna Freud (daughter of Sigmund Freud), is well-known for his conception of socialization over the entire life cycle, from birth to death. Erickson felt that the social problems encountered in the course of development were more important than biological ones. He described a progression of *psychosocial stages* in which the individual faces a wider range of human relationships as they mature and have specific socialization issues to solve at each of these stages (refer to Table 4:2). Successful transition and development at each stage requires that the individual resolve the particular issues that are faced. Inadequate resolution of issues at each stage leads to incomplete development and possible problems in the future.

For Erickson, it is not a question of the individual adapting to society nor of society moulding the individual. The individual and the society form a unity which cannot be artificially separated. According to Erickson, the separation of individual development from society is impossible since both are necessary for socialization.

The Symbolic Interaction Explanation

At the turn of the century American sociologists attempted to establish the discipline of sociology by theorizing about the social self from a perspective that came to be known as symbolic interaction. This theorizing differed from that done in psychology since it focused on the social individual interacting with society rather than on the individual and the internal development of psyche. These symbolic interactionists argued that individuals possess only a general capacity for thought. This capacity, therefore, must be shaped and reshaped in the process of social interaction. Such a view leads the symbolic interactionists to focus on a special form of social interaction—socialization (Ritzer, 1988). To the symbolic interactionists, socialization is a dynamic process that enables individuals to think, learn, and act. Furthermore, socialization is not simply a unidirectional process whereby individuals receive information, but is a dynamic process in which the individual shapes and adapts the information to their own needs (Manis and Meltzer, 1978:6).

The intellectual roots of this perspective are most often associated with Charles Horton Cooley (1864-1929) and George Herbert Mead (1863–1931). Cooley is best known for his conception of the **looking-glass self,** while Mead is best known for his work on **role-taking.** In general, both argue that the self could not exist without society since society is in the mind. In this section, we will specifically focus our attention on

Table 4:2
Erickson's Psychosocial Stages of Development

Stage/Age	Psychosocial Issue	Characterization
1. Birth–first year	Trust vs. mistrust	Emotional attachment to the mother is vital for a favorable outcome. Infants need to recognize that even though the mother is not in sight, they have not been abandoned.
2. Second year	Autonomy vs. shame and doubt	Children during this stage begin to physically grow and gain control over bowel functions. This provides the child with a sense of autonomy and control. If the child is unable to control bowel movement and is subjected to too much parental control, they are vulnerable to shame or doubt for not having self-control and willpower.
3. Third year– fifth year	Initiative vs. guilt	Children during this stage seek direction and purpose. The capacity for language and understanding is sufficient enough to relate to parents and significant others, though they frequently misunderstand. Children explore continuously, both verbally and in their actions. Children who are made to feel that exploration is desirable will move through this stage successfully. Children who are made to feel that exploration is undesirable may experience guilt for their desire to do so.
4. Sixth year– onset of puberty	Industry vs. inferiority	During this stage, children are ready to learn, cooperate and form attachments to parents, relatives, teachers, and other children. Children are able to relate to roles that they can identify, i.e., policeman, firefighters, astronauts, and so on. Successful development during this stage enables the child to feel that they can work at tasks. Children who do not experience success during this stage may develop a sense of inferiority.
5. Adolescence	Identity and repudiation vs. identity diffusion	For Erickson, the adolescent period is a crucial stage in the socialization process. During this stage adolescents are maturing physically, mentally, and sexually. Success at this point requires that individuals establish roles for themselves, develop a coherent sense of self, and find their place in society.
6. Early adulthood	Intimacy and solidarity vs. isolation	As individuals begin to emerge from their identity struggles, they are faced with developing the ability to establish relationships such as intimate love and friendship.
7. Young and middle adulthood	Generativity vs. stagnation	This stage involves the establishment of satisfying social roles. Generativity, according to Erickson, is the interest in directing and guiding the next generation. Naturally, this is not a satisfying interest for all adults. Stagnation occurs if the individual is not involved with some role that fosters development, whether that be raising children, involvement in research and development, planting a garden, etc.
8. Later adulthood	Integrity vs. despair	This stage involves individuals reflecting back on their lives. Feelings of integrity, a sense of wholeness/ completeness, or a sense of despair, lost opportunities and incompleteness.

Source: Modified from original; Erickson, Erik. 1963. *Childhood and Society*, second edition. New York: Norton.

these two theorists and their views on how children experience the socialization process in our society.

Charles Horton Cooley: The Looking-Glass Self

Cooley began his work by observing children playing with what appeared to be imaginary friends. To Cooley, children may appear to be physically by themselves, but in their imaginations they are in the presence of others. Cooley suggests that this is how the mind initially develops because thinking consists of imaginary conversation that is carried on silently in the mind, even among adults. The mind, then, interacts with external stimuli from the social world through silent talk and interpretation of what is received.

Cooley called his social model *the looking-glass self* because the mind is like a mirror in that individuals receive from others what they believe others to think and see. The general premise is that we see ourselves as others see us and we depend on some reasonable consensus of friends and associates to maintain a consistent sense of self *(self image)*. According to Cooley, there are three components to the looking-glass self:

1. we imagine how we appear to others;
2. we imagine what their judgement of that appearance must be;
3. we develop some self-feeling, such as pride or mortification, as a result of our imagining other's judgement (Cooley, 1902).

Therefore, the development of self is not individual in nature as it is within the psycho-analytic models since the "mirror in the mind" is based on social interaction with the external world. For instance, when young children tell adults a story, their satisfaction with the storytelling experience is not with the story itself but with the response they receive from those that are present. If the adults were not to say anything to the child after the story was told, the child receives the message—through the looking-glass self—that (s)he did not please the adults or what (s)he had to say was not valued.

The power of the looking-glass self has both short and long term effects. Children who are told they are attractive, intelligent, funny, and creative throughout their childhood may internalize that they are. Similarly, children who are told that they are fat, stupid, dull, and have no creativity may also internalize that image of themselves in their personality structure. This is also true of adults who experience relationships where they are continually made to feel inadequate and worthless as human beings. If this view is received from those that they encounter repeatedly, there is a much reduced opportunity that they will sustain or develop a positive self.

The empirical evidence available tends to support Cooley's conception of the looking-glass self. Rosenberg (1981) has shown that individuals do see themselves as others see them. Similarly, there is evidence that individuals believe others think more highly of them than they actually do. Individuals, then, tend to side in the egocentric direction in their views of how others see them, unless they are repeatedly made to feel differently. Finally, many individuals from minority groups that have suffered discrimination such as Blacks in the U.S. and Jews around the world, tend not to have negative views of themselves. The reason for this is that they tend to identify with other group members, resulting in a realistic appraisal of self (Rosenberg, 1981).

George Herbert Mead: Taking the Role of the Other (Role-Taking)

Mead, a philosopher by training, was one of the most influential figures to carve out the groundwork for the symbolic interaction perspective. As one of the most notable figures in this tradition, it is interesting to note that he never went to graduate school. Nevertheless, Mead was best known during his career as having a powerful impact on his students. It was not until after his death that his most famous work was published, *Mind, Self, and Society: From the Standpoint of a Social Behaviourist (1934/1962).* This publication, however, was not written by Mead himself but was compiled from lecture notes taken by his former graduate students. One of his former students, T.V. Smith, once stated, "Conversation was his best medium, writing was a poor second" (Ritzer, 1988:176).

Mead's general theory of the stages of socialization begins with Cooley's description of children's imaginary friends. According to Mead, children's play moves through two distinguishable stages. The earliest form of play, known as the play stage, is characterized by children playing make-believe. Undoubtedly you have seen young children pretend to be a mother or a father by imitating behaviour and conversation. In the play stage children take on the roles of people who are significant to them. They will play as doctors, police officers, astronauts, and the like because they identify with them. At times, children will take on two complementary roles at once. Thus, children may say things to themselves that their mothers have said to them, then reply in their own words (Elkin and Handel, 1984).

The second stage of play is known as the game stage because children as they develop learn the organization of roles. Children learn how to distinguish one role from another. They learn how they should act at school with teachers, how to act around their friends, and how to act with their parents. Very young children are not capable of making this distinction. Let me try and clarify this point. If you ever have been to a young child's t-ball game you probably remember laughing after a child finally hit the ball because all the children on the playing field would chase the ball simultaneously or one would catch the ball and chase the base runner around the bases instead of throwing the ball to another player ahead of the runner. To Mead, very young children have not yet learned that for organized games to be properly played requires that people play various positions (roles). Mead also emphasizes that during this stage children learn the norms and values of society from their parents and significant others.

During the game stage children also become cognizant of the **generalized other.** By this, Mead is referring to the child's ability to take the role of the other. In our baseball example, older children know that if the ball is hit to the left field, the left fielder alone will chase the ball while the other players bold their positions and await the throw from the fielder after the ball has been caught. The generalized other represents our capacity to take a viewpoint by putting ourselves mentally in the role of the other. That is, we know what the left fielder will do by understanding the role of the left fielder on certain plays. The self to Mead is at first unsocialized since it is poorly developed and external to children. It is established once children learn to take the role of the other and internalize society's norms and values. In other words, the socialized self emerges once society is internalized which occurs in the game stage of socialization.

Mead also goes beyond Cooley by partitioning the self into two components: the "**I**" and the "**Me**"; however, he later identifies a third component, the **generalized other** which completes the process of developing a socialized self. For Mead, one of the essential qualities of the self is its reflexive ability: the ability to be self conscious (White, 1977). This quality enables individuals to stand apart from themselves (that is, as they see themselves) in order to see how others view them. The reflexive nature of the self enables individuals to react to the imagined "other person's judgement." According to Mead, individuals acquire a sense of self through the processes of communication and interaction with others.

The "**I**" in Mead's self represents the individual's ability to project oneself outside of the body. In other words, the "**I**" is that part of the self that we usually do not think about. For example, when you are chasing a baseball you do not think of what your body is doing during the action. To do so would make you clumsy, therefore, you concentrate on chasing the ball. The "**I**" as a component of self is the part of which we are unaware until the act is completed. You probably remember as a child—as I do—rolling your eyes after your parents stated something that you did not like or could not agree with. This act often occurred unknowingly to you, but was usually brought to your awareness by your parents. Restated, this part of the self is spontaneous, provides us with our individuality, and expresses itself without our conscious awareness until after the act.

The "**Me**" in Mead's conception of the self consists of those conscious thoughts and actions that are in our awareness. More accurately, it is the organized set of attitudes of others which individuals assume themselves. The "**Me**" is our ability to be appropriate and meet societal expectations. For example, when you are invited out on a dinner date to a lavish restaurant, you usually know how to behave—even if you have never been to a lavish restaurant—and what silverware is used for what purpose. On the other hand, when you go out with your friends for pizza, how you behave and whether or not you eat your pizza in hand or with a knife and fork is usually not of any real consequence. The "**Me**," then, attempts to adopt the proper response to the situation encountered. The "**I**," the spontaneous side of self, and the "**Me**," the social self, represent separated but complementary components of the same self. In our previous example of rolling your eyes at a comment made by your parents, the "**I**" is expressing itself since you were not aware of it, even though your social self, the "**Me**," recognizes that this is not acceptable behaviour toward your parents. The self-reflexive nature of the self is evident when the act is made conscious to you since you recognize that this is not considered appropriate behaviour when you put yourself in the role of the other.

Theories of Development: A Recapitulation

In this section we discussed a variety of theoretical views on child development. Although each of these views are different in detail, each emphasize that the self emerges through social interaction with others. Each view attempts to demonstrate how the individual comes to understand societal standards. Piaget specifically dealt with the cognitive development and morality in children. Freud was particularly interested in the unconscious and its effect on the human personality. Erickson's work takes us beyond Freud since it explores stages in personality development over the life cycle. Finally, Cooley and Mead suggest how society is internalized in us through social interaction with others.

Each of these theoretical views should not be perceived as competing views of socialization but complementary since each theorist addresses different components of development and socialization. The theories of Freud, Erickson, Cooley, and Mead, however, tend to be more applicable to adulthood socialization than Piaget's. Overall, the importance of these theoretical views on childhood socialization become especially relevant once we explore the types of socialization experienced by individuals in our society. More importantly, these views lay the foundation for understanding the processes of socialization experienced by members of any society.

Types of Socialization

As suggested earlier, socialization is not a uniform concept but one that has enormous range over the life cycle. Socialization processes vary over the life cycle resulting in a cumulative effect that enables us to function in pro-social ways rather than in anti-social ways. To fully understand the processes of socialization, we need to further delineate the types of socialization experienced by all individuals during their lifetimes.

Primary Socialization

Primary socialization takes place during infancy and early childhood usually within the family. Initially, children's view of the social world is very general and primarily seen through the eyes of their parents. It is through primary socialization that individuals learn language, symbols, mores, norms, and values and develop a diverse set of cognitive skills, enabling them to act productively in society.

As children move through the primary socialization process, their referent shifts from the specific to the general. This abstraction is necessary for them to come to understand what others in general expect. Children slowly begin to learn that the views they hear first about the social world may not necessarily be consistent with others they are now in contact with. According to Berger and Luckmann (1967), primary socialization is the most important since it is during the early years that an individual's social construction of the world takes place. Primary socialization alone, however, cannot entirely prepare children for roles and experiences in the adult world.

Secondary Socialization

Secondary socialization refers to the social training received by children, often in institutional or formal school settings and which continues throughout their lives. In contrast to primary socialization, secondary socialization typically involves socialization by other adults, i.e., teachers. Secondary socialization later in life (also known as *adult socialization*) takes place when individual's become involved with new dimensions of life: raising a family, entering a professional school, starting a job, and retiring. You will recall that we suggested that socialization in adulthood requires individuals to adapt to changing circumstances. This is especially apparent in such cases as marital breakdown (see Family chapter) and occupational obsolescence (see The Organization of Work chapter). In general, the skills initially developed through primary socialization provides adults with the basis to acquire the adaptation skills necessary during their life time experience with secondary socialization. We will return to the notion of adult socialization later in this chapter in section five.

Anticipatory Socialization

Anticipatory socialization is considered by sociologists a rehearsal or preparatory process enabling individuals to anticipate what it will be like to play particular roles in life. For example, if you were to enter nursing school or teaching, you probably have anticipated what it would be like to be a nurse or a teacher. Often, imagery operates to enable individuals to consider how they will play out social roles prior to engaging in them; including, what will be worn and used (symbols of the position), anticipation of how various situations that may arise would be handled, and the language (technical jargon) that is necessarily attributed to the occupation. Anticipatory socialization can be an intermediary stage between primary socialization and secondary socialization. Most often, however, anticipatory socialization occurs during the period most often associated with secondary socialization.

Wheeler (1967) argues:

A practical question facing most agencies of socialization [i.e., the school system] is how to manage the advance preparation so as to increase the probability of successful outcome....Since much activity may go on between the decision to enter a program and actual participation, it seems likely that a considerable amount of socialization affect is achieved before the person enters. (p.84)

Simply put, the agencies of socialization, such as the school system (teachers and guidance counsellors) and the mass media, are actually providing individuals with preparation for anticipated future social roles as a way to ensure that individuals are socialized to carry them out as expected.

Resocialization

Resocialization is based upon unlearning and replacing old attitudes, beliefs, and behaviours with new ones. This type of socialization is especially relevant to adults since throughout the adulthood life cycle, people are constantly required to adapt to changing circumstances and situations. Resocialization is usually more difficult than the original socialization experience since it entails the unlearning of old and familiar ways of behaving. This is obvious when we think of how adults adapt to changing job roles that have been instituted by organizations, i.e., the transition to computer technology. Similarly, individuals who lose their jobs, retire, or go back to school after a prolonged absence, experience the process of resocialization. In each case, the identity of the individual may change, or at minimum, their social role may become altered leading to the necessity to adapt to changed circumstances.

The resocialization process is also evident among individuals who enter **total institutions** (Goffman, 1967) or **carceral organizations** such as correctional or psychiatric institutions for any length of time. In most respects, individuality and freedom to act as one desires is removed. Individuals living under such circumstances lose the freedom to eat, sleep and exercise when they so choose, express themselves freely, and leave when they would like. Prior to and immediately following discharges after prolonged incarceration from such institutions obviously requires that the individual undergoes the process of resocialization in order to adapt to community life once again.

Individuals in extreme situational isolation and stress, usually known as **critical situations** are also subject to the process of resocialization. Bettelheim (1943) and Cohen (1953) studied concentration camp behaviour of individuals imprisoned in Nazi concentration camps during the second world war. Bettelheim, imprisoned himself, witnessed in many of his fellow prisoners a continuous resocialization process taking place. In the camps the first response of many prisoners was to pay the minutest attention to every sign of harm, to each guard, to the prisoner foreman, to each noise in the distance, and to each abrupt or large-scale movement. Finally, after long-term stress caused by such concerns, prisoners either "converted" themselves from their Judaic religion to a synthetic faith and action or moved on to a form of psychological adaptation which involved paying less attention to lethal danger and more to self-preservation actions such as trying to find "safe" or less difficult job assignments, making friends to share a confidence with, and finding a better place to sleep. Cohen's research confirms Bettelheim's findings and suggests that extreme situational isolation leads to a deculturation process. According to Cohen, prisoners strive to adjust new and peculiar circumstances to be congruent with values ordinarily learned in the process of socialization.

Atypical Cases: Blocked Socialization

To this point we have described socialization patterns common to most children and adults. These patterns typically involve situations that are established to enable individuals to become productive members of society. Many individuals, in particular children, are not so fortunate. Some children are raised in crowded institutions, others are raised by unresponsive adults or parents who are absent for long periods of time. Studies of these less than ideal situations provide contrasting evidence for understanding the importance of primary socialization.

Blocked socialization, represents one type of socialization which results when the child is withheld social interaction and social support for prolonged periods of time. One study, among many aimed at determining the effects of parental deprivation, compared the development of infants with and without maternal stimulation. In this study, Spitz (1964) compared infants who were abandoned and receiving hospital care with infants who resided in a nursery for infants who had mothers incarcerated in prison. Spitz found that the infants who were abandoned received minimal stimulation in the hospital setting since nurses were responsible for numerous children at once. In fact, of the 45 infants under the age of eighteen months, 6 died in a measles epidemic. In another ward containing 43 infants eighteen to thirty months of age, 17 died of measles and only two of the 26 surviving infants could speak.

In contrast, the children who were in the prison nursery and were placed with their mothers for a portion of each day, were reported to be healthy, vigorous, and developmentally on track. Spinx's study showed that physical stimulation alone is insufficient to ensure adequate development and socialization. Those infants that were in contact with an adult who cared and provided consistent emotional support were able to acquire the primary socialization necessary to develop emotional and social attachments.

Studies have also traced the long-term effects of children deprived of adult attention. Children raised in isolation or near isolation are termed *feral* (or unsocialized) children. Such cases as the "Wild Boy of Aveyron" and the "Wolf Girls of Agra" have been reported in the literature. These were purported cases of children raised by wolves and who were later found by humans. Bettelheim (1959) has studied the documentation of these cases and has concluded that the reports actually suggest cases of abandoned children suffering from autism or feeble-mindedness. Bettelheim concludes that there is no scientific evidence available to demonstrate that any animal, including adult primates, could care adequately for a human infant, especially in terms of meeting the demands of species-characteristic behaviour, reflexes, and drives, to enable them simply to survive the time of their utter dependency.

More recent reports of feral children point to instances of children who were raised in the attics of houses with little to no human social contact. The best known case of a feral child raised in social isolation was reported in the United States by Kingsley Davis (1940). The girl in this case became known as "Anna of the Attic" since she was raised since birth in a dark attic by her grandfather because she was an illegitimate child. Anna reportedly received minimal physical care and virtually no social or emotional care. At age six Anna was discovered by social workers who reported that she could not walk, talk or feed herself. Prior to her death, approximately five years later, Anna was able to walk and could communicate in a limited way. This case, however bizarre it may seem, points to the importance of human social contact for child development and socialization.

Blocked socialization most frequently occurs in less extreme situations. It may occur to individuals living in situations where sexual and verbal abuse is a constant feature of everyday life. Cooley's looking-glass self may help us understand how individuals develop inadequate senses of self and emotional attachments to others in these situations. You will recall that Cooley suggested that we develop a sense of self through our experiences with the social world as well as in silent talk and interpretation of what others say to us. Individuals living in the situations alluded to may develop a distorted view of human relationships in the social world.

For an example of blocked socialization, see Inset 4:1.

Inset 4:1
Child Needs a Family

The following newspaper clipping is based on a neglected child in need of an adoptive family. The description demonstrates the negative effects of a child neglected early in life. Even short-term blocked socialization can impede a child's development and ability to socialize with others.

Melissa is a three-year old who needs an adoptive family. She has come a long way in the past year but functions at the level of a one-year-old.

This little girl enjoys good physical health. She can drink from a cup and can feed herself with a spoon. Despite significant delays, Melissa has responded well to a daily infant stimulation program and to a caring and structured home.

While Melissa does not yet interact with other people, as she gains confidence, her eye contact with those around her improves. She is learning to talk with the help of a speech therapist.

Melissa will need continued stimulation programs and medical supervision. She also needs a family who will provide her with love, understanding and patience.

The Calgary Sun, Sunday, June 9, 1991, p. 4.

Socialization and Society

Socialization and Social Control

Society requires that the individual should respond in appropriate ways to certain stimuli. From this single premise it is reasonable to conclude that the socialization process is closely related to a system of social control. According to White (1977), "...it might be possible to conceive of socialization as a pervasive yet covert mechanism designed to ensure cultural continuity, and social control as its more overt counterpart" (p.16). By way of the mechanisms of socialization social control can operate. In childhood, patterns of attitudes and action are established which suit the need for people to interact meaningfully and harmoniously. Later in life after some view of "self" has become well established, mechanisms of socialization still operate to dispose individuals to behave in appropriate ways, and to help them either to select the right attitudes and actions from their mental bank, or to learn new appropriate responses. The notion of oneself becomes enhanced throughout socialization, and both childhood and adulthood can become part of an overt social control system. For example, parents and teachers will often appeal to what they believe is an adolescent's self image by invoking standards of adult behaviour (i.e., "As an adult, what do you think are the consequences?"), or readiness to accept responsibility (i.e., "Since you're an adult now, I'll leave you in charge"), when trying to coerce the young person into what may be considered a desired behaviour. The social control form in this respect attempts to appeal to the individual in terms of what she perceives as being worthy of herself.

The internalized controls which are established throughout socialization ensure that individuals know in broad terms how to behave in any social situation, or at least have the necessary knowledge potential for proper behaviour. Ultimately, social control is achieved when self-control (or, the *internalized social conscience*) is mastered, and individuals are able to exercise discipline over their own actions and behaviour. This does not mean that the social conscience is necessarily obeyed each time, nor even does this conscience provide the individual with the precise response demanded by the particular social circumstances, only that what is plausible is available. For instance, individuals in our society understand that driving under the influence of alcohol violates both social and legal codes of conduct, nevertheless, many still do drink and drive; even though the appropriate response is evident and available to them. Nevertheless the socialization process plays a vital social control function and helps to ensure the reasonably smooth continuity of society.

If socialization responds to the needs of society the question of who does the socializing is of considerable importance. It is likely that socialization will greatly be influenced by the individuals and institutions conducting it. Let us now turn to these agencies of socialization in our society.

Agencies of Socialization

The process of socialization obviously does not occur in a vacuum. Throughout the lives of children, as well as adults, various individuals and institutions participate in influencing future attitudes and actions. An important aspect of socialization is the acquisition of social meaning and behaviour from experiences with families, schools, peer groups, work settings, and the mass media (Peterson and Peters, 1983). The separate influences of these and other *socializing agents* have been the focus of most of the existing scholarship on socialization (Gecas, 1981; Inkeles, 1968). Initially, the family is the primary socialization agent during the early years. As children come into contact with the larger society, the school system, peer groups, and the mass media affect how they learn about society and future social expectations. These agencies, however, do not have a sequential influence on children, with the exception of the first two or three years of a child's life. Most of the agencies influence children in a concurrent and complementary fashion.

The Family

The first agent of socialization for infants is their immediate family. Children are not only provided with physical care but also care that initiates emotional bonds with their parents. Almost immediately, most infants learn that they can rely on their parents for care, security and comfort. As infants grow older parents begin to take on the role of educating them to human and social ways. This process is extensive and requires that children attain requisite levels of cognitive development before they can acquire language, become toilet trained, learn how to delay gratification, and so on. Initially, children are socialized to familial ways, rather than what is socially acceptable to society at large. Parents, in particular, teach their children about society based on their own experiences, biases, and modes of conduct. Later children learn that their parents ways may not necessarily be the universal way to achieve functional membership in society. Nevertheless, children are still strongly influenced by their parents as agents of socialization.

The family into which children are born act as their first reference group (commonly called the *family of orientation*). The family, as a social institution, stresses particular values, norms, and attitudes specific to itself and are used as referents for children in enunciating and evaluating their own values, norms, and attitudes. Parsons and Bales (1955) have suggested that children identify with the family as a group; therefore, their practices become part of children's conception of self. Specifically, Parsons and Bales suggest that not only do children identify with individual members of the group as role models, but they use interaction within and between group members as models for future ways of acting and building strong identities of themselves. The pattern of interaction that takes place within the family setting has future implications for how the individual will act in the future. Interestingly, during the late adolescence and into the early twenties young people can readily identify those qualities of their parents or interactions within the family unit that they will exclude from their own family life in the future. Nevertheless, many will fall into similar patterns of behavior simply because they have learned from their parents only certain ways of resolving a problem or accomplishing a task. For example, if a parent turns to alcohol every time there is a crisis, it is not unusual for children of that parent to turn to similar vices to deal with conflicts in their lives. Often, the interaction patterns developed within a family are not practiced by the offspring, but frequently they will marry someone who does cope in similar ways without immediately recognizing it.

At birth children inherit the status (or statuses) of their parents, in the community and in society. Most importantly, the family's position in the social class structure becomes the child's position. This affects not only bow the child will be responded to during the childhood years but their status as an adult as well (Elkin and Handel, 1984). One of the first major studies looking at the factors affecting occupational attainment in the United States was that by Blau and Duncan (1967). These researchers found that "the family into which a man is born exerts a profound influence on his career, because his occupational life is conditioned by his education, and his education depends to a considerable extent on his family" (p. 330). Evidence in Canada would suggest that this is even more true compared to the United States (Wanner, 1986). Wanner's study comparing the educational attainment of individuals in Canada and the U.S. found that "in Canada parental SES [socioeconomic status] is a more potent determinant of the likelihood of extending schooling beyond high school, particularly to university" (p. 62). The evidence shows that the family does influence the values, attitudes, and future actions of children. Children born into more affluent and educated families tend to adopt similar values that emphasize the necessity of future education throughout children's lives. Children born into families of less affluence and education tend to adopt value structures geared towards obtaining "good paying and secure" employment.

More recently, sociologists have come to recognize that much of their work on families as socialization agents has been centered on the nuclear family, married adults and their offspring. Today, however, our nation has experienced what has been termed as *pluralistic* family structures. Some of these family structures include: single parent headed families, blended families, homosexual headed families, and so on (for a more comprehensive discussion on changing family structures see chapter 10). Conventional wisdom suggests that children from these families will be maladjusted to "normal" functioning in society. Presently, there is no compelling evidence that these family structures result in more or less well-adjusted children than the typical nuclear family. In fact, the evidence would suggest that the adjustment of children to these alternative family structures typically depends on the ability of adults to adjust to them and how they deal with these relationships with children (Eiduson et al, 1988).

Our knowledge of child socialization within the family usually led us to believe that socialization was a one-way process: parent-to-child. During the last fifteen years or so we have come to realize that children are not passive recipients to the influence of their parents, but do in fact act as socialization agents to their parents (Bell and Harper, 1977; Mackie, 1984). As much as parents impart knowledge and the ways of society to their children, the process is reciprocated by children. Many parents of adolescent children learn the ways of the changing world through the eyes and experiences of their children. Times change and parents tend not to experience the changing realities confronted by their offspring. This phenomenon is commonly called the "generation gap" implying that parents seldom understand the pressures experienced by youth today. Pressures such as early sexual and drug exploration, conflicting values, development of self-concept, or changing gender roles, were not experienced to the same degree by many of their parents; consequently, they are not understood.

Although families are still perceived as having a major influence on the socialization of their children, parental involvement with children in the last decade has declined. More recently, parents argue back and forth that it is not the amount of time spent with children that is important, but the quality of time. We will not debate this point here, but will emphasize that alternative agents of socialization have replaced the parent to a greater or lesser extent in socializing children. Some of these include day care centres (see Inset 4:2), mass media (i.e., television), school, and organized activity and sports clubs.

The Peer Group

Up until about the age of two, children who are seemingly playing together, are essentially only playing in close proximity with each other; which consists of them doing their own particular things. By the time this independence ends, children have learned how to respond to the orders, requests or needs of other children (White, 1977). Peer groups tend to be the first contact children have with others outside of their family. It is in these groups that children socialize through playing with each other and begin to exert their independence from family. During the early years of childhood, children usually play together under the supervision of an adult or an older child, to whom reference is frequently made for direction, assistance, approval, and mediation as disagreements emerge between playmates. Play between very young children tends to be *egocentric,* all vying to exert their own interests and desires. Adults and older children while supervising young children act as agents of socialization, establishing how children should play together. As children mature, adult supervision is required to a lesser extent as children learn the social rules of play, cooperation, and negotiation.

The peer group, according to Elkin and Handel (1984), has certain distinctive characteristics:

1. by definition, it consists of similar ages;
2. participants in the group have varied power and prestige;
3. the peer group establishes its own interests and concerns, quite apart from adults concerns with appropriate social values, norms, and expectations; and,
4. their intent for long-term socialization is unintentional, yet their interactions serve an important function for preparing them for the adult world.

Children usually participate in more than one peer group. Sometimes they include siblings and cousins, others consist of neighbourbood children, still others involve schoolmates. Participation in a variety of peer groups prepare children for future relations with a variety of adults. Each peer group usually has its own rules, norms, and purpose. Children learn to adapt to varying circumstances and roles that they assume within each group, much in the same way that adults adjust to groups that they are in contact with.

Inset 4:2
Child Day Care Provision: Socializing Agent?

Since World War II one of the most striking demographic changes in North America has been the number of women entering the work force. During the first half of this century, few women worked outside of the home after starting a family. Today, this is no longer true. A major consequence of this development is that infants and pre-school children (ranging from three weeks to five years of age) are being placed in various types of day care; receiving primary care from adults other than parents, at least for a portion of each day.

The number of licensed day care spaces in Canada in 1990 was 320,624, an increase of 22,541 spaces from the year before (Health and Welfare Canada, 1991). These day care spaces, however, do not include the number of children receiving primary care from non-licensed private or casual day care arrangements established between parents and care providers (i.e., babysitters).

Professionals and parents alike have debated the consequences and benefits of children receiving care from adults other than the parents of procreation.

Here, our concern is not with entering into this debate but to suggest that this new form of child care for our nation's children has resulted in the creation of a new socialization agent. Care providers today receive children during their informative years. Many are responsible for providing care to many children at once.

Presently, we have little empircal data to confirm or disconfirm the effects that these arrangements have on child development and socialization to familiy and societal values. Part of the problem, of course, is that children cared for in private and casual day care arrangements are difficult to assess and access. Further, longitudinal studies would be required to determine if children in day care facilities develop differently than children receiving care from their parents on a full-time basis.

What do you think? Does it make a difference if children are cared for by adults other than their parents?

Peer groups for older children serve some very important functions. First, it is in these groups that children establish their own rules for dealing with membership inclusion/exclusion, conflicts, trust, and other forms of normative behavior. For older children, the peer group is separate from the watchful eyes of adults. In these groups, children take on adult roles such as decision-makers and leaders. In addition, children learn their own special place within the group. Children learn to be followers, leaders, comedians, negotiators, scapegoats, and so on. For this reason, children in multiple peer group situations tend to have greater opportunity to experience a variety of roles. That is, the roles they occupy may vary by peer group.

Peer groups among adolescents take on special significance since adolescence is the time period in young people's lives when they struggle between parental/family dependence and establishing their own independence and sense of self. In a national study conducted in Canada, Bibby and Posterski (1985) found that adolescents commonly perceived adults to be insensitive to their problems. Many claimed that they were not taken seriously. Whether these views are real or perceived is irrelevant to the fact that they are felt. Peer group socialization then, is most prominent during adolescence because it is in the peer group that teenagers sense self-importance and acceptance.

Socialization during this stage of the life cycle involves dealing with both positive and negative peer influences. Adolescents tend to deal with issues around "fitting in," dating, sexuality, drugs and alcohol use, personal independence, future educational and occupational prospects, and so on. Peer influence plays a major role in how these issues are resolved. Parents of adolescents tend to want to help their children make decisions, but often their values are initially rejected as adolescents exercise their own individual identity and independence.

As a socialization agent adolescent peer groups not only develop their own understandings of the world but complement the views of their families in many respects, particularly in late adolescence. Adolescents, although often rejecting many of their familial values also accept many others. These values are usually shared in discussions with their peers resulting in a socialization process that broadens adolescents' views of society beyond that of their parents. Overall, the peer group is an influential socialization agent, but it is still not the primary socialization agency in our society. According to Mackie (1983), the peer group is the second most potent socialization agency behind that of the family. Bibby and Posterski found support for Mackie's insight. Table 4:3 shows that even during adolescence, teenagers still perceive their family as having a major influence on their lives. Teachers and the media have a less perceived influence on the lives of adolescents. Although parents have the greatest influence on their adolescent children, many adolescents reportedly receive more satisfaction from their peer group than their families (see Table 4:4). Most of this satisfaction stems from adolescents feeling that their parents do not understand them nor treat them as adults, whereas their peer group is "in touch" with them, according to Bibby and Posterski. Nonetheless, the family is still the predominant socialization agent.

Table 4:3

Perceived Sources of Influence among Adolescents, Canada, 1984[1]

"To what extent do you think your life is influenced by:"

	A Great Deal	Quite a Bit	Some	Little or None	Totals
Family	55%	30%	11%	4%	100%
Your Friends	30	43	23	4	100
Teachers	9	32	43	16	100
Media	8	26	45	21	100

[1]Number of respondents = 3500

Source: Modified from original. Bibby, Reginald W. and Posterski, Donald C. (1985). *The Emerging Generation: An Inside Look at Canada's Teenagers*. Toronto: Irwin Publishing, p.101.

Table 4:4

Perceived Sources of Enjoyment among Adolescents, Canada, 1984[1]

"How much enjoyment do you receive from the following:"

	Canada	B.C.	Prairies	Ontario	Quebec	Atlantic
Peer Group	59.7%	59.7%	58.7%	62.3%	56.0	61.7
Family	33.0	33.4	28.6	34.4	35.8	31.0
Television	29.0	30.0	27.0	31.0	26.0	36.0
School	15.0	17.0	11.0	17.0	15.0	16.0

[1]Number of respondents = 3500

Source: Modified from original. Bibby, Reginald W. and Posterski, Donald C. (1985). *The Emerging Generation: An Inside Look at Canada's Teenagers*. Toronto: Irwin Publishing, p.32.

The School

With the increase in the social complexity of our society, socializing experiences within the family setting and the peer group alone are insufficient to prepare children for later experiences in the adult world. Consequently, it is in school that children systematically are taught the ways of the whole culture. "From entry in the first grade until entry in the labour force or marriage the school class may be regarded as the focal socializing agency" (Parsons, 1964:130). Ishwarin (1979) estimates that from kindergarten through grade six children spend approximately 7,000 hours in school (p. 23). Evidently, the school system has the potential to influence children.

According to Parsons (1964) the school system simultaneously serves four functions:

1. It emancipates the child from primary emotional attachment to the family;
2. it drives home societal values and norms beyond those that can be given in the family;
3. it imposes a differential valuation and reward of achievement; and,

4. from society's point of view it provides a selection and allocation of its human resources relative to the adult role system (p. 143).

The school system, then, as a formal socialization agency imparts more to children than just knowledge about reading, writing, and arithmetic. It is also a time and place for developing those social skills that are necessary if they are to use the formally learned knowledge in satisfying ways for themselves and in acceptable way for others. It is also the place where children experience a whole set of new constraints. Children must adapt to new and unfamiliar surroundings, new people, time-tabled work and play, and possibly a new range of behavioral expectations.

As children move through school, they slowly adapt their processes of thought and logic to a more objective recognition of others in their social environment. Children learn to recognize the difference and the independence of their own views and feelings from those of others. More importantly, children begin to experience in the school system their relative abilities compared to the students around them. Prior to the school years, children may have been raised with praise and feelings of their importance as members of a family. During the school years however, they come into contact with other children vying for similar praise and attention. Teachers tend to reinforce the differences between children through grading and providing rewards to the "better" students, while offering few incentives for "weaker" students, whether intentionally or not, to compete in the educational marketplace. Typically, class size is very large limiting the amount of time that a teacher can spend with a child experiencing difficulty mastering the fundamentals of a subject matter. Often, these processes lead to feelings of low self-worth, competitiveness, and, finally, to future roles in life becoming clearer to children well before they actually assume them.

Children initially experience extrafamilial social control and authority in the school system. Early in the school career children learn that the teacher has authority and control over them. Most often, teachers must maintain uniform standards in terms of evaluation, behaviour, and social expectations to which all students must adhere to. The effect of this process is that students learn to be constrained in their attitudes so they are accepted by both the authority figure and their peers. Children also learn about authority figures and social control outside of both the classroom and their families while they are in the school system. For instance, older children in the school system come into contact with even more teachers than they experienced during their earlier school years. These teachers, along with teachers involved with extracurricular activities such as sports teams and activity clubs, act as socializing agents in moulding students to societal expectations. Children learn how to compete with others in socially appropriate ways. They learn the pleasure of winning and the pain of losing. This process prepares them to adapt to adult life with flexibility and recognition that winning and losing will be constants in the years to come.

The socializing influence of the school system is not only experienced by children but also by young adults pursuing post-secondary school training. Numerous studies have shown that young adults are socialized in nursing schools (Davis, 1968; Ross, 1961; Simpson, 1967), graduate training (Bates, 1967; Becker and Carper, 1956), and to professional training such as medical schools (Bucher and Stelling, 1977; Friedson, 1970; Haas and Shaffir, 1981), chiropractic schools (Kelner et al, 1980; Mills and Larson, 1981), and law schools (Lortie, 1968), to assume the occupational roles that they are being trained for. All of these studies point to the way that self-identity is transformed, feelings of competency are developed, collegiality and competitiveness are reinforced, and how uncertainty is managed, during the schooling years.

The school system as a formal socialization agent begins early in children's lives and lasts upwards of twenty or more years for some. It not only teaches the knowledge necessary for individuals to function adequately in adult life, but also operates as a primary disseminator of appropriate values, norms, and social expectations to members of society. Functionally, this is important to society but not necessarily to all of its members. The school system as a socialization agent also acts as a credential granting agency; that is one that grants certification to individuals for succeeding on their terms. Employers in the work world have passed through this system and accept its legitimacy. Unfortunately, many students are not able to remain in the school system until they reach the minimal level of education—high school diploma—for a variety of reasons. Individuals who fall into this category tend to receive fewer employment prospects compared to their graduating counterparts. For example, individuals with grade twelve diplomas tend to have greater employment opportunities compared to individuals who have grade ten or eleven completed. Presently, there is no compelling evidence to suggest that an extra year in school actually leads to higher calibre labourers or salespersons. Nonetheless, individuals who do not achieve the minimum standards accepted today, often find themselves at a disadvantage when seeking employment.

The Mass Media

The influence of the mass media (i.e., television, music videos, magazines, newspapers, and advertisements) has unquestionably been a powerful socializing force of both the young and old in our society. The mass media invades our senses while we are at home and when we are out in public areas. In today's society, it has become increasingly difficult not to have been exposed to the mass media in one form or another on a daily basis. According to Rosengren and Windahl (1989), the mass media play very important roles:

1. as carriers of society's overall culture and also of specific subcultures;
2. as political arenas of conflict and consensus;
3. as evermore ubiquitous and powerful agents of socialization;
4. as a means to express group identity and group affiliation; and,
5. as individual instruments of knowledge and pleasure, power and subjugation (p. xix).

Our concern here is with how the mass media *acts* as a potential socialization agent in society. We will pay particular attention to the medium of television since it is the most potent catalyst in disseminating and reinforcing cultural values, norms, and attitudes in modern day life.

When a medium such as television has the power to transmit and reflect the values of society and when, as Leifer *et al.* (1974) suggest, it serves a normative reference point, it assumes some of the characteristics of an agent of socialization. If the premise that television has some of these characteristics is accepted, it becomes crucial to examine television's impact on the minds of those who are subjected to its influence. The statistics on the television viewing patterns of children have stimulated much interest. Comstock (1975), synthesizing the findings of a number of studies, points out that:

1. Children typically begin viewing television regularly 3 or 4 years before entering the first grade.
2. Most children watch some television every day, and most watch 2 hours or more per day.

Spurlock (1982:73) further suggests that the evidence on television viewing shows that by the time children are 16, they have watched from 12,000 to 15,000 hours of television. This is equivalent to viewing approximately 15-20 months of television, 24 hours a day! The influence of television for socializing children cannot be repudiated. Rosengren and Windahl (1989) went as far to say that television as a source of general information may have a greater impact on children's social development than school. This is alarming considering that the television programs viewed by children seldom serve an educational function. According to Spurlock (1982), the heaviest period of television viewing by children is during prime time. Frequent television viewers can testify to the fact that there are far more half-hour sitcoms, game shows, sporting events, and "cops and robbers" shows during prime time than programs that would serve educational value to children.

The invention of the television has also met with mixed blessings in our society since it not only provides us with needed up-to-date information on what is happening around the world, across the country, and in our city, but it also reinforces cultural stereotypes, codifies social roles, and constructs gender identity (see Estep, 1982; Lindsey, 1990; Mackie, 1991; Rosengren and Windahl, 1989). Television shows typically portray men in positions of power, domination, and control; whereas women are typically portrayed as weak, submissive, emotional, and as sex-objects (Lindsey, 1990). Moreover, both adult and children's shows revolve around men, with male characters outnumbering females 3 to 1 (Signorielli, 1982 quoted in Lindsey, 1990). When females do outnumber males it is usually in the context of multiple females hanging off the arms of a male, with the accent on women as object. Studies (Fruch and McGhee, 1975; Gross and Jeffries-Fox, 1978) have shown that the degree of television viewing is associated with conceptions of gender stereotypes. These studies show that both pre-schoolers and older children who are heavy consumers of television viewing hold more traditional gender stereotypes than pre-schoolers and children who view television less frequently. Coupled with the gender stereotypes are children's perceptions of social roles available to them in the future. Heavy consumers of television programming often felt that men performed instrumental roles (i.e., providers and decision-makers) while women performed expressive roles (i.e., nurturers and childrearing functions), which limited their conceptions of occupations available to men and women and contributed toward a view that males were superior to females. The major consequence of these findings is that the vulnerability of children leads them to believe that what is on television is an accurate depiction of reality.

Television also acts as an agent that reinforces the values and norms of a society. Most programming emphasizes the importance of the family, the consequences of deviant behaviour, and the extent of cultural diversity in our society. More recently, television networks have taken steps to address these issues, however, most of these efforts are ineffective since the majority of the programming still exhibit sexism and violent acts. Until television network executives realize the impact of their programming on viewers, little progress will be made toward the advancement of the equality of the sexes and sensitizing us toward the consequences of the victimization of others.

Patterns of Subcultural Variation in Canada

Throughout this chapter we have alluded to socialization as a complex process. You should be aware, however, that the patterns of socialization, or the ways that individuals become socialized to society can, and often do, vary by such factors as ethnic background, social class, and region of the country. In this section we will briefly convey how these factors contribute to different socialization practices and their effects on society and the individual.

Ethnicity

Canada as a nation was founded on immigrants. Today, Canada is considered to be a multicultural society with distinct ethnic subcultures remaining intact. Since 1980 19% of Canada's immigrant population have predominantly come from Asian and other non-European countries (McKie and Thompson, 1990). This fact accompanied with our aboriginal population, French Canadian and English Canadian distinction, and earlier immigrant populations, has resulted in a cultural mix unseen in many industrialized nations. Naturally, then, this process leads to varied cultural and socialization patterns among the various ethnic groupings in the country. Here our concern is with bringing to your attention that the socialization patterns discussed throughout this chapter differs by ethnic grouping. It is true that most members in our population do support the general values and norms in our society, however, many do vary in terms of socializing their children, the importance of the family, the value of education, and strength of their cultural identity.

One of the consequences of a rich cultural mix is tension between various ethnic and race groups. As pointed out in McGuigan's chapter on Culture, ethnic and race relations has been a source of tension and common misconceptions between groups. Prejudicial and discriminatory attitudes and actions tend to be reinforced during childhood socialization. For example, think of yourself as a young child overhearing your parents discussing the violent behaviour of some Asian gangs or the French separatist movement. If your parents believe that the violent actions of some Asian gang members represents the violent nature of Asians in general or that we should let Quebec separate because they are nothing but a society of complainers, then you too as an impressionable young child may adopt similar beliefs about these groups without having a clear understanding of the issues and problems faced by these groups. Socialization, then, not only is a necessary and beneficial societal requirement, it also has detrimental effects when the socializee is influenced by socializers who maintain egocentric postures or base their views of others on generalizations.

Social Class

The concept social class is a complex concept that has been variously defined in sociology and related disciplines. The concept of social class, however, invariably suggests that different groups possess unequal amounts of wealth, influence, prestige, and "life chances" (Elkin and Handel, 1983). For our purpose we will define social class as the social standing an individual has in their community based on their education, occupational prestige, and income level. Undoubtedly, you have heard of such classes as lower class, working class, middle class, and upper class groups in society. Social class becomes an important factor in understanding how individuals are socialized to society since it contributes toward self-identity, extent of political influence, social contacts, as well as economic and educational aspirations and opportunities.

Research in social class differences in Canada and elsewhere frequently point to the varied socialization practices across the classes. For example, in a study conducted in Hamilton, Ontario, Pineo and Looker (1983) found evidence to suggest that the socioeconomic status of parents had bearing on whether or not the value of self-direction in children was supported by parents. The researchers found that middle-class parents were more likely to encourage self-direction in their adolescent children than working-class parents. Lambert (1981) in his study of the social influences among English-Canadian and French-Canadian parents on child development found that there were more similarities between French-Canadian and English-Canadian parents of the same social class in child-rearing values than either group are with same-ethnic parents of a different social class.

Earlier we discussed the work of Blau and Duncan (1967) and Wanner (1983) showing that the education level of parents influenced the educational aspirations of their children. These studies demonstrated indirectly that the social experiences of children from families to different social classes are socialized differently, resulting in divergent values toward education.

Oversocialization

Our discussion on socialization may lead you to conclude that the individual is a more or less passive object of socialization by society as represented by its various socialization agents. It is true that individuals are often constrained in their actions because of these socialization forces, but they still have free will to act on their own. If individuals did not have the free will to act, then we would have a society with very little variation in personality and action. In one of the most quoted articles dealing with this concern "The Oversocialized Conception of Man in Modern Sociology," Dennis Wrong (1961) argues in a complex way that the individual is not totally driven by internalized norms and values. In other words, Wrong suggests (not to the extent that Freud did in earlier writings) that the individual is a social, but never a fully socialized creature. If the norms and values of the environment that they experienced growing up, then all actions would not be the responsibility of the individual. In other words, if an individual were raised in a poor neighbourhood and had negative role models, does this mean that they should not be held responsible for their actions in society?

In our society, most individuals are socialized by the various agencies discussed. However, we also know that all agencies do not socialize all individuals in the same way. For example, the school system socializes children in different ways depending on the attentiveness of the student and their individual academic ability. Similarly, not all families are the same; therefore, we should expect variation in the content of socialization to society. Wrong is quite right in his argument: we do place too much emphasis on the internalization of values and norms, and less on the variety of ways that individuals experience these influences. It seems reasonable to conclude that the internalization of societal norms and values are experienced by most individuals in our society but that the process by which it is experienced, as well as, the personalities of the individuals subjected to these processes will affect the extent of social constraint internalized.

Socialization and Social Roles

Socialization to society from early infancy onward is important in preparing individuals for future social roles. In primary socialization, children learn the general aspects of participating in society. As children mature, secondary socialization enables children to learn the specific elements of the activities and social roles that people play in society. In this section, we will briefly discuss the concept of social roles and how socialization enables individuals to carry them out. We will also discuss the effects of gender role socialization as well as socialization to occupational roles.

Performing Social Roles

> All the world's a stage,
> And all the men and women merely players:
> They all have their exits and their entrances;
> And one man in his life time plays many parts.
>   (*As You Like It,* Act II, Scene VII)

This excerpt from William Shakespeare's 1599 play, *As You Like It,* summarizes what we engage in on a daily basis. All the world is a stage in the sense that we play many roles that demand certain requirements of us. As a mother you act differently to your children than you do toward your husband, employer, closest friend, parents, and those you meet at school. Each time we enter a social encounter with others, we wear different hats depending on who it is we are interacting with at the time. The act of wearing different hats is called performing **social roles.** *Social roles* can be defined as "a pattern of behaviour, structured around specific rights and duties and associated with a particular status position within a group or social situation" (Theodorson and Theodorson, 1969). Notice that social roles are not people but are the parts played by people in social situations. Social roles enable us to predict the behaviour of others and for individuals to pattern their actions accordingly. Social roles, then, are sets of norms that allow and limit our behaviour.

Erving Goffman, an Albertan-born sociologist, is probably the best known theorist who has worked in the area of social role performances. Goffman in an important work *Presentation of Self in Everyday Life* (1959) frequently used the analogy that everyday interactions with others was similar to performing on a stage. According to Goffman, there were **front stages** and **backstages.** The *front-stage* was that part of yourself that you acted out for social audiences. If you were talking to your employer, for example, you would probably act confident, knowledgeable, and skilled. Away from your employer, the *backstage,* is where you drop the "act" or take off the mask, perhaps even tell a loved one how worried you are about being able to do the tasks ahead of you. Goffman believed that performing social roles represented the "crucial discrepancy between our all-too-human selves and our socialized selves" (1959:56). According to Goffman, we spend a good part of every day playing multiple social roles and have to take off and put on the different masks warranted to play the role required. For Goffman, this was all a part of **impression management,** the art of guarding against a series of unexpected actions, such as unintended gestures, verbal slips, and inappropriate behaviour required by the situation. *Impression management* requires that we maintain the social role intact until we leave the setting or situation. In addition, impression management requires that we do not allow others into our backstage since it then becomes frontstage knowledge about ourselves. For instance, even if you invite your employer over to your house for dinner, you still do not act as you normally would when your employer was not present. In general, we attempt to keep a controlled front of who we are to others. Only certain individuals have the opportunity to see other sides of our same self, but no one ever really has the opportunity to see all our backstage behaviour. Overall Goffman does recognize that some backstage parts of ourselves are revealed on occasion. Instructors will sometimes communicate differently to students when they see them in the cafeteria, in contrast to the way they act in the lecture hall. Similarly, if you frequent the same night spot, the waiter or waitress may act differently to you, in contrast to a patron they have not served before.

Social role performance is possible since individuals are socialized to the society they live in. We learn all about social roles through secondary socialization processes and the agents of socialization. In addition, particular norms, values, and attitudes are adopted and reinforced by the different groups to which we belong. As you learned in the chapter on culture, norm violations are recognized by members of social groups. We learn through our own errors, and those of others, how to play social roles and control what it is we want others to see of ourselves.

Gender Role Socialization

Gender role socialization, unlike social roles, begins at the moment of birth. Whether you liked it or not, your parents in all probability treated you different than your opposite sex sibling. Since parents are socialized into the same society, albeit at a different period of time, they react differently towards you depending on whether you were a boy or a girl. Fox (1977:809) found that studies of gender learning show that "even as infants, girls are expected to be, thought to be, and rewarded for being quieter, more passive, more controlled—in short, 'nicer' babies—than are boys" (quoted in Mackie, 1991). This process, no matter how harmless it may appear at first, is the beginning stages of gender role socialization. Gender *role socialization is* the process whereby individuals are socialized to take on the roles that are deemed "sex-appropriate" for the society they live in. These roles are often defined in terms of their degree of masculinity and femininity. This process limits the range of possible behaviour seen to be acceptable of a man or a woman. Boys learn not to cry, girls learn that crying is acceptable. Boys learn that aggressive play is natural and fun, girls learn that aggressive play is not lady-like and unacceptable. Boys learn that playing house with dolls is sissy-like and girls learn that playing house with dolls is rewarded with praise—"you're a good little mother." Each of these situations socializes boys and girls to particular gender roles. Boys learn to hold back their emotions, to be aggressive and competitive, and to believe that they cannot nurture like a female. Similarly, females learn to express their emotions, be passive and pacify, and to believe that it is their mothering "instinct" to be good nurturers.

At school boys and girls learn that their abilities are differentially assessed by teachers. Boys are good at mathematics and sciences, girls are better at english and spelling. Until recently, textbooks assigned to school classes reinforced sex role stereotypes; often portraying women as intellectual inferiors to men (Weitzman, 1979). In addition, vocational tracking often resulted in males and females entering classes that reflected stereotypical biases of their predecessors—boys learned machine shop, woodwork, and automobile mechanics; girls learned home economics, secretarial skills, and hairdressing—under the guise that it would be useful to them later in life. What children actually learned was a narrow range of skills that made them dependent on the other sex. In addition, boys were able to learn the skills that paid better later in life compared to those of girls.

As boys and girls become young adults, boys are perceived as a "good catch" if they are single and educated; females, on the other hand, are considered to be "old maids" and must be undesirable if they are still single at a certain age. Even though times are changing, these descriptions of men and women are still common perceptions of many individuals in our society. Young men and women, even if they do not accept these stereotypical notions, are often the envy of others or the recipient of sympathy of others because of their status—which is usually sex-based.

More recently in the sociological literature there has been discussion on the connection between the early socialization of males and violence. Given that the vast majority of violent crimes are committed by males, researchers have looked for possible sources of violent behaviour in the particular expectations of parents and significant others have for young boys; that is, expectations that will lead them to become a particular type of "man."

A recent example of such research is Myriam Miedzian's work, *Boys Will Be Boys: Breaking the Link between Masculinity and Violence* (1991). Miedzian continues the tradition established by Chodorow (1978) and Dinnerstein (1977) which argues that it is exclusive female mothering which is a major factor in the creation and maintenance of a violent masculinity. Miedzian maintains that young boys must deny the warmer, softer, and more intimate world of the mother if they are to take on a masculine identity. Because

92

males have been absent from the world of nurturing, masculinity is understood by young boys as that which is not feminine, and given that the feminine is so strongly tied to mothering, that which is not warm, soft, intimate, and nurturing. According to Miedzian, young boys must separate themselves from the world of women and mothers, denying all that is feminine inside of them, in order to take on the fruits of masculinity which are concerned with toughness, domination, and the suppression of emotions. Miedzian documents how these tendencies, established in the family context, are translated into violence and reinforced by contemporary sports, television, music videos, and toys.

Miedzian calls for a wholesale change in how adults parent. In particular, that it is crucial that fathers become more actively involved in nurturing children so that young boys identify with nurturing and caring as normal human action and emotion. Miedzian also points to concrete programs in schools and elsewhere that could be instituted to encourage young boys to take on care-giving roles and to develop nurturing skills. In this way the masculine mystique will lose its violent edge.

For some, gender role socialization is not perceived to be problematic, for others it is deleterious to both males and females and has made our society less rich than it could otherwise be. Our intent here is not to take issue with this practice but simply to point out that gender role socialization from birth onward affects how men and women view the world, their perception of the opportunities available to them, and so on (later chapters in this book specifically address the issues pertinent to this process). Gender role socialization, particularly during adult life, takes the form of social roles. Men and women play different social roles primarily because they were socialized into them (see chapters of The Family and The Organization of Work).

Socialization to Occupational Roles

Socialization to occupational roles consists of both psychological and social adjustments of people to their work and work setting. This process often originates well before people actively enact the role that they will play at work and will be an ongoing feature throughout their careers. Naturally, socialization to occupational roles does not imply that all people are content and satisfied with their careers, but it does suggest how people learn to adapt to the formal and informal norms, values, and codes of conduct of the role they will or presently do occupy. Socialization to work roles consists of three phases according to Chen and Regan (1985). These phases consist of

1. the neophyte learning the knowledge and skills of the work that is necessary to perform the activities of the occupational role;
2. the neophyte learning the subculture of the work setting, including the code of conduct that is shared by the work group; and,
3. the neophyte's transformation of identity, whether recognized or not, through the internalization of the occupational role (pp. 63–73).

These phases are equally applicable to janitors, ministers, steel workers, salespersons, librarians, and physicians since each must learn the skills, adapt to the ways of the work setting, and identify with the work group and occupational role. In *Men and Their Work* (1958) Everett C. Hughes identified that all of these occupational roles are occupied by actors facing similar kinds of problems associated with adapting to a different status, unfamiliar expectations, and new work environments when moving into new occupational roles. Let us clarify this point by looking at two different examples.

In their study of medical students, Haas and Shaffir (1980) found that the socialization of medical students to the profession involved two sets of problems. The first problem was based on acquiring the vast body of knowledge and skill necessary to become a competent physician. The second, and more immediate, was to convince their evaluators that they were competent in their knowledge and skills. According to Haas and Shaffir, these medical students attempted on a daily basis to direct their evaluators away from the areas in which they felt least competent during hospital rounds and volunteered to answer or raise insights or express knowledge when they knew the area under discussion. Haas and Shaffir suggested that these students were becoming socialized to demonstrate their competence through impression management either by being competent (*instrumental abilities*) or by appearing to be competent (*expressive abilities*). Eventually, as the medical students acquired greater areas of competence they spent less time managing their expressive demonstration of competence and more time demonstrating their instrumental abilities. Finally, as the medical students gained greater levels of competency, their self-identity was transformed through detaching themselves from emotional involvement with their patients, enabling them to align themselves with their occupational role and away from that of a lay person.

The work of Jack Haas in 1977 studying high steel ironworkers, those individuals who construct the structural beams for high-story buildings, demonstrates the socialization experiences of newcomers and experienced ironworkers in managing their personal fears and work conditions in a highly dangerous occupation. These workers, like the medical students, managed their role competency by never discussing their fears and inadequacies. Haas suggested that these workers depended on each other for safety, resulting in a culture that required workers to manage their feelings of fear while on the job. According to Haas, apprentices are ridiculed and are expected to perform some of the most demeaning and dangerous jobs. For the ironworker, apprentices are treated in this fashion to test their ability to "take it" and to determine if they were "made of the right stuff." Apprentices, on the other hand, take many calculated risks in demonstrating their acts of bravado. Most of these risks, however, demonstrated to the experienced ironworkers that the apprentice was fearless, dependable, and could be trusted while "running the iron"—the colloquial term for assembling beams.

The two examples provided illustrate that although the demands of the occupational roles are different, both require managing the presentation of self in demonstrating ability to others. It is through the process of socialization that individuals learn to acquire the knowledge, skills, abilities, motivations, and attitudes to successfully transform their identity to be consistent with the occupational role performed.

Socialization to occupational roles is an ongoing process during the work career. Many organizations indoctrinate incoming employees with orientation sessions directed at the operation, policies, and procedures of the setting. Similarly, most organizations today have ongoing training seminars for employees to retrain or reorient employees to changes in the work setting. All of these formal practices are developed to socialize employees to the ways of the organization.

One area of socialization to be discussed later in this book is that of the informal socialization to deviant occupations. During the last twenty years, sociologists working in the area of deviant subcultures have analyzed how individuals are recruited and trained for deviant occupational roles such as illicit drug trafficking, prostitution, exotic dancing, street gang membership, and so on. In this book, Brannigan *et al* discuss, among other things, the occupational careers of prostitutes; in particular, how they are socialized into the business and manage their identities which are in direct conflict with the wider mainstream society.

Summary

1. Socialization may be defined as the process by which individuals develop a sense of self and acquire the knowledge, skills, attitudes, motivations, and behaviour required to participate in a given society or social group so that they can function within it. It is a process that helps to explain two different types of phenomena: (i) the way that an individual is capable of participating in society; and, (ii) how society is possible at all (Elkin and Handel, 1984). The socialization process is not confined to childhood. It is a lifelong cumulative process requiring individuals to adapt to changing circumstances.

2. Piaget's cognitive development approach to child development emphasizes that children move through four stages of development. Each stage usually requires the former since cognitive development requires that children achieve certain mental abilities to move to the next level. Piaget also contributed to our understanding of child development by studying moral reasoning in children. Piaget found that children under the age of nine exercise moral realism in judging the acts of others: that is, the severity of punishment should depend on the amount of damage done. Children around nine years of age believe that the severity of the punishment should depend on the intent of the act. For Piaget, this is a direct outgrowth of what he calls *moral autonomy*. Piaget believes that the development of children's cognitive capacities enables them to reach a level of moral thought that is consistent with society's.

3. The psychoanalytic explanation is best exemplified by the works of Sigmund Freud. According to Freud, the roots of human behaviour lie in the unconscious (instinctive) aspect of the human mind. Consequently, for the individual to function effectively in society, personality development requires that the unconscious aspects of the mind be tempered and controlled. According to Freud, the human personality has three major energy systems: the *id, ego,* and *superego*. The distinction between the three energy systems of the personality can best be thought of as the difference between the child (id), the adult (ego), and the parent (superego); wherein the child

is spontaneous, the adult is responsible, and the parent imparts appropriate morals, values and constraints.

4. Erik Erickson's psychoanalytic theory of personality development extends Freud's work. He describes a series of psychosocial stages in which the individual faces a wide range of human relationships as they mature and have specific socialization issues to solve at each of these stages. Successful transition at each state requires that the individual resolve the particular issues that are faced. Inadequate resolution of issues at any stage leads to incomplete development and possible problems in the future.

5. The symbolic interaction explanation of socialization is best exemplified by the works of Charles Horton Cooley and George Herbert Mead. Cooley's model is based on the *looking-glass self.* According to Cooley, the mind is like a mirror in that individuals receive from others what they believe others to think and see. The general premise is that we see ourselves as others see us and we depend on some reasonable consensus of friends and associates to maintain a consistent sense of self. Mead's work starts with Cooley's description of children's imaginary friends. According to Mead, children's play moves through two distinguishable stages: the *play stage* and the *game stage.* The play stage is characterized by children playing make-believe, while the game stage is characterized by children learning the organization of roles. During the game stage children become cognizant of the *generalized other.* Mead also goes beyond Cooley by partitioning the self into two components: the "I" and the "Me." The "I" represents the spontaneous side of self, and the "Me," the social self.

6. Socialization is not a unitary concept. In our discussion, we identified four types of socialization experienced by individuals: *primary, secondary, anticipatory, and resocialization.* In addition, we suggested that some individuals experience what is known as *blocked* socialization. Primary socialization is probably the most important of the types identified but it is not enough to complete the socialization process.

7. Four agencies of socialization were identified: the *family,* the *peer group,* the *school,* and the *mass media.* Each of these agencies influences the development of the child's personality and socialization to society. In addition, each agency may be a more potent socialization agent than the others during certain periods of the life cycle. Overall, however, the family is still the most important socialization agent in our society today.

8. Variation in socialization practices is evident across social class and ethnic groups. Overall, the studies suggest that social class in Canada seems to be more influential when we look at child development between French-Canadian and English-Canadian families.

9. Dennis Wrong argues that sociologists have what he calls an "oversocialized conception of man," whereby the influence of the socialization process is exaggerated in effect. Wrong suggests that individuals do have free will to act and that all individuals do not experience society in the same way. For Wrong, individuals do internalize societal values and norms, but do so to varying degrees.

10. Social roles can be defined as a pattern of behaviour, structured around specific rights and duties and associated with a particular status position within a group or social situation (Theodorson and Theodorson, 1969). Social roles are the parts played by actors on a daily basis governed by sets of norms that allow and limit behaviour. Goffman's analysis of social roles led him to conclude that the self orchestrates frontstage and backstage behaviour. Frontstage behaviour is that which others see when we are acting out our social roles. Backstage behaviour is that which particular others do not see. The difference between the two, according to Goffman, is that we guide our behaviour around our socialized self, whereas, few people see our all-too-human self. For Goffman, frontstage behaviour required impression management whereby we maintain the social role intact until we leave the setting or situation.

11. Gender role socialization is the process whereby individuals are socialized to take on the roles that are deemed "sex-appropriate" for the society they live in. These roles are often defined in terms of the degree of masculinity and femininity. Generally, this process begins at birth at which time the newborn is sex-typed a boy or a girl.

12. Socialization to occupational roles consists of psychological and social adjustments of people to their work and work setting. Socialization to work roles consists of the novice learning the knowledge and skills of the work, learning the subculture of the work setting, and a transformation of self-identity. All individuals who work are subject to these adjustments. In addition, many individuals will experience a variety of occupational roles throughout their work careers.

References

Bates, Alan P.
1967   *The Sociological Enterprise.* Boston: Houghton Mifflin.

Becker, Howard S. and James W. Carper
1956   "The Development of Identification with a Profession." *American Journal of Sociology,* 61:289–298.

Bell, Richard O. and Laurence V. Harper
1977   *Child Effects on Adults.* New York: John Wiley.

Berger, Peter and Thomas Luckmann
1967   *The Social Construction of Reality.* New York: Doubleday.

Berry, Gordon L. and Claudia Mitchell-Kernan eds.
1982   *Television and the Socialization of the Minority Child.* New York: Academic Press.

Bettelheim, Bruno
1943   "Individual and Mass Behavior in Extreme Situations." *Journal of Abnormal and Social Psychology,* 38:417–452.

1959   "Feral Children and Autistic Children." *American Journal of Sociology,* 64:455–467.

Bibby, Reginald W. and Donald C. Posterski
1985   *The Emerging Generation: An Inside Look at Canada's Teenagers.* Toronto: Irwin Publishing.

Blau, Peter and Otis D. Duncan
1967   *The American Occupational Structure.* New York: Wiley.

Borgatta, E. and M. Borgatta eds.
1992   *Enclycodpedia of Sociology.* New York: MacMillan Publishing Company.

Bucher, Rue and Joan Stelling
1977   *Becoming Professional.* Beverly Hills: Sage Publications.

Campbell, Ernest Q.
1975   *Socialization: Culture and Personality.* Iowa: Wm. C. Brown Company Publishers.

Chen, Mervin Y. T. and Thomas G. Regan
1985   *Work in the Changing Canadian Context.* Toronto: Butterworths.

Chodorow, Nancy
1978   *The Reproduction of Mothering: Psychoanalysis and the Sociology of Gender.* Berkeley: The University of California Press.

Comstock, George A.
1975   *Television and Human Behavior: The Key Studies.* Santa Monica, Calif.: Rand Corporation.

Cooley, Charles H.
1902/   *Human Nature and the Social Order.* New York: Scribner's.

1964

Davis, Fred
1968   "Professional Socialization as Subjective Experience: The Process of Doctrinal Conversion among Nursing Students," in Howard S. Becker, Blanche Geer, Davis Reisman, and Robert S. Weiss eds. *Institutions and the Person: Papers Presented to Everett C. Hughes.* Chicago: Aldine.

Dinnerstein, Dorothy
1977   *The Mermaid and the Minoteur: Sexual Arrangements and the Human Malaise.* New York: Harper and Row.

Eiduson, Bernice T., M. Kornfein, I. L. Zimmerman, and T. Weisner
1988   "Comparative Socialization Practices in Traditional and Alternative Families," in Gerald Handel ed. *Childhood Socialization.* New York: Aldine De Gruyter.

Elkin, Frederick and Gerald Handel
1984   *The Child and Society: The Process of Socialization,* Fourth edition. New York: Random House.

Erickson, Erik
1963   *Childhood and Society,* Second edition. New York: Norton

1968   *Identity: Youth and Crisis.* New York: Norton.

Estep, Rhoda
1982   "Women's Roles in Crimes as Depicted by Television and Newspapers." *Journal of Popular Culture,* 16(Winter):151–56.

Fox, Greer Litton
1977   "Nice Girl: Social Control of Women through a Value Construct." Signs, 2:805–817.

Freidson, Eliot
1970   *Profession of Medicine: A Study of the Sociology of Applied Knowledge.* New York: Harper and Row Publishers.

Fruch, T. and P. McGhee
1975   "TraditionAl Sex Role Development and the Amount of Time Watching Television." *Developmental Psychology,* 11:109.

Gamble, Thomas J. and Edward Zigler
1986   "Effects of Infant Day Care: Another Look at the Evidence," *American Journal of Orthopsychiatry,* 56(1):26–42.

Gecas, Victor
1981   "Contexts of Socialization," in Rosenberg, M. and Turner, R. eds. *Sociological Perspectives in Social Psychology.* New York: Basic Books.

Goffman, Erving
1967   *Interaction Ritual: Essays on Face-to-Face Behaviour.* Garden City, New York: Doubleday Anchor Books.

1959   *The Presentation of Self in Everyday Life.* Garden City, New York: Doubleday Anchor Books.

Gross, L. and S. Jeffries-Fox
1978   "What Do You Want to Be When You Grow Up, Little Girl?" in Tuchman, G., Daniels A., and Benet, J. eds. *Hearth and Home.* New York: Oxford University Press.

Haas, Jack and William Shaffir
1978   *Shaping Identity in Canadian Society.* Scarborough: Prentice-Hall.

1981   "The Professionalization of Medical Students: Developing Competence and a Cloak of Competence," in David Coburn, Carl D'Arcy, Peter New and George Torrance eds. *Health and Canadian Society: Sociological Perspectives.* Don Mills, Ont.: Fitzhenry and Whiteside.

Haas, Jack
1977   "Learning Real Feelings: A Study of High Steel Ironworkers' Reactions to Fear and Danger." *Sociology of Work and Occupations*, 4(2):147–170.

Handel, Gerald
1988   *Childhood Socialization.* New York: Aldine De Gruyter.

Health and Welfare Canada

1991   *Status of Day Care in Canada 1990: A Review of the Major Findings of the National Day Care Study.* Ottawa: National Child Care Information Centre, Child Care Programs Division.

Inkeles, Alex

1968   "Society, Social Structure and Child Socialization," in Claussen, J. A. ed. *Socialization and Society.* Boston: Little, Brown.

Ishwarin, K

1979   "Childhood and Adolescence in Canada: An Overview of Theory and Research," in Ishwarin K ed. *Childhood and Adolescence in Canada.* Toronto: McGraw-Hill Ryerson.

Kelner, Merrijoy, Oswald Hall and Ian Coulter

1980   *Chiropractors: A Study of Their Education and Practice.* Toronto: Fitzhenry and Whiteside.

Lambert, Wallace

1981   "Social Influences on the Child's Development," in Gardner, Robert C. and Kalin, Rudolf eds. *A Canadian Social Psychology of Ethnic Relations.* Toronto: Metheun.

Leifer, A. D., N. J. Gordon and S.B. Graves

1974   "Children's Television: More Than Mere Entertainment." *Harvard Educational Review,* 44(2):213–245.

Lindsey, Linda L.

1990   *Gender Roles: A Sociological Perspective.* Englewood Cliffs, New Jersey: Prentice Hall.

Lortie, Dan C.

1968   "Shared Ordeal and Induction to Work," in Howard S. Becker, Blanche Geer, Davis Reisman, and Robert S. Weiss eds. *Institutions and the Person: Papers Presented to Everett C. Hughes.* Chicago: Aldine.

Mackie, Marlene

1983   "Socialization." Chapter 3 in Robert Hagedorn ed. *Sociology.* Toronto. Holt, Rinehart, and Winston.

1984   "Socialization: Changing Views of Child Rearing and Adolescence," in Maureen Baker ed. *The Family: Changing Trends in Canada.* Toronto: McGraw-Hill Ryerson Limited, pp. 35–62.

1991   *Gender Relations in Canada: Further Explorations,* Second edition. Toronto: Butterworths.

Mandell, Nancy

1988   "Socialization, Subcultures, and Identity," in Curtis, James and Tepperman, Lorne eds. *Understanding Canadian Society.* Toronto: McGraw-Hill Ryerson Limited, pp. 395–422.

Manis, Jerome and Bernard Meltzer
1978   *Symbolic Interaction: A Reader in Social Psychology,* third edition. Boston: Allyn and Bacon.

McKie, Craig and Keith Thompson
1990   *Canadian Social Trends.* Toronto: Thompson Educational Publishing Inc.

Mead, George Herbert
1934   *Mind, Self, and Society: From the Standpoint of a Social Behaviorist.* Chicago: The University of Chicago Press.

Miedziam, Myriam
1991   *Boys Will Be Boys: Breaking the Link between Masculinity and Violence.* New York: Doubleday.

Mills, Donald L. and Donald E. Larson
1981   "The Professionalization of Canadian Chiropractic," in David Coburn, Carl D'Arcy, Peter New and George Torrance eds. *Health and Canadian Society: Sociological Perspectives.* Don Mills, Ont.: Fitzhenry and Whiteside.

Parsons, Talcott
1964   *Social Structure and Personality.* Glencoe, Illinois: The Free Press.

Parsons, Talcott and Robert F. Bales
1955   *Family, Socialization and Interaction Process.* Glencoe, Illinois: The Free Press.

Peterson, Gary W. and David F. Peters
1983   "Adolescents' Construction of Social Reality: The Impact of Television and Peers." *Youth and Society,* 15(1):67–85.

Piaget, Jean
1928   *Judgement and Reasoning in the Child.* New York: Harcourt.

1960   *The Moral Judgement of the Child* [1932], 3rd Impression. New York: Harcourt.

1962   *Play, Dreams and Imitation in Children.* New York: W. W. Norton and Company.

Pineo, Peter C. and E. Dianne Looker
1983   "Class and Conformity in the Canadian Setting." *Canadian Journal of Sociology,* 8:293–317.

Ramu, G. N.
1979   *Courtship, Marriage and the Family in Canada.* Toronto: The Macmillan Company of Canada.

Ritzer, George
1988   *Contemporary Social Theory,* second edition. New York: Alfred A. Knopf

Rosengren, Karl Erik and Sven Windahl
1989   *Media Matter: TV Use in Childhood and Adolescence.* Norwood, New Jersey: Ablex Publishing Corporation.

Ross, Aileen D.
1961   *Becoming a Nurse: Professional Nurses in Canadian Hospitals.* Toronto
            Macmillan Company of Canada.

Simpson, Ida Harper
1967   "Patterns of Socialization into Professions: The Case of Student Nurses," *Sociological Inquiry,* 37:47–54.

Spurlock, Jeanne
1982   "Television, Ethnic Minorities and Mental Health: An Overview," in Berry,
            Gordon L. and Mitchell-Kernan, Claudia eds. *Television and the Socialization
            of the Minority Child.* New York: Academic Press.

Wanner, Richard A.
1986   "Educational inequality: Trends in twentieth century Canada and the United
            States." *Comparative Social Research,* 9:47–66.

Weitzman, Lenore J.
1979   *Sex Role Socialization.* Palo Alto, Calif.: Mayfield Publishing Company.

White, Graham
1977   *Socialisation.* London: Longman Group Limited.

Williams, Thomas Rhys
1972   *Introduction to Socialization: Human Culture Transmitted.* Saint Louis: The C.
            V. Mosby Company.

```
┌─────────────┐
│             │
│  SECTION 2  │
│             │
│             │
└─────────────┘
```

Social Stratification

Introduction

Mahfooz Kanwar and Don Swenson

Social stratification is an inclusive term that describes a wide range of equality and inequality that we experience as social beings in any society. We are equal (or unequal) to one another on a wide range of characteristics: age, gender, family type, race, ethnicity, income, education, geographical location and the like. In this section, we are going to investigate three different types of social stratification: social class, ethnicity and race, and gender.

In Chapter Five, Bruce Arai examines some of the major characteristics of class formation and class relations in Canada. He maintains, that in comparison to the United States and Britain, most Canadians consider themselves to be middle class. In general, Canadians are protected by a number of social safety nets in the event of ill health and loss of employment. Even though this has been threatened by recent fiscal restraints, there are signs that this is going to be strengthened again.

Arai points out that those who earn the least amount of income in Canada still acquire a slightly greater proportion of national income than the lowest quintile of American earners. On the other hand, the higher quintile in the United States receives a larger share of the national income than its counterpart in Canada. By using national data provided by Statistics Canada, he demonstrates a wide range of issues related to the distribution of wealth, social class structure, and social mobility in Canadian society during the past few decades. Further, he shows the concentration of political power among the working class, the middle class, and the corporate elites within the political party establishments in Canada.

Chapter Six is devoted to the issues of race and ethnicity. Fredrick Ulmer provides the reader with an extended definition both of race and ethnicity. His review of the literature leads him to argue that race is, essentially, a social construction that has little basis in society. He does, however, show that racism, in all its various forms, is a social reality that needs to be challenged. His case history is the Aboriginal peoples of Canada and how they have suffered from so much racism. The author continues with an extended definition of ethnicity that includes many of its variants. He provides case examples of when ethnic differences do not enhance the human mosaic but evoke prejudice, hatred, and various kinds of "ethnic cleansing" of the kind we are seeing in the former Yugoslavia in the spring of 1999.

A central issue of social stratification in any society is that of gender. In general, the contributions of women have been consistently undervalued by most known human societies except, possibly, in the early years of our human history. Gisele Thibault addresses some of these inequalities.

She points out in Chapter Seven, that the women's movement, particularly since the 1960s in Canada and the United States, has contributed to the development of political consciousness among women for a greater campaign to win their equality with men. She examines the development of women's studies in post-secondary education and its influence on the understanding of women's issues. These programs have been able to demonstrate a number of social, political, and economic concerns of women. By examining the inherent limitations of these classical and contemporary sociological theories to interpret women's concerns, Thibault demonstrates the emerging theoretical orientations in feminist scholarship. However, she recognizes the need for further theoretical expansion in feminist studies in order to provide an in depth understanding of women's issues.

These three chapters discuss micro and macro levels of social inequalities in Canada. However, these are not the only aspects of possible inequality among Canadians. As noted above, there are many others. We limit our discussion to these three.

5

Class Patterns
and Life Chances in Canada

A. Bruce Arai

Introduction

In this chapter some of the basic issues involved in the study of social class and economic inequality are introduced. The chapter consists of four broad sections. First, class divisions in Canada are examined—do classes exist? A "classless" vision of Canada is presented, and some "common-sense" reasons often used to dispute the existence of different social classes in Canada are outlined. Second, after showing that, at the very least, there are significant economic inequalities between Canadians, some of the major formulations of class analysis, as proposed by people such as Karl Marx, Max Weber, and Eric Olin Wright are summarized. The third section deals with mobility—the movement of people within and between classes. The final section explores how class analysis can be used to understand various aspects of Canadian society, such as economic development, the pension system, and other social services.

The Classless Vision of Canada

When many people think about Canada, they see a country without large class differences, even when compared to similar countries such as Britain or the United States. For example, there is no Canadian nobility of very rich lords as there is in Britain (e.g. the Duke of Wellington). Nor do there seem to be very many wealthy Canadians comparable to the Rockefellers, Carnegies, or Bill Gates of the United States.

Similarly, Canada supposedly does not have many poor people. Inhabitants of inner-city neighbourhoods in Canada are significantly better off than those who live in the ghettoes of the larger British and American cities. Homelessness in Canada is a minor concern compared to the rapidly rising number of Americans forced onto the street. The overall impression of Canadians is that the vast majority of us are "middle-class." We can afford a car, and often a house. Almost everyone lives a comfortable life. This perception meshes nicely with the fact that for the past several years, Canada has consistently been judged by the United Nations as the best country in the world in which to live.

Most of us are able to give reasons as to why we do not see the extremes of rich and poor in Canada. For example, we share with Britain and the United States a system of government based on democracy and equality. This allows us as individuals to pursue our goals to the best of our abilities and it gives us a say in how our society is organized.

In addition, Canada, the U.S. and Britain all have free market economies. In the market, all people can compete on an equal basis to earn their living. On those occasions when the market has failed, politicians in all three countries have drafted laws to preclude some people from gaining an unfair advantage over others. There are laws preventing people from fixing the prices of their goods or services at artificially high levels, or forming monopolies to control the market. We also have minimum wage laws to ensure that people are paid a fair wage, and a taxation system whereby rich people redistribute a portion of their income to the less fortunate.

Furthermore, in comparison to Britain and the U.S., we often perceive that there is less inequality in Canada because of our extensive social service "safety net" to protect people against the possibility of poverty. Our social services generally compare very favourably to those in the U.S. or the U.K., which mitigates against the class divisions we see in these other two countries. When people lose their job in Canada they are entitled to employment insurance (formerly called "unemployment insurance"), and, as a last resort when they cannot get a job, we have a generous welfare system. When Canadians fall ill, their medical costs are paid by the government to ensure that people are not ruined financially by an illness. In addition, educational institutions in Canada are predominantly funded by the state to allow everyone an equal opportunity to attain their desired level of training.

This situation is markedly different from the U.S. and Britain. In some cases in the U.S., paying for hospital bills has reduced families to absolute poverty. Similarly, many British and American schools, colleges and universities are privately run, and access to these educational opportunities depends in large part upon one's ability to pay high tuition fees. Therefore, inequalities are entrenched as the rich can afford to send their children to "the better schools," which gives them an advantage over poorer kids who attend regular schools.

In sum, in the classless vision of Canada, the free market combined with the Canadian social services system and the ideals of equality and democracy ensure that class divisions in Canada are minor in comparison to other countries. Further, any economic divisions which do exist are thought to be the result of the normal operation of the economy and therefore justifiable. Those who are rich have earned their money on the basis of their hard work and they are entitled to a fair reward. Those who are poor have simply not applied themselves with sufficient vigour, and raising their standard of living is simply a matter of effort and determination.

Reasons for Studying Social Class

Although many of us may subscribe to the notion of Canada as a classless and relatively equal society, that belief rests largely on our impressions, without reliable data to back up these claims. But by studying social class, as opposed to relying on conjecture, we are able to get a better picture of the extent of economic inequality, and refute or confirm the classless vision of Canada. The study of social class also allows us to compare Canada with other countries in actual, not speculative terms. Is it true that there is more economic inequality in Britain or the U.S. than in Canada? This question is difficult to answer without looking at social class.

Finally, studying social class gives us insight into other sources of inequality which are often expressed in class or economic terms. For example, women, members of ethnic minorities and the elderly often receive less income than white men, not because they are less competent, but because they are victims of systematic discrimination.

Canada in Comparison with Other Countries

One way to examine differences in the degree of economic inequality between different countries is to look at the proportion of the total income earned by all earners in each country that falls to various "percentile groups." Percentile groups, as shown in Table 5.1 are constructed by ranking all income earners in each country from highest to lowest, and then dividing these people by the appropriate percentage of the total number of earners. Thus, for example, the 20% of earners who earn the least amount of income comprise the "lowest quintile." Table 5.1 shows the percentage of total national income which falls to the various percentile groups in six selected countries.

Our impression of Canada as more egalitarian than the U.S. in terms of income distribution is marginally confirmed in Table 5.1. Those Canadians who earn the least acquire a slightly greater proportion (5.7%) of national income than the lowest quintile of American earners (4.7%). Moreover, the highest quintile in the U.S. receives 1.7% (41.9–40.2) more national income than its Canadian counterpart.

Table 5.1. Percentage Distribution of Income in Lowest Quintile, Highest Quintile and Highest Decile for Selected Countries.

Country	Year	Lowest 20%	Top 20%	Top 10%
Brazil	1989	2.1	67.5	51.3
Canada	1987	5.7	40.2	24.1
Japan	1979	8.7	37.5	22.4
Sweden	1981	8.0	36.9	20.8
United Kingdom	1988	4.6	44.3	27.8
United States	1985	4.7	41.9	25.0

Source: Adapted from *World Development Report 1996: From Plan to Market*. p. 197.

The distribution of income in Canada is also very similar to that in the United Kingdom. The bottom quintile in the U.K. receives almost exactly the same proportion of income as in the US. However, income distribution in the U.K. is slightly more concentrated at the upper end than in Canada and the U.S., with the top 20% receiving 44.2% of the total income. Therefore, we can conclude that economic inequality in Canada, despite our impressions, is not very different from the situation in the U.S. or the U.K., and it may even be more unequal (see Banting, 1987).

What Is the Extent of Economic Inequality in Canada?

If we focus attention specifically on Canada and examine income distribution over the past decade, we find quite striking differences between the rich and the poor. Table 5.2 shows the percentages of total personal income which accrues to each quintile for selected years between 1979 and 1996. What this table shows is that, over the entire period, those Canadians in the lowest quintile earn less than 5% of the total income earned by all individuals and families. In contrast, those people in the highest quintile consistently earned over 40% of the total personal income. Put another way, on average, each individual or family in the highest income quintile earns approximately eight times the amount of money of each individual or family in the lowest bracket. Not only has this income distribution persisted over the last seventeen years, it has remained fixed ever since World War II (see Hunter, 1993).

Table 5.3, which shows the upper dividing lines between each quintile, also reveals a large gap between the lower and higher income brackets. For example, in 1980 the highest earners in the lowest quintile had a gross income of $17,282, which is roughly one-quarter what the highest earners in the fourth quintile accumulated. This gap stays constant, and in fact increases over the period.

Table 5.2. Percentage Distribution of Income of Families and Unattached Individuals by Quintile, 1979-1989.

Year	Lowest Quintile	Second Quintile	Middle Quintile	Fourth Quintile	Highest Quintile
1979	4.3	10.8	17.7	25.2	41.9
1985	4.6	10.4	17.0	24.9	43.0
1991	4.7	10.3	16.6	24.7	43.8
1996	4.6	10.0	16.3	24.7	44.5

Source: Adapted from Statistics Canada, Cat. No. 13–207 1996, p. 161.

Table 5.3. Upper Income Dividing Lines between Quintiles, in Current (1996) Dollars.

Year	Lowest Quintile	Second Quintile	Middle Quintile	Fourth Quintile	Highest Quintile
1980	17,282	33,122	49,763	69,169	N O
1985	17,007	30,693	46,851	67,736	L I
1991	17,149	30,818	46,496	69,194	M I
1996	16,478	29,938	46,252	69,943	T

Source: Adapted from Statistics Canada, Cat. No. 13-207-XPB1996, p. 160.

Rich Canadians

These tables clearly show that there is a high degree of economic inequality in Canada. This idea is further supported when we examine the average compensation of top Canadian executives. For example, in 1986, the average total compensation for various types of chief executive officers (CEOs) ranged from $88,941 for Canadian Operations Managers to $160, 174 for CEOs in finance/banking and insurance (Sobeco-Chapman, 1986:4). Further, the average total compensation for second executive officers (just below CEOs) was $107,460 (Sobeco-Chapman, 1988:64).

These compensation figures may seem minuscule in relation to the vast wealth held by people such as Bill Gates or even the annual salaries of entertainers and professional athletes. However, when we examine a list of the ten richest people in the world, we find that three of them are Canadians! Albert Reichmann, Kenneth Colin Irving and Kenneth R. Thompson all possess over six billion dollars worth of assets, while professional athletes do not even make the list (see Grabb, 1990; Davies, 1993).

Poor Canadians

In contrast to the very rich, there are also a large number of poor people in Canada, many of whom are forced to rely on food banks and/or transient houses for sustenance and shelter. In the 1986/87 fiscal year, 26 transient houses provided beds for 110,061 people (Health Reports, 1989).

The rise in the number of food banks since 1981 also points to the existence of a substantial number of poor people in Canada. For example, in 1989 an average of 175,000 families per month depended on food bank grocery bundles to supplement their inadequate food supplies (Bolaria and Wotherspoon, 1991:473). The majority of these people (72%) were also forced to rely on welfare assistance to cover their other costs of living.

A final measure of the condition of the poor in Canada is provided in Table 5.4 which documents the incidence of families and individuals who are forced to live on "low income." Low income families and individuals are defined as those people who spend more than a certain portion of their total income on food, clothing and shelter (in 1992 the percentage was 54.7%). This official definition is often taken by researchers as an estimate of the amount of poverty in Canada (Ross and Shillington, 1989:6).

Table 5.4. Incidence of Low Income by Family Type and Age, Various Years.

	1980	1989	1994	1996
All people	16.0	14.1	17.1	17.9
Men	13.9	12.2	15.0	16.0
Women	18.1	16.0	19.1	19.9
Children under 18 years	15.8	15.3	19.5	21.1
Elderly, 65 years and older	34.0	22.4	19.3	20.8
All others	13.6	12.3	15.9	16.2
Persons in families	12.7	10.8	13.5	14.5
Men	11.6	9.9	12.2	13.2
Women	13.7	11.7	14.7	15.8
Children under 18 years	15.8	15.3	19.5	21.1
Elderly, 65 years and older	17.8	8.9	6.1	7.6
All others	10.5	9.0	11.9	12.6
Unattached individuals	43.5	37.1	40.6	40.2
Men	33.9	28.6	33.1	33.9
Women	52.2	48.7	48.2	46.6
Elderly, 65 years and older	68.6	51.5	47.6	47.9
Non-elderly, less than 65	34.5	31.7	38.0	37.1

Source: Adapted from Statistics Canada, Catalogue No. 13-207-XPB 1996, p. 30–34.

The table shows that the incidence of poverty across the population has risen from 16% in 1980 to 17.9% in 1996. Put another way, 5.3 million Canadians lived in poverty in 1996. Over the same period, the incidence of poverty has gone up among people living in families, but gone down for unattached individuals. However, poverty among unattached individuals is still much higher than among those living in families.

If we break these figures down by age and sex, we can see evidence of the operation of other sources of inequality expressed in class or economic terms. Poverty is more prevalent among children in 1996 than in 1980, rising by 34% (from 15.8% to 21.1%). Women are also more likely than men to live in poverty, regardless of whether they live in families or are unattached. Overall, the disturbing message of the table is that poverty has gone up for people in most groups over the 1980 to 1996 period. The main exceptions to this trend are among unattached individuals, who comprise less than 30% of the population over the sixteen years.

As indicators of poverty in Canada, the number of transients in transient houses, the percentages of low income families and individuals, and the extent of food bank use, clearly show that many Canadians fall well below the "middle class." Also, the salaries of CEOs and top managers, the wealth of prominent families like the Reichmann's, Irvings, and Thompsons, and the proportion of the country's total income garnered by the top quintile reveals the existence of a distinct upper stratum in Canadian society. How, then, are we to explain these differences between Canadians? One of the most useful approaches is that of class analysis.

Class Analysis

The concept of class is rooted in the writings of Karl Marx. Marx was born in 1818 and lived through the turmoil of the "Industrial Revolution" in his native Germany, France and England. He was expelled from both Germany and France for his writings and participation in protest movements. In 1848 he moved to England which at the time was the world's most advanced industrial economy.

The British economy presented Marx with an extraordinary contradiction. On the one hand Marx saw the tremendous wealth that was generated through the application of machinery to the process of goods production. On the other hand he also saw that most of this wealth accrued to a small group of people while others lived in abject poverty. The wealthy often lived extremely well while the poor worked up to eighteen hours a day in the dangerous working conditions of mines and factories. In many cases, women and children were forced to find jobs, usually in "sweatshops" or mines, just to provide the family with the bare minimum of food, clothing and shelter.

What could possibly account for these incredible differences in wealth, prestige and lifestyle? For Marx, the answer lay in the power that a person derived from their **relationship to the means of production**. Marx saw that the people who owned the land, factories and machines were generally wealthy while those who did not were poor. Thus, he reasoned that the private ownership of productive property was the basis for the creation of two great classes in capitalist society; the class of rich owners known as the **bourgeoisie**, and the class of poor workers called the **proletariat**.[1]

Marx argued that on the basis of its ownership of productive property, the bourgeoisie was able to exploit the proletariat through the mechanism of profit. He, like Adam Smith before him, argued that the labour power of workers was the source of the extra value of a commodity after it had been transformed from raw materials into a finished product. Therefore, he thought that these workers should be compensated for their efforts. However, in capitalist production this extra value is appropriated by the bourgeoisie in the form of profits.

According to Marx, private ownership gave the bourgeoisie tremendous power over the proletariat because the working people could only make a living through the sale of their labour power (i.e. they had to become employees). They did not own the land or equipment to produce commodities, and therefore were forced to work for others to survive. Conversely, the bourgeoisie did not need the aid of others because they could work their own property to make a living.

The implication of this situation was that owners could deny workers an ability to survive, simply by not allowing others to use their productive property. In order to live, then, workers were forced to compete with each other for the right to work. The surest way to "win" a job in this situation was to offer the most amount of work for the least amount of money. Under these conditions, owners were quite happy to lend out their productive property because they could make more money by hiring workers at low wages.

Marx also claimed that there was another reason that owners paid the lowest possible wages to their workers. This was because intense competition also existed within the bourgeoisie. Owners were forced to generate as much profit as possible to protect themselves from their competitors. If an owner paid her/his workers "excess" wages s/he might not have enough capital to buy cost-cutting machinery, which would put that owner at a disadvantage in relation to her/his competition. Marx felt that capitalism inevitably tended towards monopoly as the less successful businesses went bankrupt or were bought out by more successful companies. This tendency swelled the ranks of the working class as more and more people were forced to sell off their holdings and work for others.

As working people became more aware of the increasing gap between the rich and the poor, members of this class would begin to understand the real nature of capitalism. This understanding, known as *class consciousness*, involved an identification of the real problem of capitalism (i.e. ownership of private property) and a recognition of the means by which the problem could be solved. According to Marx, this usually involved a violent revolution in which the power of the owning class was wrested away by force.

The crux of this revolution, for Marx, was the abolition of private property, because this was the way in which owners exploited workers. Once private property was eliminated, exploitation would cease to exist and a more egalitarian, communist society could be created.

As is clear from this brief review of Marx's thought, his major focus is on the power that people derive from their position in the economic sphere. For him, one's power was determined by one's class, and all social inequality can ultimately be reduced to one's relationship to the economy, as either an owner or worker. Many people have criticised him as an *economic determinist*, arguing that he paid too little attention to other sources of power and social change.

Max Weber was one of the first people to argue that while Marx's ideas were generally right, his understanding of the sources of social change was too narrow. Weber felt that people derived power from two other sources besides their economic position. First, people gained power from the prestige they held among members of their community. The more prestige a person had, the more ability that person had to influence the decisions of others. Weber identified this as power based upon one's *status*. The second alternate source of power which Weber identified was the arena of politics. A person's connection with politics and political figures at all levels also influenced their ability to affect change. This power, Weber called *party*. For him, the triumvirate of class, status and party provided a much better explanation of inequality in social life than a reliance on one single factor (Giddens, [1979] provides a good discussion of class analysis, and he offers a more detailed examination of the views of Marx and Weber).

More recently, others have criticised many of Marx's ideas as being outdated. Dahrendorf (1959) for example, has argued that Marx's theories may have been applicable to nineteenth century Britain, but they are inadequate for the study of modern societies. Marx's notions of class cannot explain the development of the joint-stock company and the "middle classes" of managers, supervisors and professionals. How, Dahrendorf asks, can we fit supervisors into Marx's notions of class? They are not part of the ownership class because they are not owners, yet neither are they members of the working class because they control other workers. Additionally, how do we classify people who own stocks in a company while working for that company at the same time?

Marx has also been criticised on other grounds. On the one hand, the rise of feminist sociology has questioned the usefulness of the concept of class in explaining inequalities between men and women in two ways. First, is it true, as Marx claimed, that all inequality can be reduced to a class basis? Many feminists argue convincingly that gender is an important source of power and difference in its own right. One of the best examples of this is that many women, whether they are owners or workers, remain subject to abuse and oppression at the hands of men.

The second criticism raised in the feminist literature concerns the class position of someone who does not participate in the paid labour force (for example, housewives). Do these women just assume the class position of their husbands, in the same way in which they have traditionally taken on their husbands' surnames? If so, then the concept of class is inherently sexist because it does not recognize the value of women's work to either the family, or industrial capitalism.

In a similar vein, many researchers have questioned the applicability of class analysis to numerous other groups who have only indirect ties to paid employment and the market. Do retirees maintain the class position they occupied during their working lives, or do they fall into a different class, reflecting their changed circumstances? Similarly, what is the class position of students who are, in many cases, simply training themselves for labour force participation? Can we assume, for example, that business students will become business people and therefore should be in a higher class than say, forestry or nursing students?

Finally, the tremendous growth in state bureaucracies calls into question Marx's basic two-class system. Are public-sector workers exploited in the same way as private-sector labourers, even though the majority of them do not work in organizations run for profit? That is, if profit is the mechanism by which the surplus value of workers is extracted, do public-sector employees retain the value of their work? The question then becomes whether or not public-sector workers are members of the same class as private-sector workers.

The numerous criticisms of the Marxian definition of class would seem to render the concept ineffectual. However, ideas of class have undergone a resurgence due to the work of people like Eric Olin Wright (1985). Wright modified Marx's two class system to accommodate some of the changes brought on by the rise of monopoly or finance capitalism.

Wright accepts Marx's basic distinction between owners and workers, but further subdivides these two "great classes" to account for what he calls "contradictory class locations." The bourgeoisie can be split into three groups based roughly on the amount of assets they own and control. The proletariat can be separated into numerous groups or class locations based on control over two specific types of assets: "assets in skill" and "assets in organization."

People may possess assets in skill which differentiate them from other workers. For example, secretaries and factory workers possess more skills assets than garbage collectors, and thus occupy different class locations. Additionally, people may possess assets in organization in that they are located higher in an organizational hierarchy. For instance, managers and supervisors possess more organizational assets than secretaries, factory workers or manual labourers. The acquisition of both types of assets usually involves formal schooling or apprenticeship followed by job experience.

While Wright's ideas are tied closely to Marx's, other understandings of social class have built more on the work of Max Weber. John Goldthorpe (Goldthorpe et.al., 1980) for instance has proposed a rather complicated conception of social class. For him, class analysis is concerned with how employment relations structure or affect the life chances of individuals over time. He has no grand theory of class, nor of the importance of class. Rather, Goldthorpe focuses on specific concepts such as class location (different structural positions within labour markets), and mobility (whether individuals move to different class locations over their lifetimes, or in relation to their ancestors). He also does not presume that class is relevant in all situations, and argues that the relevance of class, and indeed any other concept, must be determined empirically in each situation.

Goldthorpe's ideas are very closely related to Weber's in several key respects. He deliberately tries to eschew particular political commitments, which is very similar to Weber's commitment to a "value-free" sociology. He also insists on multi-causal and contextual explanations, which are also a hallmark of Weber's writings.

Unlike Marx, Wright and many others, Goldthorpe does not believe that exploitation is an integral element of class relations. That is, classes are not always and necessarily in conflict, nor do the gains of one class always come at the expense of another. Rather, he argues that classes can coexist, and gains by one class can be accompanied by gains for other classes. Similarly, losses by one class can go hand in hand with losses by other classes (Goldthorpe and Marshall, 1992).

The point of this discussion is that sociologists have employed numerous definitions of social class. Marx, Weber, Wright and Goldthorpe are four men whose ideas have been particularly influential. However, there is no one "right" definition of the concept which can be employed in all situations. Moreover, there is extensive debate about the amount of explanatory weight which should be given to social class versus other social categories such as race and gender. In the following sections we will illustrate the ways in which various definitions of social class have been used, in connection with race and especially gender, to explain different issues of inequality in Canada.

The Canadian Class Structure

The pie chart (Figure 5.1) gives estimates of the percentages of workers and owners in the Canadian economy. Very few Canadians are principally owners, only about 4%. The size of the working class is about ten times larger (43%), although still a minority. Indeed, the other three groups combined, what might loosely be called the middle class, comprise the majority of participants in the economy (53%).

Figure 5.1. The Canadian Class Structure

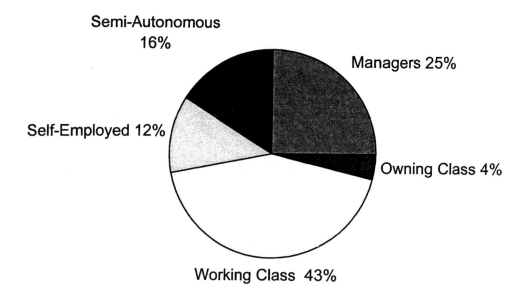

Semi-Autonomous 16%

Managers 25%

Self-Employed 12%

Owning Class 4%

Working Class 43%

Managers and supervisors (25%) make up the bulk of this middle group. These are people who control the work of others but who are not owners. Another large middle class contingent is semi-autonomous workers, people like college teachers, social workers, and engineers, who do not supervise the employment of others, but who are themselves employees. The last segment of the middle class is the "own-account" self-employed, people who work for themselves and employ no helpers (e.g., many farmers, artists).

This chart captures at a glance both what Marx foresaw and what he missed. The concentrated form of ownership which Marx predicted has emerged. Very few Canadians are the outright owners of large business enterprises, employing the labour of others to generate profit. But the growing working class that Marx also predicted is not in evidence. While a significant number of Canadians are workers, there are important divisions within this group, especially around issues of authority, supervision, and education.

In spite of these divisions, Canadian workers have all experienced relatively high standards of living. Most Canadian families own their own home and enjoy vacation travel. Almost every Canadian family owns a car, a television set, and a score of other household appliances. While the quality of housing and leisure varies enormously, patterns of consumption, not patterns of class, seem to matter most to Canadians. In the age of advertising and mass marketing, allegiance to consumption over class is hardly surprising.

Opportunities and Mobility

Issues of class may be less important to Canadians because, as we noted above, the ideal of equality is a strong part of our heritage. Canadian's pride themselves on being fair-minded, on stressing issues of equality. Canada is seen as a good place to live because of the opportunities available. Equality of opportunity captures this stress. But just how equal are the opportunities of Canadians? Does the child of a wealthy, urban family have opportunities equal to those of a child from a poor, farming family?

In a qualified manner, the answer to this question must be yes. All Canadians attend schools. The public funds to support education are also relatively equal across all school boards, whether the neighbourhood is rich or poor, rural or urban. In this manner, equality of educational opportunity exists. We are also fortunate in this country to have a health care system which provides access to quality care independent of the size of our bank accounts.

These examples demonstrate that opportunities to participate are equal, everyone has access. This does not, however, mean that everyone has an equal opportunity at success. Here is an analogy to illustrate the difference between participation and the likelihood of success. Any horse can enter a horse race (there is equality of opportunity). But all bettor's know that the likelihood of victory (success) is not equal, and consequently some horses have better odds than others.

A parallel situation exists in the school system. All children may participate, but the likelihood of success differs. The children of poorer parents face many hurdles, all of which diminish their chances of success. Relative to children from more wealthy homes they have poorer nutrition, they have fewer (if any) educated role models, they are exposed to fewer educational resources (e.g., reading material, travel experiences), and their families have less money to spend on tutors, private lessons, and other educational experiences (e.g., summer camps, pre-schools). Some of these differences are being recognized by Canadian governments, and attempts made to eliminate them. In Ontario for example, many school boards have introduced "junior kindergarten" for four-year-olds because they have found that kids who attend daycare perform better in school than kids who have not attended daycare. The idea is that if all kids go to junior kindergarten, then the advantage of daycare children over non-daycare children will be wiped out.

Certainly the hurdles mentioned above do not prevent children from less privileged backgrounds from succeeding at school. Just as the long-shot at the horse race occasionally wins, so too do some children from poor families excel at college and university. The point is that the odds of succeeding are stacked against children from poorer backgrounds.

Sociologists talk about these hurdles in terms of equality of condition. The skills and abilities that children bring to the school environment differ, their initial conditions are unequal, and so their chances of success in the school system vary. Figure 5.2 illustrates these differences by examining the effect of a mother's education on the schooling of her sons and daughters.

The levels of education of mothers are divided into four groups: those mothers with grade 8 or less, those mothers with less than high school, mothers who have completed high school, and mothers with post-secondary education. The likelihood of a daughter attaining

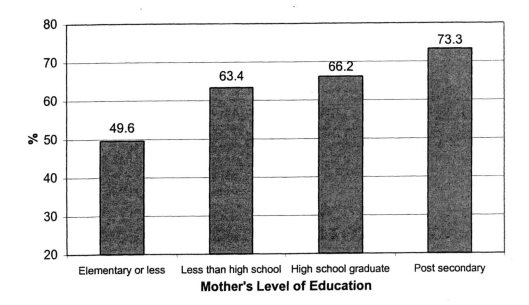

post-secondary schooling rises from 44.3% to 73.6% across the four categories of mother's schooling, a difference of 29.3% between the two extremes.

The figure also shows that a son's schooling is influenced by his mother's education, although the effect is not quite as strong (a 23.7% difference between the extremes). This is clear evidence that mother's schooling has a strong bearing on the educational attainment of her daughters and sons. While Figure 5.2 does not tell us which of the hurdles listed above are operative, it provides compelling evidence that barriers to educational attainment exist. The importance of these barriers to educational attainment is not limited just to a person's level of formal training. Past research has shown that one's level of educational achievement is strongly related to both their occupation and amount of income (Boyd, 1982). Consequently, the existence of obstacles to educational attainment not only prevents people from less educated backgrounds from acquiring superior schooling, it also perpetuates economic and occupational inequality between Canadians.

An alternative perspective on issues of opportunity in Canadian society focuses upon occupational mobility. By comparing the occupations of parents and their children, we can identify how much social mobility occurs. The mobility process is more open, more democratic if someone's occupational position does not depend upon the social class into which they were born.

Table 5.5 provides some evidence on the degree of occupational mobility among Canadian men. The table is constructed in order to examine the occupational destinies of the sons of fathers who held either professional/managerial jobs or blue collar jobs (for simplicity we ignore the range of other jobs held by fathers, e.g., white collar, farm). An obvious

117

feature of the table is that not all sons follow in the occupational footsteps of their fathers. However, there is a substantial amount of occupational "inheritance" since 55% of the sons of blue collar fathers are themselves blue collar workers and 50% of the sons of fathers in professional and managerial positions hold similar jobs.

The general lessons from mobility research can be summarized as follows. First, many more people are mobile than immobile. Second, there is generally more upward than downward mobility in Canada, because historically jobs in the professional, managerial, and white collar sector have expanded while work in farming and blue collar jobs has shrunk. Third, most of the mobility that does occur is short range, with very few people going from "rags to riches" (or vice versa).

In addition, patterns of mobility in Canada are relatively similar to those in the U.K. or the U.S. Nevertheless, one notable difference between Canada and the U.S. is the relative lack of mobility of Canadians into senior management. The reason for this is that many companies in Canada are foreign owned and/or controlled, with the result that many top management positions are filled by non-Canadians.

Finally, the evidence points to a modest increase in the openness of the occupational structure, suggesting that over time an individual's life chances have become less tied to their social origins. Although inequality of opportunity continues, this evidence suggests it is declining, possibly because of the expanded opportunities available from the growing numbers of people attaining post-secondary education (see Wanner, 1993).

Ascription and Achievement

It is important that two issues be kept separate: the *amount of inequality* versus patterns of *change in inequality*. It is very important not to think of decreases in inequality as equivalent to the eradication of inequality. The gap in pay between women and men is a useful way of illustrating this point.

Table 5.5. Occupational Mobility in Canada: Father to Son Mobility in Selected Occupational Groups

Father's Occupational Group	Son's Occupational Group			
	Prof/Managerial	White Collar	Blue Collar	Row%
Professional/ Managerial	50%	25%	25%	100%
Blue Collar	20%	25%	55%	100%

Source: Summarized from Creese, Guppy, and Meissner, 1991.

118

Table 5.6 shows, for the period 1967 to 1989, the average wages paid to women and men who worked full-time, full-year. In 1967 the average wage paid to women was 58.4% of the average wage of men. Put another way, the *amount* of pay inequality between women and men in 1967 was 42¢ ($1.00 – $0.58). This gap in average wages has *changed* over time, but clearly a significant difference remains by 1996 with women still earning only 73.4% of men's average pay.

Some of the earnings difference between the sexes is attributable to differences in the occupations women hold, the greater frequency of career interruptions among women (for children mainly), and the greater likelihood of women to be in the service sector labour market. But even when relative earnings are adjusted for these factors, women still earn 20-30% less than men (Robb, 1987).

These comparisons of average wages between women and men add a further dimension to the patterns of poverty we documented in Table 5.4. That is, not only do women have a greater chance than men of living in poverty, even when they live above the poverty line the average woman can expect to earn only a portion of the income of the average man.

Sociologists have typically interpreted gender inequalities of this sort by distinguishing between *ascription* and *achievement*. Ascription refers to characteristics of groups based on birthright and/or personal attributes determined at conception. To the extent that others interact with us, or make judgements about us, based on our sex or race (for example), then ascriptive processes are at work.

Table 5.6. Historical Change in the Earnings of Women Relative to Men (for full-time, full-year workers)

Year	Relative Earnings
1967	58.4
1971	59.6
1975	60.1
1979	63.3
1983	64.6
1987	65.9
1989	65.8
1990	67.7
1991	69.6
1992	71.9
1993	72.2
1994	69.8
1995	73.1
1996	73.4

Source: *Earnings of Men & Women*, Statistics Canada (13–217) Annual.

119

In contrast, when people judge us on the basis of what we do, as opposed to who we are, they are evaluating us according to principles of achievement. A frequent measure of social progress, of enlightenment, is the degree to which performance and ability indicators (achievement) take preference over ascribed stereotypes in judging or evaluating people.

The very, very slow erosion of pay differences between women and men suggests that many women are judged on the basis of their sex not their abilities. Here is an important contrast to put these pay differences in perspective. Recently 10,000 more women than men have earned university degrees each year. Yet a sizeable wage gap remains. In fact, even among women and men who have recently graduated from university, a wage gap of between $2300 and $8400 exists (Davies, Mosher and O'Grady, 1996). Since these women and men were of similar age, all university graduates, possessing equivalent years of experience, the earnings gap is hard to explain using achievement principles.

Class, Social Movements, and the State

The distribution of income is a key measure of the extent of inequality in a country. As shown in Table 5.1, income distributions vary considerably in different countries. This variability suggests that different national policies influence income distribution. For example, by altering tax policies (e.g., income taxes, wealth taxes, sales taxes) and public expenditures (e.g., welfare, family allowance, state pensions), governments can influence the national income distribution.

Governments, however, do not have an entirely free hand in taxation and expenditure decisions. Taxpayers are also voters. As well, business owners resist attempts by governments to intervene in the economic marketplace, arguing that the free market is the best means of insuring fair income distribution. Organized labour also applies pressure to governments, lobbying for social legislation such as unemployment and universal health insurance to provide a social safety net when the blind forces of the market deal harsh blows to particular individuals or families.

Government strategy is thus the product of bargaining and negotiation between contending parties. On the one hand business groups such as the Business Council on National Issues, the Canadian Manufacturers Association, and the Canadian Chamber of Commerce press the government to pursue policies sensitive to the needs of business. This is effectively the voice of capital, the lobbying arm of an ownership class. In contrast, the Canadian Labour Congress (CLC) puts forward a labour agenda, speaking on behalf of the approximately 3.5 million union members in Canada. On issues of income distribution and economic inequality the CLC is often joined by the Canadian Council on Social Development and the National Anti-Poverty Organization. This is effectively the voice of working people, the pressure groups urging a redistribution of income and wealth in Canada.

A concrete example of the struggle between business and labour occurs over pension entitlements. Labour views pensions as a form of deferred wage, a pot of money set aside to provide working people with a source of economic support upon retirement. Business leaders share that view but worry that pension income drains funds out of business investment and increases government deficits.

What makes the pension question particularly contentious now is the growing size of Canada's elderly population. One view is that a demographic time bomb is ticking and that as the baby boomers of the 1950s and 1960s reach retirement age (in 2010 to 2030), the amount of money required to fund their pensions will bankrupt the Canadian state. Business leaders worry that unless the state drastically reduces public pension provisions (e.g., the Canada Pension Plan, the Guaranteed Income Supplement, and Old Age Security), current financial obligations for these pensions will greatly inflate government debt.

Labour groups counter by arguing that adequate pension packages were freely negotiated and that any rearrangements would violate the democratic process by which these provisions were made. Government and business leaders helped devise and implement current pension provisions. Labour argues that to alter those agreements now, just prior to many workers retiring, would be to effectively, and unfairly, change the rules of the game at the last minute. For labour the problem is one of democracy, not one of demography.

Assessing the quality of pension provisions in fifteen capitalist democracies, John Myles (1989) has shown that the power of the working class to mobilize and assert its influence dramatically improves pension quality. The single most important factor effecting the quality of nation's pension system is working class mobilization (e.g., the size and organization of the labour movement), not corporate concentration, the size of the elderly population, or the level of economic development. Myles found that the quality of Canadian pensions is relatively low in comparative perspective and he argues that if the government were to emphasize a business agenda even more than it now does, then poverty among the elderly (see Table 5.4) would significantly worsen.

If these government policies are to be understood as the result of struggles between owners and workers, between capital and labour, then it is important to consider the relationship between these three groups—owners, workers, and political leaders. First, the two federal parties which have formed recent governments are financed primarily by business. The large election budgets of both the Conservative and Liberal parties come primarily from corporations or individual business people. It would be wrong to see these donations as direct bribes for political favours, but the funding clearly is given in the expectation that the ruling party will favour business interests. And despite the fact that the NDP receives money from various labour groups, our point is that business, rather than labour, has, at least in terms of financial support, a greater influence on federal parties (see Stanbury, 1986).

Second, politicians are not recruited equally from the different social classes. In the 1980s federally elected politicians were overwhelmingly (almost 90%) from upper class origins (Guppy, *et al.*, 1987). At the level of Cabinet Ministers, the concentration of upper class representation was even higher. In addition, Ornstein and Fox (1986) demonstrate the existence of direct linkages between politicians and private corporations. They show that, for the period 1946 to 1976, strong ties were present between both federal and provincial cabinets and private organizations (a trend that has not weakened in the last two decades). These linkages add further evidence to the argument that business holds a stronger position than labour in influencing political decisions.

Now, of course, politicians are influenced by groups other than capital and labour. Over the past few decades many other groups have formed to press for specific political concessions. These groups include the National Action Committee for the Status of Women, the Assembly of First Nations, the National Advisory Council on Aging, and the Canadian Civil Liberties Association. One tangible result of this growth of *new social movements* (i.e., pressure groups not aligned with capital or labour) can be seen in section 15.1 of the *Canadian Charter of Rights and Freedoms*:

> Every individual is equal before and under the law and has the right to the equal protection and equal benefit of the law without discrimination and, in particular, without discrimination based on race, national or ethnic origin, colour, religion, sex, age or mental or physical disability.

The policies of various federal and provincial governments introducing laws on employment and pay equity, on family matters, and on sexual harassment have been inspired in large part by the women's movement. Feminists looking at trends such as those in Table 5.6, have argued that equality for women will not come if market forces are allowed to dictate the relative wage rates of women and men (Armstrong and Armstrong, 1990). Due to the obstacles women face in the workplace (e.g., promotion), in education (e.g., male bias as in engineering), or in the home (e.g., wife abuse), women cannot be expected to attain wages that truly reflect their levels of productivity (see Abella, 1984).

Consequences of Inequality—Real Life Chances

We are all aware of social inequality. We all share some idea of what it means to be rich or to be poor. Here, though, is a graphic way of depicting just what consequences follow from inequality. Above we showed how your *life chances* are influenced by your social background. In contrast, Figure 5.3 shows how your *chances of life* are influenced by your social background. The likelihood of surviving at birth varies dramatically by social class origins. Twice as many children born in poor neighbourhoods die in comparison to children born in the richest of Canadian neighbourhoods.

Comparing these infant mortality rates for various racial and ethnic groups produces still larger differences. Among Native Indians in Canada the infant mortality rate for children up to 12 months of age was 17.2 deaths per thousand live births in 1986 (Bobet, 1989). Alternatively, the life expectancy of Native Indian women is 73 years as compared to an average for all Canadian women of 81.4 years. For men the respective differences are 65.7 versus 74.1 years.

Furthermore the link between *life* expectancy and income also occurs for *health* expectancy and income. People from low-income families experience many more health ailments than do individuals born to more affluent families. For example, Jerrett, Eyles and Cole (1998) found that low income among males, and low education (which as we saw above is often linked to low income) among females are important predictors of premature mortality in Ontario. Further, the health problems of poor children begin before birth and often continue to plague them throughout their life. There is a poverty of health as well as a poverty of income (see the National Council of Welfare, 1990).

122

Figure 5.3. Infant Deaths per 1,000 Births by Neighbourhood Income (1986)

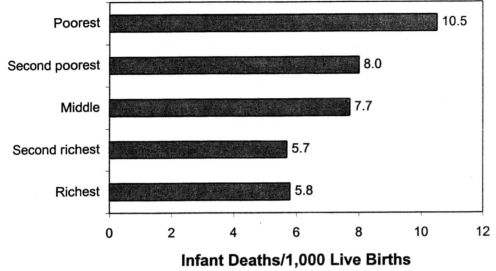

"*There but for the grace of God go I*": of all life's unknowns, the lottery of birth is the most telling. We do not choose our parents, but fortune is on our side if we are so lucky as to be born in a privileged family. This is a real life chance that we have all experienced, although too few of us reflect on the consequences.

The lottery of birth is a personal problem or personal fortune, depending upon your luck in the lottery. It is also something over which an individual has no control. Children born in poor families have no choice in the matter, they cannot be faulted for their personal misfortune any more than can children born to wealthy families be lauded for their foresight. Sociologists view these different real life chances not as *personal troubles*, but as *public issues*.

We cannot adequately explain the fact that over a million children in Canada currently live in poverty by blaming them. Poor children are the victims of poverty, and they deserve no blame for their misfortune. Issues of effort, or motivation, or personality are totally inadequate labels to account for their predicament. Rather the explanation must lie with the way in which we collectively have allowed the distribution of income to occur. It is thus a public issue, an issue of social organization in which we all share.

High rates of poverty result not from some deficit or some inadequacy among the victims of poverty. To argue so is to blame the victim (Ryan, 1976). The growing feminization of poverty (depicted in Table 5.4) is not the fault of poor women, it is the result of practices (e.g., domestic responsibilities, lower pay for work of equal value) and policies (e.g., alimony defaulting) that we all permit to continue.

123

Conclusion

In this chapter we have attempted to provide an idea of the way sociologists examine the inequalities of Canada. We began by showing that a "classless" or middle-class vision of Canada is naive and unrealistic. We then outlined the notion of social class, and showed how it has evolved and been used in different ways to help make sense of differences in wealth. However, throughout the chapter we have tried to show that while some forms of inequality are expressed in class terms (e.g. pay differentials between women and men), other social divisions such as sex and race also remain fundamental to the creation and maintenance of these inequalities. Finally, we have tried to make it clear that the victims of inequality deserve no blame for their plight. Rather, the causes of these disadvantages lie in the social organization of Canadian society, which we all help create, and for which we all share responsibility.

Note

1. Marx made mention of two other classes which are unimportant for the present discussion: the petite bourgeoisie, which was a class of people who owned their own productive property but did not employ anyone (e.g., small shopkeepers and farmers); and the lumpenproletariat, made up of people whom Marx said did not contribute anything to society, such as criminals and the mentally ill.

References

Abella, Rosalie
1984   *Equality in Employment: A Royal Commission Report* Ottawa: Supply and Services.

Armstrong, Pat and Hugh Armstrong
1990   *Theorizing Women's Work* Toronto: Garamond.

Banting, Keith
1987   "The Welfare State and Inequality in the 1980s" *Canadian Review of Sociology and Anthropology* Vol. 24(3), 309–38.

Black, Don and John Myles
1986   "Dependent Industrialization and the Canadian Class Structure: A Comparative Analysis of Canada, the United States and Sweden" *Canadian Review of Sociology and Anthropology* Vol. 23(2), 157–81.

Bobet, Ellen
1989   "Indian Mortality" *Canadian Social Trends* Winter, 12–13.

Bolaria, Singh and Terry Wotherspoon
1991   "Income Inequality, Poverty, and Hunger" in S. Bolaria (ed) *Social Issues and Contradictions in Canadian Society* Toronto: Harcourt Brace Jovanovich.

Boyd, Monica
1982   "Sex Differences in the Canadian Occupational Attainment Process." *Canadian Review of Sociology and Anthropology* Vol. 19(1), 1–28.

Clement, Wallace and John Myles
1992   *Relations of Ruling: Class, Gender and Postindustrialism in Comparative Perspective* (forthcoming).

Dahrendorf, Ralph
1959   *Classes and Class Conflict in Industrial Society* Stanford: Stanford University Press.

Davies, James
1993   "The Distribution of Wealth and Economic Inequality in Canada" in J. Curtis *et al.* (eds) *Social Inequality in Canada: Patterns, Problems, Policies*, 2nd edition, Toronto: Prentice-Hall.

Davies, Scott, Clayton Mosher and Bill O'Grady
1996   "Educating Women: Gender Inequalities among Canadian University Graduates." *The Canadian Review of Sociology and Anthropology,* 33(2):125–42.

Giddens, Anthony
1979   *The Class Structure of Advanced Societies* 2nd edition, New York: Harper and Row.

Goldthorpe, John with Catriona Llewellyn and Clive Payne
1980   *Social Mobility and Class Structure in Modern Britain.* Oxford: Clarendon Press.

Goldthorpe, John and Gordon Marshall
1992   "The Promising Future of Class Analysis: A Response to Recent Critiques." *Sociology,* 26(3):381–400.

Grabb, Ed
1990   "Who Owns Canada? Concentration of Ownership and the Distribution of Economic Assets, 1975–1985" *Journal of Canadian Studies* Vol 25(2), 72–93.

Guppy, Neil and Bruce Arai
1993   "Who Benefits from Higher Education? Differences by Sex, Social Class, and Ethnic Background" in J. Curtis *et al.* (eds) *Social Inequality in Canada: Patterns, Problems, Policies*, 2nd edition, Toronto: Prentice-Hall.

Guppy, Neil, Sabrina Freeman, and Shari Buchan
1987   "Representing Canadians: Changes in the Economic Backgrounds of Federal Politicians" *Canadian Review of Sociology and Anthropology,* Vol. 24(3), 417–30.

Health Reports
1989   *Health Reports* Vol 1(1), Ottawa: Statistics Canada, Cat. # 82–003 S19.

Hunter, Alfred
1993   "The Changing Distribution of Income" in J. Curtis *et al.* (eds) *Social Inequality in Canada: Patterns, Problems, Policies*, 2nd edition, Toronto: Prentice-Hall.

Jerrett, Michael, John Eyles and Donald Cole.
1998   "Socioeconomic and Environmental Covariates of Premature Mortality in On-
          tario" *Social Science and Medicine*, 47(1):33–49.

Myles, John
1989   *Old Age in the Welfare State: The Political Economy of Public Pensions*
          Lawrence, Kansas: University of Kansas Press.

National Council of Welfare
1990   *Health, Health Care and Medicare* Ottawa: National Council of Welfare.

Ross, David and Richard Shillington
1989   *The Canadian Fact Book on Poverty* Toronto: Canadian Council for Social De-
          velopment.

Ryan, William
1976   *Blaming the Victim* New York: Vintage Press.

Sobeco-Chapman
Annual   "Sobeco Management Compensation in Canada" Toronto: Sobeco-Chapman
          Inc.

Stanbury, William
1986   *Business-Government Relations in Canada* Toronto: Methuen.

Turritin, Anton, Paul Anisef, and Neil MacKinnon
1983   "Gender Differences in Educational Attainment: A Study of Social Inequality"
          Canadian Journal of Sociology, Vol. 8(4), 395–319.

Wanner, Richard
1993   "Patterns and Trends in Occupational Mobility" in J. Curtis *et al.* (eds) *Social
          Inequality in Canada: Patterns, Problems, Policies*, 2nd edition, Toronto: Pren-
          tice-Hall.

Wright, Erik-Olin
1985   *Classes* London: Verso.

6

Race, Ethnicity, and Group Relations

Fredrick Ulmer

It is a cliché now to say that we live in a global world, and that race and ethnic relations are a serious concern all over the world. Multi-ethnic societies—societies comprising a number of different racial, ethnic, religious and/or cultural groups—are common today. In fact they are the norm, not the exception. The difficulties of getting along with Others, those who do not share your culture, who do not look like you, have been and continue to be a subject of interest and importance to scholars, politicians, and everyday folk. In recent years the gravity and potential cost of failing to deal effectively with difference has made itself clear in such places as Rwanda and the former Yugoslavia. Here, various groups have resorted to extreme violence in their efforts to proclaim their identities and remove those defined as "different" from their societies. In such places groups make claim to unique, unchanging and permanent identities, as though they were somehow biological and not social. The words "ethnicity" and "race," and their extensions or counterparts "racism" and "ethnicism" are today far too often associated with cataclysmic events such as "ethnic cleansing" or "ethnocide," and/or "genocide." Ethnicity and race in modern times seem to have become markers of exclusivity, opposition, antagonism, and competition.

The study of ancient societies in the Old and New Worlds seems to show that the "problem" of getting along with Others is not a new one, however. The historical and archaeological records reveal a great deal of interaction among very different peoples. Despite the difficulties and hardships, people did travel and did make contact with Others for most of the same reasons Others are contacted today—to trade, to make war, to create alliances and to make peace. But, the concepts of "race" and "ethnicity" as markers of a fixed human identity seem not to have been part of their awareness. Rather, there seems to have been an understanding that cultural characteristics, social identity, were learned forms of behavior, not inherited. "Others" could become "us" simply by learning our language and adopting our customs and values. During the first years of contact in North America, for example, "Europeans" could become "Indians" simply by dressing and acting as they did. And some did. Identity was not constrained or imposed by biology.

The purpose of this work, then, is twofold: first to provide working definitions of "race" and "ethnicity" as they are currently used and understood, and second to document the development and rise of "racism" and "ethnicism" as ideologies in the modern world.

Race and Racism

Race—The Concept

The concept of "race" is very much a loaded term today. It carries a strong emotional charge and is not used lightly, even by "objective" social scientists. The idea of race is now so commonplace that it is easy to believe that it has always been around. It does not appear, however, that the concept has as long a history as was once supposed. Audrey Smedley (1998, 1993), an anthropologist, discusses the history of identity construction in human societies. She points out that in ancient societies social identity was based largely on place of birth and language, and could change as individuals or groups moved to new locations and became part of new groups. Other important diagnostics of identity included kinship and descent (primary features of one's social identity in pre-industrial societies), occupation, and religion. Rank[1] and class[2] were also important markers, but not in quite the same ways as they are now. For example, the status of slaves in ancient (and indigenous) societies was not necessarily a permanent one, nor was it associated with a particular ethnicity, geographical place of origin, or physical characteristics.

Smedley describes recurring situations of intercultural tolerance and minimal strife, even when states or empires expanded through the use, or threatened use, of military force. Analysing historical sources (including the Bible), she proposes that the worldview of ancient societies saw even "barbarians" as transformable. The dominance and exploitation typical of the growth and development of complex societies thus included means by which Others could, at least potentially, become Us. Smedley argues that early conflicts between complex, state societies, regardless of how brutal or bloody, did not create conditions for what she calls a "racial" worldview. "There are no racial designations in the literature of the ancients and few references even to such human features as skin colour" (1998:693). Furthermore, there was no form of inequality based on skin colour or other physical features.

The concept of race apparently did not surface until the eighteenth century, in the American colonies. Smedley notes that the term *race* can be found in English sources as far back as the sixteenth century, but it was typically not used to refer to slave peoples; rather it was "a mere classificatory term like *kind*, *type*, or even *breed*, or *stock*" (1998:694). "Race" took on its present meaning as a social classification of difference as English settlers in North America attempted to maintain their position of superiority over indigenous peoples in North America ("Indians"), African slaves and servants, and other European immigrants (most notably the Irish). Smedley suggests that the binary opposition between "savage" Irish and "civilised" English which the settlers brought with them to

North America was the basis for the development of the racial worldview. Bacon's Rebellion in 1676, an unsuccessful colonial revolt of servants, poor freedmen and slaves, was the event which solidified "race" in colonial consciousness. In response to the rebellion, colonial administrators devised and passed laws that divided people along clear, artificial, racial lines; these laws "provided resources and benefits to poor, white freedmen and restricted the rights of 'Africans,' 'mulattoes,' and 'Indians'" (1998:694).

These English settlers justified their actions in a number of ways. They appealed to the Chain of Being, invoking reason, logic and "science" in their defence. There was also the concept of *manifest destiny*, the notion that "Whites" (the English), because of their cultural, moral, religious, technological and "biological" superiority, should (had the right to) control the world, or at least large parts of it. And there was the *Hamlite Rationalisation*, the belief, taken from the Bible, that Ham was cursed by God and turned into a non-White person so that he and his descendants should remain cursed and be subservient to Whites from then on (Frideres 1998). In this way a new form of social identity was created, one which defended the conquest and cruel treatment of Native Americans, and the imposition of slavery on Africans brought to North America. "American society had made 'race' (and the physical features connected to it) equivalent to, and the dominant source of, human identity, superseding all other aspects of identity" (Smedley 1998:695).

Smedley maintains that the "invention of whiteness" had taken hold in the United States by the mid-nineteenth century. By this time, she argues, virtually all Americans had been conditioned to this arbitrary ranking of American peoples. Racial thinking was accepted, "proper." In America, the black-white opposition came to be seen as "natural." Racial ideologies of various sorts then diffused around much of the world, affecting the lives of (at least) European peoples and the colonised peoples of the Third World.

Such beliefs subsequently became an all-too-often unquestioned part of both (global) public consciousness and scholarly tradition. In *The Mismeasure of Man* (1981) Stephen J. Gould provides several examples of famous and influential scholars who subscribed to the notion of "race" and allowed it to affect and bias their work. Three or four of the more striking will be noted here. George Cuvier, the famed French naturalist, founder of modern comparative anatomy, described the indigenous people of Africa as "the most degraded of human races, whose form approaches that of the beast and whose intelligence is nowhere great enough to arrive at regular government" (1812:105 in Gould 1981:36). And, Charles Lyell, founder of modern geology and proponent of *uniformitarianism*,[3] one of the accepted "facts" of the scientific community today, wrote the following of the Bushmen (nomadic hunter-gatherers in the Kalahari desert in South Africa, formerly known as the !Kung and now known the Ju/'hoansi, a term they prefer): "The brain of the Busham leads towards the brain of the Simiadae [monkeys]. This implies a connexion between want of intelligence and structural assimilation. Each race of Man has its place, like the inferior in animals" (in Gould 1981:36). Charles Darwin, in his *Descent of Man* (1871:201 in Gould 1981:36), spoke about a future when the process of natural evolution would lead to an increase in the evolutionary distance between human and ape because current intermediary forms such as the chimpanzee and Hottentots (pastoralists, herders of sheep and cattle, in southern Africa, currently known as the Khoikhoi) would be extinct. Finally, Paul Broca, professor of clinical surgery in the faculty of medicine at the University of Paris and founder of the Anthropological Society of Paris in 1859, wrote extensively about the relative brain size of men, women, and the different races of mankind. His data came from *craniometry*, the measuring of the skull and its contents. He related brain size to intelligence, and found that "the brain is larger in mature adults than in the elderly, in men than in women, in eminent men than in men of mediocre talent, **in superior races than in inferior races**" (emphasis added, 1861:304 in Gould 1981:83).

The concept of "race" developed in the United States during the eighteenth century was, then, solidly based in biology. It proposed that there are clearly bounded categories of people sharing the same biological traits and that any given individual can be unequivocally placed into one of these groups. *The Dictionary of Anthropology* (Winick 1970) clearly demonstrates this biological basis in the definitions it offers: "*race*: a major division of mankind with distinctive, hereditary, transmissible physical characteristics; for example the Negroid, Caucasoid, Mongoloid races; a breeding group with gene organisation different from that of other intraspecies groups. Thus the morphological and metrical features which members of a race have in common derive from their common descent" (1970:448). Richard Schaefer (1988:11) provides a similar definition of a *"biological race"*: "a genetically isolated group characterised by a high degree of inbreeding that leads to distinctive gene frequencies. This distinctiveness is made most apparent by the presence of hereditary physical characteristics that differentiate members of a group from other human groups." Schaefer notes that such a definition follows the definition of race adopted in the 1950 UNESCO Statement on Race.

In the *Dictionary of Anthropology* Winick goes on from his original definitions to note that each race has a tremendous range of internal variability, that there are no completely pure races, and that the criteria for a given race may not be manifested by all the members (although any one member will "probably manifest most"). The vagaries and internal contradictions inherent in such definitions are neither noted nor discussed.

Criteria popularly used to mark races are skin colour, hair and eye colour, prognathism,[4] cephalic index,[5] nasal index,[6] skull capacity, hair texture, degree of hirsuteness, and lip eversion. More "scientific" criteria "currently used for determining whether characteristics are racial" include hereditary transmission, comparative unalterability, lack of variability from external causes, and comparative independence of age and sex (Winick 1970:448).

According to Winick (1970), J.F. Blumenbach provided the first division of the human species into races in 1825: Ethiopian, American, Malayan, Caucasian. He attributed racial differences to differences in climate. In Von Eickstedt's classification there are now usually said to be three main races, 29 subraces, and three special races. Carleton Coon (1965) distinguishes 30 races. Stanley Garn (1969, 1971) attempted to confine his definition of race to groups limited to a small, localised area. He developed the concept of a *geographical race*—the largest taxonomic unit below the Linnean category of species (Garn 1971)—and identified nine geographical races:

1. the Amerindian race
2. the Polynesian race
3. the Micronesian race
4. the Melanesian-Papuan race

130

5. the Australian race
6. the Asiatic race
7. the Indian race
8. the European race
9. the African race

Obviously, then, there is and has been no agreed upon classification of human "races." As noted in the *Dictionary* definition above, the three races found most commonly in popular and scholarly discussions are Mongoloid, Caucasoid, and Negroid. The Caucasoids originally inhabited Western Europe, northern Africa, and western Asia; their distinguishing characteristics include light skin pigmentation, frequent balding, prominent chins, and relatively long trunks. The Mongoloids originally inhabited northern and Eastern Asia; they have yellow to brown skin, black hair, broad cheekbones, low nose bridges, and epicanthic folds of the eyelids (giving the impression—from a European perspective—of slanting eyes). The Negroids are the original inhabitants of Africa; they have dark pigmentation, low-bridged noses, and kinky or curly hair (Schaefer 1988:11).

There are also the notions of "composite race" and "secondary race" (Winick 1970:449). A composite race is defined as a "race that is a stable blend of two or more primary races [whatever they may be] and represent combinations of feature from the different racial stocks involved. There are often geographic areas in which the blend has been stabilised." A secondary race is a "race which results from two primary races mingling."

Many scholars in the twentieth century have pointed out the various problems of trying to define biologically separate human races. A basic list will be provided here. First, there are no discrete boundaries between racial groups (however they are defined). Racial groups merge at their peripheries. This is in large part because all humans, regardless of physical "type" can interbreed, so distinct populations cannot exist. Second, from all the traits available to define a race, the traits selected tend to be very few and easily seen (such as skin colour and head shape) but not important biologically. Furthermore, little is known about the actual "inheritability" of most of these characteristics. Third, racial categories are too narrow. Variations among people in the same "race" are very great; in fact, individuals in the same "race" are as different genetically as are individuals of different "races." Fourth, the notion of common origin for people who appear to be of the same "race" is false. Social scientists have found that similar "racial characteristics" evolve repeatedly in genetically unrelated peoples. The people from Central Africa and New Guinea, for example, look alike but are not linked biologically. Finally, racial classifications tend to be used for political purposes, to distinguish inferior and superior peoples, even when the author of the classification had no such original intention.

For these reasons many anthropologists and sociologists would like to dispense with the word "race" altogether. In anthropology, for example, Franz Boas was a key figure in the critique of the biological concept of race. Around 1900 he stressed the biopsychological equality of all human beings—the idea that individuals differ but all have equal capacity for culture. The work of his students, Ruth Benedict (1940), Margaret Mead (1942), Ashley Montagu (1942) conclusively demonstrated that the concept of race has no basis in biological fact. Montagu, Gerald Berreman (1988), and Martin Marger (1991), among others, have gone on to propose that we use *ethnic group* to describe what were previously talked of as races. They argue that it is reasonable to invoke this usage because such groups always shared cultural traits as well as physical characteristics. Montagu (1974:129) also argues that using *ethnic group* "eliminates all question-begging emphases on physical factors or differences and leaves that question completely open, while the emphasis is now shifted to the fact—though it is not restricted to it—that man is predominantly a cultural creature."

The scholarly analysis of and challenges to the idea of race in the first half of the century thus tended to focus on the "bad science" of the concept but largely ignored the "*social construction* of race" (Harrington 1998:611) which has proven extremely resistant to eradication. Implicit in the discussions of the scientifically questionable nature of race was the belief that education and objective knowledge would somehow change the beliefs and prejudices of those who believed in the concept of race and/or its concomitant, racism. However, the idea of race has continued (and continues) to have currency in the media and popular discussions. In the late 1960s and early 1970s, for example, educational psychologist Arthur Jensen, a professor at the University of California at Berkeley, brought discussions of race back to centre stage when he published "How Much Can We Boost IQ and Scholastic Achievement?" in 1969. In this study he maintains that 80 percent of general intelligence is inherited. Noting the generally poorer performance of African Americans on IQ tests (they score on average one standard deviation lower than whites on IQ tests) and in school, Jensen argued that such performance was the result of innate racial differences and not subject to intervention on the part of schools. His conclusion was that intervention programs were useless, as African Americans were simply mentally inferior for genetic reasons. According to Jensen, what should be provided to African Americans—and presumably to other "low IQ" minorities as well—is basic skills training using rote, drill-and-practice methods of instruction. His study caused a storm of controversy; academics and the public became embroiled once again in discussions of "race" and racial attributes.

Most scholars criticised Jensen's work and his findings (see Gould [1981] for example), but a few supported them and research investigating relationships among intelligence, class and race continued. Among the more prominent recent works in this vein is *The Bell Curve: Intelligence and Class Structure in American Life* (1994) by Richard J. Herrrnstein and Charles Murray. In it they unquestioningly use the concepts of "black" and "white." The abstract concepts have become "real," concrete (reified). Herrnstein and Murray also offer more data that would seem to support a "natural" hierarchy, based on the distribution of "intelligence" among races and classes. At the same time, however, they state that there is a close connection between demonstrated cognitive ability, socio-economic conditions, and political environment. The debate goes on.

It is perhaps because of the durability of the "social myth" of race (Schaefer 1988:15) that, after a period of relative inattention when many scholars seemed to think the matter to have been dealt with or turned their attention to the study of *ethnic groups*, social scientists are once again focusing on "race." And, race is now emphatically distinguished from *ethnic group* by many (see Harrington, 1993, 1998; Smedley, 1998). Berreman (1988), for example, maintains that race must be understood as a social concept in the last half of the twentieth century. He calls race an "invidious" distinction. It is an *ascribed* characteristic, something one is born with, that one cannot change, and that is perceived as a source of inherent inequality. Invidious distinctions such as race, he states, categorise people into groups and stereotype them on the basis of socially perceived group characteristics, whether or not those characteristics are manifested by any particular individual and regardless of the individual abilities or achievements of individual members of the group. "Everyone is sentenced for life to a social cell shared by others of like birth, separated from and ranked relative to all other social cells" (Berreman 1988:485). More recently, Kyeyoung Park (1996:445), analysing Korean-African American relations in the United States, proposes that the biological notion of race is now typically reconfigured as "culture," and urges researchers to "unravel culture" in terms of an "underlying racial hierarchy" so that "race" can be recognised even when the term itself is not used.

Racism

With the development of the new social identity of "race" in the eighteenth and nineteenth centuries came a new set of beliefs about relations between groups defined as "races"—racism. Although race has no scientific validity as a way of classifying human beings, the idea of race—using physical differences to categorise people—was and is still used in many cultures as a basis for prejudice, discrimination, and social stratification. In the United States and Canada, for example, the tendency has been to divide people into cultural categories based on colour: "black," and "white." Such classification does not accurately describe the reality of the variation of skin colours in North America, nor does it deal with the fact that some of those categorised as "black" have lighter skin than those culturally classified as "white" or even "brown." It is the result of the imposition of an ideology—racism—on reality, creating the cultural category of race in North America which, like categories of race everywhere, does not correspond to any objectively measurable physical characteristics. Such classification is used to support the separation and relative ranking or stratification of groups on this continent. This separation and ranking is known as *racial stratification*.

Racism,[7] or more specifically biological racism, is generally agreed to be structured around three basic ideas, all of which are objectively incorrect:

1. Humans are divided naturally, or are divisible into different physical types.
2. The physical traits displayed by each physical type are intrinsically related to their culture, personality, and intelligence (Race determines a person's capabilities).
3. On the basis of their genetic inheritance (their physical type), some groups are innately superior to others.
   (Banton, 1970; Benedict 1959; Mantagu, 1972; Shibutani and Kwan, 1965 in Marger 1991:27).

Thus, *racism* is the belief that humans are subdivided, or can be subdivided, into distinct hereditary groups that are innately different in social behaviour and mental capacities. Therefore, some groups may be superior or inferior to others.

Racist ideologies assume that differences among groups are inborn and immutable. Racist thought maintains that intelligence, character, behaviour, even attitudes, ideologies and convictions are biologically based; they cannot be greatly influenced by the environment. Thus groups at the bottom of the social ladder are believed to occupy their inferior social position because of their inferior (genetically inherited) abilities and not because they have been exploited and subjugated by the dominant group over a long period. And, the dominant group[8] is argued to be at the top of the social hierarchy because of their (genetically inherited) superior abilities—they are the superior race—and not because of social advantages such as better education and job opportunities that have accrued over time.

Racism is associated with both *prejudice* and *discrimination*.[9] Prejudice is an arbitrary feeling or belief, a judgement "based on a fixed mental image of some group or class of people and applied to all individuals of that class without being tested against reality" (Mason 1970:52). Prejudice involves thoughts, attitudes, beliefs, and emotions, not actions. Prejudicial beliefs are *categorical*; individuals are not evaluated on the basis of their personal attributes or achievements, but rather on the basis of their group membership. Prejudices are usually, but not always, negative judgements about a group based on *stereotypes*[10] of that group. Prejudice is also relatively inflexible and tends not to change with exposure to new, differing knowledge. "Objective" evidence that is contrary to a prejudice is ignored or explained away as exceptional.

Discrimination is action, behaviour that excludes all members of a group from certain rights, opportunities or privileges. Like prejudice, discrimination is categorical and has a negative impact on targeted groups or group members. Discrimination may involve *ethnopaulisms*, derogatory terms or slurs such as "honkie," "nigger," or "Injun." It may also involve denial of access to life chances—education, job opportunities, housing, and so on. And, discrimination may be expressed through acts of violence, either in isolated incidents or through group violence against group (i.e., genocide). Discrimination is not always overt or intentional, however. *Individual discrimination* is action taken by an individual against a member or members of a group. It is both intentional and overt, and is the acting out of prejudicial beliefs. *Institutional discrimination* is overt discrimination that has become legitimised, either as custom or as part of the legal system. *Structural discrimination* is covert, unintentional—often unconscious—discrimination that exists because of the structure of society and societal institutions. It perpetuates the existence of certain groups at the bottom of the societal ladder. The discrimination associated with racial stratification is associated with limited expectations of the marked group (or groups) by the dominant group(s) in society, and such expectations are often internalised by members of the marked group(s) themselves (with disastrous consequences).

Racist ideologies are intrinsically *ethnocentric*.[11] Out-groups are judged as inferior. Such thought pursued to its logical conclusion leads to the idea that racial groups must be kept apart both socially and physically. Social interaction between the races needs to be minimised, de-personalised and/or highly structured. "Unregulated" social interaction might lead to social "union" of some sort which might lead to physical mixing which (a) *could* result in the political downfall of the superior group, and (b) *would* result in its biological degradation. The superior group would no longer be "pure;" thus they would lose the "right" to their claim of biological superiority.

This belief is, of course, contrary to reality. In truth, offspring of parents from greatly different genetic pools—parents from different "races"—are as likely to be superior in genetic makeup to their parents (to have superior mental and/or physical abilities) as offspring of parents with largely similar genetic pools—parents from the same "race." Furthermore, contact and interbreeding between different peoples has historically given rise to some of the greatest of human civilisations, including the Mesopotamian, Egyptian, Incan, Mayan, and Greek (Schaeffer 1988).

Racism, like many other ideologies, then, does not accurately describe reality. Rather, racism is composed of a set of beliefs that become accepted as descriptions of "reality," the way things really are. Manning Nash (1962) points out that racist ideologies depend on three logical confusions:

1. identifying racial with cultural and social differences
2. the assumption that cultural achievement is directly, and chiefly, determined by the racial characteristics of a population
3. the belief that physical characteristics of a population limit and define the sorts of culture and society they are able to create or participate in

Historically, racism tends to be found where groups are competing (or have competed) for economic resources or power, or both. The successful group becomes dominant and institutes the ideology of racism to justify its position of superiority and to prevent the less successful, minority, group or groups from "taking over." Racism is easiest to maintain when physical differences between groups are marked, such as between English settlers and First Nations people in Canada. But, for many social scientists, racism applies to any situation where social behaviour is said to derive from or be generated by innate, hereditary sources. Racist ideologies are thus arguably at work when any group—racial, ethnic, class- or gender-based—is singled out on the basis of their biological characteristics and subject to prejudice and discrimination.

Racism merges in Western cultures with an ideology of *racialism* (Todorov 1993:90–96). With racialism, the presumed superiority or inferiority of some groups is used to legitimate the unequal distribution of resources, specifically wealth, power, and prestige. Racialism involves political action to ensure that the structure of society reflects the hierarchy of the races. Racialism like race, is based on weak scientific reasoning; it is a social construction. It has never been shown, for example, that groups have differing biologically based abilities. But, like racism, the lack of an objective or scientific basis for racialism does not limit its existence or minimise its consequences.

Biological racism peaked during the nineteenth century with "scientific racism." The theory of evolution outlined by Charles Darwin in his *On the Origin of Species by Means of Natural Selection* (1859) was a powerful influence on Western European thought. Darwin's theory had to do with the biological evolution of physical organisms but some proposed that his theory, particularly the concept of natural selection,[12] could be applied to humans and human culture as well. The movement called Social Darwinism arose.

Sociologists such as Herbert Spencer (1873) in England and William Graham Sumner (1906) in the United States argued that natural selection was the mechanism for creating superior and inferior human cultures, socioeconomic classes and races. Herbert Spencer coined the phrase "the survival of the fittest" to describe what he saw as the "natural" free play of competitive forces in the struggle of individual against individual, nation against nation, and race against race. Spencer went so far as to advocate the end of all attempts to provide charity and relief for the unemployed and impoverished classes and the so-called backward races on the grounds that such assistance interfered with the operation of his law of "the survival of the fittest" and merely prolonged the agony and deepened the misery of those who were "unfit." Spencer used Social Darwinism to justify the capitalist free enterprise system, and his influence continues to be felt among advocates of unrestrained capitalism as well as among advocates of white supremacy.

In the twentieth century, as the concept of race shifted from its biologically based origins, nineteenth century *biological racism* has gradually been replaced with other, new forms. These new forms focus on the inferiority of a group's way of life (culture), their fundamental character or spirit, and their assumptions about the world. Notions of cultural superiority have replaced the concept of biological supremacy.

Many of the "new" forms of racism developed in the twentieth century have been incorporated directly and completely into societal institutions and systems of power. This is known as *structural* or *institutional racism*. With biological racism, individual thought and behaviour in the forms of prejudice and discrimination were necessary components of racism. With structural racism, prejudice and discrimination are "built in" to the system and may be unintended by any particular individual or group. Structural racism is not the result of the prejudicial beliefs or discriminatory actions of individuals. Nor are there specific laws or rules deliberately established by one group with the intention of denying or depriving another group or groups of particular rights or privileges. Analysis of this form of racism suggests that "rules, regulations, and norms [can be] 'set up in such a way that they automatically operate to the disadvantage of some racial group' despite the absence of deliberate intent" (Drake 1987:34 in Harrison 1998:611).

Institutional or structural racism does not require the use of group identity as the means by which to subordinate. It is often the product of past inequalities—that is, racism—in a society. Marger (1991) offers the example of schools and schooling in North America. The "inner city" of most North American cities tends to be occupied by "nonWhites," most of whom have migrated to the city looking for employment. They have historically been rural people with little education and few job skills. They have gravitated to the inner city to take advantage of low-cost housing. Thus, inner city schools throughout North America are attended primarily by the children of these nonWhites. Such schools generally provide lower quality education than schools in the suburbs attended which are attended largely by Whites. Those who attend inner city schools are therefore automatically placed at a disadvantage as they attempt to qualify for and be hired in well-paying and promising jobs. In the same way, gaining entrance to top-ranking colleges and universities is more difficult for nonWhite graduates of inner city schools because they are not adequately prepared to meet the rigid academic requirements of the better schools. Intentional prejudice or discrimination against nonWhites is not necessary. On the contrary, decisions made by those

136

in positions of power, "gatekeepers," in the business or educational sectors may be made solely on the basis of rational "neutral" criteria. But nonWhite minority group members are still effectively and repeatedly disadvantaged and racism—the "ideological and material forces that categorically mark and stigmatise certain peoples as essentially and irreconcilably different while treating the privileges of others as normative" (Harrison 1998:613)—is perpetuated.

Why Racism?

A number of social scientists have attempted to explain the existence and persistence of racism. Their explanations generally reflect their general theoretical perspective on how society as a whole works. Two major theoretical orientations in anthropology and sociology are *functionalism*[13] and *conflict theory*. The following presents a brief outline of functionalism and conflict theory and the explanations offered by proponents of each for *racism*.

Bronislaw Malinowski (1929) and A.R. Radcliffe-Brown (1965) were the main proponents of functionalism in anthropology; Talcott Parsons (1951) and Robert K. Merton (1968) its major advocates in sociology. From the functionalist perspective generally, cultures are assumed to be discrete, wholes, with fixed or at least determinable boundaries. The analogy of an organism is often invoked. It is proposed that within the whole, each part has a function: specifically, to contribute to the smooth functioning of the whole. Typically, avoidance of conflict is normal and indicative of cultures in good health. Cultures function smoothly at both the *manifest* and *latent* level. (*Manifest functions* are intended and recognised; *latent functions* are unintended and unrecognised.)

Cultures are also assumed to be homogeneous and consensual. Invoking Durkheim's (1915) notion of social facts as "things," as well as his concept of a "collective consciousness," functionalist theory proposes more or less "fixed" pan-cultural norms. As they are taught these norms, members of a group are socialised to behave and believe in appropriate and accepted ways.

It is an organic, mechanical model. Norms, "out there," part of the collective consciousness, are internalised and thus predictive of individual behaviour. This process, what might be described as *cultural transmission*, is held to be imperative to the continuation of healthy cultures. Equilibrium, or a tendency toward equilibrium, is also assumed. Variation, departure from the norm, is thought of as deviation, usually pathological, and in need of "fixing." The fixing may take the form of adjustment of the individual, the norm, or both. Robert F. Murphy (1971) describes it as a kind of "normative determinism."

With regard to race and racism, the question for functionalists would thus seem to be what "function" racism serves. Manning Nash (1962) proposes four "positive" functions of racism (from the perspective of the dominant group):

1. It provides a moral justification for an unjust social system that systematically deprives a minority group or groups of basic human rights.

2. Because it describes the social hierarchy as "natural" and based in biology, it discourages questioning of the social order, most importantly on the part of the subjugated.

3. It can provide the focus for a political cause or political action, identifying "scapegoat" minorities in times of social uncertainty.

4. It sustains the status quo by arguing that change would lead to even worse conditions for the (biologically inferior, "inept") minority and a general lowering of the standard of living for all (as the biologically superior dominant group becomes tainted).

Nash suggests that because racist ideologies "function" in these ways for dominant groups, such ideologies will be extremely resistant to change and will persist over time.

Ralf Dahrendorf (1959) and Randall Collins (1975) propose to look at human social groups in another way. Their approach is called *conflict theory*. Conflict theory looks at relations—co-operation and especially conflict—between groups within society. It does not assume an over-riding goal or purpose for society; it does not assume integration and maintenance as basic to society; it does not assume equilibrium and stability for society; it rejects the analogy of organism commonly invoked by functionalists. Conflict theory proposes that human action is a consequence of the relationship of the structures (or groups) to which humans belong, and the force(s) creating (and/or destroying) those groups and structures.

Conflict theorists tend to attempt to answer the question *cui bono*—who benefits?—in their analyses of social systems. For them, the major scarce resource over which groups compete is power. They argue that as one group attains dominance over others in its competition with them for economic and political resources, that dominant group will attempt to sustain its position. To do this it centralises control of social and political institutions, particularly those that have to do with the use of force. In effect, the dominant group monopolises the legitimate use of force in society. Thus, for conflict theorists reproduction of the social structure and its system of (unequal) stratification is a primary "function" of society's major institutions. Conflict is inevitable.

With regard to racism and racist ideologies, the obvious answer to the question *cui bono* would seem to be the dominant group. Members of the dominant group reap the lion's share of the material, social and psychological rewards from the social system. Minority groups are exploited and subjugated; they are paid less for their labour (if they are paid at all); they are provided with lower quality food, clothing, housing and/or education; they are denied access to life chances. The perspective of conflict theory proposes that criticisms of minority groups for their subordinate status—"blaming the victim," as it were—is part of the mythology created by the dominant group to justify their superior position. By shifting responsibility onto the subjugated minority, this ideology ignores the roles the dominant group has played in creating (and maintaining) an unequal and unjust social system.

Racism in Canada—The Example of First Nations Peoples[14]

Over time, Europeans and later Euro-Canadians ("Whites") have evidenced apparently contradictory attitudes and behaviours toward First Nations people. At times Europeans seemed to have wished to assimilate First Nations peoples, at other times they appeared to want to annihilate them, and at still other times it looks as though they would have liked to segregate and marginalize them, hoping First Nations people would just "go away." Throughout the history of contact between the two groups, however, Europeans have always assumed superiority over First Nations peoples. James Frideres (1998) and others maintain that this belief has taken the form of racism in Canada. Racism, they argue, has provided the underlying basis for the relations of Whites and First Nations people and for the policies developed by White governments to deal with First Nations people.

At first contact Europeans questioned the basic humanity of the aboriginal inhabitants of the Americas. It was a serious matter with important political, social, and economic ramifications. If the indigenous peoples of the Americas were *not* found to be "human," then they could (and would, it was made clear) be treated very differently than if they were found to be "human." The question was taken to the highest courts and argued before Pope Pius III. Sepulveda, one of the most brilliant legal minds of his time, was given the task of proving that aboriginal Americans were *not* human. They therefore could be freely exploited and enslaved. In the end, a *Papal Bull* in 1545 decreed that "Indians" were indeed "human" (and consequently worthy of converting to Christianity).

When First Nations peoples and Europeans first came into contact in Canada, two very different worlds and worldviews were brought together. First Nations peoples were either hunters and gatherers[15] or "gardeners" (extensive agriculturalists or horticulturalists).[16] They seem to have lived in harmony with their physical environment. There is evidence that they had a conscious conservation ethic, firmly rooted in their very spiritual worldview.[17] "Limited" technological developments inflicted little damage on the ecology, and relatively small numbers of people meant that population pressures were light. Europeans, on the other hand, were agriculturalists, farmers. It was a biblical imperative. Europeans were continually developing their technology to achieve superiority over nature. This, too, was an imperative with biblical justification (see Genesis). Europeans had over-populated and over-utilised their homelands and were looking for new lands to exploit and new places to house their "excess population." They also had a mission to Christianise the world.

Not unexpectedly, both Europeans and First Nations people were ethnocentric in their outlook. Each thought their own way of life to be superior and viewed the other with a mixture of fascination and horror. The first Europeans in what is now Canada, the French, described the First Nations people they encountered as handsome and "comely," and admired some aspects of their cultures, particularly what they saw as the "freedom" in the aboriginal lifestyle. They also found many of their customs, such as their practice of torturing captives of war, loathsome and detestable. In the same way, First Nations people admired French technology but were very unappreciative of their political system and social organisation. Representatives of First Nations people taken to France, for example, could not understand the existence of so much poverty when there was such (obvious) wealth. They also found the French to be personally extremely dirty and disgusting. The *Jesuit Recollections*[18] document at least one incident where a Chief took a French man aside and asked how the French were able to reproduce—their women, he said, found the hairy faces and odour of the French men so disgusting that they could not understand how French women would allow themselves to be touched by them.

Initially the French were interested in the New World as a source of wealth for wartime activities. It was hoped the land would hold precious metals like those found in Spanish

America. By the end of the 16th century, however, the fur trade began to grow into an important economic activity.

There was no well-defined policy established to govern French-Native relations. Generally, the French were attempting to exploit the land and to continue *pseudo-colonisation*. At first they did not intend to settle New France with any large stable population. Also, only a small number of French people wished to emigrate to New France. In addition, the Roman Catholic Church had found the Indians to be human and worthy of conversion. Finally, the dominant economic theory in France and most of Europe at the time was *mercantilism*.[19] Thus there was no policy of cultural or physical genocide on the part of the French.

French policy did not treat "Indians" as distinct or inherently inferior. French policy, at least at first, was to make Indians over into French, Catholic, civilised citizens. The idea was to create a new bi-racial empire, French in language and culture but populated largely by Indians, mixed-bloods, and some French: *Our sons shall marry your daughters*. It was perhaps for this reason that the French never discussed aboriginal land rights. The French assumed that the Indians would assimilate to French culture, convert to Christianity, and thus become full French citizens, with all the rights and responsibilities of any French citizen. To discuss special aboriginal rights of any kind therefore seemed unnecessary, redundant. This policy of assimilation was expressly favoured by Colbert, Talon and the King.

The French saw "Indians" as *sauvages*. A *sauvage* was an uncivilised, unsophisticated, natural being. Indians were thus seen as *inferior*, but their inferiority was not innate. In this the French practised what might be called *minimal racism*, the belief that Others are quantitatively different, different in degree but not in kind. From this perspective, Others are capable of being raised up to a status of equality with the dominant group through training and education. The French policy of assimilation aimed to lead the "Indian" to the same cultural level as the Europeans. First Nations peoples were required—and expected—to convert to Catholicism, to adopt French manners and customs, and to subordinate themselves to French laws and political jurisdiction.

Assimilation, of course, required the co-operation and consent of First Nations people. The French foresaw no resistance in this matter. The assumption was that over time, through association with Europeans, the Indians would become "civilised" and with the French language, they would also acquire "a French heart and spirit." Through this policy of assimilation rather than genocide the French were able to maintain relatively amiable relations with the Native population for awhile.

When war broke out with England in the eighteenth century, the demand for furs decreased, and the French mercantilistic philosophy came to an end. War also changed French policy toward the Indians. Native land rights began to be systematically ignored. Letters signed by Louis XV at this time gave companies headed for New France full ownership of the land, coasts, ports and havens of New France, and full right to dispose of these properties in any way they desired.

By the time the English made a serious bid to control New France, mercantilism economics was finished, and the importance of the fur trade was diminishing. *Colonisation* in the true sense was now important. In addition, British religious ideology was different: the notion of *Manifest destiny*, and the *Hamlite rationalisation* pervaded the British way of life. These were exemplified in the *Protestant work ethic* that basically said hard work and no play would lead to salvation. ("Idle hands are the devil's plaything.") The belief was that success in this world (the logical result of hard work) was demonstrable evidence that one was in a "state of grace" with God. The corollary belief, of course, was that those who did not evidence hard work—as, in English eyes, First Nations people obviously did not—could not possibly be in a state of grace with God. Such people were not "worthy," and English treatment of them did not have to conform to normal Christian standards.

During the initial contact period between the English and First Nations people in Canada, the concerns of the latter were almost completely ignored. Little control was exerted over the British settlers as they expanded westward. "Indians" were not even mentioned in discussions when land was given to companies. For example, the letters patent of James I to Sir Thomas Gage and others for "two several colonies," dated April 10, 1606, although granting away two vast areas of territory greater than England, inhabited by thousands of First Nations people, the existence of whom the Kind had knowledge both officially and unofficially, do not contain the slightest allusion to them. Although later charters recognised the existence of Natives, they did so in an extremely racist fashion. Charles I, for example, authorised the state "to collect troops and wage wars on the barbarians, and to pursue them even beyond the limits of their province and if God shall grant it, to vanquish and captivate them; and the captive put to death...."

When ignoring First Nations people was no longer feasible due to the need for westward expansion, the English chose to isolate Indians through a reserve system, or to annihilate them. But the British regime recognised some Native claims to the land. First Nations people were *granted* Aboriginal rights by the British Crown (at the will and pleasure of the Crown and not as an inherent aboriginal right) in the *Royal Proclamation* of 1763. From that point on, land was usually purchased from First Nations people in formal treaties between the British government and First Nations people, with the First Nations people agreeing to settle on reserves and to take up farming.

In 1775, "Indian agents" were appointed, formally establishing Canada's policy of treating First Nations people as *wards of the state*. Significantly, the Indian agents initially placed in control of reserves were always military men. With the constant threat of invasion from the United States, Indians continued to be important as military allies. Control of and responsibility for Indians remained a military matter. The military importance of the Indians to British North America was evident in 1812. It was the First Nations peoples' military forces, primarily the Iroquois, which repelled the southern invaders and helped to establish the 49th parallel as the border between the United States and Canada right across the North American continent.

The Iroquois were an exception, however. As White settlement spread West, most of the Indians of southern Ontario signed away their lands and moved West and North. Most of the British, Scottish and Irish immigrants who came to Canada came in search of land. The fur trade had lost much of its importance; agriculture was paramount. Immigrant settlers cleared the land, fenced it in and farmed it. This meant the rapid displacement of the Natives. As the Whiteman moved westward First Nations peoples were forced, usually under threat of military action, to surrender their lands to him.

By 1830, the federal government was questioning the value of the "Indian" for Canada's future. Invasion from the south by the United States was no longer a direct and immediate threat. Because there were no other political attackers, Indians were not likely to be needed as military allies. Indians were therefore considered irrelevant to Canada and its future development. Thus in 1830 responsibility for Indians, the Department of Indian Affairs, was removed from military control and became a branch of the public service.

Shortly after Confederation, the first comprehensive *Indian Act* was passed in 1876. Through this legislation First Nations people were segregated from the dominant society and subjected to paternalistic control over all aspects of their lives. As a Parliamentary statute the *Indian Act* cannot violate either the *Constitution* or the *Charter of Rights and Freedoms*. However, because Section 91 (24) of the *British North America Act* and the *Constitution* declares that Indians and lands reserved for Indians fall under the exclusive legislative authority of Parliament, "equality before the law" as guaranteed by the *Charter* has been difficult to achieve in practice, in large part due to the very broad definition of "equality" accepted in the Canadian courts. In effect, then, the *Indian Act* still defines the rights of "Indians"[20] in Canada and denies these First Nations peoples basic recognition as human beings.

Frideres (1998:9) uses the proceedings of the federal Parliament with regard to issues of First Nations People as an indicator of the fundamentally racist nature of the relationship between the dominant group and First Nations people. He maintains that these proceedings are "shot through with racist dogma" and provides a number of examples of racist commentary and conclusion, two of which will be noted here. The first is a statement made by a Commission that was appointed to enquire into the conditions of First Nations people of the Northwest Coast:

"the Indians having acquired a little mental activity and a very partial knowledge of some of the things about which they are agitating, probably imagine that they know a great deal and are thoroughly able to say what is good for them" (1888:32–33 in Frideres 1998:9).

The second is a statement made by the Minister of the Interior in 1902:

Our position with reference to the Indian is this: We have them with us, and we have to deal with them as wards of the country. There is no question that the method we have adopted [will bring] these people to an improved state . . . There is a difference between the savage and a person who has become civilised, though perhaps not of a high type (Debate of the House of Commons, 2nd sess. 9th Parl., 1902:3046 in Frideres 1998:9).

Frideres admits it could be argued that these are not representative statements, and that they are, in any event, simply a matter of "history" now, but argues that racism towards First Nations peoples has not disappeared in Canada. Frideres points out that First Nations people were not granted a social identity as Canadians in the full sense of the word until after World War II. For example, they were not allowed to vote unless they gave up their legal status as Indians; at times they were required to carry passes when they left their reserves;[21] and women could (and did) lose their status simply by marrying someone who was not a status Indian.[22] Furthermore, basic rights recognised and claimed by most

Canadians such as the right to quality education and health care have historically been denied them.

Racism in Canada thus has followed the evolution of racism in other parts of the world, shifting from biological racism to other forms, including structural racism, in the twentieth century. Wilhelm (1969 in Frideres 1988:378) argues that Canadians adopted a new strategy of racism during the 1960s, what he calls "the myth of equality." "The myth's basic premise is that all humans are equal no matter how diverse they appear to be. This acts as a rationale for denying special privileges and affirmative action programs to various minority groups."

The idea that all ethnic and racial groups are equal, regardless of the impact of historical discrimination on the group arose as Prime Minister Pierre Elliot Trudeau attempted to implement his concept of a *just society* in Canada. In order to justify his position of no special treatment of or special status for Quebec, Trudeau was forced to define "equal" as "same," and in the process perpetuate—apparently unintentionally—institutionally legitimised racist government policies. The infamous *White Paper*, the Trudeau government's position paper on Indian issues, was touted by the Liberal government (and then Minister of Indian Affairs Jean Chretien) as a sweeping new approach to the Indian "problem." However, the *White Paper* recommended that reserves be terminated and special status for Indian people be revoked. The advantages enjoyed by Indian people in Canada as a result of their status as aboriginal peoples were thus to be taken away from them in the name of equality.

A justification for the continued racist treatment of First Nations peoples in Canada during the latter part of the twentieth century arose with the characterisation of Canada's resources as "limited." Frideres (1988:379) argues that this notion was similar to one which had developed in the United States concerning Black-White relations. He sums up the argument in this way: "More for Natives translates as less for Whites." Dixon elaborates:

> If I am pro-Black, then I must be anti-White. If I am pro-White, then I must be anti-Black. Another way of stating the either-or concept is the two-person, zero-sum game. According to the strategy of this game, if, for example, a sum of 100 units of some commodity is to be distributed between two people, then any changes in a given distribution means than increasing one side causes a corresponding decrease in the other. Similarly, in the context of ... race relations, any gain for Black is viewed as a loss for White and vice versa. (1971:29 in Frideres 1988:379)[23]

Finally, Frideres (1998) maintains that most Canadians still believe—overtly or covertly—that First Nations peoples are inferior. Thus they believe that there good reasons for discrimination against First Nations peoples at both individual and institutional levels. For example, it is true that there has been public recognition of First Nations peoples' rights. "Existing Aboriginal rights" were officially recognised by the Canadian government in the *Charter of Rights and Freedoms* in 1982. But little has been done to address the discrimination and bias present in the Canadian legal and social systems that continue to deny them equality with other Canadians. Frideres points out that the sort of recognition provided in the Charter has not gone very far towards mitigating the political, economic and social consequences of several hundred years of exploitation, subjugation, and colonialism.[24]

143

Frideres' model describing the colonisation of First Nations people offers a persuasive argument for the racist treatment of First Nations people in Canada and clearly demonstrates the relationship of colonialism to the development of racism in Canada. He describes First Nations people in terms of *internal colonies* and, refining Blauner's (1969) description of basic components of internal colonialism, outlines seven steps or parts in the colonisation process of First Nations people in Canada.

The first step is the incursion of a coloniser into a geographical area. The incursion usually takes the form of *forced-voluntary entry*, such as the French entry into Canada or the English entry into the USA.

The second step has to do with the destructive effect of contact with the coloniser on the social and cultural systems of indigenous groups. In Canada, for example, White colonisers destroyed the political, kinship, social and religious systems of First Nations peoples. The values and norms of First Nations peoples were also ignored or violated.

In the third step there is the development of external political control of indigenous communities. For example, in Canada, until the 1940s DIAND decided which Natives could/not leave reserve lands, the Minister of Indian Affairs can (still) suspend almost any right set out in the *Indian Act*, and reserve land can be expropriated by the government (with *appropriate* compensation).

In the fourth step there is the development of economic dependence on the part of First Nations people. Nock (1978) documents the proletarianization of Native peoples in nineteenth century Ontario. He describes the effect if not the intent of schools on nineteenth century Ontario Natives as producing "a breed of sub-proletarians who were at home neither on the reserve nor in urban industrial society." They were "fated" to work for others as tradesmen, unskilled workers, farmhands, or domestic servants. Frideres argues that First Nations people have remained economically dependent in large part because reserves are exploited for primary resources by metropolitan business for the benefit of metropolitan business.

The fifth step involves the provision of low quality social services for the colonised in such areas as health and education. First Nations people in Canada have a life expectancy on average ten years shorter than other Canadians. They are much more likely to die from violent causes. One in three families lives in crowded conditions, often with two or three families sharing a house. Social problems, such as drug and alcohol abuse and welfare, are of epidemic proportions in many First Nations communities.

The sixth and seventh steps are the two most important to this discussion. With the sixth step comes the ideology of racism. Frideres argues that the ideology of racism is used to justify the social position of the coloniser and colonised, and to legitimise the treatment, the exploitation and subjugation of the colonised by the coloniser. With the seventh step comes the development of a colour line. Skin pigmentation, and/or body structure become the basis for determining inferiority and superiority. Interaction is then limited to members of the same group: Whites interact with Whites; First Nations people interact with First Nations people.

Colonisation, states Frideres, has lead to the development of a *two-tier system* in Canada. Colonisers own, direct and profit from industries that depend upon the exploitation of the colonised, First Nations people, who provide an unskilled, seasonal workforce for the coloniser. Profits made from reserve resources and on the reserve itself go elsewhere, outside the reserve. The rewards of a colonial system, then, seem clearly economic. And racism, as one of the major ideologies associated with colonialism, serves to justify and legitimise the systematic economic exploitation of one group by another in Canada.

Ethnic Groups—Ethnicity and Ethnicism

The terms *ethnicity* and *ethnic group* are relatively new. Maybury-Lewis (1997) notes that they began to be systematically used in the 1950s. Glazer and Moynihan (1975) point out that these terms did not appear in standard dictionaries until the 1960s. Groups that are now defined as "ethnic" were previously defined as races or nations. The terms came into use because social scientists began to recognize that they needed a term, or set of terms, that would describe groups in frequent conflict within nation-states composed of people who felt common ties that were beyond kinship but less widespread than national ties. The need for such terms was made greater by the fact that these groups were most emphatically not disappearing into the various "melting pots" of the nation-states in which they lived.

The development of "ethnicity" historically, then, involved the social recognition and marking of a number of characteristics. In anthropology and sociology ethnicity has often been defined first and foremost in terms of shared cultural characteristics. Ethnic groups are groups within a larger society that display unique cultural characteristics. They are *subcultures*,[25] divisions of society distinguished from others by their names, language, traditional foods, holiday rituals, occupations, folklore, patterns of child rearing, and loyalties.

Ethnicity as "Primordial"

An important feature of ethnic groups is that they think of themselves as "different." Members of ethnic groups see themselves as having common roots. There is an often emotionally charged awareness of an in-group versus out-group distinction. Clifford Geertz (1973:277) terms these sorts of ties "primordial bonds," ties stemming from common blood, religion, language, attachment to a place, or customs. For Geertz, these ethnic ties are passed down from generation to generation and serve to differentiate group members from non-group members. They are the expression of a basic self and group identity. From this *primordialist perspective*, ethnic ties are natural, inherent, basic to human social life. One's ethnic group is a fundamental reference group: self-identification comes from it. Behaviour is also influenced by ethnicity. For example, for most ethnic group members, ethnicity plays a significant role in shaping one's primary relations. Family, friends, peer group, marriage partner, place of residence may all be determined, or at least affected, by one's ethnic group identity. There are other important groups in our lives—for example groups based on class, age, sex, and/or occupation—but primordialists maintain that one's ethnic group is the primary group, and often overlaps with these others. Ethnic group identity also accounts for collective mobilisation of group members in their political or economic interests. In this way, primordialists argue, ethnicity and ethnic ties exert an independent, powerful force on human behaviour.

145

Primordialists propose that the highly emotional nature of ethnic ties is a major factor in explaining the persistence of ethnic groups and ethnic group identity despite forces of modernisation such as urbanisation, education, and the mass media, which could be expected to weaken them. Emotional ties to childhood and to the past, they argue, have the ability to withstand the trends toward homogenisation of the global market and "information age." From this perspective the existence of ethnic groups and ethnic group conflict in contemporary societies is explained as either "clinging to old loyalties" on the part of ethnic group members, or "resisting change" on the part of members of traditional, aboriginal societies (within both developed and developing nation-states).

People outside any given ethnic group also, necessarily, recognise differences between themselves and ethnic group members. Ethnic group membership is created, at least in part, by the beliefs and behaviours of members of the larger society. Ethnic group identity may not be the single most important variable in all social interactions, nor must ethnic identity be prominent in an individual's awareness all of the time, but ethnic group boundaries are based on a social recognition of cultural differences between groups. One need not be strongly conscious of one's ethnic identity, nor must one's ethnicity be a major factor influencing one's interrelations with others for ethnic group membership to have a powerful effect on one's life. And, ethnic group identity is very often a basis for ranking or stratification[26] within a society. Thus ethnicity is a dominant force in human society.

Ethnic groups (and ethnic identity) are characterised by *ethnocentrism*. As with all social groups, ethnocentrism plays an important role in the creation and maintenance of ethnic identity. Ethnocentrism provides a basis for group solidarity and fosters cohesion within the group. Ethnocentrism also, however, contributes to hostility between groups. The negative valuation of groups other than one's own that is the inevitable result of viewing "others" in terms of the values and norms of one's own culture does little to promote understanding of or tolerance for other groups. Thus, from the primordialist perspective, ethnocentrism—in conjunction with the emotional aspects of ethnic group identity noted above—makes conflict among ethnic groups "pervasive and intractable" (Marger 1991:15).

For primordialists, ethnic group membership is *ascribed*. One is born into an ethnic group; one does not "become" ethnic.[27] If the physical characteristics of any given ethnic group do not differ significantly from those of the dominant group, it is possible at different times and in different places to "pass" as a non-ethnic, *dominant group* member. But because of the enculturation/socialisation process whereby group identification, group values and group customs are internalised, it is not easy to abandon or change one's ethnicity. In addition, at the same time as one internalises the values and customs of one's own group, the various categories provided by the larger society for classifying people into ethnic groups are also internalised. Once internalised, classification becomes unconscious, automatic. This, too, makes it difficult to change ethnic identification. Finally, the larger society rarely permits full integration of (identifiable) ethnic group members into the mainstream. Ethnic group members are not usually allowed to deny their ethnicity. Ethnicity in modern multiethnic nation-states in fact tends to be one of the primary identification markers of an individual.

From the primordialist perspective, geographic (not just social) "isolation" is an important factor in sustaining ethnic group identity over time. Most ethnic groups, they point out, are concentrated in a particular geographical area. In North America generally, the tendency is for ethnic groups to occupy relatively small areas of land within a larger geographical (often urban) area. In Canada, for example, there is a "Chinatown," or "Little Italy," (to name but two such groupings) in virtually all of the larger cities. Mahfooz Kanwar (1996) describes North-East Calgary as an ethnic "ghetto," an area "heavily occupied by South Asian Canadians who seem to have segregated themselves on the basis of their ethnicity." He points out that virtually all South Asian social activities take place within North-East Calgary, and that this physical and social isolation works to prevent the *functional assimilation*[28] of South East Asians into the larger Canadian (Calgarian) society. "Ghettos can create barriers in social participation with outsiders, which in turn can restrain the process of functional assimilation."

Occasionally ethnic groups in North America do occupy larger tracts of land—the Hutterite colonies in Alberta, the Québecois in Québec, and First Nation reserves and reservations in Canada and the United States, for example—but these are exceptions to the rule. In Europe, on the other hand, it is not uncommon for much larger areas of land to be occupied by particular ethnic groups: the Basque in Spain and France, and the Serbs, Croats, *et al.* in the former Yugoslavia are two examples. Many ethnic groups occupying larger tracts of land in both North America and Europe aspire to political autonomy. They wish recognition of their separateness to take the form of an independent entity of some sort. Québec separatists in Canada, Basque separatists in Spain and France, Bretons in France, and a significant number of First Nations peoples currently seek the right to control their own destinies.

Finally, those who see ethnicity as primordial point out that even where ethnic groups have ceased to be territorially based, group members usually maintain emotional ties to their society and place of origin. Thus they continue to see themselves as somehow different and apart.

Ethnicity as "Emergent"

The primordialist description of ethnicity and ethnic groups presented above describes many undeniable components of ethnicity in the modern world, but a major criticism of this account is that it does not sufficiently concern itself with history, social structure, and class conflict. Treating ethnic ties as inherent in human social life, for example, does not explain why ethnic ties manifest differently under varying social, political, and economic conditions. A definition of ethnicity and ethnic groups which emphasizes their social and geographic isolation, and their fundamentally static, unchanging character does not provide a satisfactory description, analysis or explanation of their reality in the modern world.

One of the features of ethnicity that is difficult to explain from the primordialist perspective is the fact that an ethnic group may be granted status as a separate group whether or not there is in fact a shared ancestry for ethnic group members that can be objectively documented. Martin Marger (1991:13) notes that groups claiming or being accorded separate ethnic status may be "objectively" quite similar and groups that claim to be similar may be "objectively" quite different. The extent to which ethnic groups will be noticed or marked by non-group members, and the degree to which ethnic group members will insist on their ethnic identity is variable. Both in-group and out-group response play a role. Ultimately, then, ethnic group identity seems to be primarily a social creation.

In an attempt to describe this aspect of ethnicity, sociologist Robin Williams (1964) distinguishes ethnic "collectivities" and ethnic "categories." Ethnic collectivities are people who have a recognisable culture, are aware of themselves as a unit, are recognised as a unit by outsiders, interact with other group members, and feel a sense of obligation to defend and support one another. Ethnic categories are people who have similar (cultural) characteristics but have little sense of themselves as a group, little interaction with other group members, and minimal obligations to support or defend other group members. Williams notes that ethnic groups may constitute themselves as collectivities or categories at different points in time (but he does not explain why or how they do this).

David Maybury-Lewis (1997:60) also marks this characteristic of ethnic groups in his discussion of the differences between kinship or "family ties" and ethnic ties. He notes that "everybody everywhere starts life as the member of a family and must some time or other act as one." Family ties, then, could be said to be truly "primordial" ties. But this is not the case with ethnic identity. In the sense that everyone speaks a particular language, has a skin color, lives in a place that has a history, and so on, every human has the "latent qualification" for ethnic association. But such criteria do not necessarily make individuals members of ethnic groups. Ethnic identity develops only when one or more of the criteria for ethnicity are "activated" and perceived to be "the defining characteristics of a group." For Maybury-Lewis and others, manipulation of ethnicity is an essential aspect of both ethnic identity and scholarly discussions of ethnicity.

Frederik Barth (1969) argues against the "primordialist" notions of ethnic group geographic and social isolation. He maintains that positing these as critical factors in maintaining ethnic group identity is too simplistic. Barth points out that ethnic boundaries persist *despite* interaction among ethnic groups over time. And, what is more, he shows that there are often important social relations across ethnic boundaries. Thus, a crucial element of ethnicity for Barth and those who share his views is the *boundary maintenance mechanisms* that develop to enable the ethnic group to persist over time. Ethnic groups never exist in isolation. Group members always have contact with Others and interact across group boundaries, even where there is hostility between groups. Ethnic group members must know whether Others can join the group, how much one can think and act like an Other, and how much and what kind(s) of interaction ethnic group members may have with Others. However "too much" is defined, too much interaction with or "being like" Others can pose a danger not only to an individual's right to remain a group member but also to the identity of the group as a whole.

Barth agreed with the primordialisits that ethnicity has an important cultural aspect, but he maintained that there is no simple one-to-one relationship between ethnic units and "objectively defined" cultural differences. He proposed that ethnicity is *emergent* in the process of social interaction. Ethnic identity is not natural, inherent, "primordial"—basic to human life—but instead emerges in a particular form under particular social circumstances. For Barth ethnic groups do not exist because people share the same culture but rather because people who share these characteristics either decide they are members of a distinct group or are perceived and treated by out-group members as "different," members of a distinct group. He argues that ethnic group identity develops after or because a group of people is considered by others to be ethnically related. Once that happens, the "ethnic group" begins the process of establishing "rules and understandings concerning the essence and limits of what they have in common and who belongs and who does not" (Maybury-Lewis 1997:61).

From the *emergent* perspective, then, ethnicity is not seen as atavistic, or a "survival."[29] Ethnic group members are not perceived to be "clinging to old loyalties" or "resisting change," continuing an earlier cultural tradition. Rather, an ethnic group's identity is understood to be a product of both the contemporary situation with which the ethnic group must deal **and** cultural continuity from the past. Ethnicity is an artifact of group interaction in specific circumstances.

This perspective on ethnicity has been developed by anthropologists and sociologists who lean towards materialism and conflict theory. As previously noted, for them the study of ethnicity is necessarily part of the study of social relations within and between groups. Conflict theorists maintain that power and class relations are key variables in social relations, particularly those that involve inequality. They propose that ethnic groups are social groups in competition for access to or control over political power or economic resources. Thus the assertion or identification of ethnicity varies over time and depends on social circumstances. Ethnic identities and ethnic groups appear, transform, and disappear as the social and economic environment changes. Ethnicity from this perspective, "entails the assertion, revitalization, and elevation of ethnic cultural identity" (Harrison 1998:613). Furthermore, they argue that ethnic identity "may operate as a form of cultural resistance against racism and the denigration of the racial subordinates' cultural past and present" (Harrison 1998:613). Thus ethnicity is (necessarily) fluid, a historically constituted social identity.

One example of this sort of *emergent ethnicity* in modern societies is offered by David Maybury-Lewis (1997:99-107). His discussion of the 1994 massacre in Rwanda—where more than a half a million people were killed during the month of April—shows clearly that the conflict between the Tutsi and the Hutu was caused by European colonialist intervention which resulted in the creation of separate, opposing ethnic groups.

Maybury-Lewis notes that in pre-colonial times, the population of Ruanda-Urundi (Rwanda and Burundi) was roughly one-fifth Tutsi, four-fifths Hutu, and one-to-two percent Twa. It was more or less a feudal system with Tutsi lords ruling Hutu peasants. (The Twa were "aboriginals" and pretty much outside—marginal to and "below"—the social system.) Tutsi, Hutu and Twa speak the same language and share the same religion and culture. Furthermore, it was (and is) rarely possible to tell whether individuals are Twa, Hutu or Tutsi from their physical characteristics. Those identified as Tutsi and Hutu had different social statuses and were associated with different occupations. Tutsi was a term applied to lineages[30] that controlled wealth (particularly in cattle) and power. Hutu lineages were those who did not possess the wealth and were not closely tied to the powerful. Poor Tutsi could be considered Hutu and wealth Hutu lineages could over time become Tutsi.

When the Belgians made the area of Ruanda-Urundi into a colony they governed it by indirect rule. They co-opted the Tutsi rulers and used them as administrators. This meant that the Tutsi now had more power than ever before. And, because it was difficult to distinguish individual Hutu and Tutsi based on physical characteristics, the Belgians required everyone in the colony to carry an identity card which specified the group to which s/he belonged. "Where there was doubt, a man owning ten or more head of cattle was classified as Tutsi, while one owning less was classified as Hutu!" (Maybury-Lewis 1997:102).

The Belgians thus fabricated rigid, static social identities in what had been a fluid social system. By the end of the colonial era these "ethnic groups" created by the Belgians were involved in civil war against one another. In the newly created nation-state of Burundi the Tutsi managed to maintain control, but in the newly independent Rwanda the Hutu took power. In 1972 the Tutsi rulers of Burundi put down a Hutu rebellion, slaughtering between 100,000 and 200,000 Hutu. Later in Rwanda, a civil war broke out, with Tutsi rebels challenging the Hutu regime. In that conflict the Hutu massacred more than half a million.

Maybury-Lewis argues that "[t]hese repeated genocides in Rwanda and Burundi are not spontaneous eruptions of mutual hatred between contending ethnic groups" (1997:105). He proposes that they are in large part the result of European intrusion, action and inaction. Europeans created the rigid ethnic identities of Tutsi, Hutu and Twa, and made them exclusive, opposing categories. Pre-colonial antipathy between these groups was made worse by the imposition of both Western perceptions of ethnicity and Western political systems enforcing the perpetual dominance of those designated Tutsi. But, at the same time, the Western world has been extremely reluctant to interfere in what have been defined as "internal" problems. Thus Hutu and Tutsi extremists were left to invoke "ethnic identity" as a key part of their radical and violent agendas designed to realise political power for them. Moderates on any side were annihilated and the justification for their murders was much the same as that used by racists against those who would tolerate the blurring of racial lines through intermarriage.

Conclusion

The preceding has outlined the several and various definitions of race and ethnic group identity. It has been argued that race and ethnicity are social constructs, specific to particular times and places in history. They are "emergent." It has also been proposed that the "isms" associated with the social categories of race and ethnicity—racism and ethnicism—develop and persist over time in the same ways, as part of the social creation of reality. The experiences of First Nations peoples in Canada and the Hutu and Tutsi in Rwanda-Burundi plainly demonstrate the artificial and arbitrary "fabrication" of identities involved in the marking of racial and ethnic categories.

It is clear that "race" and "racism," as well as "ethnicity" and "ethnicism" have not gone away, nor are they likely to in the foreseeable future. These sorts of ideologies have shown themselves to be particularly persistent and to have the ability to reinvent themselves in new (and often unanticipated) ways. Contrary to the expectations of some social scientists and politicians (see Wilson (1980), for example), the "social significance" of race and ethnicity has not declined. Some have gone so far as to suggest that racism and ethnicism are "permanent," and will persist whether or not "race" or "ethnicity" exist as specific, explicit classificatory devices demarcating difference (Bell 1992; Winant 1994). Others point to the development of "reverse racism" that now discriminates against Whites and Asians (Custred 1998).

Social scientists have done quite well in understanding, analysing and challenging the biological concept of race. They have also offered descriptions of the parameters used to define ethnic group identity. However, as Harrison (1998:610ff) notes, there has been and is no consensus across the disciplines on how to explain the "social realities" of race or ethnicity. There is, for example, the "problem" of the black-white "folk dichotomy" in North America. It persists despite the realities of the colour continuum and is increasingly applied to and by members of groups that are neither "white" nor "black." "Whiteness" is associated with things positive and desirable; "blackness" with things negative and undesirable. According to Ong (1996), among Asians in America there is a distinction between "model minorities"—primarily Chinese and Japanese who are hard-working and highly educated and therefore worthy of "cultural citizenship"—and "minorities"— mostly Cambodians who tend to be on welfare and are therefore unworthy of "cultural citizenship." Model minorities tend to be described as "white" while minorities tend to be discussed in terms of "blackness." Harrison also remarks on research which has begun to document the "divergent experiences and forms of ethnicity for white ethnics ... and ethnics of colour, particularly historically subjugated groups such as African Americans, Native Americans and certain categories of Latinos (particularly Puerto Ricans and Chicanos)" (1998:613). Such work, she states, constitutes only a "good beginning."

As racism assumes new forms in the post-colonial and post-modern era, researchers may not even agree whether race or racism apply in any given case. Harrison (1998) describes the debate within anthropology regarding the interethnic, immigrant-host relations in contemporary France and Germany: that debate asks whether those social relations constitute a new form of racism or an altogether new order of power and knowledge that represents a fundamental shift in the structure of difference-making. She also remarks on the debate among anthropologists in the United States who cannot agree whether or not current political discourse, welfare reform and the criminal justice system "encode race and reinforce racial domination by pathologizing what are being represented as irreconcilable sociocultural differences" (1998:610). The challenge for the twenty-first century will be to construct new kinds of social analysis that will allow social scientists to deal with the new ideological forms that justify inequality and exploitation. And then those analyses must be communicated to the general public to become part of global awareness. Perhaps, as Foucault said, in the end we must see the study of "race [and by extension, ethnicity] as part of the discourse of power within which it is endlessly reconceived, redefined and reconstrued" (in Shanklin 1998:675).

151

Notes

1. Ranking refers to differential access to prestige, but not wealth or power, within a society.

2. A *social class* is a group who have generally similar educational histories, job opportunities, and social standing. Because of the number of different variables which define social class, and because the variables may not correlate neatly, social class is a somewhat ambiguous category. An *economic class* is defined by the similar access of its members to wealth and economic control. Most researchers today have found it useful to combine the definitions of these two types of class; they speak of *socio-economic classes*.

3. Uniformitarianism is the idea that if the earth's mantle is now affected by natural forces (wind, flowing water, frost, volcanic activity, and so on), then it stands to reason that such forces operated in a similar, or *uniform,* fashion in the past. "The present is the key to the past."

4. Prognathism refers to the degree to which one's jaw projects forward.

5. The cephalic index is the ratio of the maximum width of the head to its maximum length times 100.

6. Nasal index refers to the relative flatness, "pointedness," length, and width of the nose.

7. The following discussion of *biological racism* is taken largely from Marger (1991:27-35) and Schaefer (1988:11-18).

8. A *dominant* or *majority group* is a group that controls the majority of the wealth, power and prestige in a particular culture. It is not necessarily superior in numbers. A *minority group* is a subgroup whose members have significantly less power or control over their own lives than members of the dominant group. A minority group has five characteristics: unequal treatment, distinguishing physical or cultural traits, involuntary membership, in-group marriage, and awareness of subordination (Schaeffer 1988:5-8).

9. This discussion is adapted from Marger (1991:74-92) and Schaefer (1988:55-68).

10. Stereotypes were first described by Walter Lippmann in 1922 as "pictures in our heads" not acquired through personal experience. Stereotypes are based in partial, inadequate and exaggerated descriptions of a group. They may focus on positive or negative features of a group but generalize these features to all members of the group. Schaefer (1988:27) defines stereotypes as "unreliable generalizations about all members of a group that do not take into account individual differences within the group."

11. Ethnocentrism is the process by which each group assesses its own values and folkways to be the only and right ones, and each individual views (evaluates) alien cultures and cultural activities in terms of the values and norms of his/her own specific "culture."

12. Natural selection is the result of differential reproduction. Differential reproduction is the ability, in a given environment, of certain individuals to produce more surviving offspring and thereby to increase in the population genetically-derived traits that enhance that ability. As a result of natural selection the characteristics of species change over time. Eventually new species emerge as populations of the same species diverge by adapting to

different environments. The genetic basis for natural selection was discovered by Gregor Mendel. Currently the theory of evolution is known as the "evolutionary synthesis."

The Theory of Evolution by Natural Selection as proposed by Charles Darwin may be summarised as follows: Organisms produce far more offspring than required to maintain their population size, and yet their population size generally remains more or less constant over long periods of time. From this, as well as from observation, it seems clear that there is a high rate of mortality among individuals. Individuals in any population show much variation, and those that survive probably do so to some extent because of their particular characteristics. That is, individuals with certain characteristics can be considered better adapted to their particular environment. Since offspring resemble their parents closely, though not exactly, successive generations will maintain and improve on the degree of adaptation, by gradual changes in every generation.

Therefore this process of variation and selection by the environment for better suited individuals is called *natural selection,* and the change in the nature of populations that follows upon selection through differential mortality is the process of *organic evolution.*

13. The term *functionalism* is used here in a generic sense, and the commonalities among the various "versions" of functionalism will be stressed. The differences between Malinowski's functionalism and the structural-functionalism of Radcliffe-Brown, Parsons and Merton, for example, are not relevant for this discussion. For a more complete discussion of functionalism readers are urged to consult introductory texts in sociology **and** cultural anthropology.

14. Since contact, Europeans have used a number of terms to refer to the indigenous peoples of North America. Originally they tended to adopt the misnomer applied by Christopher Columbus: Indian. That singular label obscured the tremendous variety and difference among aboriginal people, and provided Europeans with a single cognitive category for a very diverse group. Over time aboriginal peoples in Canada have begun to demand that non-aboriginals refer to aboriginal peoples with the term(s) that they, the aboriginal people, have themselves chosen. The term of reference preferred by most aboriginal people in Canada today seems to be "First Nations people." It is this term that will be used through most of this discussion. However, because this is also a discussion of history, the term historically used—Indian—will also appear from time to time and should be considered synonymous.

15. The hunter-gatherer adaptation is the most flexible of all subsistence patterns, adapting to the existing environment rather than seeking to transform and control the environment. Most hunter-gatherers are organised into small nomadic groups known as bands. The optimum size of a band for efficient use of resources is between 15 and 25 persons, depending on the environment. Kinship is important in band membership. Through kinship a person will likely acquire the right to use specific territories for foraging. The members of a band may range over a territory from less than one hundred to up to a few thousand square miles. Hunter-gatherer groups are *egalitarian.* Division of labour is based on age and sex. Men *hunt* large marine and land animals, and usually fish. Women *gather* wild plant foods, process food, bear and care for the young; may hunt small animals. There are no full-time specialists: every woman/man can do what every other woman/man can

do. Hunter-gatherers are generally well-fed, comfortably sheltered, and enjoy ample leisure time. A key in social relations is reciprocity, sharing with the local group the food that any member has collected. Decisions affecting groups are made by *consensus*. Those who disagree may move away. The *settlement pattern* of h-g depends on the abundance and reliability of food resources. Hunter-gatherers adapt to variability in resources by mobility, and adjusting local group size to food availability. Among hunter-gatherers there is no formal political system. Leadership is informal and situational. Leaders acquire their *positions* because they possess qualities admired by the group. Leaders have no coercive powers; they must convince and cajole their followers. Typically, leaders of h-g groups are *headmen.*

16. Horticulture is the growing of plants using simple, non-mechanised technology such as hoes and digging sticks. There are no draft animals or ploughs and no irrigation techniques or fertilisers. Fields are not permanently cultivated; after two or three years of productivity the land must be left to lie fallow (for up to twenty years) and new gardens must be created. Typically several varieties of crops (in North America the "three sisters": corn, beans and squash) are cultivated together in small gardens. The small plots of land are cleared by hand using what is called the "slash and burn" method. The forest is cut down and the felled trees are left to dry out. Once dry, they are burned. The residual ash provides nutrients for the soil. Horticulture provides a low yield per acre of land. Horticulturalists provide food mainly for their own households; they do not produce a surplus for sale or trade.

17. The Montagnais-Naskapi (Cree) of northern Québec, for example, have a strong and continuing oral tradition which clearly indicates awareness of and concern for maintaining an ecological balance in their environment. Trappers regularly survey the animal populations on their trap lines and if animal populations appear diminished, they will leave the land lie fallow until populations regain sufficient numbers to allow a safe harvesting of them.

18. The *Jesuit Recollections* are the diaries of Jesuit missionaries sent back to France and then Italy. They were a source of information for the higher echelons in the Jesuit Order and are often used by historians as primary sources in their investigations of the past.

19. Mercantilism was an economic theory which proposed the following: 1) that the mother country was entitled to accumulate wealth in any form, and 2) that the mother country was entitled to exploit its colonies as a source for raw materials and a market for finished products, thereby maintaining a favourable balance of trade for the mother country.

20. It is important to note that the term "Indian" as defined in the *Indian Act* refers only to those people recognised by the federal government of Canada to have legal status as Indians. Such *status-Indians* make up a little less than half of the First Nations population in Canada. The remainder, *non-status Indians,* are socially and/or physically identified as "Indian" but are not classified as Indian by the federal government and consequently have no (recognised) aboriginal rights, receive no benefits from the federal government, and are not subject to the provisions of the *Indian Act.* Status Indians became legally "Indian" because they were on a list compiled by government Indian agents, or because they or their ancestors signed a treaty with the federal government. "Indians" who failed to get their

name on a list or who refused to take treaty were not (and are not) considered to be Indians by the federal government. Historically, then, legal status as "Indian" was not necessarily related to social, cultural, physical, or biological characteristics.

21. On the Prairies during the 1930s Indians were required to carry an identification card when, if, they left their reserve.

22. The requirement that an Indian woman give up her legal status as an Indian in Canada upon marriage to someone other than a status Indian ended in 1985 with the passing of *Bill C-31 (An Act to Amend the Indian Act)*.

23. Interestingly, in another context anthropologists have described such a zero-sum worldview as the *image of limited good*. They generally describe it in negative terms, as a "limiting" factor preventing peasant peoples from taking advantage of new opportunities and/or technologies that would allow to improve production, increase their wealth, and eventually move themselves out of their powerless, dependent, subordinate position as peasants.

24. A *colony* is a territory for which final governmental and policy authority is located in another country, or (by extension to fit the North American internal situation) in institutions whose interests are outside of, and not controlled by, the communities governed. *Colonisation* is the operative process. *Colonialism* is the ideological orientation toward such action. The *coloniser* is the exploiter, the intruder. The *colonised* is the exploited; the indigenous or aboriginal inhabitants of the area.

25. It should be noted that the term *subculture* does not apply only to ethnic groups. A subculture is generally thought of as a group in the complex relationship of being both part of the larger society, yet in some ways marked off from it; participating in a larger culture yet having a distinctive version of it. The term may be applied to such diverse groups as biker gangs, missionaries, university and college students, and so on.

26. Stratification refers to differential access to wealth, power and prestige within a society. Societies may be stratified according to socioeconomic class, caste, race, ethnicity, and/or gender.

27. There is, of course, the notable exception of the many hyphenated Canadians who over the past twenty years or so have either decided to stop "passing," or are making efforts to return to ethnic roots of their ancestors that had been abandoned by parents or grandparents. In both cases there is a new recognition of and claim laid to their "ethnicity."

28. Functional assimilation refers to the integration of diverse ethnic groups into the institutions of the larger society. This form of assimilation involves elimination of group discrimination based on ethnicity. Ethnic groups may continue to remain distinct and be recognized by Others to be "different," but there is political and economic equality and a basis for social interaction within the larger society.

29. A "survival" is a cultural trait from a previous time that persists into modern times. The term is often associated with cultural traits that seem to be either dysfunctional or non-functional in the present.

30. *A lineage* is a group of kin who trace descent from a common ancestor through known links. They can demonstrate the genealogical links among the members of the

lineage. A *patrilineage* is formed when descent is traced through males. A *matrilineage* is formed when descent is traced through females. Lineages are generally corporate kin groups that can serve a primary role in the distribution of wealth and political power. Often land is held jointly by lineage members. Lineage members often co-operate economically. Better-off lineage members are often responsible for ensuring that others who are poor, infirm, or elderly are cared for. Religious life in lineage-based societies frequently emphasises the worship of lineage ancestors.

References

Barth, Frederik
1969   *Ethnic Groups and Boundaries*. New York: Allen and Unwin.

Bell, Derrick
1992   *Faces at the Bottom of the Well*. New York: Basic Books.

Benedict, Ruth
1940   *Race: Science and Politics*. New York: Viking.

Berger, Thomas; et al.
1989   *The Arctic: Choices for peace and security—a public inquiry*. West Vancouver, BC: Gordon Soules Book Publishers.

Berreman, Gerald
1988   Race, Caste and Other Invidious Distinctions in Social Stratification. In *Anthropology for the Nineties: Introductory Readings*. Johnetta Cole (editor):485–518. New York: Free Press.

Blauner, Robert
1969   Internal Colonialism and Ghetto Revolt. *Social Problems* 16:393–408.

Cartmill, Matt
1998   The Status of the Race Concept in Physical Anthropology. *American Anthropologists* 100(3): 651–660.

Collins, Randall
1975   *Conflict Sociology: Toward an Explanatory Science*. New York: Academic Press.

Coon, Carleton
1965   *The Living Races of Man*. New York: Knopf.

Custred, Glynn
1998   Our National Obsession with Race. *Anthropology Newsletter* 39(2):16–17.

Dahrendorf, Ralf
1959   *Class and Class Conflict in Industrial Society*. Stanford, California: Stanford University Press.

De Waal, Alex
1994   Genocide in Rwanda. *Anthropology Today* 10(3):1–2.

Durkheim, Emile
1961[1915]   *The Elementary Forms of the Religious Life*. New York: Collier.

Frideres, James S.
1998   *Aboriginal Peoples in Canada: Contemporary Conflicts* (fifth edition). Scarborough, Ontario: Prentice Hall Allyn and Bacon.

1988   *Native Peoples in Canada: Contemporary Conflicts* (third edition). Scarborough, Ontario: Prentice Hall.

Garn, Stanley M.
1969   *Human Races*. Springfield, Illinois: Charles C. Thomas.

Geertz, Clifford
1973   *The Interpretation of Cultures*. New York: Basic Books.

Glazer, Nathan and Daniel P. Moynihan
1975   *Ethnicity: Theory and Experience*. Cambridge: Harvard University Press.

Gould, Stephen J.
1981   *The Mismeasure of Man*. New York: WW Norton and Company.

Harrington, Faye V.
1998   Introduction: Expanding the Discourse on "Race." *American Anthropologist* 100(3): 609–631.

Hernnstein, Richard J. and Charles Murray
1994   *The Bell Curve: Intelligence and Class Structure in American Life*. New York: The Free Press.

Hill, Jane H.
1998   Language, Race, and White Space. *American Anthropologist* 100(3):680–689.

Isajiw, Wsevolod W.
1999   *Understanding Diversity: Ethnicity and Race in the Canadian Context*. Toronto: Thompson Educational Publishing, Inc.

Jensen, Arthur
1969   How Much Can We Boost IQ and Scholastic Achievement? *Harvard Educational Review* 39(1).

Kanwar, Mahfooz
1996   Policies Fuelling Divisions. *Calgary Herald*. November 5.

Lippman, Walter
1922   *Public Opinion*. New York: Macmillan.

Malinowski, Bronislaw
1929   *The Sexual Life of Savages in North-Western Melanesia: An ethnographic account of courtship, marriage and family life among the natives of the Trobriand Islands,* British New Guinea. New York: Liveright.

Marger, Martin
1991   *Race and Ethnic Relations: American and Global Perspectives* (second edition). Belmont, California: Wadsworth Publishing Company.

Mason, Philip
1970   *Patterns of Dominance*. New York: Oxford University Press.
Maybury-Lewis, David
1997   *Indigenous Peoples, Ethnic Groups, and the State*. Toronto, Ontario: Allyn and
            Bacon.
Mead, Margaret
1942   *And Keep Your Powder Dry: An Anthropologist Looks at America*. New York:
            Morrow.
1935   *Sex and Temperament in Three Primitive Societies*. New York: Dell.
Merton, Robert K.
1968   *Social Theory and Social Structure*. New York: Free Press.
Montagu, Ashley
1974   *Man's Most Dangerous Myth: The Fallacy of Race* (fifth edition). New York:
            Oxford University Press.
1942   *Man's Most Dangerous Myth: The Fallacy of Race*. New York: Oxford Univer-
            sity Press.
Murphy, Robert F.
1971   *The Dialectics of Social Life: Alarms and Excursions in Anthropological Theory*.
            New York: Basic Books.
Nock, David A.
1978   The Social Effects of Missionary Education: A Victorian Case Study. In R. W.
            Nelson and D. A. Nock (editors), *Reading, Writing, and Riches: Education and
            the Socio-Economic Order in North America*. Kitchener, Ontario: Between the
            Lines.
Nash, Manning
1962   Race and the Ideology of Race. *Current Anthropology* 3:258–288.
Ong, Aihwa
1996   Cultural Citizenship as Subject-Making: Immigrants Negotiate Racial and Cul-
            tural Boundaries in the United States. *Current Anthropology* 37(5):737–762.
Orser, Charles E., Jr.
1998   The Challenge of Race to American Historical Archaeology. *American Anthro-
            pologist* 100(3):661–668.
Park, Kyeyoung
1996   Use and Abuse of Race and Culture: Black-Korean Tension in America. *Ameri-
            can Anthropologist* 98(3):492–505.
Parsons, Talcott
1951   *The Social System*. Glencoe, Illinois: Free Press.
Porter, John
1965   *The Vertical Mosaic*. Toronto: University of Toronto Press.

Radcliffe-Brown, A. R.
1965   *Structure and Function in Primitive Society: Essays and Addresses*. New York: Free Press.

Schaeffer, Richard T.
1988   *Racial and Ethnic Groups* (third edition). Glenview, Illinois: Scott, Foresman and Company.

Shanklin, Eugenia
1998   The Profession of the Colour-Blind: Sociocultural Anthropology and Racism in the 21st Century. *American Anthropologist* 100(3):669–679.

Smedley, Audrey
1998   "Race" and the Construction of Human Identity. *American Anthropologist* 100(3): 690–702.

1993   *Race in North America: Origin and Evolution of a Worldview*. Boulder, Colorado: Westview.

Spencer, Herbert
1933[1873] *Descriptive Sociology*. New York: D. Appleton.

Sumner, William Graham
1906   *Folkways*. New York: Ginn.

Todorov, Tzvetan
1993   *On Human Diversity: Nationalism, Racism, and Exotism in French Thought*. Catherine Porter, translator. Cambridge, Massachusetts: Harvard University Press.

Williams, Robin
1964   *Strangers Next Door: Ethnic Relations in American Communities*. Englewood Cliffs, New Jersey: Prentice Hall.

Wilson, William Julius
1980   *The Declining Significance of Race: Blacks and Changing American Institutions* (second edition). Chicago: University of Chicago Press.

Winant, Howard
1994   *Racial Conditions: Politics, Theory, Comparisons*. Minneapolis: University of Minnesota Press.

Winick, Charles (editor)
1970   *The Dictionary of Anthropology*. Totowa, New Jersey: Littlefield, Adams and Company.

7

Gender Relations

Gisele Marie Thibault

The goal of this chapter is to provide the reader with an introductory understanding of the sociology of gender—how men and women are structured in society because of social definitions of biological sexual differences that structure how men and women relate to each other in personal, collective, economic and political ways. The chapter extends our understanding of how social life is structured in context of the various networks of relationships that we are embedded within. Many of these networks are interpersonal but many are also forged into linkages within geographical regions, economic sectors, and political institutions.

The chapter begins with a look at how the sociology of gender relationships emerged in Canadian sociology and then continues to outline the basic concepts of sex and gender. The chapter proceeds to present a theoretical understanding of gender, and then presents the various kinds of feminism: liberal, radical and socialist. The chapter concludes with the linkages between gender and a number of social institutions.

What Is the Sociology of Gender Relations?

The Background

In order to derive a systematic basis for understanding gender relations as an academic study, it is necessary to ask how the field emerged in sociology. While it is impossible to provide an entire analysis of the evolution of gender studies or the women's movement in the scope of this chapter, some general background information enables one to better appreciate the implications that gender analyses have had on the discipline as a whole.

The recognition of sexual divisions within sociology, and the development of gender relations as a distinct field of study; both owe an enormous debt to the ideas and political activism of the women's movement. The sociology of gender relations has its origins in the grass-roots feminist movement. The feminist movement (or women's movement) has a long history stemming from the nineteenth century in Canada, but took on a more vocal, visible and collective presence in the general ferment of the late 1960s and early 1970s, or what has been referred to as "the second wave" (Thibault, 1987).

The social context of the late 1960s affected women's consciousness in a number of significant ways. First, the period was one of social and political change in the United States and Canada, and in many other parts of the world. The continuing movement for civil rights, protests against the war in Southeast Asia, the women's movement, and somewhat later the gay movement, were principal events that called into question the authority and values of Canadian and American institutions. Since a significant segment of the participants in these movements were students and faculty at universities across the continent, the educational establishment itself became subject to scrutiny and challenge (DuBoise et al., 1987). Both students and faculty began to politicize a number of issues including gender, race, and class. The time period also affected middle-class women in two ways: the growth and composition of universities had changed to include more women and industry was booming which brought about a rapid increase in the percentage of women working outside (Hole and Levine, 1971).

Those social movements most active during this time were demanding a reallocation of societal power, and argued for equitable treatment for blacks, native Canadians, the poor, students, and women (Wilson, 1991). The "New Left" protested the Vietnam war, the alienation of humans and their labour, the dehumanization of an automated and technocratic society, and the appropriation of identity by mass consumerism and the world of the corporate elite (Marcuse, 1972; Miles, 1982). Coupled with these issues was a concern for identity and freedom which became reflected in a criticism of all social institutions. Radical groups began to criticize the "establishment" for attempting to restrict radical political activity to a separate and narrow political sphere—a sphere that would be less threatening to the existing social structure or status quo.

Within the context of these struggles, feminist radicalism emerged (Hole and Levine, 1971). For feminists, the question of male dominance and an essentially masculine "humanity" was addressed as women realized that what they were experiencing as "personal" was political. While sexist practices in other radical movements were a powerful cause for anger and disillusionment among women, their critique of male dominated institutions was generally applauded by feminists. However, they came to view their subordinate position in these movements as indicative of a general failure to create an independent statement about women and for women (Wine and Ristock, 1991).

Concurrent with the political movements that led women and men to reexamine patriarchal society were political movements that challenged hierarchies of academe. These movements set out to demystify the illusion that the university, as an institution, could be isolated from the mainstream of national power. The problems of education on all levels were connected to the perpetuation of social class inequalities. For many faculty and students, the ivory tower of academe reflected the interests of government, corporations, and military political machines (Rozak, 1967). At the same time there were charges that scientific and technological research ultimately served the military rather than the progress of human knowledge. Further, scholarship in the social sciences was criticized for its neglect of urgent social issues, the working class, minority groups, and of most importance to this discussion, women (DuBoise et al., 1987).

The first women's campus groups to emerge in the late 1960s were those composed of students and faculty who began organizing to confront and challenge the inequities they were experiencing in academe (Freeman, 1973). Their criticisms were directed at both the structure of university and the practices and content of scholarly research. Feminists complained that as a subject of research in all disciplines, women were being neglected, overlooked, or distorted by existing scholarship.

It was at this juncture that sociology "discovered women" (Mackie, 1991). Women showed that biases existed in the way women were researched and analyzed. Research did not focus on the myriad examples of sexual divisions in society, nor did it center on gender as an organizing feature of social life. "Gendering" was not seen as an essential feature of what role all our social institutions play in society—the school, the medical system, the family, the judicial system, and the economy. In terms of the subject matter of sociology, women as a topic of research were "confined to a special section" (Mackie, 1986:15) or "appeared in male related roles" (Huber, 1976). Similarly, it was demonstrated that women had been systematically omitted or presented in distorted and pejorative ways in both theoretical models and in the interpretation of research studies (Thibault, 1987;1988). As Mackie (1991) points out,

> What had been accepted, until then, as the sociology of human behaviour was consequently discovered to be the sociology of male behaviour. Research had been conducted primarily on males (and females who had been socialized to accept the masculine ruling ideas), on topics that interested men, using methods congenial to men. (1991:20)

Since sociological theories had also been developed with reference to males alone, women's experiences had been left out and misrepresented.

The recognition of these problems, in turn led to what Hesse and Ferree (1987) refer to as a "feminist revolution in the social sciences." From this revolution arose a struggle to restructure the various academic disciplines in ways that more readily permitted the study of women and their experiences. Mackie (1991) suggests that as a result of the rapidly expanding post-secondary education system in the 1970s, and the increasing numbers of women in academia (particularly in sociology), gender and the study of gender relations became a component of the sociological curriculum.

The Current Status

The popularization of the term "gender relations" in the current sense is associated with feminist research. A more precise designation is the specific form of sociopsychological behaviourism linked originally with women scholars working in psychology and sociology—influenced heavily by radical sociologists and the growth of women's studies as an academic discipline (Bowles and Duelli-Klein, 1977).

Today, the term gender studies has assumed various distinctive forms. This diversity has provoked numerous efforts at developing a definition. One definition that seems to provide a satisfactory starting point is Mackie (1991), where she proposes that gender relations applies to the study of the causes and consequences of the cultural identification of emotional, attitudinal, intellectual, and behaviourial traits as either masculine or feminine. The causes and consequences, she explains, are examined from the point of view of individuals, groups, and society as a whole. The term relations emphasizes the interdependence among individuals, groups, and societal institutions. Consequently, the field of gender relations attempts to encompass the situation and experiences of women and men, both individually and in relation to one another. Due to the fact the women have generally been neglected in the sociological account of the social world, more emphasis is placed on the position of women.

Since the late 1970s, major transformations have taken place in sociology, of which the emergence of gender studies has been a vital part. The last decade, in particular, has seen considerable shifts both within the organization of the discipline itself and the structure of the profession. These changes are the result of a greater awareness of gender issues brought about by the women's movement and through the work of gender theorists.

Studying gender from a sociological perspective involves examining both the social differences between men and women as well as the resulting inequalities that these differences entail. Women and men in most societies are socialized differently, assume different roles, and have different experiences of the social world. They live out their lives in a social environment that is separate at some junctures and overlapping in others. Accordingly, some questions that feminist sociologists may ask include: What are gender roles and what purpose do they serve? How is gender part of the very fabric of Canadian institutions? What assumptions are behind the assignment of gender roles, tasks, and behaviours? How and in what ways are women placed in a disadvantaged position in comparison to men? What forms does this inequality take?

To address these questions, the sociology of gender relations, first and foremost, attempts to provide theoretical explanations by critically examining social patterns of inequality. This is accomplished by carefully reevaluating existing theories and providing an alternative knowledge base that includes the experiences of women. As a distinct field of study, it seeks to investigate the consequences of the gender system with respect to the division of labour in societies and the marginalization of women.

Conceptualizing Gender Relations:
Some Basic Concepts

In order to fully grasp the importance of feminist research to sociology, it is necessary to define some of the basic concepts used to explain and analyze gender inequality. The following are the most fundamental concepts that must be clearly understood, as they represent the building blocks of gender analyses; sex, gender, role, stereotype, feminism, and patriarchy.

Sex is a term used by social scientists and biologists to refer to certain biological categories—female and male. In the biological sense, a "woman" is thought to be a person whose chromosomes, internal and external organs, and hormonal chemistry come together to make them "female"—a label which is prescribed to them at birth. Overall, the term sex is considered to represent the biological aspects of a person which differentiates females and males using anatomical, reproductive, hormonal, and other physiological characteristics (Lindsey, 1990). Generally, a person's sex cannot be changed—the anatomical differences of males and females cannot be denied. However, the rich variety of social arrangements that exist in North American cultures and others, suggests that biological sex differences cannot, by themselves, explain the social patterns of inequality that exist between men and women in virtually all societies. There is much more than biological or physiological differences that determine who is a man and who is a woman.

Gender is a social not a biological concept. It refers to neither a "natural" nor innate characteristic—people are not born with a gender. Rather, gender is a social construct, which involves a set of cultural and psychological traits linked to females and males in particular social contexts. Femininity and masculinity, terms used to denote a person's gender, refer to a complex set of characteristics and behaviours that are prescribed for a particular sex by a society and learned through socialization. For example, femininity for certain groups of women in various cultures refers to those qualities associated with passivity, fragility, and the inclination toward nurturing behaviours. Consequently, a little girl is given a doll to play with, dressed in frilly or constrictive clothing, and rebuked for so-called unladylike behaviour. These serve to reinforce behaviour patterns thought to be feminine, and learns to be passive, dependent, and nurturing. Thus, gender refers to what is socially recognized as femininity or masculinity and can therefore be seen as socially created or constructed.

The cultural norms of a particular society at a certain point in time identify ways of thinking, behaving, and feeling as "appropriate" for females and other ways of thinking, feeling and behaving as "appropriate" for males (Mackie, 1986). Furthermore, as Mackie argues, "The momentous impact of gender stems from the direct translation of the greater social prestige enjoyed by males into a monopoly of **power** [emphasis mine] at both institutional and interpersonal levels" (1990:7). In this sense, a "woman" and a "man" are social constructs. An important part of this social definition is the fact that a "woman" is capable of bearing children (or that most women are capable of bearing children). Consequently, in order to fulfill personal and societal expectations, a woman must bear a child. Even though many women never marry, bear children, or nurse them, we are socially defined by our capacity to do so and by the social expectation that this capacity is an intrinsic, "natural" characteristic of our existence.

Similarly, social definitions of "man" include many physical, psychological, and behavioral characteristics, the sum of which, for any one society, represents the gender label "man" for that group. To understand the social definition of men, one must untangle men's biological "manhood" or their sex with their "historically specific, socially constructed and personally embodied notions of masculinity" (Kaufman, 1987a:xiv).

Roles are composed of a pattern of behaviours prescribed for individuals playing a certain part in the "drama of life" (Lindsey, 1990). Roles can also be defined as the "organized actions of a person in a given position" (Sarbin, 1954:225). For example, the role of a teacher in our society requires actions such as imparting knowledge to the student, attending classes, advising students, or grading papers.

In almost every society, females and males are assigned separate and specific roles on the basis of their sex. These roles are referred to as gender roles. Varying from culture to culture, and within a culture by a variety of factors (class, religion, age, sexual orientation and so on), gender roles are made up of a set of expected behaviours with accompanying gender traits. The role of a middle-class white female in our society typically includes playing with dolls, helping mother, getting married, having children, doing the house-keeping work, striving to be attractive as defined by a male dominated society, and so on. Many of these behaviours in their turn form other role configurations or role sets. Thus, the role of a woman may include several subroles such as daughter, wife, mother, and grandmother to name a few. A key point here is that gender roles refer to the specific attitudes and behaviours that women and men are expected to adopt. There is nothing biological about the roles people play. The role concept places the reference squarely on the sociocultural level.

On a final note, the nomenclature commonly including "sex roles" or "gender roles" is now considered unsatisfactory (Mackie, 1991). Since objections have been raised to the concepts of "role" and "sex" both have fallen into disuse. We will go into further elaboration on this point in the section on analyzing gender.

Stereotype is a concept related to role. Simply put, a stereotype is a composite image of traits and expectations pertaining to a group—an image that is persistent in the social mind though it is inaccurate or built upon prejudicial beliefs. Or as one author suggests, it is a "picture in our heads." Typically, the stereotype is an over-generalization of charac-teristics that may or may not have any basis in reality.

Not all stereotypes are pejorative, but many become images that are tinged with negative connotations—connotations that are often reinforced through the media. For example, a stereotypical image of a "women's libber" or more recently a "feminist" often involves viewing these women as incapable of fulfilling the traditional gender role requirements for "proper" femininity, or that all are "man-haters" who are generally homely, dirty, aggressive, strident, shrill, sexually promiscuous (or frigid, or a lesbian, or all three) making speeches, carrying banners, and burning underwear. The fact that many feminists are not middle class or white or college educated, that feminists wear a variety of dress and have differing sexual codes and identities are pieces of reality that do little to change media-produced images (Ruth, 1980). Stereotypes, often born and maintained in ignorance and fear, can and do have wide-reaching effects on both the stereotyped group and those with whom the members of the group interact. Stereotypes can and do dictate gender behaviour to a great extent.

In order to further clarify the nature of gender relations and how it is analyzed, it is vital to de-mystify the preconceived notions about who or what is a feminist. First, **feminism** is not a monolith, but rather it represents a collection of ideas, theories, and divergent approaches which can be loosely defined as a movement and an ideology, and insofar as many have engaged in extended philosophic, sociological analyses, it gives rise to theories about the way gende—masculinity and femininity—are constructed and so-cially produced in our society (Pierson and Prentice, 1982). Second, intrinsic to feminism is the understanding of social inequality and polarity between women and men imposed not by individual men, but by an institutional and state system of masculine dominance. This system of power and domination is referred to as **patriarchy**.

The concept of **patriarchy**, or "rule of the fathers" is usually used to mean all systems of male dominance (Jaggar, 1983:103). Instead of seeing patriarchy as a trait of one or several individuals, feminist scholars insist that it is a system in which both men and women are exploited—albeit in differing forms. Kaufman (1987a) explains patriarchy as something that involves "Domination by men based on, and perpetuated by, a wide range of social structures, from the most intimate of sexual relations to the organization of economic and political life" (1987a:xiv).

While feminism has been defined in various ways, feminists share an ideal of a world in which men and women could be different without these differences becoming value laden and sources of inequality. In general, feminist scholarship proposes that to attain this ideal, patriarchy must be dismantled. From a feminist perspective, patriarchy is a system and an ideology that is reflected in all social institutions. While some women maintain some power, influence, and autonomy in society, the majority are subject to the authority of men. Patriarchy does not refer so much to the specific activities of men and women but rather the value society attaches to particular activities—primarily the greater value attached to activities performed by men. Such is the nature of patriarchy according to feminist thinking, and therein lies its importance to understanding the organization of gender inequalities.

Finally, fundamental to feminists' work in sociology is the analysis of how political, economic and social systems, and their accompanying ideologies, work to perpetuate women's subordinate status. However, feminist research argues that an exclusive preoccupation with the exploitation of women can lead to a purely negative picture of women as passive victims. Therefore, feminist scholars emphasize that women should be viewed as active agents who can resist domination individually and collectively.

All of these concepts are involved in the analyses of gender relations and in explaining the social positions of women and men. In the next section, a short synopsis of various feminist theories used in sociology is presented to help explain gender oppression and the relations of domination and subordination which they create.

Feminist Scholarship

As part of the challenge to mainstream research in sociology, feminist scholarship has made it clear that traditional sociological theories assume an androcentric view of the world where women are seen as the deviation from the norm, the exception to the rule, or the "other." This represents a critique of traditional scholarship and forms the basis for the emergence of new modes of analysis. Feminists have attempted to both modify existing sociological paradigms to include women and an analysis of gender inequality, and focus attention on forging new theoretical models which differ from sociological theories in several ways.

Traditionally, sociology has studied social behaviour and the connections between individual experience to the social organization of society. It has analyzed how individual experiences are created and transformed through social, political, and economic institutions. Consequently, the impact of sociology proper on feminist insights cannot be denied. As Epstein (1984) proposes:

> The methodological and theoretical perspectives offered in ethnomethodology, structural-functional analysis (with its focus on systematic analysis), conflict analysis and other sociological approaches are not **intrinsically** [emphasis mine] unsuited for analyzing

women in society. Rather the problem has been that most social scientists of diverse conceptual persuasions have not considered women to be important or interesting subjects of study. (Epstein, 1984:153)

While not all would necessarily agree with Epstein, feminist sociologists have found many established theories and methodologies helpful in understanding gender relations. For example, feminists have utilized theories of gender socialization or social psychological perspectives to establish the significance of learning in the acquisition of gender (Mackie, 1991). As most of the psychosocial differences between men and women are not innate, theories of learning grounded in psychology, have helped explain how gender relations are acquired through our culture and through agents of socialization such as the family, the school, the media.

In general, socialization theorists have relied on three explanatory models which delineate the way in which cultural expectations about gender are transmitted to the individuals in a society. These models are: the identification model; the social learning model; and the cognitive-development model.[1]

It is important to note that socialization takes place in the context of social institutions and these institutions pass on gender expectations that are consistent with institutional needs (Anderson, 1983). Both Anderson (1983) and Mackie (1991) emphasize that understanding the influence of socialization on the development of our gender identities encourages us to perceive how gender roles contour our behaviour and our beliefs (Anderson, 1983:70). It is equally important, however, to recognize that socialization cannot fully account for all of the complexities of gender inequalities. As Anderson (1983) writes,

> If we limit our understanding of gender relations to a perspective on sex roles, we tend to downplay the significance of gender in the social-institutional framework of society. To illustrate this point, consider how absurd it would be to explain racism in society in terms of a role perspective. No one uses the term race roles to describe patterns of inequality between blacks and whites, although surely it is true that, because of racism, blacks and whites establish expectations of each other. Similarly, to assume that roles are the only appropriate framework for studying gender is to assume that consciousness, not structured inequality, is the sole basis for women's subordination. (1983:71)

The "sex role" perspective neglects the institutional basis for gender inequality and tends to view women and men as the "passive victims" of social messages, rather than active agents in their social relations. As a result, gender theorists have looked to other theoretical and methodological approaches to aid them in explaining gender relations. One cluster of approaches, coined "micro-sociological" perspectives, have proven to be useful in this regard.

The use of symbolic interactionism or symbolic interaction theory has provided feminist research with a conceptual framework that facilitates a deeper understanding of the socialization process involved in psycho-sociological theory. This approach explores the reflexive character of all interaction as people respond to their interpretation of the meanings of others (Hale, 1991:33). Generally, advocates of this perspective argue that behaviour is symbolic. Consequently, roles such as gender roles are not adopted uncritically as taught to them by various socialization agents but rather they are actively created by the participants—women and men. According to the symbolic interactionist perspective, the process of socialization rests on the ability of people to take the role of others. It is suggested that through a reflective process of envisioning oneself from the perspective of others, that people form their self-concepts (Anderson, 1983).

While the symbolic interactionist perspective has been helpful in the study of gender identity formation, it tends to remain within the confines of sex role socialization paradigms created by men. Consequently, it still fails to explain the motivation people have to comply to socially prescribed roles, "or how the world, made up of mundane typifications, actually exerts itself upon the perceptions, actions, and interactions of people" (Hale, 1991:37). As a result, feminists have turned to ethnomethodology and ethnomethodological research because it reveals the way in which sociologists and others actively work at creating their versions of reality that they claim to be studying "objectively." For example, some feminist scholars argue that much of the research data on male-female differences succeeds only in identifying patterns already built into the way the research was conducted. When the findings are reported as "scientific evidence," they come to represent authoritative fact and become the basis for organizing people's expectations, where "people who do not fit such experiences come to consider themselves deviant" (Hale, 1991:39).

Put simply, ethnomethodology focuses on the ways in which women and men, in their everyday lives, use their "common sense" knowledge and understandings to make sense of themselves and the world around them. Hale (1991) proposes that the central contribution of ethnomethodology is its focus on the practices by which people actively create a sense of what is happening in their interactions and how they actively construct their own actions to make them sensible to others (1991:101). However, this method does not take into account how larger social structures are created and simultaneously shape the experiences of women and men. Feminist theorists have recently turned their attention to examining how society is socially created to explain this process.

The social construction of reality, as a conceptual framework, begins with the premise that ideas emerge from particular social and historical settings and that this social structural context shapes—not determines—human consciousness and interpretations of reality (Anderson, 1983). Rooted in the ideas of Karl Marx and Karl Mannheim, the social world and how it is experienced in the form of ideas and consciousness, is related to the social structure, social institutions, and human culture—how experience is socially located. Feminist sociologists have used this framework to criticize sociology on the grounds that knowledge varies according to the social location of the "knower," and because one's social experience and consciousness are conditioned by the social location of one's existence, males (who have generally been the dominant figures in sociology) have developed a different view of the social world than women. To the extent that their situations or "locations" differ, their culture, consciousness, ideas, and conceptions of the world are also different.

By examining the social construction of reality, it is possible to recognize that what people come to know and experience as women and men is not just a product of social learning, but rather something that is actually socially produced by the practices and processes of institutions and the people working in them. Dorothy Smith (1974a; 1974b;

1975; 1977a; 1977b; 1987), who insists that knowledge and the social production of knowledge be socially located, argues that men and women live in worlds that are subjectively and objectively different. These insights question the whole notion of "objective truth" as an abstraction from reality. From this perspective, "truth" is in fact, constituted by real people in their everyday lives. However, as Smith (1977b) points out, this does not dismiss the centrality of macro social structures and their interaction with social consciousness. She suggests that people's everyday worlds are shaped by macro structures (social, political, and economic institutions) which are in themselves configured by socio-historical specifics.

To summarize, feminists have found axioms and postulates of several existing sociological models useful for considering new problems and incorporating women with their unique experiences to the study of gender inequality. The feminist dialogue with sociology has enabled scholars to examine the emergence and persistence of unequal and problematic gender relations in novel ways. There are currently several distinctive features of feminist theory and practice which can be summarized as follows:

> Feminist theory is that part of the new scholarship on women that implicitly or formally presents a generalized, wide-ranging system of ideas about the basic features of social life and of human experience as these can be understood from a women-centered perspective. (Lengermann and Niebrugge-Brantley, 1988:282)

Feminist theory is woman-centered in three ways. First, the starting point of investigation is always the situation and position of women in society. Second, women are treated as "subjects" not objects of research. Third, feminist theory is critical of existing gender relations and the inequalities they entail and works to produce not only better explanatory systems of the social world but to bring about changes in the social structure of society. Consequently, feminist theory is inextricably linked to practice.

The Feminist Perspective

It is important to recognize that just as there is no one sociological interpretation of the social world, there is no single feminist perspective. Within feminist thought, different assumptions and observations have created rich and varied analyses of women. For example, differences can be found "in political strategy, in visions about what constitutes women's liberation, in attitudes toward men, in understanding the roots of women's oppression, in setting priorities, in identifying constituencies and allies" (Adamson et al., 1988:9). Differences also exist in the theoretical explanations of how and why contemporary gender relations take their current forms.

Although it is not possible to present every feminist theory or political philosophy here, the following section outlines three particular currents of feminist theory that can be found in the literature.[2] They are as follows: liberal feminism, radical feminism, and socialist feminism. Each current represents a different interpretation of gender inequality and gender oppression though they share some common themes. This review provides an overview of the variety of interpretations found in feminist theory as to how social institutions reproduce gender and actually sustain gender inequality.

Liberal Feminism

Liberal feminism's explanations of gender inequality begins with the identification of the sexual division of labour, the existence of private and public spheres of social activity, the primary location of women in the private sphere and men in the public sphere, and the systematic socialization of children into adult roles and spheres appropriate to their gender (Lengermann and Niebrugge-Brantley, 1988:296).

The central theme of liberal feminism, or the cluster of writings and ideas categorized as "liberal feminism," is "equality of opportunity" which proposes that

> each individual in society should have an equal chance to compete for the resources of that society in order to rise within it as far as talents permit, unhindered by law and custom; wealth, position, and power should not be distributed on the basis of inherited qualities such as race and sex. (Adamson et al., 1988:9)

Liberal feminists are generally considered to be the more moderate feminists and base their philosophy on the proposition that all people are created equal and should not be denied equality of opportunity because of gender. Rooted in the tenets of the liberal political philosophies of John Locke and Thomas Hobbes, liberal feminism shares a belief that women and men have the same rational faculties, a belief that education is the best means to change and modify society, and a belief in the doctrine of natural rights.

Liberal feminist thinking has been called "mainstream thinking" because of its conviction that the existing social system is not problematic requiring revolutionary changes, but rather requires some modification and reform. In general, liberal feminism accepts the existing social framework (Adamson et al., 1988:190). Unlike their counterparts, liberal feminists do not regard the oppression of women as an inherent problem of the capitalist economic system. They believe that it is possible to eliminate sources of inequality by working within the system. By working within the existing social framework, liberal feminists have pressed for important reforms to benefit women. Such things as equal pay for work of equal value, maternity leave, provisions for daycare, and services for abused and battered women all represent improvements to the current system, brought about by the efforts of liberal feminists working on the inside (Mackie, 1991:257).

Contemporary liberal feminists, while tolerant of the existing system, are particularly critical of women's relegation to the private sphere. Betty Friedan's classic book, *The Feminine Mystique* (1963), was one of the first liberal feminist critiques of the ideology which defined women as primarily wives and mothers. Friedan argued that such an ideology was oppressive to women because it prevented them from developing their own identities. As a liberal feminist, she is critical of motherhood, marriage, and housework, but does not include in her analysis the possibility of structural factors involved in the oppression of women. Instead, Friedan examines the individual character of gender inequality.

As a result of their philosophical orientation, liberal feminist strategies for ending unequal gender relations often include the following: mobilizing women using the existing political and legal channels to initiate change (including having equal numbers of women in positions of power and authority); lobbying for equal economic opportunities; and introducing changes to the major socialization agents such as the family, the school, and the mass media to break the rigid gender roles in society. Those critical of liberal feminism suggest that these reforms only serve to make women a part of the existing structure, and do little to abolish gender inequality. It is argued that liberal feminists do not recognize the ways in which the patriarchal social structure, in and of itself, promotes inequality of opportunity.

Radical Feminism

Radical feminism is the antithesis of liberal feminist theory. As mentioned above, the liberal feminist framework emphasizes the enactment of sex role, the socialization process, and the denial of opportunities as central to the existence of gender inequalities. The radical feminists focus attention on how gender develops and persists as a social, political, and economic category in a particular social structure. The radical analysis of gender relations goes beyond the method of "adding women and stirring" proposed by liberal feminism (Bunch, 1977). Radical feminism argues that all dominant social institutions are characterized by gender, race, and class oppression, and therefore, reforming the existing cannot and will not eliminate inequality (Anderson, 1983:264). Furthermore, radical feminists view the social structure as something that is dominated by men, and used to systematically exploit, control, and suppress women (Hartman, 1981). This is in sharp contrast to liberal feminist thinking which views individual attitudes, not the social structure, as the primary factor that governs gender relations.

Radical feminist thinking begins by identifying women's unique capacity to give birth to children and how this is central to both their life experiences and their oppression (Adamson et al., 1987:10). Put simply, radical feminists argue that the social relations that determine the fate of women are the relations of reproduction. Central to the theory of radical feminism is the primacy of sexual, rather than economic power, and the power which men, or patriarchal society has over women.

This has allowed feminist research to move beyond studying the biological basis of the sexual division of labour and examine the larger issue of female sexuality and the issue of violence against women. In addition, radical feminism has been instrumental in identifying the emotional, social, and political differences between women and men. Finally, and perhaps its most significant contribution to the study of gender, lies in its analysis of power and power relationships. Patriarchy rather than capitalism is viewed as the main system of power, where it is defined as "a sexual system of power in which males have more power and privileges than females" (Lacombe, 1988:27). By adopting this explanation of power, radical feminists suggest that "the personal is political," or that there can be no separation between the private and public. Sex moves from the private to the public, where sex becomes part of the political landscape where women come to share in their oppression based on the expropriation of their sexuality as women.

In sum, radical feminists see all of society as characterized by oppression. Every institution, even society's most basic structures, are assumed to be systems by which some people dominate others. They suggest that their is a continual pattern of domination and submission between classes, castes, racial and ethnic groups, religious groups, and age and gender categories (Lengermann and Niebrugge-Brantley, 1988:306). The existing arrangements are said to benefit men—sexually, economically and politically—at the expense of women.

However, as mentioned previously, patriarchy is a pervasive and ubiquitous source of domination. Patriarchy shapes socialization practices and is embedded in institutional practices and ideologies. Consequently, radical feminists posit that it is often the least noticed and the most significant structure of oppression. To alter and transform the unequal relations between women and men, or break the pattern of domination and submission, radical feminists suggest that only by making women aware of the inherent inequalities of the existing social structure can they be free from the present patriarchal rule. They propose consciousness-raising groups to provide women with new opportunities to gain a sense of who they are and what are their roles—a process based less on adapting to or imitating current role models and more on recognizing the unique potential of being a liberated woman through interaction with women who share common experiences. Then together, women can create a new social structure, as opposed to adopting a new role in the old social system.

Socialist Feminism

A third current found in feminist writings has been coined "socialist feminism." This position represents a synthesis of traditional marxism and radical feminism "unified more by a theoretical agenda and less by substantive theoretical conclusions" (Lengermann and Niebrugge-Brantley, 1988:307). According to Adamson et al. (1988), the basic tenets of the socialist feminist position can be summed up as follows. First, socialist feminism is concerned with transforming the relations of domination between men and women and redistributing political and economic power more equitably across class and racial lines. In addition, this form of feminist thinking assumes that there are fundamental interconnections between the structures of political and economic power—capitalism and the organization of male power—which require a dramatic reorganization of all social institutions that perpetuate unequal social relations. Further, it is posited that because the domination of men over women is not biologically based but rather rooted in the social and economic structures, resistance and conflict are very real means through which social change can be brought about. Finally, socialist feminism values cooperation over competition, need over profit, and emphasizes the need for collective rather than individual action. In this way, socialist feminist analyses put forward a view in which the relations of power inherent in gender, class, race, and sexual orientation are not prioritized, but rather examined in terms of how they are interrelated, and how they reinforce and contradict each other.

Recent development in socialist feminism have been instrumental in distinguishing between the everyday gendered lives of women and men and the larger socio-economic, political, and ideological structures that are at once shaping and are shaped by human action. For example, socialist feminists contend that the sexual division of labour is a major organizing principle of capitalist patriarchies. The sexual division, in simple terms, refers to the processes of social, political, and economic activity which separates and divides the world into two seeming different spheres—the private (or the domestic) and the public (the political world of economics, business, and commerce). Or as Luxton

(1980) puts it, the sexual division of labour is "a distinct separation between workplace and home, between workers and family and between work and leisure." What makes the sexual division of labour important to socialist feminist analyses is the fact the women are often regulated to the private sphere and men to the public sphere, which works to place women in a disadvantage position. The following excerpt from Adamson et al. (1988) illustrates this where they write:

> Inside the workplace women are segregated [from men] in a few occupational classifications (in particular, clerical, sales and service work) where the wages, degree of unionization, extent of benefits, and chances for promotion are low. The current sexual division of labour between the household and the workplace in Canada means, for example, that the care of young infants is generally located inside the household and is a form of unpaid labour performed mostly by women. Finally, the sexual division of labour inside the household assigns women disproportionate responsibility for housework, despite the fact that increasing numbers of women are working for wages [outside the home]. (1988:110-111)

As feminists, theorists who have adopted this position oppose the conventional gender (or sexual) division of labour which places women in the home and thus excludes them from being full participants in the economic system (most of their work is unpaid labour) and the political system (reflected in the inferior legal status of women). The socialist feminists have played a vital role in focusing attention on the various aspects of women's work. For example, the fact that women's labour in the home is devalued, not respected, and generally not recognized as work because it is unpaid labour are just a few of the concerns raised by these feminist scholars (Luxton, 1980; Adamson et al., 1988).

In addition, socialist feminism has contributed significantly to understanding how gender relation are perpetuated by focusing attention on bow the state—as a source of patriarchy capitalist domination—affects the power relationships in other social institutions. They argue that the state (the government) is not politically neutral, but rather grants privileges to men over women, whites over people of colour, middleclass over working-class, and heterosexuals over lesbians and gay men. Further, these biases are said to exist at the very foundation of government policies, legislation, and institutional practices. Consequently, the state is posited to affect virtually every facet of people's lives, from welfare benefits to educational funding, immigration, housing, the administration of justice. All of which, they suggest actively produce gender, as well as class and race inequalities.

In short, socialist feminism develops an analysis of the social world in which the oppression stemming from patriarchy and capitalism is seen as an integrated whole that forms a set of unequal relations between genders, classes, races, and people with different sexual orientations. Further, the sexual division of labour, both inside the home and outside the home is considered to be detrimental to women because their work and the contribution it makes to the functioning of society is diminished. Finally, the functioning of the state is viewed as a process by which inequality is actively produced by intruding into people's lives and determining their fate through discriminatory policies, procedures, and practices. The socialist feminist solution to abolish inequality calls for the complete restructuring of all social institutions to eliminate barriers to opportunity, whether it be gender, race, ethnicity, religion, or sexual orientation.

In concluding this overview of the various currents of feminist thinking, two key issues must be addressed. First, as Mackie (1991) points out, "a fine line must be drawn between appreciating the ideological and tactical distinction we have just made, and exaggerating the divisive forces within the Canadian women's movement" (1991:260). In other words, students of gender relations should not rely on these arbitrary categories to define feminism, categories that tend to stress the differences between feminist ideas at the expense of thinking about the common concerns that have been brought to light through their collective efforts. Rather, students should focus attention on how these concerns have propelled women of all political persuasions and theoretical orientations to organize and actively seek the elimination of gender inequality.

A second, equally important issue, is the apparent neglect of ethnic differences and inequality in much of the predominantly white feminist writings (Hooks, 1984; Moraga and Anzaldua, 1981; Rollins, 1985). In general, feminist theory is representative of white, middle-class, heterosexual interests and therefore is subject to criticism for being inherently biased towards this population of women. All three currents of feminist thought are increasingly cognizant of this problem and are taking steps to deal with the experiences of Third World women, women of various racial and ethnic groups, and lesbian women.

Gender and Social Institutions

Feminist sociologists have used the varying theories and concepts discussed earlier in this chapter to examine the institutional structuring of gender that occurs in the many social institutions that make up any given society. All social institutions establish and organize patterns of gender relations that often result in gender inequalities. An analysis of gender relations in one of the most central institutions in contemporary society—namely the education system—illustrates this process.

Education is a pivotal social institution in modern societies. It plays a crucial role in gender socialization and the reproduction of gender inequality and oppression. Paradoxically, education is seen as one of the most equitable and progressive institutions—as the path to upward mobility in an ever increasing "credentials oriented" society. At the same time, however, it has been the sight of resistance and rebellion against the status quo as evidenced by the emergence of radical social movements on university campuses (Thibault, 1987). In this "most equitable" and progressive social institution, the gender of a child continues to be a key determinant of his or her educational experience and future life chances (Lindsey, 1990). The following discussion examines gender development and reproduction within the context of this apparent contraction.

First, the education system is one of the most significant sources of gender stereotypes and gender "consciousness" in modern society, beginning in kindergarten and ending in graduate school. The feminist critique of the education system has centered on socialization issues and structural issues. Conventional wisdom suggests that the business of education is the "teaching and learning" of knowledge, norms, and the dominant beliefs of a particular culture-that is socialization. Feminists argue that what is taught and the values that are imparted to students represent patriarchal, capitalist interests. Consequently, they propose that what is taught and learned in the education system is ''man made'' (Spender, 1985). Or as Gaskell (1988) and McLaren (1988) suggest, school curricula is not socially and politically neutral, nor is knowledge merely unbiased information presented in such a way that meets the needs of all students. Instead, curricula and knowledge tend to exclude women altogether and portray them in a stereotypical manner.

Evidence has generally supported this view. A number of studies have shown that the illustrations, language and the depiction of gender roles in textbooks provide children with explicitly differentiated gender imagery (Mackie, 1991). Other related empirical findings suggest that textbooks which teach reading skills, social studies, and even mathematics consistently reinforce the idea that females are less important (Spender, 1985). Research that has examined school readers has revealed that stories about females are rare in comparison to those about males. Further, the contributions of females in history, science, or government are rarely included in school readers. Finally, where female characters are present, they tend to reflect the stereotypical views of women—they are generally portrayed in nurturing—caregiving roles such as mothers, nurses, and teachers.

The curriculum involves what is officially taught but also what education theorists have called ''the hidden curriculum.'' A considerable body of literature exists that suggests that the inequalities between the sexes is related to the hidden as well as official school curricula.

For example, little girls ''learn'' through their texts and the teacher's treatment of the material to be nurturant, passive, and dependent. They are encouraged, through the content of the course and the usage of certain language (i.e. mankind), and by example, to assume a subordinate role in a patriarchal society. In particular, women are taught that physical beauty, domestic competency, and their future roles as mothers and wives are of utmost importance to their future well being. Consequently, feminists argue that education is central to the perpetuation of the present inequalities that exist between men and women. Through the preferential treatment of boys found in the reading material and the presentation of course material, teachers' differential expectations of performance, the role of guidance counsellors in streaming boys and girls into sex-segregated programs, the pressures of peer cultures to conform, the gender inequality which places men in a superior position and women in a subordinate position is maintained (Frank, 1990).

To summarize, the education system plays an important part in stereotyping men and women into very static roles. Through the differential allocation of resources, differential curricula (both official and hidden), and the actual formation of educational settings, gender is used to both manage and regulate childhood socialization processes. At all levels of education, higher valuation is placed upon the male gender, by both females and males.

Notes

1. See Mackie (1991) for a thorough discussion of these models.

2. To find a good overview of the various feminist theories and political philosophies see Jaggar (1983) and Walby (1990).

References

Adamson, Nancy, Linda Briskin, and Margaret McPhail
1988   *Feminist Organizing for Change: The Contemporary Women's Movement in Canada*. Toronto: Oxford University Press.

Anderson, Margaret
1983   *Thinking About Women: Sociological and Feminist Perspectives*. New York: Macmillan.

Bowles, G. and Renata Duelli-Klein, eds.
1977   *Theories of Women's Studies*. Berkeley: University Press.

Bunch, Charlotte
1977   "Beyond Either/Or: Feminist Options." *Quest: A Feminist Quarterly*. 3(1): 2-17.

DuBoise, Ellen and Gail Kelley, et al., eds.
1987   *Feminist Scholarship: Kindling in the Groves of Academe*. Chicago: University of Illinois Press.

Epstein, C. F.
1984   "Ideal Images and Real Roles." *Dissent*. 31: 441–447.

Frank, Blye.
1990   "Hegemonic Heterosexual Masculinity." *Studies in Political Economy*. 24 (Autumn): 159–170.

Freeman, Jo
1973   "The Origins of the Women's Liberation Movement," *American Journal of Sociology*. 78: 792–811.

Friedan, Betty
1963   *The Feminine Mystique*. New York: Laurel.

Gaskell, Jane
1988   "The Reproduction of Family Life: Perspectives of Male and Female Adolescents," in *Gender and Society: Creating a Canadian Women's Sociology*, edited by Arlene Tigar McLaren. Toronto: Copp Clark Pitman

Hale, Sylvia
1991   *Controversies in Sociology: A Canadian Introduction*. Toronto: Copp Clark Pitman.

Hartman, Heidi
1981   "The Family as the Focus of Gender, Class and Political Struggle: The Example of Housework." *Signs* 6: 366–394.

Hess, Beth B. and Myra Marx Ferree, eds.
1987   *Analyzing Gender: A Handbook of Social Science Research*. Newbury: Sage Publications.

Hole, J. and E. Levine
1971   *The Rebirth of Feminism*. New York: Quandrangle Books.

Hooks, Bell
1984   *Feminist Theory: From Margin to Center.* Boston: South End Press.

Huber, Joan, ed.
1976   "Sociology." *Signs.* 1: 685–697.

Jaggar, Alison
1983   *Feminist Politics and Human Nature.* Totowa: Rowman and Allanheld.

Kaufman, Michael
1987a   "The Construction of Masculinity and the Triad of Men's Violence," in *Beyond Patriarchy: Essays by Men on Pleasure, Power and Change,* edited by Michael Kaufman. Toronto: Oxford University Press.

Kaufman, Michael, ed.
1987b   *Beyond Patriarchy: Essays by Men on Pleasure, Power and Change.* Toronto: Oxford University Press.

LaCombe, Dany
1988   *Ideology and Public Policy: The Case Against Pornography.* Toronto: Garamond Press.

Lengermann, Patricia Madoo and Jill Niebrugge-Brantley
1988   "Contemporary Feminist Theory," in *Contemporary Sociological Theory,* by George Ritzer. New York: Alfred A. Knopf.

Lindsey, Linda
1990   *Gender Roles: A Sociological Perspective.* Toronto: Prentice-Hall.

Luxton, Meg
1980   *More Than a Labour of Love: Three Generations of Women's Work in the Home.* Toronto: The Women's Press.

Mackie, Marlene
1986   *Exploring Gender Relations: A Canadian Perspective,* Second Edition. Toronto: Butterworths.

Mackie, Marlene
1991   *Gender Relations in Canada: Further Explorations.* Toronto: Butterworths.

Marcuse, Herbert
1972   *Counterrevolution and Revolt.* Boston: Beacon Press.

McLaren, Arlene Tigar, ed.
1988   *Gender and Society: Creating a Canadian Women's Sociology.* Toronto: Copp Clark Pitman.

Miles, Angela
1982   "Ideological Hegemony in Political Discourse: Women's Specificity and Equality," in *Feminism in Canada: From Pressure to Politics,* edited by A. Miles and G. Finn. Montreal: Black Rose Books.

Moraga, Cherrie and Gloria Anzaldua
1981   *This Bridge Called My Back: Writings by Radical Women of Colour.* Watertown: Persephone Press.

Pierson, Ruth and Alison Prentice
1982   "Feminism and the Writing and Teaching of History," in *Feminism in Canada*, edited by Miles and Finn. Montreal: Black Rose Books.

Rollins, Judith
1985   *Between Women: Domestics and Their Employees.* Philadelphia: Temple University Press,

Rozak, Theodore, ed.
1967   *The Dissenting Academy.* New York: Pantheon Books.

Ruth, S., ed.
1980   *Issues in Feminism: A First Course in Women's Studies.* Boston: Houghton Mifflin.

Sarbin, R. T.
1954   "Role Theory," in *Handbook of Social Psychology,* edited by Gardner Lindzey. Reading: Addison-Wesley.

Smith, Dorothy E.
1974a   "The Social Construction of Documentary Reality." *Sociological Inquiry.* 44(4): 257–268.

1974b   "Women's Perspectives as a Radical Critique of Sociology." *Sociological Inquiry.* 44(1): 7-13.

Smith, Dorothy E.
1975   "An Analysis of Ideological Structures and How Women Are Excluded: Considerations for Academic Women." *Canadian Review of Sociology and Anthopology.* 12 (Part I): 353–369.

1977a   *Feminism and Marxism—A Place to Begin, A Way to Go.* Vancouver: New Star Books.

1977b   "Some Implications of a Sociology for Women," in *Woman in a Man-Made World,* edited by N. Glazer and H. Y. Waehrer. Chicago: Rand McNally.

1987   *The Everyday World as Problematic: A Feminist Sociology.* Toronto: University of Toronto Press.

Spender, Dale
1985   *Man Made Language,* Second Edition. London: Routledge and Kegan Paul.

Thibault, Gisele
1987   *This Dissenting Feminist Academy: A History of the Barriers to Feminist Scholarship.* New York: Peter Lang Publishing.

1988   "Women and Education: On Being Female in Male Places," in *Gender Bias in Scholarship: The Pervasive Prejudice,* edited by Winnifred Tomm and Gordon Hamilton. Waterloo: Wilfred Laurier University Press.

Walby, Sylvia
1990   *Theorizing Patriarchy.* Oxford: Basil Blackwell.

Wilson, S. J.
1991   *Women, Families, and Work* , Third Edition. Toronto: McGraw-Hill Ryerson.
Wine, Jeri Dawn and Janice L. Ristock
1991   *Women and Social Change: Feminist Activism in Canada.* Toronto: James
          Lorimer.

Deviance and Social Control

Introduction

Mahfooz Kanwar and Don Swenson

Behavior that departs from group or societal expectations and/or violates social norms is usually considered to be deviant behavior. Common images of deviant behavior that frequently come to mind are acts of crime. However, criminal acts as deviant behavior account for only a portion of all deviants. For example, a homicidal act is both a criminal and a deviant act, while becoming intoxicated at home every morning is considered a deviant act but not a criminal act since it only violates socially acceptable conduct, not legally sanctioned rules.

Deviance is often defined as a breach of trust, ignoring or defying social expectations that society defines for its members. We are expected to play by the rules. Those who cut corners may be considered as deviants. In any given society, most people conform to the normative system. However, some people, in every society, do not adhere to, and do not obey society's norms. They are the rule breakers; they are deviants.

Nonconformity to social norms can result in either severe or minor consequences depending on a number of factors and circumstances. If a deviant form of behavior is considered dangerous, societal reaction may be severe. This is particularly true for acts that are premeditated. On the other hand, acts that are not considered to be dangerous or straying too far from societal expectations result in only minor reactions from others. In Canada, for example, picking your nose as you walk down the street may result in strange and disgusting looks from others. But this type of reaction is different from robbing an elderly woman or walking into a school and killing students as happened in the spring of 1999 in Tabor, Alberta and in Littleton, Colorado. Therefore, relatively minor deviations from

181

social norms do not cause special concern to society, while significant deviations result in societal intervention to control the behavior and to punish the rule breaker.

It is not a simple matter for any society to divide its people into conformists and nonconformists. Most people, at any given time, are considered as conformists not necessarily because they have never deviated from any specific norm considered important by their society, but because their deviant acts have not been detected. Some people have more means to deny, or to defend their violations of norms. Consequently, they do not become part of the statistics. It is asserted that those who violate social standards, or legal norms for that matter, and are able either to hide their violations or defend themselves successfully, are not considered, or defined, as non-conformists, deviants, or criminal persons, but their behaviors are deviant or criminal depending on the definition of the norm in question. For example, if a person smokes marijuana or commits adultery and does not get caught or proven guilty, the person is not a criminal or a deviant but his or her behavior is criminal or deviant.

Social control is to maintain conformity and to prevent and reduce nonconformity in society. Social agencies or institutions will go to great lengths to encourage its members to live up to its standards whether they are social or legal norms. Every society tries to help its members to learn, internalize and obey its rules. Social control is easier and more effective if and when people internalize voluntarily the important norms of their society. Once internalized, the norms and values are considered as personal standards and as personal codes of conduct. In this case, they become part of one's conscience and morality. If they are not internalized, and enforced externally, some individuals may not feel guilty about violating them.

Social control is applied formally as well as informally. The presence of police, courts, prisons, remand centers, and halfway houses, to mention a few, reminds us to conform to important and written rules. Socialization in the family, school, religious organizations, and peer groups, to mention a few, provides us with social persuasion and moral influence to obey social norms. Some people will argue that social control takes many different forms such as socio-legal attempts at preventing deviance, or threatening the deviants with punishment to deter them from deviance. Some may argue that, especially in Canada, the emphasis of social control is on punishment more than it is on reform. Some even go as far as suggesting that the agencies of social control are bent upon revenge, and not on justice. Whatever is the argument, the function of social control is to induce conformity of members of a social system.

Socialization, not coercion, is considered to be an integral part of social control. We learn and teach what is considered to be right in our society. Coercion may turn people away from conformity. Socialization, be it formal or informal, can persuade individuals to conform to socio-legal norms. It is considered to be one of the most effective ways to help people to internalize norms, rules, and expectations. Learning from others in intimate relationships in families, schools, and religious organizations may help us to internalize society's norms more than the threat of retaliation from the police, the courts, and prisons. However, one needs to know that socialization is a life-long process and is never complete. Nevertheless, socialization sometimes is defective. Parents are imperfect parents, teachers are learners as well, and peers may be significant but not almighty. This may leave individuals in a state of *anomie* as Durkheim would have it. Also, there are conflicting norms. A powerful pornographic industry hails freedom of speech in touting its smut in film, magazines and over the Internet. Many parents (and a sizable number of social scientists) proclaim how harmful pornography is to children, women and family life. The differential expectation of what is normative can, therefore, create confusion. This may happen frequently with new immigrants who are confronted with conflicting values from their homeland and their host society.

Social control cannot function without sanctions. The positive sanction is rewards and approval, where as the negative sanction is punishment and disapproval. Conformity is rewarded and non-conformity is punished in every known society. These sanctions may be formal or informal. A stare from a parent to a child for the latter's misbehavior functions as an informal sanction. The same child who grows up into adulthood and then rapes someone is punished formally by the justice system of a particular society. On the other hand, a husband who privately honors his wife is informally rewarding her. In contrast, when *Time Magazine* honored Pope John Paul II as the man of the year in 1994, the company was rewarding him with formal recognition.

In our teaching experience, several students have tried to do research and write essays in the field of general deviance and crime in society. We have, therefore, included two chapters on deviance, and crime and punishment in Canada.

In chapter eight, Bernard Schiesel explains what constitutes deviant behavior and what the associated sanctions are. He also discusses variations of deviance and crime: who is more deviant-the intoxicated driver or the automobile business executive who knowingly sells a defective product. Schissel introduces various theories of deviance as he refers to some of the pioneers such as Emile Durkheim. He provides a very good explanation and a review of the related literature, as well as systematic critique of the various points of view in this area. He makes it easier for the reader to understand the relativity of defining deviant behavior. In this regard, the discussion on labeling theory and ethnomethodology is very useful for our readers. Also discussed in this chapter is the social dimensions of deviant behavior. This includes mental disorder, substance abuse, alcohol related deviance, youth crime, and sex related deviance.

In the final chapter of this section, John Winterdyk treats crime as a serious social problem. He debates the issue of crime being related to social control and defines punishment for crime as he discusses its functional and dysfunctional effects. Winterdyk provides details on how the justice system justifies sentencing for the purposes of deterrence, rehabilitation, or retribution.

He also comments on statistics and keeping track of crime and punishment. In the light of recent tragedies in schools in the United States (Littleton, Colorado) and Canada (Tabor, Alberta)* where, in total, fourteen students were killed, the issue of violent crime is salient. This chapter provides a timely discussion on violent crime trends in Canada. He also addresses property crime, the risk of criminal victimization, and the patterns of punishment in Canada. Winterdyk further explains the characteristics of adult and young offenders, women and crime, and the sociological causes of crime.

* In April of 1999, two teenage boys entered a suburban high school in Littleton and proceeded to murder 12 students and one teacher. They then turned their weapons on themselves and inflicted fatal wounds. Their intent, however, was more massive. They had planted bombs throughout the school and some of which had the potential of destroying the whole school. Since that times (as of April 30, 1999), there have been 450 bomb threats in schools throughout the United States. In Tabor, a fourteen year old teenager entered the local high school and killed a student and inflicted serious wounds on another (NBC, April 29, 1999).

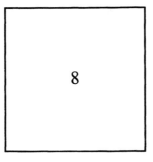

Deviance

Bernard Schissel

In the introduction to sociology, we found that the concept of culture was central to understanding society. To remind ourselves again, in our relationships with others, we interact with them channelled or framed by social structures. In addition to that, however, we are thinking persons who view our social behaviours through world views and mental maps. Within these world views, we have a sense of what we consider to be "right" behaviour and what is "wrong" behaviour. This helps us to "map" our relationships with others according to some predefined codes that are constructed both by ourselves and cultural systems.

However, we all know so well that, because we are free agents, we have freedom, at least relative freedom, to follow these codes or not. It is thus that we meet the concept of deviance which may be generally defined as deviation from cultural codes.

Then, in the chapter on culture, we were introduced into what McGuigan calls "cultural as code," which is the normative element of a culture. They are, again, codes which direct people to what is considered good or bad, normal or abnormal, acceptable or unacceptable, and desirable or undesirable. Deviance, then, is understood to be the breaking of society's rules or codes of behaviour.

Introduction

We know that social life involves people breaking society's rules. Some people violate the formal rules by assaulting others while some violate the informal rules by persistent staring in elevators or by chronically arriving late to class. Both types of **norm violation** are considered as **deviance** and have penalties attached to them.

As we will come to see, however, the issues of what constitutes deviant behaviour and what are the associated penalties are difficult to define. The degree of consensus regarding what is acceptable behaviour is highly variable. Who is more deviant, for example, the intoxicated driver who threatens the lives of pedestrians or the automobile business executive who knowingly neglects to rectify defects in a new product.

Variations, then, as to what is defined as deviant occur over time, over social group, and over society. For Durkheim (original 1897, 1964), for example, deviance depends on the characteristics of the individual, the social context, and the historical period. Others, such as Stanley Cohen (1985) and Michel Foucault (1979), argue that the definition of deviance is closely associated with social control—society's need or tendency to categorize and control the behaviour of certain types of individuals. Historical studies of conditions such as mental illness and homosexuality illustrate that definitions of abnormal behaviour have ranged from sin, to sickness to lifestyle, coinciding with the influences of religion, science, and the law.

The theoretical or philosophical approaches to deviant behavior are premised on one of two basic ways of viewing such behaviour: the **absolutist** and the **relativist.** The absolutist stance assumes that morality, and the rules that prescribe the morality, are inherent and unchangeable. Furthermore, the rules of conduct—definitions of good and evil, right and wrong—are assumed to be shared by most people. The basic problem facing the society, from this perspective, is the rule breaker herself and the focus of social control, then, is on either punishing or reforming the violator. As we will see in subsequent discussions, the absolutist explanations of deviant behavior are encompassed by a general category of theories called **consensus theories** and the focus of attention is on deviance **as norm violation.**

The relativist perspective challenges the absolutist. This approach, which is held by many contemporary sociologists, argues that because societies are complex, definitions of right and wrong are not generally shared, but arise from one group exerting its power over another, or arise from accommodation resulting from unequal groups in conflict. Morality is not a given but changes relative to time, place, context, social standing, political power, economic influence, etc. The basic problem facing the society is not the rule breaker but the rule itself. Relativist theories can generally be subsumed under the general category of theories called **conflict theory.** The focus is on deviance as **social constructed.**

The **interactionist** perspectives can include both relativist and absolutist perspectives. The interactionist perspective, however, is less concerned with the structure of the society and the origins of rules and more concerned with how individuals come to accept or reject rules. The focus is on shared meanings and values and the interchanges between people that result in deviance behaviour. This perspective is micro-sociological in that the object of study is primarily the individual, while consensus and conflict theories which are macro-sociological, concentrate on the structure of the society. As we will see in subsequent discussions, interactionist theories, like the macro theories, fall into absolutist or relativist categories based on assumptions about origins of rules.

Theories of Deviant Behaviour

Although the primary focus in this chapter is on sociological explanations of deviant behaviour, it is important to realize that there are other levels of explanation that are characteristic of other scientific disciplines. The basic levels of explanation other than the social, are the biological and the psychological.

Biological Theories

Biological theories fall into the general category of consensus theories. The underlying assumption in this general body of theories is that certain biological conditions cause bad behaviour and that certain types of deviant behaviour can be "cured" through medical intervention.

The original research using a biological perspective is typified by the work of Cesare Lombroso (1911) who argued that criminal behaviour was a symptom of a lower position on the evolutionary scale. Based on comparison of a sample of inmates and a sample of Italian soldiers, Lombroso found that, relative to the soldiers, inmates were typified by physical anomalies, such as high cheekbones, protruding foreheads, eye defects, poor dentition, and bodily malformations such as excessively long arms. Deviants were viewed as evolutionary throwbacks (atavists) which could be identified by bodily characteristics. The flaws in this type of logic can be readily seen when we consider the effects that prison may have on the physical body, and especially when we consider that the physiological traits that Lombroso identified may be stigmatized and may prevent individuals from leading a normal productive life or that poverty and malnutrition may produce both physical abnormalities and a need to engage in criminal activity. Lombroso's faulty logic and poor research design coupled with future research that failed to support his findings, discredited these particular types of biotheories and Lombroso's work is only of historical interest today. Despite this, we will see that altered versions of the biological approach continued to flourish.

The work of William Sheldon (1949) is one of the most noteworthy extensions of biological theories. In the 1940s Sheldon attempted to link body type to criminal and deviant behaviour arguing that certain body types—the ectomorph who is skinny and fragile, the mesomorph who is muscular, stocky and athletic, and the endomorph who is soft, round and fat—are associated with temperament and behavior. An excessively high percentage of criminals, especially juvenile gang members, were found to be mesomorphs which led Sheldon to argue that there was a cause and effect relationship between physiology and behaviour. Again, faulty logic seems to be at play; mesomorphs are more likely to be recruited to delinquent gangs, or judges may see strong athletic boys as more of a threat than other types. Like Lombroso's theories, the supporting evidence was weak.

Later, research into genetic abnormalities, created excitement in the medical and crime control communities with the claim that deviants were more characterized by genetic abnormalities than non-deviants. Specifically, Klinefelter's Syndrome was identified as a genetic abnormality where an extra Y chromosome is present. Where ordinary men have a typical XY chromosome composition; violent criminals were argued to have an abnormal XYY combination, and this defect was manifested in aggressive behaviour, large (excessively tall) body types, and mental deficiency. The resulting argument was that there must be a casual connection between the genetic abnormality and criminal behaviour (Shah and Roth, 1974). Once again, the subsequent evidence has suggested that the research and the casual logic underpinning these studies may be faulty. Even if the association between chromosome composition and deviant tendencies can be made, it does not suggest how or why the abnormality leads to deviance. It may be that the physical difference isolates individuals and restricts them from conventional society. If

XYY individuals have lower mental capacities, for example, it may be that they find it impossible to engage in conventional social and economic activities and that they are "driven" into the world of deviance. The underlying assumption is that the stigmatizing effects of an intolerant world may force deviant behaviour.

Despite the flaws in earlier bio-studies, biological research has currently gained a new life. Current sociobiological research in alcoholism concentrates on identifying the neurological or genetic traits of individuals with high risk propensities to alcoholism (Pollock et. al., 1986; Goodwin, 1986). As well, recent work on male predispositions to violence attempts to link evolutionary concepts, such as reproductive competition—which are characteristics of our lower primate ancestors—and status competition, with homicidal behaviour in male gangs (Wilson and Daly 1985). An interest in biological phenomena is also seen in recent twin studies comparing identical (monozygotic) and non-identical (dizygotic) twins. The basic research question in these studies is the degree to which twins of different types share criminal or deviant tendencies (Mednick and Volavka, 1980), and the overall findings suggest a greater similarity in deviant behaviour for identical compared to non-identical twins.

Although biological studies are compelling and persistent, they have gained little favour in sociological research primarily because the research has failed to control psychological and social factors which interact with biology, and, most importantly, because the implications of such research appear to be rather frightening. Certain policy implications such as genetic engineering and selective abortions of defective foetuses are considered objectionable goals by many people.

Psychological Theories

Psychological explanations of deviant behaviour, like biological theories, adopt the absolutist view of deviant behaviour and focus on the causes of the violation as originating within the individual. Unlike biological theories, however, psychological theories argue that character and personality is acquired in early life and is not primarily biologically inherited; the emphasis is on the mind and not the body.

For example, psychoanalytical theories concentrate on the improper development of conscience. Sigmund Freud suggested that personality is comprised of the id, the ego, and the superego. The id was envisioned as a part of the personality that all people had and that led us to aggressive, self-destructive, and antisocial tendencies, the more animalistic side of human nature. The ego, or the social self, and the superego (the conscience) were the dimensions of personality that held the id in check. Deviants, then were those whose ego and superego development was impaired. For Freud, this impairment starts at the earliest stages of infant development and is influenced by degree and type of parental training.

Some psychological theories suggest that deviance results from the frustration that results from unmet needs. According to the frustration-aggression hypothesis (Berkowitz, 1969), frustration leads to aggressive behaviour that may be manifested in outward deviant behaviour or in self-destructive behaviour. Bandura and Walters (1963) extended this explanation of aggression in a **theory of social learning** which suggested that people come to behave aggressively through a process called modelling, whereby individuals who observe the behaviour of others being rewarded, are prone to internalize the rewarded behaviour as acceptable. For example, much of this research focused on the influence that violence on television has on deviant behaviour. Simply put, if the viewer is exposed to depictions of deviance that are socially acceptable, then he or she may become insensitive to the deviance and may no longer see acts of violence, for example, as negative.

The types of vicarious conditioning that social learning theorists discussed were seen to be fundamental to the **theory of behaviourism**. Beginning with the work of B. F. Skinner (1953), behaviourism assumed that behaviour was instilled through reward and punishment and that, because behaviour is learned, bad behaviour can be unlearned. Eysenck (1977) argued that immoral behaviour is the result of improper conditioning; children never learn to associate fear and pain with bad conduct. Eysenck considered this conditioned fear as the basis of conscience. In this general arena of psychological research which stressed the effect of fear and punishment on moral development, the **theory of cognitive development** focused on how moral development coincides with stages of psychological and physical maturity. For psychologists like Jean Piaget (1932) and Lawrence Kohlberg (1969), the individual is the source of "badness' and as in psychoanalytic theories, deviants are characterized by deficits in moral reasoning. These deficits occur at certain stages of psychic development and deviant tendencies can be rectified by redirecting the individual through the appropriate stages of development.

Psychological theories have maintained their appeal in the study and control of deviance primarily because the emphasis on the individual permits the development of a treatment program based on psychotherapy. Therapies such as behaviour modification are still used in prison to establish conformist behaviour. The main criticism of psychological theories, however, is that they ignore the relative nature of deviance, that definitions and reactions to deviant behaviour depend on social power, social context, etc. As well, psychological theories have been criticized for ignoring certain major forms of deviant behaviour including violations committed by organizations (corporate crime), political crimes, and certain types of rational individual crimes such as credit card fraud. The sociological theories, some of which include elements of biology and psychology, tend to consider factors other than the act and the actor.

Sociological Theories

As mentioned previously, sociological theories of deviant behaviour can be broadly categorized into consensus (absolutist) and relativist (conflict) paradigms. This distinction, however, tends to ignore the **interactionist** tradition in sociology which is concerned less with the structure of the society and more with how the individual interacts with others in creating his or her "reality." Nonetheless, interactionist theories can be associated with the broad categories of either consensus or conflict theory and, in the following discussion I will locate the interactionist theories under these two categories.

Consensus Theories of Deviance

Consensus theories concentrate primarily on deviant behaviour and make the assumption that the rules and norms by which we conduct ourselves are shared and therefore correct. Morality is a given, and as such, the basic problem facing society is that certain people fail to conform.

Structural Theories

Structural Functionalism

Structural functionalist theories can be traced to the tradition of Emile Durkheim. For Durkheim and successive functionalists, deviance stems from lack of conformity and societies with a low level of social cohesion are characterized by high rates of deviance. According to Durkheim, suicide is a deviant activity that can be attributed primarily to lack of social integration and conformity. Societies which experience rapid social change are less likely to integrate and regulate their citizens, and will, as a consequence, experience high rates of deviance. The psychological state that disrupted societies engender is *anomie* or normlessness. Anomic conditions exist when value consensus is low and when societies fail to regulate or control their members.

Robert Merton (1938) extended Durkheim's work by emphasizing the influence that social pressures have on certain relatively vulnerable people. This more contemporary body of research has been discussed under the label of **anomie** or **strain theory.** Merton argued that anomic societies do not provide adequate legitimate means for people to achieve the culturally defined and accepted goals. The discrepancy between goals and the actual means to achieve those goals creates strain, and this strain, in turn, produces various non-legitimate innovations for circumventing **blocked opportunity.** Merton categorized five types of responses to the strain of blocked opportunity: conformity, innovation, ritualism, retreatism, and rebellion. Conformity is the only non-deviant response and requires no further discussion. Innovation, however, involves the acceptance of shared goals but not acceptance of the legitimate means of achievement. For example, an unsuccessful student may cheat on an exam or a fired corporate executive may decide to defraud his company. Most types of criminal behaviour fall into the category of innovation. Ritualism identifies activity wherein the means are accepted and the goals are rejected or altered. For example, Merton considered individuals who simply show up for work but do not accomplish as much as they can as deviant in industrial societies. This type of goal de-escalation is considered somewhat harmless and has received very little attention in research. Retreatism, on the other hand, as a response to blocked opportunity, has received considerable attention in research on deviance. Retreatists reject the goals and the means of achieving by "dropping out" of society. Mental illness, substance abuse, and compulsive gambling may all be forms of retreatist behaviour, and as we will see further on in this chapter, retreatist forms of deviance are highly visible in studies on social control and deviance, despite the likelihood that these forms of deviance are primarily victimless activities. Lastly, rebellion signifies a form of deviance much like retreatism wherein the goals and mean are rejected. Rebellion, however, constitutes behaviour which advocates new forms of achievement. Merton might argue that political rebellion, for example, is born of blocked opportunity, and that revolutionary activity on university campuses or the activities of the Black Panther civil rights organization typify forms of rebellion in response to blocked opportunity.

Social Control Theory

Like structural functionalism, **social control** or **deterrence theory** assumes that norms are shared by everyone, and, as a consequence, the proper subject for study is the investigating of why some people violate norms and others do not. Unlike other consensus theories, however, social control theory assumes that norm violations are attractive and that most people are motivated to engage in deviant behaviour. Simply put, man is a rational, calculating being, and he will choose to deviate if it is in his best interests to do so. This theory, then, is concerned with why so few people engage in illegal or abnormal behaviour, given that such behaviour has high utility.

The answer to this question lies in two forms of social control: inner and outer control. The former refers to the internalization of the rules and norms that are shared and valued by a majority in society. The acceptance of such rules controls behaviour because people experience guilt and remorse when they act in a deviant manner. Deviance results from a lack of moral socialization, a lack of conscience. Psychopathology, for example, may result from a complete lack of morality or conscience—the deviant is not moral nor immoral, but rather amoral.

Travis Hirschi (1969) focused on the degree of bonding to conventional society as a general determinant of inner control and moral conduct. He introduced the dimensions of attachment, involvement, commitment, and belief as components of bonding—as they relate to family, education and peer group. Hirschi's theoretical model suggests a behavioural as well as an attitudinal component to bonding, and measures elements of inner control, tapping the strength of conscience/morality and outer control by measuring the degree to which individuals respond to social pressure and proscription. Attachment is defined in terms of attraction to parents, school, and peers. Commitment involves an attitude to conventional aspirations in terms of occupation and education. Involvement is viewed as participation in conventional goal-oriented activities. The belief component involves an attitude toward consensual moral values, values which are perceived as generated by society as a whole, in essence, a measure of morality or conscience. For Hirschi, then, the greater the degree of bonding—as measured by the four dimensions——he less likely is youth deviance.

Outer control involves the various types of positive and negative sanctions that encourage normal behaviour and discourage or deter deviant behaviour. From this perspective, people who deviate forego social rewards like job promotion and respect from peers and may also suffer punishment, such as fines and imprisonment. Deterrence theory is a special case of outer control theory which looks at how people are constrained by official, state-administered punishment. For example, deterrence theory investigates the degree to which a certain form of punishment will inhibit (a) the individual violator (specific deterrence), and (b) the general public (general deterrence) from engaging in a targeted behaviour. Punishment is a concrete event and individuals are aware that it can happen to them—this information is taken into account when individuals rationally choose to commit or refrain from deviant behaviour. One of the basic premises of our system of law and punishment is the principle of deterrence/cost-benefit.

Socio-Cultural Theory

Socio-cultural theories of deviant behaviour focus on the processes by which individuals learn deviant behaviour. Cultures and sub-cultures are targeted as the "transmitters" of deviant values. This body of research originated with the ecological theories of crime and deviance attributed to the Chicago School of sociology. This approach concentrated on the spatial or geographical patterns of urban areas, and how these patterns were associated with levels of deviant activity. *Cultural transmission theory,* otherwise known as subcultural theory, arose from Chicago sociology and argued that deviance and crime were concentrated in certain urban areas and that deviance becomes part of the culture of urban areas. The deviant values that were attributed primarily to inner city subcultures, were said to be passed on from generation to generation and deviance was, then, based on conformity to subcultural norms. *Social disorganization theory* explained urban patterns with high deviancy rates as a consequence of poorly organized communities which resulted from disruptions associated with rapid in- and out-migration. Unstable populations contributed to inner city areas, for example, that had unstable cultural values and poorly defined mechanisms of inner and outer control.

Interactionist Theories

Differential Association Theory

Differential association theory extended both social disorganization and cultural transmission theories to explain how deviant values become part of certain subcultures. Sutherland (1939) maintained that criminal and deviant behaviour was learned in intimate association, and that if an individual is exposed to deviant influences that are viewed as favourable, then deviant behaviour is likely—the higher the ratio of exposure to deviant versus non-deviant definitions the more likely deviant behaviour will be exhibited. This theory then stresses the psychological process of socialization into a deviant lifestyle, and focuses attentions on the process of learning and evaluating moral definitions.

Neutralization Theory

Neutralization theory, which drew on the premises of social control theory argued that norms are not as rigid and well-defined as most sociologists have perceived. Sykes and Matza (1957) defined neutralization as a psychological technique whereby individuals use justifications for engaging in deviant behaviour that remove guilt and shame. These individuals do not lack inner control, but they do use certain techniques to neutralize inner controls. Deviance is not the result of attitudes and values that stand in contrast to those of conventional society; deviance occurs because of learned justifications which temporarily neutralize the restraints of conscience. Young offenders typify this type of behaviour, and were viewed by Sykes and Matza as characterizing justifications for typical kinds of deviance in youths, such as vandalism, substance abuse, and truancy.

Conflict Theories of Deviance

Conflict theories stand in contrast to consensus theories by arguing that society does not necessarily share a single set of values. Conflict theory can be traced to the works of Karl Marx and Max Weber (1969); Marx (original 1848, 1964) for his arguments that social inequality is part and parcel of the capitalist economic system, that conflict between social classes is the basic social process in society, and that deviant definitions are determined largely by the dominant class; and, Weber for his insistence that conflict can arise from sources other than class, sources such as political, organizational and professional groups. Nonetheless, Weberian conflict theory maintains that deviance and the corresponding mechanisms of social control are the result of conflict and compromise.

Structural Theories

Conventional **Marxist** theories of deviance argue that social conflict exists between those who control the means of production and those who do not. Those in control constitute a ruling class which controls relationships in arenas other than economy. This class is responsible for defining, identifying and sanctioning those whom it defines as unacceptable. Richard Quinney (1977), for example, argues that the ruling class uses the law to define certain types of activity such as prostitution and theft as deviant, while tolerating or at least minimizing the seriousness of corporate and organizational deviances, including price-fixing, safety violations, and workplace safety violations. The law, then, as determined by ruling class interests, can be selectively applied to maintain advantage for wealthy, powerful people. Chambliss (1969) has argued that we punish those people who can be tried and convicted with the least difficulty, namely, the socially and economically disadvantaged.

Pluralistic conflict theorists, like Marxist theorists, suggest that deviance and crime result from the use and abuse of power. Unlike Marxist theorists, however, pluralists see conflict and accommodation stemming from other than economic bases. Status groups, as defined by Weber, may gain power and privilege because of wealth, status, political power, occupational authority, etc. These multi-dimensions of power and inequality are the bases on which groups are formed and on which privileged or powerful groups try to influence the content and application of our systems of laws. The drama that is played out is one of constant struggle for influence.

Austin Turk (1969) argued that the law, rather than being an impartial arbiter of disputes, is a mechanism for expressing power and influence. Turk viewed status groups as dichotomized into authority and subject groups, and maintained that conflict arises when cultural, educational, and political differences between authorities and subjects are so vast that conflict inevitably results. Ultimately, in the struggle for influence, authority groups are most successful in influencing the type and direction of social control. For example, medical practitioners and researchers command a good deal of authority and respect, but they have, as well, a vested interest in ensuring that certain forms of deviant behaviour are defined as medical problems in need of medical intervention or control. The security of this status group depends on the successful definition and control of certain forms of deviant behaviour, exemplified by the increasing intervention of medicine into problems of the workplace; problems stemming from poor work environments are redefined as individual medical problems.

Interactionist Theories

Labelling Theory

Labelling theory, although microsociological in nature, accepts the conflict premise that social inequality is a primary condition when studying the definition and control of abnormal behaviour. Labelling theory, however, takes the notion of social inequality and the abuse of power, and searches for the process by which individuals come to see themselves as deviant or criminal. Central to the process of the *internalization* of deviant definitions is the argument that deviance is not naturally bad behaviour but that the deviant is one to whom the deviant label has been successfully applied. Howard Becker (1963) has suggested that "social groups create deviance by making the rules whose infraction constitutes deviance . . . deviance is not a quality of the act the person commits, but rather a consequence of the application by others of rule and sanctions to an offender" (Becker 1963:9).

Edwin Lemert (1951) has expanded this perspective by suggesting that initial acts of deviant behaviour, **primary deviance** comes from diverse sources which may include biology, psychology or social circumstance. For Lemert, however, such inconsequential and fleeting acts become important only when they are defined as abnormal. *Secondary deviance* is internalized behaviour which results in response to societal identification. As Lemert argues, "When a person begins to employ his deviant behaviour or role based upon it as a means of defense, attack or adjustment to the overt and covert problems created by the consequent societal reaction to him, his deviation is secondary" (Lemert 1951:76). Edwin Schur (1971) has extended this argument by suggesting that the process of becoming a secondary deviant is determined by negotiation, and that some people who so are labelled successfully defend themselves against negative labels. For Schur, the power to negotiate positive labels is based on individual self-concept rather than on social status or social power.

The social policy implications of labelling theory can be seen in Canada's Young Offenders Act of 1984. This legal reform stressed that the law must not contribute to the negative labelling especially of first time young offenders, for fear that legal identification was the first step on the road to a criminal career. The act, as a result, contains provisions for diverting youth from the formal justice system, and also specifies that the names and identities of youth must be confidential. The premise of this legal approach is that the police, lawyers, judges, court workers, and society in general, by identifying and publicizing the names and identities of young offenders who are relatively powerless, may contribute to further criminal involvement.

Ethnomethodology

The second conflict-based interactionist approach is similar in many respects to labelling theory but makes few assumptions about social inequality and the rightness or wrongness of definitions of deviance. **Ethnomethodology**, like labelling theory, is concerned with the social construction of deviance: abnormal behaviour is neither right nor wrong, but is defined by different people in different contexts. Ethnomethodologists study how we come to create typifications (stereotypes), and how these collective images of deviance are applied in specific situations.

D. L. Rosenhan (1973) and a group of research colleagues gained admission to mental hospitals as false patients whose false claim was that they heard voices. None of the pseudopatients was detected as a liar; all gained admittance to the hospitals. Rosenhan reported that although they all conducted themselves normally, they were diagnosed and treated as mental patients. Rosenhan illustrated how the hospital behaviour of the pseudopatients was reinterpreted by hospital staff to conform to the original diagnoses, and was further confirmed when the patients were released with their illnesses defined as "in remission." Such research illustrates how images of deviance, like mental illness, are held in common by people in authority, like doctors, who used these predefined images to reinterpret and reinforce initial labels or definitions. Although ethnomethodological research in theory does not concentrate on power and inequality, much of the research stresses the effectiveness of people in authority—psychiatrists, police, judges—in judging and typifying people of lower status, and as a result, falls under the general category of conflict theory.

Whatever theoretical perspective we choose to study deviance, the reality is that some rules are just while others are unfair, some rules are applied without prejudice while others discriminate against the underprivileged, and, certain types of deviance are more prevalent amongst certain categories of people than others. In this next section, we will discuss the social dimensions of rules and behaviours.

The Social Dimensions of Deviant Behaviour

Mental Disorders

Defining mental disorder is not as straightforward as we might think. Mental disorder is a condition which is exhibited in a wide range of behaviours. The DSM Ill-R diagnostic manual for psychiatry covers a wide range of diagnoses from the extreme **psychoses** of psychopathy or schizophrenia to the much less severe neuroses of phobias and anxiety. These disorders range from biologically based—mental impairment, organic brain disorders, schizophrenia—to the socially determined—alcohol dependence, traumatic shock disorder, hypochondria. Although I have implied that the origins of these disorders are either biological or social, there is a continuing controversy whether, for example, alcoholism is triggered by a biological intolerance or whether alcohol consumption is a learned behaviour that results in physical dependency.

Despite the ongoing nature/nurture debate in the field of mental health, we can show that incidence of certain types of disorder occur more often in some groups than others. For example, mental illness occurs most often in the 30-40 age group and then declines until the advanced years when age-related mental disorders occur. Social class also appears to be related to certain forms of mental illness—psychoses or the more serious forms of mental disorder are more prevalent amongst lower class individuals while the less serious types of neuroses are more prevalent in the higher classes. We might argue that poverty may lead to mental illness—through lack of health care, poor nutrition, physical injury—or we could claim that mental illness causes poverty by blocking legitimate channels for success. A third possibility might be that low status individuals are more likely to come to the attention of public psychiatric practitioners and are more likely to be recorded as mentally ill. Simply put, wealthier individuals can provide alternatives to institutional psychiatry, including private psychiatrists, private clinics and personal caregivers, and as a consequence, more financially solvent individuals seldom show up in official statistics.

An historical analysis of mental illness shows quite clearly that all societies and historical epochs are characterized by some type of mental deviance, and that the social control of the mentally disordered differs across time periods. The historical "development" might be best described as a transformation from sin to sickness to lifestyle and back to sickness. Szasz (1970) discusses the dominance of religion in the Middle Ages and the predominance of the belief that disease was a form of sin. The famous Inquisition and the organized witch-hunts that resulted sought out the mad and eradicated the evils of madness by eradicating witches. Many historians hold that witches were really the mentally ill of the Middle Ages, and that when science took over from religion during the Renaissance, medicine took over the control of the mad (Szasz, 1970). Szasz, like many others envisions the growth of the psychiatric profession as a social control agent; mental illness thus became the new concept to explain certain types of behaviour. From a typical relativist position, medical historians argue that scientific conceptions of madness are invented at certain historical junctures and that science and the needs of industry demand that unproductive and threatening people be controlled. The mental health industry thus developed as a rational response to the scientific orientation of the time, and asylums were to be the utopian "hospital" for sick minds (Foucault, 1965). As the science of mental illness developed, physicians increasingly looked to the organic brain and nervous system for the origins of madness. For Szasz (1970) the incorporation of science into the control of madness was a deliberate attempt by psychiatry to take and maintain control over the mad; psychiatry's purpose, he says, was to define and seek out new types of mentally ill people.

With the popularization of Freudianism, the scientific method gained new respectability in relation to madness. Freud and the whole psychoanalysis movement introduced the assumption that psychiatric symptoms arose from conflicts between biological impulses and socio-cultural forces. These conflicts were either resolved in the context of family socialization or exacerbated by improper child rearing. Freud was successful, as a result, in introducing the psycho-social into the arena of madness. The resulting "psychotherapy" model attempted to meld the medical/scientific model with the conception that medical illness not only resulted from bio-genetic causes but also from "lifestyle."

Conrad and Schneider (1980) argue that since the 1950s, there has been a resurgence of the medical model of mental illness. These authors suggest that the involvement of drug companies in the cure and control of mental disorder has ushered in a new era of mental health control that once again stresses the biological disorder and the curative/pharmaceutical response. Despite the decline of the asylum/mental hospital and the rise of community methods of help for the mentally sick, psychiatry has persisted in its search for the genetic origins of madness.

The historical research on mental disorder illustrates quite clearly that what we consider sick or deviant is not necessarily absolute, that institutional, political and social influences help determine the definition of madness as well as the acceptable means of its control. As this body of critical literature suggests, like the typical witch—women, the poor, the homeless—people most often diagnosed as suffering from mental health problems exist at the margins of society.

Substance Abuse

Deviance and Drug Use

The concern about the use of illegal drugs has become one of the prominent political issues of our time. Election campaign rhetoric brims with fear and panic regarding street drugs and moral decay. As we will see, however, the abhorrence of drugs such as heroine, cocaine, and marijuana is specific to this historical period and to our typical first-world, industrial society. As well, the definition of dangerous drugs is very closely tied to the medical/pharmaceutical definition of legal drugs, substances claimed to have medical usefulness.

An historical analysis of Canadian drug legislation illustrates quite clearly that at one time in Canada drugs like opium were accepted as part of cultural and medical practice. Comack (1986) shows that up until 1908, there were no restrictions in Canada regarding the manufacture, sale, or use of opium. Furthermore, opium was used primarily by the Chinese community and medicine. The prohibition of this drug, however, did not occur until Chinese immigration came to be seen as a threat to employment opportunities. Simply put, Comack argues that the Canadian state "created" the opium problem (which was directed against the Chinese immigrant and was facilitated by racist sentiments) as a means of diverting attention away from problems of unemployment and labour unrest. A similar history of the Marijuana Tax Act of 1937 in the United States shows that marijuana use was defined as a problem only at a certain historical juncture, coinciding with increased Latin American immigration and the expansion of the Federal Bureau of Narcotics (Schaller 1970).

While certain drugs seem to be targeted for control at certain times in history, other drugs seem to be immune from being labeled dangerous, and so remain part of the "legal drug trade" despite addictive qualities and harmful side effects. The pharmaceutical industry is responsible for dispensing medicinal remedies that alter moods and behaviour as much as illegal drugs do. Legal drugs, however, have worked their way into mainstream use and suffer very little prohibition despite their potential harmful qualities. Some of these drugs are abused through improper usage by patients and doctors, through attempts by pharmaceutical companies to find and market a pill for all human problems, and through the redirection of prescription drugs into underground drug trade. Stuart Hills (1980) reveals that legitimate drugs, because they are used primarily by mainstream society and are given legitimacy by medicine, are a real social problem but they remain uncondemned.

Alcohol and Deviance

Probably the most dangerous of abused substances in our society is alcohol. More deaths occur as a direct or indirect result of excessive drinking, more work hours are lost because of alcohol abuse, and more money is spent on curing alcohol addiction than any other type of substance addiction. Why, then, do we tolerate and perpetuate this social problem by advocating drinking as normal and acceptable and condemning excessive drinking as sickness? The answer may lie in one or more of the following. Firstly, the powerful brewing industry has a large influence on definitions of acceptable behaviour; through advertising and the corporate sponsorship of athletics, social drinking is associated with the good life. The brewing industry is a major player in the corporate world and much of the marketing of alcohol is based on advertising alcohol consumption as a means to popularity and social enjoyment. In essence, through the media and cultural socialization we are taught that drinking is a preferred activity. Secondly, the medical model of substance abuse suggests that the individual is responsible for excessive drinking because of his/her weak will or genetic predisposition. Overall, the medical model of alcoholism is based on excessive drinking as a disease and the therapeutic response is treatment of the individual. Psychiatric medicine, for example, treats alcoholism as a psychiatric illness that is treatable by drug or psycho therapy. So, despite the influence of socialization and media campaigns to encourage drinking, our society has decided that excessive drinking is solely an individual pathology. This is not to say, though, that individual cures are not effective. Alcoholics Anonymous has been very successful in treating the individual alcoholic. Thirdly, in western culture "taking time out" has become a social convention that is tied to success in the business, social, and occupational worlds. Lastly, alcohol consumption creates tremendous amounts of revenue for governments. In light of the aforementioned reasons for the tolerance of alcohol, little has been done to resolve the contradiction between society's encouraging of drinking on the one hand, and its branding people who drink excessively as sick or weak-willed on the other.

Youth Deviance

To understand the nature of youth misconduct and societal reactions to such conduct, we must first recognize that the types of deviance that create fear and revulsion in society are not typical of youth deviance. We must also recognize that rule-breaking behaviour amongst youth is quite universal, especially non-serious types of behaviour. Reports of a 93 percent delinquency rate in Sweden (Elmhorn, 1965, quoted in Corrado, LeBlanc, and Trepanier, 1983:33), an 88 percent rate for a national sample of 13-16 year olds in the United States (Williams and Gold, 1972), and a 96 percent rate for working class adolescents in England (Farrington, 1979) illustrate the point. In Canada, Frechette and LeBlanc (1978) have determined that 92.8 percent of adolescents between the ages of 12 and 18 had committed one deviant act and that 81.8 percent had contravened the criminal code. From a labelling theory perspective, inconsequential types of behaviour become important only when the violator is isolated for punishment and public degradation. Such treatment may affect the individual's self-concept and foster the internalization of a criminal self-image.

The assumption of universality must not, however, ignore the fact that certain types of deviance, such as murder, sexual assault, and gang violence are of considerable concern and importance to society. What is more important however, is that most acts of deviance, especially those committed by juveniles, are relatively inconsequential and transitory. Such a statement gains credibility when one realizes that most juveniles at one time or another, violate drug and alcohol abuse laws and vandalism laws. In fact, in certain contexts such as high school peer groups, types of norm-violating behaviour are outwardly condoned as acceptable. Most important, then, to any discussion of youth deviance is the concern that only certain types of deviance and certain types of youth are isolated for detection and punishment. To this end, we must realize that relativist views like labelling theory offer great insight into youth deviance because they suggest that underprivileged or marginalized youth come under the severest labeling and control. The mechanism of such discrimination is best illustrated by the landmark research of Chambliss (1973).

As we observe the historical development of juvenile delinquency we gain further insight into the changing and discriminatory definition and control of youth deviance and the changing nature of the causal origins ascribed to juvenile delinquency. Prior to the nineteenth century, no legal distinctions were made between juveniles and adults. Most historical accounts of pre-modern, pre-nineteenth century society, reveal the absence of an acknowledged stage of adolescence in human development. Simply put, teenagers did not exist. As Aries (1962) suggests, the family in pre-industrial life, especially the lower-class family, was much more community-centred than the modern family. As a consequence, childhood autonomy and independence fostered a rapid transformation from childhood to adult responsibility: "lower class children were mixed with adults ... They immediately went straight into the great community of men, sharing in the work and play of their companions, old and young alike" (1962:411).

With the onset of the Industrial Revolution, exploitation of children became commonplace. It is likely that the initial motivation to create a juvenile justice system was based on generally humanitarian and philanthropic concerns directed against child exploitation and that the concept of adolescence arose as a result of the "Child Saving Movement" (Platt, 1969) which was based on the principle of *patens patriae* the state was the ultimate guardian of the child. The Juvenile Delinquency Act of 1908 in Canada gave the state the absolute authority to intervene forcibly in family life, denying the family's right to due process in the law. Blame for juvenile deviance was placed squarely on the shoulders of families, and the reasons thought to cause bad behaviour were defective intelligence, uncaring parents, and poor home environments. The defective families were assumed by people with political influence to predominate in poor, working class and immigrant families. The juvenile justice system came to determine delinquency on the basis of unclear definitions such as truancy, immoral behaviour, and incorrigibility—definitions which served to provide the system with a wide range of discretionary power. A rather large body of research shows quite clearly that this discretionary power was used against poorer, marginalized youth and their families.

The Civil Rights Movement, coupled with the whole social reform era of the 1960s, gradually led to a reform of the juvenile system, the seminal stages of which have now been determined by the Young Offenders Act in Canada, passed by parliament in 1982.

The Young Offenders Act was implemented to correct the inequities of the Juvenile Delinquency Act which were responsible for discrimination against the powerless. Specifically, the new act addressed the problems of lack of access to legal resources and knowledge for certain people. In the spirit of the new act, implemented in 1985, young offenders were to have the same legal rights as adults. As well, in response to labelling theory, trivial acts of deviance (status offences) which were covered by the Juvenile Delinquency Act were no longer under the purview of the youth court. In essence, the new act melded the best of the due process model of justice, which was characteristic of the adult system, with the child welfare model, which was retained from the former juvenile court system. The underlying philosophy of our current approach to youth deviance is that young people are like adults; they are responsible for their behaviour and they should receive the legal rights that are accorded to adults. Our definition of adolescence has historically come full circle to a pre-industrial revolution view of youth as accountable citizens.

Sexuality and Deviance

The legal status of homosexuality is rather straightforward in Canada. As of 1968 when sexual activities between consenting adults were excepted from the Criminal Code, the Canadian state has had no legal right to intervene in the private lives of individuals. In the United States, the same trends toward legal tolerance are evident except that in some states, making love to someone of the same sex still carries criminal penalties. The historical trends toward legal tolerance, however, have not been accompanied by social acceptance or institutional tolerance. As we will see, the history of the social control of homosexuality is similar to histories of other forms of deviance such as mental disorder and drug abuse. Fear and loathing and state intervention have been based on ideas regarding the causal origins ascribed to the deviant behaviour and to the assumed dangerousness of such behaviour to society.

The history of homosexuality in the Western world is best described as the transformation from normal to sinful to sick to lifestyle difference. In pre-biblical time in ancient Greece, bisexuality was commonplace and homosexual behaviour was considered quite normal. With the onset of Judeo-Christianity, however, homosexuality was condemned as a crime against God. This redefinition and re-moralization of sexuality resulted in extreme forms of punishment from the burning of homosexual witches in the Middle Ages to the execution of a quarter million homosexuals in Nazi Germany—justified mostly by biblical teachings.

The institution of medicine is currently active in the search for the causes of and the "cure" for homosexuality. The origins of the medical model of sexuality dates back to the turn of the century when physicians addressed the problem of same-sex conduct from a genetic perspective. Homosexuality as a genetic phenomenon, was originally viewed as biological degeneration; it is currently viewed as a neurological difference (Time, 1991). Despite our view of homosexuality being somewhat less harsh than it was in the past, the search for its cause still implies a persistent belief that homosexuality is abnormal conduct. The medical assumption of disease/abnormality is best illustrated in psychiatric medicine which has only recently shifted its view of homosexuality from sickness to lifestyle variation. In 1973, the American Psychiatric Association endorsed changing the DSM-III diagnostic manual for psychiatry by removing the designation of homosexuality as a disease and replacing it with the designation of lifestyle. "Sexual orientation disturbance" was to be diagnosed only to those who were dissatisfied with their sexual orientation. Despite this enlightened transformation, subsequent studies reveal that psychiatrists persist in viewing homosexuality as a sickness.

The research of Alfred Kinsey has had a substantial impact on society's perceptions of sexual conduct. Kinsey's work in 1948 and 1953, and subsequent studies, startled North American society with evidence that 1) a considerable proportion of men, and a smaller proportion of women, had some form of homosexual experience (Kinsey reports 37% from men), 2) a substantial portion of those who experience homosexuality engage actively in the behaviour for a continued period, and 3) homosexual orientation is not fixed and may change. From these results, Kinsey and subsequent researchers have concluded that sexual behaviour is not an either/or orientation but rather a continuum on which most people fall not at either extreme but somewhere in the middle.

Perhaps most important in understanding sexuality in a North American context is the extreme prejudice against homosexuality and the tolerated acts of violence against gays and lesbians. The legacy left by religion and medicine has provided the legitimacy that has resulted in the persistence of a mythology surrounding homosexuality that has permitted discrimination and violence against it to exist. Homosexual men, for example, are not typically effeminate (they cannot be identified by their physical appearance, are not typically sexually active or passive, and pose no particular threat to young children—in fact, child molestation is more common amongst heterosexuals (Bell and Weinberg, 1978). Despite this kind of evidence, homosexual men and women have faced official discrimination within social institutions: during World War II men caught engaging in homosexual activity were classified as "psychopathic" and were given a dishonourable discharge (Conrad and Schneider, 1980); sexual orientation may be used as reason for dismissal or prohibition from teaching positions; and homosexuals are still denied access to hierarchical positions in churches, especially ministerial appointments.

Continued discrimination has led to politicization of homosexuality by gay rights advocates. The Gay Pride Movement, which started in the late 1960s and continues to the present, was a product of the political activism of the sixties coupled with an increasing awareness that homosexuality, as defined by medicine and religion, was a label that prohibited gays and lesbians from leading normal, discrimination-free lives.

Summary

In the first part of this chapter, I have described the numerous theories that exist to explain deviant behaviour. As numerous and as varied as absolutist theories are, they are held together by the common thread that morality is shared and that the rule breaker presents a threat to social order. For the various relativist theories, the common denominator is social inequality and the basic problem facing society is that the rules themselves are unfair. As we have seen from our discussions on mental illness, substance abuse, youth deviance, and sexuality, rules regarding normal conduct change over time and place. As social investigators, our task is to try and unravel the changeability of definitions and the changeability of punishments and mechanisms of control: if our morality is shared, why, for example, are some addictive drugs considered dangerous while others are considered therapeutic?

We might look, then, to the influences that people in positions of authority have had on social control. Historical research has shown that major institutions like religion and medicine, and the attendant authority that we have given to religious leaders and doctors, have had a substantial impact at certain points in history on the explanations for deviance and on the methods of controlling or curing rule-breakers. While we have shown that the power of religion historically gave way to the power of science in defining and controlling deviant behaviour, it is apparent that the influences of religion remain in many areas of deviance control, and that medicine, in spite of the criticism surrounding biological explanations, has persisted as a major mechanism in social control.

Finally, we must mention the power of knowledge production and the power of words in the study of deviance. The term deviance, itself, implies something negative and even in this chapter, when we study homosexuality as deviance, for example, we implicity assign a negative label to a type of sexual conduct. Similarly, when deviance is defined as sin, the implication is something wicked; when defined as a medical problem, the implication is sickness. The sensitivity and objectivity that sociologists struggle to maintain in studying deviance must be based on the realization that research in this area of human behaviour, however important, can be misused and misrepresented to the detriment of certain people.

References

Aries, Philipe
1962   *Centuries of Childhood.* New York: Random House.

Bandura, A. and R. H. Walters
1963   *Social Learning and Personality Development.* New York: Holt, Rinehart and Winston.

Becker, Howard
1963   *Outsiders: Studies in the Sociology of Deviance.* New York: Free Press.

Bell, Alan P. and Martin S. Weinberg
1978   *Homosexualities: A Study in Diversity among Men and Women.* New York: Simon and Schuster.

Berkowitz, L.
1969   *Roots of Aggression: A Re-examination of the Frustration-Aggression Hypothesis.* New York: Atherton Press.

Chambliss, William
1973   "The Saints and the Roughnecks." Society. Nov.: 24–31.

Chambliss, William
1969   *Crime and Legal Process.* New York: McGraw-Hill.

Cohen, Stanley
1985   *Visions of Social Control.* Cambridge: Polity Press.

Comack, Elizabeth
1986   "'We Will Get Some Good Out of This Riot Yet': The Canadian State, Drug Legislation and Class Conflict," in Stephen Brickey and Elizabeth Comack eds. *The Social Basis of Law: Critical Readings in the Sociology of Law.* Halifax: Garamond Press.

Conrad, Peter and Joseph W. Schneider
1980   *Deviance and Medicalization: From Badness to Sickness.* St. Louis: C. V. Mosby Co.

Corrado, Raymond, Marc LeBlanc, and Jean Trepanier
1983   *Current Issues in Juvenile Justice.* Toronto:

Durkheim, Emile
1897   *1951 Suicide.* Translated by John A. Spaulding and George Simpson. New York: Free Press.

Eysenck, H. J.
1977   *Crime and Personality.* London: Routledge and Kegan Paul.

Foucault, Michel
1965   *Madness and Civilization: A History of Insanity in the Age of Reason.* New York: Vintage Books.

Foucault, Michel
1979   *Discipline and Punish: The Birth of the Prison.* New York: Vintage Books.

Goodwin, Donald W.
1986   "Studies of Familial Alcoholism: A Growth Industry." in Donald W. Goodwin, Katherin Teilman Van Dusen, and Sarnoff A. Mednick (eds) *Longitudinal Research in Alcoholism.* Boston: Kluwer Academic Publishing Group.

Hills, Stuart
1980   *Demystifying Social Deviance.* New York: McGraw-Hill.

Hirschi, Travis
1969   *Causes of Delinquency.* Los Angeles: University of California Press.

Kohlberg, Lawrence
1969   "Stage and Sequence: The Cognitive-Developmental Approach," in David A. Goslin ed. *Handbook of Socialization Theory and Research.* Chicago: Rand McNally.

Lemert, Edwin
1951   *Social Pathology.* New York: McGraw-Hill.

Lombroso, Cesare
1911   *Crime: Its Causes and Remedies.* Boston: Little, Boston,

Marx, Karl
orginal   *1964 Selected Writings in Sociology and Social Philosophy.* T. B. Bottomore
1948   and M. Rubel eds. Baltimore: Penguin.

Mednick, S. A. and J. Volavka
1980   "Biology and Crime," in N. Morris and N. Tonry eds. Chicago: University of
           Chicago Press.

Merton, Robert K.
1938   "Social Structure and Anomie." *American Sociological Review.* 3: 672–82.

Piaget, Jean
1932   *The Moral Judgement of the Child.* New York. Harcourt.

Platt, Anthony
1963   *The Child Savers: The Invention of Delinquency.* Chicago: University of Chi-
           cago Press.

Pollock, V. E., T. W. Teasdale, W. F. Gabrielli and J. Knop
1986   "Subjective and Objective Measures of Response to Alcohol among Young
           Men at Risk for Alcoholism." *Journal of Studies on Alcohol.* 47: 297–304.

Quinney, Richard
1977   *Class, State and Crime.* New York: David McKay.

Rosenhan, D. L.
1973   "On Being Sane in Insane Places." *Science.* 179: 250–258.

Schaller, M.
1970   "The Federal Prohibition of Marijuana." *Journal of Social History.* 4: 61–74.

Schur, Edwin
1971   *Labeling Deviant Behaviour.* New York: Harper and Row.

Shah, Saleem A. and Loren H. Roth
1974   "Biological and Psycbophysiological Factors in Criminology," in Daniel
           Glaser ed. *Handbook of Criminology.* Chicago: Rand McNally.

Sheldon, William
1949   *Varieties of Delinquent Youth: An Introduction to Constitutional Psychiatry.*
           New York: Harper and Row.

Skinner, B. F.
1953   *Science and Human Behaviour.* New York: MacMillan.

Sykes, Gresham and David Matza
1957   "Techniques of Neutralization: A Theory of Delinquency." *American Soci-
           ological Review.* 22: 664–70.

Sutherland, Edwin
1939   *Criminology.* Philadelphia: J. B. Lippincott.

Szasz, Thomas
1970   *The Manufacture of Madness.* New York: Harper and Row.

Turk, Austin
1969   *Criminality and the Legal Order.* Chicago: Rand McNally.

Weber, Max
1947   *The Theory of Social and Economic Organization.* New York: Free Press.

Wilson, Margo and Martin Daly
1985   "Competitiveness, Risk Taking, and Violence: The Young Male Syndrome."
        Ethology and Sociobiology. 6: 59–73.

```
┌─────────────┐
│             │
│             │
│      9      │
│             │
│             │
│             │
└─────────────┘
```

Crime and Punishment in Canada[1]

John A. Winterdyk

Perhaps our worst crime is our ignorance about crime.
Karl Menninger, 1968:3

If one can believe media reports in Canada, then crime is a pervasive, serious, and dominant social concern. Several headlines,[2] sampled over a short period of time, include: "Compensation urged for victims of LSD testing" (political crime)(March 3, 1998); "Stiffer penalties against home invasions sought" (violent crime)(February 11, 1999); "On-the-job crime combatted" (white-collar crime)(March 6, 1999); "Teachers probed for porn on e-mail" (public order crimes)(January 29, 1999), "Police bust $1M clothing scam" (organized crime)(July 18,1998), to "Workplace violence on the rise" (new forms of crime)(April 8, 1999). Among other issues, the last article points out that the rate of physical and psychological assault against Canadian women at work is 19% higher than in the United States.

As we enter the new millennium, the crime images portrayed by the media in many respects may only be the tip of the iceberg. Results from the 1981 Canadian Urban Victimization Survey (CUVS) show that based on the seven cities surveyed, 81% of the respondents said "they believed that crime had increased in their city in the year or two prior to the survey." Little has changed since the General Social Survey (GSS) was introduced in 1989 as a replacement of the CUVS. Conducted every five years, the 1993 GSS showed public fear levels remained very similar to those of the earlier CUVS. Most recently, the International Crime Victimization Survey of 1996 indicated that approximately 25% of Canadians were a victim of a crime in 1995, down from 28% in 1989 and 1992. Also of note, when compared to 11 other western industrialized countries, Canada ranked 3rd highest (30%) for fear of being victimized.[3]

A barometer of peoples' preoccupation with crime may be reflected in how much money they spend protecting themselves. Family expenditure surveys inform us that approximately 12% of all Canadian families purchase security devices and about 2% buy some kind of house alarm. By 1996, the percentage of expenditure had climbed to nearly 16%. This translates into around $195 million annually (Easton and Brantingham, 1998). Hence, it could be said that the 1985 comment of Canadian sociologist John Hagan still rings true today—crime remains a "hot topic." Furthermore, speaking at a major conference in late 1997, Federal Justice Minister Anne McLellan stated that one of the greatest challenges facing the Provinces and federal government is the increasing fear levels towards crime and their disenchantment with effectiveness of the criminal justice system. Hence, regardless of whether these impressions are real or apparent, there is no denying that crime and justice receive a great deal of attention these days.

Depending on how one evaluates the findings, the response of the Canadian Criminal Justice System (i.e., police, courts, and corrections) to this apparent increase in crime has met with varying degrees of success. In the late 1980s, it was reported that our criminal justice system is becoming 11% more costly each year, 9% less efficient, and 8.5% less effective (Menard, 1987). Demars (1984) notes that Canadians pay nearly four times as much to maintain our system than in 1960 (adjusted to Implicit Price Index). In the late 1990s, the picture has changed little. Consider the following facts taken from a selection of Statistics Canada *Juristat Bulletins*:

1. Policing in 1989–90 cost $4.7 billion vs. $5.7 billion in 1995–96. Approximately, 93% of the budget is allocated to salaries.

2. Courts in 1990–91 cost $766 million vs. $867 million in 1995–96.[4] Prosecution services account for approximately $260 million (30 percent).

3. Adult corrections cost $1.62 billion in 1990–91 vs. $1.92 billion in 1995–96. On any given day there are approximately 34,000 adults in correctional institutions.

4. Legal aid went from $341 million in 1989–90 to $646 million in 1994–95, but for 1995–96 expenditures decreased to $536 million. Less than 50% of all cases are criminal with the majority being civil cases.

5. Overall, justice spending went from $7.7 billion in 1989–90 to $9.5 billion in 1992–93 to approximately $17 billion in 1996! Depending on how one calculates the gross domestic product (GDP), the cost of crime is between 2.2 percent and 5.3 percent.

6. A study released by the conservative think tank, the Fraser Institute in Vancouver, notes that while the direct costs of justice spending are around $17 billion annually, when one takes into account pain and suffering of victims, the cost soars to $40 billion.

What does GDP mean to Canadians?
Crime costs each, and every, Canadian between $586 and $1,420 or between $2,343 and $5,680 for a family of four!
Are we getting our monies worth?

It seems increasingly evident that social control of crime and deviance is becoming increasingly more costly and less effective. From a sociological perspective, the implications of such a trend are numerous. It would appear that we are justified in viewing crime and our societal response as a serious social issue.

In this chapter, we will explore some of the trends and patterns in crime and punishment in Canada. Then we will review some of the sociological explanations that have been used to understand and respond to crime and criminality. First, however, a brief overview of the concepts of crime and punishment will be presented so that the reader can better appreciate some of the issues raised.

What Is Crime?

> The inescapable conclusion is that society secretly wants crime, needs crime, and gains satisfaction from the present mishandling of it.
>
> Karl Menninger, 1968

As Winterdyk (2000), among others, observes, defining crime is not as straightforward as might first appear. The dilemma stems from the fact that its definition allows for ambiguity. A survey of the literature will reveal at least five different definitions of crime. They include the lexical (dictionary), economic, psychological, political, and sociological. Each definition allows for a different frame of reference and perspective as to the nature of crime and its causes. They range from very broad to being relatively narrow in scope. In North America, however, because of its heritage, for most of the 20th century the sociological definition has been the dominate perspective. It asserts that crime reflects some anti-social behaviour that is injurious to those social interests which rules of behaviour (e.g., *Criminal Code*) are designed to support. The eminent French sociologist Emile Durkheim (1858–1917) argued that punishment is the defining characteristic of crime and that social harm is its corollary.[5]

Regardless of one's *frame of reference*, it should be recognized that all definitions reflect some degree of bias. Yet, the underlying theme appears to be one of (social) control and an expression of power. That is, laws are intended to encourage, or force, potential offenders to control their criminal intent in order to maintain harmony within society. British criminologist Jason Ditton (1979) has suggested that perhaps we should use the term "controlology" as it implies that the study of crime is synonymous with control or the lack thereof. For example, a few years ago, the Canadian Law Reform Commission reported that there are over 40,000 federal and provincial laws and regulations by which to regulate peoples' behaviour.[6]

The issue of crime being equated with control has spawned considerable debate. Among sociologists, these debates evolve around *conflict, critical,* or *radical* based theories. Although each perspective uses a different causal logic, collectively they tend to focus on the crime problem by examining society's social structures (e.g., institutions and/or certain relevant professions) and its control systems (i.e., criminal justice system). For example, why do some crimes such as computer crimes, embezzlement, environmental crimes, insider-trading, and political corruption, appear to go relatively undetected and unreported? In addition, why are crimes like murder, robbery and assault more likely to be reported and considered more serious when research shows that the former types of crime have a significantly greater social and economic impact on society? Those crimes commonly recorded by the police are sometimes referred to as *conventional crimes.* One explanation that has been offered purports that the likelihood of detection is related to the fact that conventional crimes represent those offences typically committed by the lower and middle social-class members of society (see below). This social-class has minimal political influence and/or power. By focusing on this group, it enables the state to exert control and divert attention away from the crimes they are prone to commit (e.g., white-collar crime).

Crimes committed by the upper-social classes tend to be *non-conventional* crimes. They are typically those types of crimes that are not regularly recorded by the police (e.g., embezzlement, fraud, corruption, etc.). Furthermore, the differences in detection reflect the *relative* and *evolutive*[7] nature of crime. By relative we mean that crime is not absolute. That is, what a crime is varies with time and place. For example, murder during times of war is often considered "acceptable," females going topless is legal in some provinces and not others, and using soft-drugs is tolerated in some European countries yet considered illegal in Canada.

Crimes that are described as evolutive refer to those behaviours/acts which at one time were not considered deviant or criminal but later become defined as such (e.g., abortion, environmental pollution, wearing of seat belts, smoking in public places, etc.).

In **summary**, the above description of crime reflects that there are very few (anti-social) behaviours that reflect unanimity, or universal consensus. Hence, defining the boundaries of crime depends on many social factors such as social harmony, economic stability, morality, ethical standards, and political ideologies. Therefore, given the framework of this chapter, suffice it to note that the subject of crime remains a challenging and enigmatic phenomenon worthy of sociological investigation.

What Is Punishment?

The concept of crime and deviance seem to connote a negative stereotype, hence we generally view crime as being synonymous with punishment. However, as will be discussed shortly, not all crimes are punished nor are all behaviours that are punishable by law necessarily crimes. In fact, for some crimes it may NOT be to our advantage to punish the individual. *Can you think of any examples?*

Durkheim once noted that crime can be either *functional* or *dysfunctional*. That is, some recurrent activity (e.g., crime) or established institution (e.g., law) may actually benefit society, or certain social groups within it. This perspective in sociology is referred to as a functionalism. One of the key contributors to this perspective was the American sociologist Robert Merton (1910–) who is perhaps best known for his theory of **anomie**. In essence, the theory asserts that there are culturally defined goals (e.g., the "American/Canadian dream") that if not legitimately attainable may lead to adaptations to avoid the strain and anger or in some cases crime.

The functional perspective has been instrumental in advancing the notion that anti-social behaviour is best corrected through neutralization processes involving counselling, guidance, and therapy. In criminology, this perspective corresponds with the *positivist* school of thought. The positivist, or functional, approach tends to downplay the notion of "punishment" in lieu of "treatment" and "resocialization" (see Box 9.1). This perspective

> **Box 9.1. Restorative Justice in lieu of punishment: Will It work?**
>
> Although its origins can be traced back to early Aboriginal practices of resolving disputes, as formal concept it gained considerable attention in the 1990s.
> The key principles and philosophy of restorative justice include:[8]
>
> 1. When someone commits a crime (wrong) the offender is required to make amends with the victim, and/or the community at large. The act requires a shift from moral accountability to accepting social responsibility.
> 2. There are positive sociological and psychological effects for the offender when engaging in the restorative process. One form of restoration involves publicly *shaming* an offender.
> 3. This proactive approach emphasizes mending violations of people rather than the conventional approach of treating a crime as a violation of the state. The process involves a shift from guilt orientation to a consequence orientation.
> 4. Crime is seen as an injury and violation to an individual and a community that deserves to be prepared. This perspective requires a shift from one of revenge and retribution to emotional, physical, social, and spiritual restitution.
> 5. The model requires that all parties should be respected equally.
>
> *Does the concept appeal to you? Do you think it can work? What might some of the challenges be?*

sometimes takes the form of sentencing and incarceration—the backbone to our judicial and correctional elements of the criminal justice system.

Some of the key principles concerning societies' justification for sentencing and/or incarcerating an offender include:

1. **Deterrence**: general, specific, and marginal. General deterrence occurs when a punishment for a crime is seen as a deterrent by a potential offender while specific deterrence is the punishment of the offender. Marginal deterrence occurs when crime rates decline in response to incremental changes in the threat sanctions. Whichever approach used, to be effective deterrence efforts strive to strike a balance between fear of punishment and justice among both the law-abiding citizen and the (potential) offender. In spite of its intuitive appeal, Canadian criminologist Julian Roberts (1999) reports that, at best, the deterrent concept is only marginally effective as a corrective strategy.

2. **Rehabilitation**: when someone commits a crime, it is sometimes believed the individual was 'misguided' somehow and can be effectively resocialized and/or treated to be lead a "crime-free" life. While rehabilitation may involve incapacitation, most rehabilitative programs take place in the community. More recent variations of the rehabilitative theme is restorative justice and transformative justice[9] (see Box 9.1). Being relatively new concepts, there is insufficient evidence to comment on the relative effectiveness of the approaches.

3. **Retribution**: Supporters of this oldest form of societal response to a wrong-doer argue that at some level, we all want to see an offender suffer for their crime

and since the law will not allow us to administer punishment, we expect and want the State to do this for us. Retributive sentencing focuses on an individual's past as the source of blameworthiness. If the crime is strongly denunciated in society, the punishment is likely to be severe. Again, what is not clear is the relative effectiveness of the retributive approach.

4. **Just deserts**: Andrew Von Hirsch (1976) was among the first to actively promote this notion. Similar to Becarria's principles of punishment in 1764, Von Hirsch was more concerned about the punishment being proportionate to the gravity of the crime as opposed to its simple imposition. Although a noble idea, Blumstein (1982) points out that the notion of just deserts is somewhat ideal when trying to account for all the mitigating circumstances surrounding an offence. The just desert approach subscribes to determinate sentences. In his examination of correctional practices in Canada and internationally, David Cayley (1998) points out how, in many ways, we have moved towards this rationale as a form of punishment.

The second dominant sociological paradigm of crime and punishment is the *conflict* perspective. The work of Karl Marx and Fredrick Engels formed the basis of conflict theory. In essence, this perspective assumes that society represents an arena of struggles over a limited amount of resources between those who have and those who do not. Hence, capitalism is seen as a criminogenic society. Since it is believed that crime is more common among the lower classes, it is left up to the ruling class to define crime. Crime is defined as behaviour that disrupts the economic and political power of those in control or who retain authoritative positions within society. Hence, violators should be punished or have their liberties restricted as such behaviour would violate class structure and *social contract*.

During the mid-1700s, the French philosopher Jean Jacques Rousseau (1712–1778) supported a number of views that have provided justification for the punishment of offenders. In his monumental work, *The Social Contract*, he argued that law and government were needed to ensure social and legal equality.

Rousseau believed that in accordance with the social contract the government had an obligation to protect the public by enforcing laws that control those actions that threaten the life, liberty, and freedom of society. In turn, the public is to understand that any violation (i.e., crime) would be subject to punishment.

Philosophers like Rousseau, Thomas Hobbes (1588–1679), John Locke (1632–1704), and Francois Voltaire (1694–1778) have been referred to as the "Enlightment philosophers" because of their concerns for social reform and their humanistic concern over societal issues. Their ideas for social reform and humanitarian principles spread throughout Europe and in Italy. Another reformer was Cesare Beccaria (1738–1794), who in his prophetic book entitled *Essay on Crimes and Punishments,* incorporated the principles of social reform and humanitarian treatment of criminals to form the basis of the Classical School of criminology. In his doctrine, he spoke against unreasonable and excessive punishment. He did believe, however, that anyone (i.e., criminal) who derives benefits without paying the price of obedience deserves some deprivation inflicted upon them in order to maintain equality—hence punishment is justified as a form of revenge and retribution. Some of his views on punishment still prevail today. For example, Becarria (1963) proposed that:

1. Punishment should fit the crime. Crime should be measured in accordance to its material gravity. "For a punishment to be just it should consist of only such graduations of intensity as suffice to deter man from committing crimes (p. 47–48). People will obey the law because the penalty will outweigh the pleasure of the crime.

2. Punishment should be certain and prompt, not necessarily severe. Severity, he argued, would defeat the utilitarian purpose of punishment. "When a crime is of such a nature that it must frequently go unpunished, the penalty assigned becomes an incentive" (p. 85).

3. Punishment should be specific and fixed by the legislature.

4. The death penalty "cannot be useful, because of the example of barbarity it gives man...it seems absurd that the laws, which are an expression of the public will, which detest and punish homicide, should themselves commit it...."(p. 50).

Many of these punishment principles have been embraced by our current criminal justice system. However, as is evident by the crime rates and level of public satisfaction with the system today, the principles do not always appear to work well. This is, in part, because we are not as rational and logical as Beccaria would have us believe. His notion of free will in choice is unverifiable, and the principle of punishment being certain and swift seems but an aberration today. Finally, regardless of how it is administered, punishment does NOT work.[10]

Therefore, when discussing the notion of crime and punishment, the two opposing perspectives should be considered.[11] Should we punish in a punitive, retributive sense or should we view criminal behaviour as an unfortunate by-product of social stressors (e.g., family, peers, school, etc.), emotional and/or cognitive difficulties, a genetic predisposition, a consequence of poor nutritional habits, etc.? How do we deal with the fact that new crimes may evolve or others become relative? As with crime, the notion of crime and punishment is not an easy issue to resolve. But, it is a fact that in Canada, as in most Western countries, we continue to punish people who violate the laws of the land whether they be Municipal, Provincial, or Federal. An understanding of this basic dilemma should help one to appreciate some of the issues confronting the justice system as well as the difficulty in defining crime and our response to it.

Having described the concepts of crime and punishment, we can now move on to looking at some of the trends and patterns of crimes and punishment in Canada.

Keeping Track of Crimes and Punishment

The most common source of crime information is official statistics as collected by the police, courts, and corrections (official elements of the criminal justice system). Before examining these statistics, however, some pitfalls of these sources need to be identified.

When using any type of official data to study crime trends either at a regional, national or international level, they have to be viewed with some degree of caution. Chambliss (1889:32) goes so far as to suggest that anyone who uses official data is "making erroneous assumptions based on unbelievable data." He further argues that cross-cultural (e.g., comparing provinces or countries) studies are even more limiting in value because of a variety of problems such as ethnocentric bias, crime definitions, recording techniques, etc. By contrast, others have suggested that while official data may have its limitations, so do any other source of data collection (e.g., self-report studies and victimization surveys). Nevertheless, despite some technical problems, official statistics provide our largest source of information and can provide insightful information about spatial and temporal patterns of crime.

Some two decades ago, Leslie Wilkins (1980) astutely noted that official crime data are not, strictly speaking, statistics of criminal events per se. Rather, they reflect police responses to social behaviour with respect to a particular set of offence categories defined by the *Criminal Code* and of political success. Therefore, the study, or use of any statistical accounts, of crime need to be viewed in a social, political, environmental, and demographic context. Although it is beyond the scope of this chapter to discuss these factors in detail, the reader should be aware of them when drawing conclusions or impressions.

The next section will explore the extent of violent and property related crimes as well as examine some facts about criminal victimization. Before you begin, consider the following questions: (1) *Is violent crime increasing in Canada?*, (2) *Who is most likely to be victimized in Canada and why?*, and (3) *What are the characteristics of a 'typical' young offender, and male/female offender?*

Violent Crime Trends in Canada

> In-spite of a six-year decline in our violent crime rate, violent crime is still 400 percent higher than 35 years ago.
>
> Easton and Brantingham, 1998

Statistics Canada classifies eight major crimes as being violent crimes (i.e., murder, attempted murder, manslaughter, rape, other sex offences, wounding, assault, and robbery). Since 1962, Statistics Canada has been using the *Uniform Crime Reporting* system for the definition and classification of offences. However, over the years, due to various legal, social, and legislative factors, the definitions and classifications have varied somewhat. Therefore, when studying anything involving a protracted period, variations are to be expected, especially given the relative nature of crime caution needs to be exercised. For example, in 1983, Bill C-127 replaced rape with three levels of sexual assault (i.e., aggravated sexual assault, sexual assault with weapon, and sexual assault). Other crimes that have been the subject of substantive legal revisions include theft, arson, and murder.[12]

Notwithstanding these issues, in 1997, the violent crime rate in Canada declined for the six consecutive year—the lowest rate since 1980 (still 400% greater than in 1962) (see Figure 9.1, 9.2, 9.3). The western provinces averaged higher violent crime rates than the eastern provinces while minor assaults account for over 60% of all reported violent crimes. Thunder Bay reported the highest rate of violent crime (1,810 per 100,000), followed by Regina and Winnipeg with Trois-Rivieres reporting the lowest violent crime rate (488).

Figure 9.1. Crime Rate, Canada, 1962–1997

Rate per 100,000 population

Source: Uniform Crime Reporting Survey, Canadian Centre for Justice Statistics, Statistics Canada

Figure 9.2. Violent crime, Canada and the provinces, 1997

Rate per 100,000 population

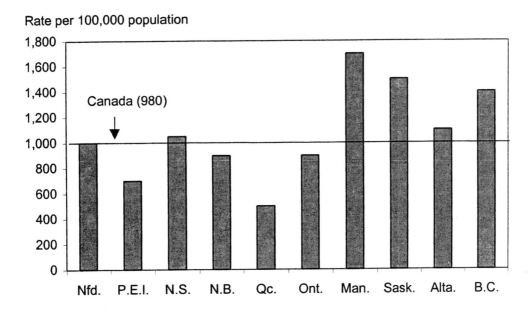

Source: Uniform Crime Reporting Survey, Canadian Centre for Justice Statistics, Statistics Canada

Figure 9.3. Violent Crime Categories, Canada, 1997

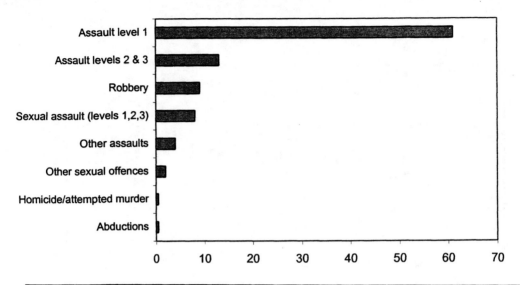

Source: Uniform Crime Reporting Survey, Canadian Centre for Justice Statistics, Statistics Canada

Aside from looking at the overall picture of violent crime in Canada, it has not grown exponentially over the years. In fact, 1998 marked the seventh consecutive year that the crime rate dropped. How might we account for this trend? A number of Canadian experts point to the changing demographics. In particular, the relative decline of those in the age group 18–24. Unfortunately, the recent spree of decline is not so much attributable to efforts by the criminal justice system but simply an article of a changing population make-up. Foot (1996) cautions however that the drop in the crime rate would not likely last as "generation X" reaches the 12–24 age group category. Edmonton, for example, already began to experience this in 1998. In 1997 and 1998, Edmonton's chief of police blames the demographic bulge of teens and young adults in their city. He points out that Edmonton's demographic trends run a few years ahead of the rest of the country (Gillis, Johnsrude, and Ovenden, 1998).

Assaults not involving a weapon or serious injury to the victim represent over half of all crimes of violence between 1989 through 1997. However, as with other violent crime categories, the rate has declined since 1992. Robberies with firearms have been declining since the early 1980s. In 1997, they account for about 1 in 10 violent crimes. However, the rate of sexual assaults more than doubled in the 1980s. In the 1990s, the rates have declined slightly.

Between 1993 and 1997, there has been a decrease in the use of weapons in violent incidents. In 1997, firearms were present in only 5.1% of violent crimes while the presence of knives constituted 9.1%.

Contrary to what some people may be led to believe, homicide rates increased only slightly between 1962 and 1975 when the rate peaked at 3.02 per 100,000. The rate remained relatively stable between 1976 and 1992 when the rate began to decline until 1996. In 1996, the homicide rate increased by 6% but in 1997 the rate declined 9% from the previous year—a record low since 1969 (see Figure 9.4).[13]

Table 9.1. Violent and Property Crime Categories: 1998

Crimes of Violence:

a. Homicide
- murder 1st and 2nd degree
- manslaughter
- infanticide

c. Assault
- assault Level 1
- assault with weapon or causing bodily harm Level 2
- aggravated assault Level 3
- unlawfully causing bodily harm
- discharge firearm with intent
- police
- other peace public officers
- other assaults

d. Abduction
- abduction of person under 14
- abduction of person under 16
- abduction contravening custody order
- abduction no custody order

e. Sexual offences
- aggravated sexual assault (level 1)
- sexual assault with weapon (level 2)
- sexual assault — aggravated (level 3)
- other sexual offences

b. Attempted murder

f. Robbery
- firearms
- other offensive weapons
- other robbery

Property Crimes:

a. Breaking and entering
- business premises and residence
- other break and enter

c. Theft over $5.000

e. Frauds
- cheques
- credit cards
- other fraud

b. Theft motor vehicles
- automobiles, trucks, etc.

d. Theft $5,000 and under

Other criminal code offences:

- prostitution
- gaming and betting
- offensive weapons
- arson

Note: In addition to there being over several hundred criminal code offences, there are also several Federal Statutes which come under criminal justice jurisdiction (e.g., *Restricted Drugs, Young Offenders Act, Liquor Act, Customs Act, Admiralty Act*, etc.). Then there are Provincial Statutes such as the *Highway Traffic Act, Fish and Wildlife Act* and Municipal By-Laws ranging from cat laws to the use of firewood. It should come as no surprise then that the laws controlling social behaviour permeate virtually every level of our life.

For example, in 1965 the rate of violent incidents per 100,000 population was 299; 501 in 1971; 666 in 1981; 1,099 in 199—an all time high. Since then the violent crime rate has declined each year through 1997 when the rate was under 970 per 100,000.

Figure 9.4. Homicide Rate, 1961–1997

Rate per 100,000 population

Source: Homicide Survey, Canadian Centre for Justice Statistics, October, 1998.

In general, homicide rates were higher in the west than the east with Manitoba continuing to have the highest rate. The lowest rates in 1996 were in PEI, New Brunswick and Newfoundland. the highest homicide rate (3.86) from 1985–1989. Winnipeg and Vancouver had the highest homicide rates while Calgary and Hamilton had the lowest rates in 1996.

Firearms, in 1997, continue to account for about one-third of all homicides with handguns comprising about half of all firearm homicides. Alcohol/drugs were involved in nearly half of all homicide cases. Youth homicides represent about 9 percent of all homicides. This figure has remained fairly stable since 1985. However, of particular interest is the fact that the incidence of children killing their parents, in 1996, has gone up.[14]

Homicide appears to be somewhat predictable in the sense that nearly 80% of solved homicides were committed by someone who previously either knew the victim in a domestic relationship (37%) or was involved as an acquaintance (41%). Not surprising perhaps is the fact that in 1997, one-half of all homicide victims (majority being women—64%) were killed in their own residences! However, males are still more likely to be victims of homicides (approximately 67%).

As with most crime categories, the age group 18–29 accounted for a higher percentage of suspects (48%) and victims (29) in 1989 than any other age group.

With respect to other types of violent crime and of particular interest to criminal justice administrators and sociology or criminology researchers is the fact that young males and adult women have increased as a proportion of all violent suspects since the early 1960s. Conversely, adult males show a corresponding decline.

As with homicide, the majority of other violent incidents occur in a private residence and between victims and offenders known to each other.

Property Crime Trends in Canada

Statistics Canada, defines property crimes as unlawful acts with the intent of gaining property (money, material goods, automobiles, etc.) but do not involve the use or threat of violence. Although most people seem more interested in violent crime rates, property related crimes occur the most frequently in Canada. In the 1990s, property crime accounts for approximately 60% of all crimes known to the police, while in the late 1970s and early '80s they represented 50% of all crimes known to police. There are approximately five property related offences for every violent crime or, a property crime occurs approximately every 3–4 seconds while violent crimes occur every few minutes. In addition, it is estimated that in addition to the financial impact of property crimes,[15] many victims suffer emotional distress long after the crime occurred. Finally, depending on the region, clearance rates average 17%.[16] Hence, the true extent of property crimes is conservative![17]

Priority in occurrence is also reflected in how Statistics Canada records such crimes. While all violent crimes known to the police are recorded, for property related crimes only those crimes for which a charge/conviction has been made are recorded. Hence, for those studying crime patterns and trends, it is important to have a sense of the *dark figure* or hidden amount of criminality, that is, the amount of crime which goes unreported and hence officially unknown to the police and the rest of the criminal justice system.

Depending on which source one reads, the dark figure problem may or may not be problematic. Anyone using official crime statistics should be aware of the dilemma, and if it is necessary they can employ other sources to enhance the validity of the data (e.g., self-report and victimization survey). This is referred to as triangulation and helps researchers to obtain a more realistic or valid picture of crime (However, researchers studying non-conventional crimes may require a different approach).

Based on the most recent data available in the *Juristat*, the following is a sampling of some property related crime trends:

1. In 1996, property crime declined 8%—marking the largest decline since crime statistics were first collected in 1962 (generally, see Figure 9.5).

2. Break and enter (B&E) represent approximately 25% of all reported property crimes with 60% being residential and 28 commercial related. Of all property crimes, B&Es are the most likely to be reported (approx. 70%). Canadians spend nearly $195 million trying to secure their residences from burglary. 1996 marked the first year of decline after two years of growth.

3. Fraud (the taking of property of another through deception—remember the Bre-X hoax?) has declined in the 1990s with the exception of credit-card fraud. Between 1983 and 1993, the rate doubled from 7% to 14%.

4. Thefts account for nearly 55% of all reported property crimes. "Theft over" $5,000 declined fairly sharply in the 1990s while "Theft Under" remained stable. The most common type of theft under items were household articles (approx. 40%) followed by personal articles (17%).

5. Arson (destruction of property using fire) is comparatively infrequent but the financial costs can be very high. One Alberta based study reported that in 1991

alone, fires knowingly set by young offenders resulted in losses of nearly $10 million. Reasons for committing arson range from mischief to arson for profit.

6. Motor vehicle theft (MVT) represents the fastest growing property crime in Canada. In North America, a car theft occurs about every 20 seconds. Youth tend to steal for kicks ("joyriding") while others steal for resale nationally and even internationally.[18] As with violent crimes, the nature of property crimes may also differ over times. For example, in 1992–93 the 2-door Ford Mustang Cobra GT was one of the most common targets while in 1995–96 it was the Honda Prelude. Similarly, depending on geographic location, motor vehicle crimes vary. France has the highest rate (2.8% of all vehicles) of car theft, Spain the highest rate of theft *from* cars (14.6%), while Canada scored the highest incident rate of car vandalism (11%) (Morrison & Ogrodnick, 1994). For the first time in over a decade, in 1997, MVT declined 3% (*Juristat*, 1998, 18(11): 8).

7. As with violent crimes, all property crimes share demographic, social, and individual differences. For example, British Columbia tends to have the highest rate of property offences while Newfoundland reported the lowest rate in 1997. However, unlike violent crimes, property offenders tend to be young and disadvantaged males. Females, however, are increasingly becoming involved in property related crimes (Ibid).

Figure 9.5. Property Crime Categories, Canada, 1997

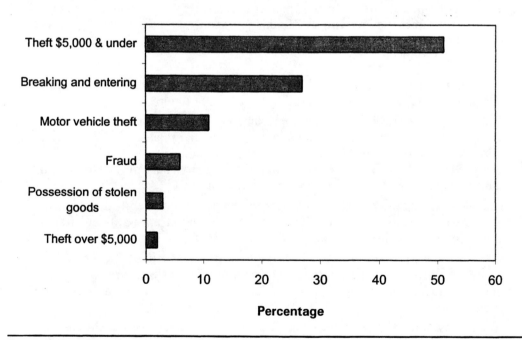

Source: Uniform Crime Reporting Survey, Canadian Centre for Justice Statistics, Statistics Canada

Before we look at patterns of punishment of crimes in Canada, a few observations need to be made about the risk of criminal (violent and property) victimization. Until recently, victims received little attention in the literature.

Risk of Criminal Victimization

Victimization surveys are designed to ask people whether they have been a victim of certain crimes. The surveys also usually gather information about the respondents' impressions of how their incident was handled as well as possible questions about their perceived level of fear of being victimized. Such data has proven invaluable in supporting theories and/or formulating criminal justice legislation.

During the early 1980s, the Solicitor General of Canada funded a national victimization survey (i.e., **Canadian Urban Victimization Survey**) involving seven major cities and over 70,000 telephone interviews. The purpose was to examine the extent to which Canadians are at risk of becoming a victim of a crime and under what conditions that victimization occurs.

The survey resulted in a series of ten bulletins beginning in 1983 (i.e., Victims and Crime) to 1988 (Multiple Victimization). In 1988, the **General Social Survey** (GSS) was introduced. It represented a standardized vicitimization survey that is administered every five years.

Some of the hi-lites from the 1993 GSS include:

1. Since 1988, there has been a small but measurable increase of fear of victimization.
2. Compared to 12 other western countries, Canada ranks in the lower third of being victimized.
3. There has been an increase in the public's perception that levels of crime have increased.
4. Actual victimization rates declined with increasing age of respondents.
5. Approximately 28% of violent victimizations are reported to the police.
6. Of those crimes reported, 64% expressed "satisfaction" with how the police respond to their incident. Females were less (54%) satisfied than males (75%).
7. Compared to official counts of crime, Canadians tend to over-estimate both the frequency and seriousness of violent crime.[19]

While Johnson and Sacco (1991:98) suggest that an accurate assessment of the way in which lifestyle, exposure, and target suitability and guardianship affect victimization is still not possible, it is apparent that social and demographic factors play a major role in ones risk of victimization.

Now that you have a sense of how serious crime is in Canada, who is committing these crimes; how does the criminal justice system respond to criminal offenders? We will explore some of these issues in the following section.

Figure 9.6. Administration of Justice in Canada: Governmental Agencies

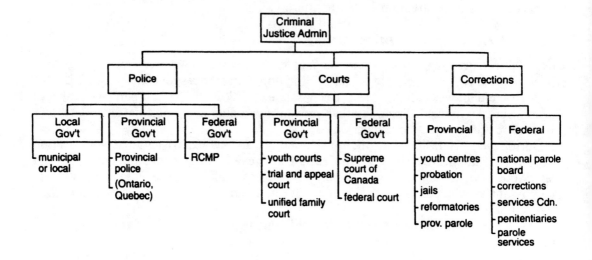

Patterns of Punishment and Descriptive Characteristics

Under the *British North America Act* (1867), criminal law is a federal responsibility. That is, the federal government in accordance with Section 91(27) of the Act has the power to legislate all criminal law for the country. However, under Section 92(14), the provinces are empowered to administer justice. The result being that Canada has a three-tier system for administering justice throughout the country (see Figure 9.6).

As noted earlier, each year Statistics Canada produces justice statistics for the country which are available to the public and will serve as the primary source of information for the trends and patterns of punishment in Canada.

Characteristics of Adult Offenders

On any given day, there are approximately 34,000 adults incarcerated in federal and provincial correctional facilities.

Although Canada borders on the United States, its crime and punishment trends and patterns do not necessarily mirror those of its neighbour. For example, Canada does not have the death penalty, parole is still used across the country, trial by jury is less frequently used and violent and property crime rates are considerably lower than in the United States. Nevertheless, similar to our southern neighbours, Canada still has a comparatively high crime rate. It is considered one of the more punitive of the western nations. For example, Corrections Service of Canada annually releases figures comparing the imprisonment rate for adults from fifteen different countries. In 1997, the United States had an incarceration

222

rate of approximately 600 per 100,000 inhabitants, Canada 115, the United Kingdom 100, Sweden 65, and the lowest being Japan at 37 per 100,000 inhabitants (*Juristat*, 1998, 18(3): 3).

According to the same report, the typical Canadian federal male inmate is:

INMATE CHARACTERISTICS	YEAR 1990/1997
MALES	
- age 20-34	64.5/46.7
- single	49.0/57.2
- common law spouse	26.0/29.7
- married	13.2/11.8
- serving his first penitentiary term	60.7/53.7
- serving a sentence for break and enter, robbery or murder	52.0/49.4
FEMALES	
- age 20-34	58.9/51.5
- single	45.0/56.3
- common law spouse	16.1/19.3
- married	15.0/10.6
- serving her first penitentiary term	83.1/74.2
- serving a sentence for murder, manslaughter, or robbery	51.2/58.0

With respect to racial/ethnic background, in 1997, 84% of the male inmate population was Caucasian while 10.6% was Native. As for the female inmate population, 75% were Caucasian and 14.4% Native.

In **summary**, it can be seen that the majority of those incarcerated are between the ages 20-34, single males, and usually first time offenders. Various research reports indicate that the Aboriginal people are over-represented in the criminal population and tend to receive longer sentences for similar offences.

Women and Crime

In August 1998, two women (ages 30 and 40 respectively) were charged with the stabbing death of an undercover Toronto police officer. He was the first Toronto officer in nearly five years to be killed in the line of duty.

One of the interesting puzzles in criminology is why do women commit fewer crimes and typically less serious crimes than men. Yet, when they do commit a serious crime they are often typified as being "sick" or the product of male victimization. Karla Holmolka tried to blame her husband Paul Bernardo for forcing her into killing her sister and another girl. Canada's youngest, and only second woman to be declared a dangerous offender, Edmonton's Lisa Neve life history is one of being constantly victimized (see Boritch, 1997). However, as Manner (1995) points out, when they are bad they are "real bad."

Gender is a powerful sociological and criminogenic variable and one that until recently has been largely ignored in the study of crime. Since the pioneering work of Rita Simon (1975), Freda Adler (1975) and Carol Smart (1976), among others, criminologists have become increasingly interested in female offenders.[20] The "sudden" interest coincided with the women's movement of the early 1970s. But, the feminist perspective did not gather true momentum until the 1980s and early 1990s when their concerns and theories began to appear in journals and textbooks.[21]

Between 1962 and 1990, women's overall involvement in violent crime went from 4% to 10%,[22] and for property offences from 7% to 23%. This converts to a rate increase from 476 to 1092 per 100,000. In terms of actual numbers, the number of women charged for all offences rose from 27,530 in 1962 to 114,770 in 1992 (Bortich, 1997). However, as Kong (1997) points out, most of the violent crimes committed by women are for minor assaults. Moreover, as with Aboriginal men, Aboriginal women are over-represented in the criminal justice system, although their representation has declined in recent years. Research also shows that Aboriginal women are more likely to commit violent crimes than non-Aboriginal women are. LaPrairie (1993:243) suggests this is due to "historical socio-economic forces and background factors" that predispose them. She also points to the long-term history of substance abuse, poor dietary history, and genetic predisposition. The bottom line is the increase in the number of women being charged has further added to an already burdened criminal justice system.

In-spite of their increased involvement in criminal activity, women, in general, do not receive the same sentence for the same crime as would a male. In 1996–97, women represented only 9% of the federal population. A trend that has remained fairly stable throughout the 1990s (Reed, 1998). Why do women receive lighter sentences? The literature is somewhat conflicting on this subject. The explanations range from women are more likely to get sentences for drug and property than are men; female offenders are more likely go seek psychological help as opposed to men; to the chivalry hypothesis which maintains that the system has a more benevolent attitude towards women than men. Whatever the reason, based on 1994 data, nearly 25% of women received maximum sentences of three years or less as compared to 18% among men while only 8.7% of women received sentences longer than 10 years vs. 14.15 among male offenders.

In **summary**, this brief overview of the female offender serves to illustrate that their presence in the system has increased in recent years. There appears to be some correlation between the women's movement and gender role socialization as well as a shift in the social and cultural mind-set within society. Yet, many of the early stereotypes still seem to prevail as women are treated and responded to differently than are male offenders. Aside from the early attempts to blame crimes committed by females on their "natural inferiority" (e.g., Otto Pollack's work of the 1950s), more contemporary theories, and in particular feminist criminology, focus on such factors as the natural oppression (e.g., economically, politically, and socially) that women encounter in society. However, with a growing awareness, we are likely to see the issue continue to evolve as society addresses the issues.

Characteristics of Young Offenders

> Sixty-four percent of young offenders in our detention centres are repeat offenders....
> There's a real problem when you have a whole group of people who feel they're above the
> law."
>
> Commissioner Jim Brown—Ontario Crime Control Commission, 1998 [On-line]

As noted at the outset of this chapter, if the media can serve as a barometer of social concern, then the issue of youth crime is a VERY "hot topic." At the time of preparing this chapter, the Federal government was considering a number of major amendments to the *Young Offenders Act* of 1984 (YOA) that would hold youth more accountable. Among the considerations are: naming young offenders of certain crimes; allowing automatic transfer to adult court for a broader spectrum of crimes, and lowering the cut-off age for youth who have committed a serious offence or are repeat offenders.

Are these amendments warranted? A 1997 survey of 150 Canadian frontline police officers indicated that 54% felt youth crime was increasing and becoming more serious. An Angus Reid poll in the same year showed that most Canadians feel similarly. Yet, since 1992/93, official statistics tell us that youth crime has been declining! However, between 1991 and 1996, violent crime increased 9% and doubled over 1981. Youth (ages 12–17) account for approximately 40% of all break and enters and auto thefts. Statistics also indicate that nearly 50% of youth crimes are unreported for a variety of reasons.[23] Therefore, whether real or perceived,[24] youth crime is drawing considerable attention and given that their numbers will increase as we enter the new millennium the attention may be warranted.

Finally, in early 1999, the Justice Minister tabled a new bill (Bill C-68) calling for the replacement of the YOA with the *Youth Criminal Justice Act*. The Act calls for new actions on three complementary levels: *prevention, meaningful consequences, and harsher punishment for violent and repeat offenders*. Although it appears to reflect the actions the Canadian public has been calling for, it remains to be seen whether it will be any more effective than its predecessors. Nevertheless, as part of this initiative in 1994 the National Strategy on Community Safety and Crime Prevention earmarked $58.8 million for crime prevention oriented programs. In April 1999 Alberta received $579,107 to help fund some 15 crime prevention projects (Mofina, 1999). These measures appear to reflect a positive and aggressive response by the federal government.

In **summary**, as with adult crime, we have seen that youth crime also presents a number of major challenges for criminologists, sociologist, and the criminal justice system in general. The economic, historical, political, and social impact can not be undermined. Crime and our efforts to control it demand public and academic attention if we wish to continue to enjoy the quality of life and sense of freedom we largely still enjoy. One method by which we can begin to address these concerns is to better understand their underlying causes. Only through such insights can we then begin to formulate policies that "will work" to control and prevent crime, and effectively address those who commit crimes. Sociological explanations have long represented one such approach.

In the next section, we will examine some of the traditional explanations as well as some of the emerging sociological theories that have been developed to explain crime and criminality.

Sociological Explanations of Crime

A review of criminological textbooks will quickly reveal that during the twentieth century the discipline of sociology is responsible for more criminological theories, the basis for more scholarly research, and writings on crime than any other discipline. Even today, most criminologists have their training in sociology. Given the vast volume of material that has been produced, it is well beyond the scope of this chapter to do them all justice. Therefore, I have chosen to provide a summative discussion of the sociological contributions.

Borrowing from Barak's (1997) analogy, the sociological contributions can be divided into three main classification schemes: (1) crime as a product of social organizations; (2) crime as a product of social processes; and (3) crime as a product of social structure. Again, given the constraints of this chapter, only a brief overview is provided for each scheme. However, in Figure 9.7, you will find a summary of some of the important sociological theories, their theoretical concerns, and their major contributors.

Social Organization

Although applying different orientations, all three perspectives seek to explain crime as a consequence of external (i.e., environmental) forces rather than individual traits or characteristics.

The first scheme identified is among the more common in sociological criminology. Social organization can include such factors as *social disorganization* (e.g., rapid social change or imbalances that compromise the legitimate norms and values of society); and *social ecology* (e.g., our actual physical environment and space can influence homogeneity within society).

Anomie/strain is another variation of social disorganization. It tends to see crime as a functional reaction to disharmony within society. That is, people do not act out unless they are dissatisfied with something.

Other variations of the social organization approach, include *subcultural* theories, *differential opportunity, middle-class measuring rod,* and others.

Individually, and collectively, each has contributed to the study of crime and its control. However, they continue to fall short of providing an adequate answer to the crime problem.

Social Process

Theories that are premised on crime as a *social process* view crime as the result of how our environment provides us with information which in turn forges our cognitive (i.e., thinking) processes. For example, how often have you heard the analogy that when in prisons, inmates learn to become "better" criminals. The extent and degree to which we associate with others is considered important. For example, Edwin Sutherland's popular theory of *differential association* focuses on the nature and context of our environment and how we learn. Other variations of the social process include *differential identification.* This theory asserts that learning does not need to involve direct contact. It only requires a degree of imagination and a desire to seek pleasure over pain. Hence, the "copy cat" syndrome where people will imitate something because it provides them with a sense of well being and/or power. Similarly, the *labelling* theory relies on a process of what is referred to as *reaction formation*. Here people are seen as responding to definitions or descriptions directed at them. If you are told often enough that you are bad, chances are you will live up to that expectation!

Therefore, in many respects, crime and criminality is seen as a *social construction*. Here sociologists focus on how "social relations and social arrangements come to be constructed" (Barak, 1997:158). This notion ties in nicely with our earlier discussion that crime is a *relative* and *evolutive* concept. Without its social construction, there would be no crime! It is only wrong because we (or someone) defines it as such.

Social Structure

The final classification scheme emphasizes crime as the product of an imbalance in the *social structure*. This schema entails a wide range of theories and can also be referred to as a *conflict perspective*. Crime and crime control is generally viewed as 'patterned variables' of social structure related to such factors as age, gender, race/ethnicity, and social-class. As Barak (1997:160) states, proponents of this perspective ask the question "why in the aggregate do we have the criminality that we do?" as opposed to the more conventional question of "why do they do it?"

Hence, crime is seen as resulting from fragmentation in the social order. This creates social struggle of social status, opportunity, and power. The *Marxist* theory, for example, blames capitalism as the source of social inequalities as it relates to the distribution of wealth and power. While there are other variations of this approach (see Table 9.2), some of the more recent variations that have influenced our perception and approach to crime control has been the *feminist* theories, *Peacemaking, British Realism,* and *Chaos Theory,* among others.

Table 9.2. Sampling of Sociologically Based Theories for Crime*

Theory**	Theoretical Concerns	Major Contributors
Anomie 1930s**	Deviance as stress generated by conflict between goals of success and structural means of achievement.	E. Durkheim R.K. Merton
Differential Association 1940s	Due to normative conflict a variety of social phenomena (e.g., subculture, social differentiation, & differential social organization) can account for deviance—behaviour is learned.	E. Sutherland
Opportunity Theory 1950s	Blocked opportunities due to limited access to legitimate means of achieving desired economic success.	R. Cloward & L. Ohlin

227

Control Theory 1960s	The importance of bonds (e.g., attachment, commitment, belief, etc.) and how they affect conformity.	T. Hirschi
Labelling 1960s	Focuses on how negative social reactions create stigmatization and isolating effects.	K. Erickson E. Lemert & H. Becker
Power Control 1970s	The distribution of power and prestige among individuals and groups in society.	J. Hagan A. Turk
"New criminology" 1970s	Similar to labelling but shifts focus from labelling the individual to society itself (e.g., class conflict, political economy and crime, power and authority).	K. Marx W. Bonger I. Taylor, R. Dahrendorf
Feminism 1970s	Examines how the patriarchal structure has limited the understanding of crime and justice, especially among women. Includes several orientations.	C. Smart M. Chesney-Lind
British (Left) Realist 1980s	Shift from focus on the role of the state to impact of crime on the victim and need to establish realistic social policy.	R. Kinsey J. Lea J. Young
General Theory Of Crime 1990s	The control theory has been modified in an attempt to explain all crimes ranging from violent crime to white-collar offences. Crime is seen as a function of poor self-control.	M. Gottfredson T. Hirschi
Peacemaking 1990s	Generally classified as a type of conflict orientation theory. It promotes the idea of equity, justice, and peace through mediation and conflict resolution vs. punishment and state control.	P. Peplinsky R. Quinney
Chaos 1990s	Also referred to as the "science of contradictions." A theory whose future remains unclear.	L. Barton D. Milovanic

* Integration and interdisciplinary approach. They are considered to offer a fuller theoretical understanding of the complexity of human behaviour.
** Dates denote the approximate time period during which the theory emerged.

In **summary**, while we have not examined any specific theory in detail, it has hopefully become evident that sociological theories of crime and criminality offer a wide range of interpretations that focus on external factors to the individual. The notion that behaviour can not function in a vacuum, or that it requires an environment to effect its actions has considerable intuitive appeal. The manner in which these external events impinge on our behaviour ("good" or "bad") remain the subject of considerable sociological inquiry. Again, as Barak (1997) describes it, sociologists/criminologists attempt to answer the questions, "why do they do it," and "why do we have the crime we have?"

As a criminologist, I view sociology as representing an integral link to our understanding of crime and criminality. Their theories help to provide a framework through which to better understand the link between individuals factors (e.g., biology and psychology) and the group, and society at large. However, this is subject to much debate as they are but a link in the puzzle of crime and crime control.

The Ethics of Crime Control and the Need for Integration

A final area worth briefly discussing involves the implications of attempting to apply theory to practice. As we have seen, crime is a social and political issue. Therefore, the study of crime by nature is an applied discipline and researchers encounter many ethical issues. For example, how do we know the individual was guilty or innocent; under what circumstances should a police officer make an arrest; what should we be studying; should the results be released, how should the results be used, etc.? Unfortunately, there are no clear-cut answers to these types of social dilemmas. A decision (e.g., labelling) can have a profound influence on both the person being labelled as well as those close to him or her. Meanwhile, researchers can try to follow the ethical guidelines of their discipline, but they are not fail-safe nor is the discretion allotted a police officer, judge, or correctional officers. So, while ethics may provide helpful guidelines, they are not a substitute for moral choice. A classical example of good intentions gone "bad" involves the now famous 1974 publication of Robert Martinson who proclaimed "nothings works" in corrections. His conclusion was widely embraced and was instrumental in our shift from a model of rehabilitation to one of retribution and revenge. In spite of several subsequent studies trying to negate the sweeping conclusion, it took nearly 30 years for criminologists and criminal justice policy to begin to move away from such punitive attitude. The shift, however, has been one driven more out of economic need than reliance on scientific evidence.

In recent years, criminology and to some degree sociologists interested in the study of crime and criminality have begun to embrace an interdisciplinary and integrated approach to criminological issues. Rather than remain provincial in their doctrines, researchers are beginning to accept that human behaviour is a complex phenomenon. Increasingly, they are beginning to acknowledge that the study of crime and criminality is best addressed from an interdisciplinary and integrated approach. Although this theme has been interwoven throughout the chapter, it is well beyond its scope to provide a detailed discussion. Rather, it is presented as "food for thought" for those serious about the social issues that continue to confront to us.

Summary

Crime is an evolving concept and will likely continue to represent a serious social dilemma for us. As we learn to handle existing crimes, new crimes will evolve to present us with new challenges. This is already being witnessed in the area of white-collar type of crimes (e.g., computer crimes, stock market frauds, real estate fraud, lawyers embezzlement, medical malpractice, even various forms of terrorism—see Winterdyk, 2000).

Historically, in Canada, our attitudes toward punishment seem to have been somewhat cyclical. As we become less efficient we risk being more conservative and with escalating costs there are fewer programs being initiated for prevention or intervention. However, as observed in the section on young offenders, there are exceptions to this trend.

From a theoretical position, our theories of crime and punishment also appear somewhat relative and evolutive. Hence, it is somewhat unclear as to whether we will ever be able to truly control crime. Yet, as Emile Durkheim once noted, crime can be functional and even necessary. Therefore, sociologists, among others, must continue our search for the answers to the dilemma and trust that through critical thinking and sound research we might someday better understand crime as well as better control it.

In order to reduce crime from a sociologic perspective, researchers must focus on the cultural and social factors underlying crime. In appreciating the frailty of the CJS in being able to control crime, it is even more paramount for sociologists to find the answers and solutions in the cultural and social conditions of society. For example, crime reduction and crime prevention can take many forms. A fundamental approach will require society to shift its current emphasis on economic gain, individual success, and competition (i.e., the primary elements of the conflict model) toward a value system that embraces co-operation and utilitarian goals (i.e., consensus model). A cross-section of viable options include: create greater economic opportunity for everyone; reduce poverty; improve social integration at the community and societal level; improve gender equality; target high-risk groups; offer support for those already victimized (e.g., battered women and abused children); a greater shift toward community based intervention and prevention programs; more humane prisons, and the elimination of controversial laws.

Although not a comprehensive list, all these ideas have been tested and found to have varying degrees of success. Their success depends largely upon the context in which they are implemented. No one program is a panacea. Readers might be interested in reading the substantial report produced Lawrence Sherman and his associates (1998). The report provides a comprehensive overview of many of the above suggestions.

While there appears to be hope for the future, we must bear in mind the ethical dilemmas discussed above. To paraphrase the noted Canadian criminologist/sociologist Gywn Nettler, society is like a social fabric that can only be mended and rewoven so many times before it is beyond repair. Perhaps it is time to release the old social fabric, the old structures, the status quo, our old ways of thinking and conceive a new order! We must be prepared to realize that we are the masters of our own destiny. We are responsible for our current social and cultural conditions that have created the crime rates we have. Only by choosing to recognize and be willing to change what is "wrong" will we be able to reduce crime. The gauntlet has been placed before you!

Notes

1. Students interested in exploring more on this subject are welcome to visit the website for the Department of Criminology, Mount Royal College. It can be reached at: www.mtroyal.ab.ca/programs/commhealth/criminology. This revised edition of the chapter reflects the evolving nature of our understanding and response to crime and punishment. And while its framework remains consistent, the theme represents a significant departure from the previous format.

2. The type of crime is included in brackets after the title of each article. Most of these headings were taken from the *Calgary Herald* newspaper.

3. France was first with 53% expressing fear of being victimized while Finland was lowest with only 11% expressing such feelings.

4. Figures for courts are collected every second year.

5. As a criminologist, I prefer a slightly modified version that has sociological overtones but also embraces the ambiguous nature of crime. *Crime is a socially constructed concept used to categorize certain behaviour as requiring formal control and warranting some form of social intervention.*

6. The number does not account for the numerous by-laws, statutes, and other regulations.

7. A term coined by American sociologist Maurice Parmalee in 1920. He is also credited with writing the first book on criminology in North America.

8. These points are drawn from Winterdyk, 2000.

9. Australia was one of the first countries to introduce transformative justice. You can visit their website at: www.tja.com.au/welcome.htm.

10. For an excellent discussion of this view see Fattah (1995) or for a summary see Winterdyk, 2000: Ch.13).

11. There are several spin-off models of the positivist and classical schools (see Winterdyk 2000). For the purpose of this chapter, we will limit our overview to the two primary schools.

12. For an interesting chronological overview of how the definition and classification of murder has changed see Neil Boyd (1988). Due to economic changes and the devaluation of the dollar, the crime of theft has been changed from theft over/under $200 to $1,000 to $2000 and most recently $5,000.

13. By contrast, the homicide rate in the United States in 1989 (8.7) was three and one-half times higher than the rate in Canada.

14. Between 1975 and 1995, an average of 19 parents were killed by their children each year. In 1996, 25 parents were killed by their children. In over 70% of the cases the homicides were the result of a quarrel or an assault. Only 15% involved financial gain (remember the Mendendez brothers case of the early 1990s in California—you can find information about their case/story on the Internet).

15. In the late 1990s, based on insurance information, it is estimated that losses due to property crimes is at least $5.7 billion.

16. In 1995, of Canada's major cities, St. John's had the highest clearance rate at 31.7% while Ottawa had a clearance rate of only 6.8% (Vancouver board..., 1997).

17. It is a well documented fact that numerous property crimes tend to go unreported. Some of the reasons include: (1) never detected, (2) too trivial to report, (3) police cannot do anything about it, (4) fear of reprisal, etc.

18. In 1996, a Toronto ring of car thieves was nabbed. The six offenders had stolen $2.5 million in luxury vehicles that were destined for Vietnam. They used youth and young adults to do the stealing.

19. For those interested in viewing the results of the first Violence Against Women Survey in 1993, you can find a summary of the results and more detailed information on the Internet at http://library.usask.ca/data/social/violence.html.

20. The father of modern criminology, Cesare Lombroso (1835–1909) was the first to write about the female offender in 1895. Lombroso suggested that women are more likely than men to have *atavistic* (i.e., evolutionary weaknesses) traits that account for any crimes they might commit. This general view was perpetuated throughout most of the first half of the 20th century.

21. Today there are several journals dedicated to the study of female offenders. For example, *Women and Criminal Justice, Canadian Journal of Women and Law, Women's Studies, Canadian Woman Studies*, and *Journal of Women in Culture and Society* among others. There are also a number of recent Canadian books on the female offender (see Pearson, 1998; Priest, 1992; and Manner, 1995).

22. In comparative terms, the female rate went up 527% in the thirty years versus an increase of 207% for men over the same period of time.

23. For a recent in-depth account of some of these issues visit the homepage of the Ontario Crime Control Commission at www.fightcrime.net/news/youthcrime.htm.

24. For an interesting expose on the youth crime trend not being as serious as the public believes it to be visit the John Howard Society of Alberta website. they can be reached through the search engine "altavistacanada.com." Simply type "youth crime" and then scroll until you find the link.

References

Adler, F.
1975   *Sisters in crime. The rise of the new female criminal*. NY: McGraw-Hill.

Barak, G.
1997   *Integrating criminologies*. Boston, MA: Allyn Bacon.

Beccaria, C.
1963   *On crimes and punishments*. Translated by H. Paolucci. Indianapolis, IN: The Bobbs-Merrill Co., Inc.

Blumstein, A.
1982   Research on sentencing. *Justice System Journal*, 307–330.

Boritch, H.
1997   *Fallen women: Female crime and criminal justice in Canada.* Scarborough: Nelson.

Boyd, N.
1988   *The last dance: Murder in Canada.* Scarborough: Prentice-Hall.

Cayley, D.
1998   *The expanding prison.* Toronto, ON: House of Anansi Press.

Chambliss, W.
1988   *Exploring criminology.* NY: Macmillan Pub. Co.

Cohen, L.E., & Felson, M.
1979   Social change and crime rate trends: A routine activity approach. *American Sociological Review*, (44), 588–608.

Demers, D.J.
1984   "Criminal justice spending in Canada: Recent trends." In Solicitor General of Canada, *IMPACT—Costs of criminal justice*, 4–12. Ottawa: Supply and Services Canada.

Ditton, J.
1979   *Controlology: Beyond the new criminology.* London: The Macmillan Press, Ltd.

Easton, S., & Brantingham, P.
1998, June   *The cost of crime.* Vancouver, B.C.: Fraser Institute.

Fattah, E.
1995   Restorative and retributive models, A comparison. In H-H. Kuhne (Ed.), *Festschrift fur Koichi Miyazawa.* Baden-Baden, Germany: Nomos Verlassgellschaft.

Fraser Institute Report
1998, June   Online: www.fraserinstitute.ca/critical-issues/crime/cost.html.

Gillis, C., Johnsrude, L., & Ovenden, N.
1998, July 23 Edmonton violent crime stats echoing upward. *Edmonton Journal.* (Online).

Johnson, H., & Sacco, V.F.
1991   "The risk of criminal victimization: Data from a national survey." In R.A. Silverman, J.J. Teevan Jr., & V.F. Sacco (Eds.). *Crime in Canadian society.* Toronto: Butterworths. (Ch. 7).

Kong, R.
1997   Canadian crime statistics, 1996. *Juristat,* 17(8).

Pearson, P.
1998   *When she was bad: Violent women and the myth of innocence.* Toronto: Random House.

Priest, L.
1992   *Woman who killed.* Toronto: McCleeland and Stweart.

Juristat Service Bulletins. Statistics Canada.
>Drug offences in Canada 1962–1987. vol 8, #2.
>Break and Enter in Canada 1962–1986. vol. 8, #1.
>Women and Crime. vol 10, #20.
>Justice spending in Canada. vol. 17(3).
>Homicide in Canada—1996. vol. 17(6).
>Youth court statistics. 1995–96 vol. 17(10).
>Criminal victimization: An international perspective. vol. 17(6).
>Adult correctional services in Canada, 1996–97. vol. 18(3).
>Adult criminal court statistics. vol. 18(7).
>Canadian crime statistics, 1997. vol. 18(11).
>Homicide in Canada—1997, vol. 18(12).

LaPrairie, C.
1993   Aboriginal women and crime in Canada: Identifying the issues. In E. Adleberg and C. Currie (Eds.), *In conflict with the law: Women and the Canadian justice system.* Vancouver, B.C.: Press Gang.

Manner, T.
1995   *Deadlier than men.* Toronto: Pan.

Martinson, R.
1974   What works?—Questions and answers about prison reform. *The Public Interest,* 35: 22–54.

Menard, S.
1987   Short-term trends in crime and delinquency: A comparison of UCR, NCR, and self-report data. *Justice Quarterly,* 4(3): 455–474.

Menninger, K.
1968   *The crime of punishment.* NY: Viking Compass Book.

Mofina, R.
1999, April 8   Minister announces funds to fight crime. *Calgary Herald,* B1, 3.

Morrision, P., & Ogrodnick, L.
1994   Motor vehcile crimes. *Canadian social trends,* 34:21–26.

Reed, M.
1998   Adult Correctional Services in Canada, 1996–97. *Juristat,* 18(3).

Roberts, J.V.
1999   Mandatory sentencing rides again. *Juristat Report,* 14(1): 1, 3.

Sherman, L, Gottfredson, D.C., MacKenzie, D.L., Eck, J., Reuter, P., & Bushman, S.D.
1998   *Preventing crime: What works, what doesn't, what's promising.* Washington: National Insititute of Justice.

Simon, R.
1975   *Women and crime.* Lexington, MA: D.C. Heath.

Smart, C.

1976   *Women, crime and criminology: A feminist critique.* London: Routledge and Kegan Paul.

Vancouver Board of Trade and Information

1997, June   Online: www.vancouver.baordoftrade.com/crime_report.html.

Von Hirsch, A.

1976   *Doing justice: The choice of punishment.* NY: Hill and Wang.

Wilkins, L.

1980   "World crime. To measure or not to measure?" In G.R. Newman (Ed.). *Crime and deviance: A comparative perspective.* Beverly Hill, CA: Sage.

Winterdyk, J.

2000   *Canadian criminology: An integrated and interdisciplinary approach.* Scarborough, ON: Prentice-Hall.

The Social Institutions of the Family, Health, Economy and Religion

Introduction

Mahfooz Kanwar and Don Swenson

The social network is an integral part of human societies. Perhaps the most important part of the social network is the family for the creation and the maintenance not only of kinship but also of the whole social system. Other social networks that are common in human societies that structure social action between people are the economy, health services, and religion. All have different functions to fulfill in human life.

The function of the family is to provide for the intimate needs of adults, and the intimate needs and socialization of dependent children. It is through the physical and social reproduction of individuals within family settings that a society reproduces itself. The family is central to the whole social system, for it is there that children become socially competent (the ability to relate well with others) which enables them to become culturally competent (the ability to earn a living) and thus contribute to a society.

The health and economic systems function to provide for the physical needs of individual members. Due to the fact that we are physically vulnerable (we have accidents and are prone to diseases and illnesses), the health system is there to respond to when we become physically incapacitated. The economic system is more general and it responds to our needs for food, clothing, and shelter. Through an intricate system of production, exchange, distribution, and consumption of goods and services, we can have these basic needs meet.

Religion's function is somewhat more illusive. However, the need for religion is evident in that there is no evidence of any human society that does not have some sort of religious expression. It may be reasoned that even after all our intimate, health, and physical needs have been met, there is still something missing: the need to make sense of our society, our world, our cosmos, and to feel connected with others. This is the role of religion. It answers the many questions we have about existence and provides an institutional setting wherein we may become intimately connected with others that we do not find in our work places, in our political system, and our schools, colleges, and universities.

In chapter ten, George Kurian discusses marriage and the family in Canada. He points out that the family system in Canada varies because Canadian society is constituted by people of different ethnic backgrounds. Kurian briefly traces the historical trends of the Canadian family. Although the nuclear family structure is the norm in Canada, he acknowledges the diversity of family forms that arises from ethnic pluralism, single parent families, common law families, and step families. He then provides a brief history of marriage, its legal framework, intermarriage, marital expectations, marital roles and conjugal power. Further, he highlights the process of communication within the family, marital satisfaction, and recent trends in the Canadian family. Lastly, he provides a timely discussion on changes in sexual mores and behaviors in the Canadian social setting.

In recent years, most Canadians have become concerned about their health, health care services, and costs. However, most introductory texts in sociology often ignore the importance of health and health care issues. This is partly due to the misunderstanding that medical sociology is a specialized sub-discipline of itself. On the contrary, in chapter eleven of this volume, Harley Dickenson provides an analysis of the causes of death, patterns of morbidity, and the distribution of health care in Canada. Further, he examines the historical background of the development of the Canadian health care system, and the rising cost of the system.

In chapter twelve, Paul Divers examines the historical development of our current economic system in the Western world and in Canada. He continues by outlining the social transformation of work and the occupational structure in Canada. In the context of the growing mechanization of the workplace and the rising unemployment in Canada, Divers emphasizes the importance of training, and the retraining of workers for the future changes at the workplace.

These three authors examine three fundamental social spaces of Canadians—the family, health, and the economy. The changing family structures, changing patterns and causes of death, health care costs, and transformations of the workplace are all important issues in current social and political discussions that Canadian sociologists cannot afford to ignore.

In the final chapter of the book, Don Swenson offers a multidimensional and synthetic definition of religion. He defines it as: "the individual and social experience of the sacred expressed in myths, rituals, ethos, and integrated into a social collective or institution." He then proceeds to expand on these dimensions by expanding on each and providing evidence for these dimensions from a wide range of historical, anthropological, and sociological literature. Where appropriate, he offers Canadian data to substantiate some of his claims.

10

Marriage and Family in Canada

George Kurian

Introduction

The Canadian Family is composed of people of various ethnic origins. The policy of the Canadian Government is to maintain the cultural diversity and not to have a homogenous type of family or a melting pot like in U.S.A. The idea that the Canadian Mosaic is beneficial to the country in the long run is an unresolved debate. What one can do here is to present some of the aspects of diversity in the Canadian Family.

The most dominant groups are the British and the French who were the first immigrants from Europe. The political domination of the British has influenced social institutions as well. Most of the other immigrant groups from Europe eventually spoke English and adjusted to British traditions. While there were people in Canada, long before the arrival of Europeans, namely the aboriginal people, they were pushed aside by the colonial powers and are still not part of modern Canadian society. The other ethnic groups began to arrive in Canada in large numbers by the middle of the past century. "In 1871, European settlers other than French and British constituted only about 7 percent of the population. By 1951 the figure had increased to 18 percent" (Emily M. Nett, 1988, p. 100).

By the turn of the 20th century non-European immigrants started arriving in Canada. This was a continuation of the process when the Canadian Pacific Railway was built across the Rocky Mountains when Chinese workers were brought in. However, the non-Europeans, who were all Asian immigrants, were never welcomed. All kinds of obstacles were placed to prevent them from bringing their families—especially in British Columbia. Legislation, like the Immigration Act of 1910, made it expensive for immigrants to come to Canada. Each person had to pay $200. In the case of Chinese, a head tax of $500 was imposed between 1885 and 1923.

However, by the end of the Second World War, Canada gradually changed the restrictive immigration laws. In 1962, a major change took place allowing immigrants to come in without quota restrictions. By 1967, the racial bias was removed and immigrants were allowed on the basis of Canadian national needs. With the realization that there was not

239

much interest for Europeans to come to Canada, the Government looked to non-European countries for immigrants. Canada cannot afford the luxury of keeping out non-white immigrants when one looks at the demographic realities. An alarming decline in birthrate from 2.1 children per woman, which is the minimum replacement number, to an average of 1.7 for the country with some provinces like Quebec showing even steeper declines.

Assuming Canada has only 10 percent of the land as habitable, it has only 26 people per square kilometer. Professor Morton Weinfeld of McGill University compared this to West Germany (247), Britain (231), Japan (318) and Netherlands (422). Canadians also have under estimated the loss through emigration. For example in 1985 though immigration was 84,000 the net growth was only 36,000 due to emigration. Many overlook the fact that immigrants are a bargain with highly qualified people who were educated at no cost to Canada (Morton Weinfeld, 1987, June 19).

The people of British and French ethnic background are the largest where 34% of the population could trace their origin in Great Britain and Ireland, and 24% representing people of French background. More than 38 percent of Canadian people belong to other ethnic groups than British and French. Finally, the aboriginal people of Canada including Canadian Indians, Inuits and Metis are about three quarters of a million forming 3% of the population (Pamela M. White, 1990, Pp. 3–6). "Canadians were ethnically diverse in 1986 with almost one third of them reporting mixed ethnic roots, Statistics Canada said yesterday." (Canadian Press, 1989, July 5). The English speaking population in the large urban areas seem to spearhead the social change in Canada like in U.S.A. The nuclear family is the norm in Canada.

In the 1996 Census, people were asked to identify themselves according to ethnic origin. "Some of the findings: more than one in 10 Canadian—11.2 percent, or 3.2 million people—identified themselves as a visible minority; of those, 30 percent were born in Canada. The most numerous were the Chinese (860,000), or 27 percent of all visible minorities, followed by South Asians (671,000, or 21 percent) and blacks (574,000, 18 percent) (Statistics Canada Report 1998).

History of Marriage

The history of marriage of the majority of Canadians who are descendants of immigrants from Europe is similar to the traditions that existed in Europe. It seems in the early days of Christianity, marriage was viewed as a civil and private affair based on Roman Civil Law. The church also emphasized the idea of free consent of partners. In the beginning, the church encouraged intermarriage with non-Christians to get more converts. Gradually the church felt strong enough to halt intermarriage with non-Christians. By the middle ages, the presence of a priest at wedding ceremonies was considered important as symbol of religiosity. They had a clear definition of the ideal spouse, "The ideal wife was expected always to submit humbly to her lord, raise his bastards if he desired, never utter a word of disapproval and by earnest efforts of love try to win him back from distracting influences" (Bernard J. Murstein, 1974, p. 145). Women were expected to be virgin before marriage.

In Canada, the early settlers were not influenced by aboriginal people whose social customs considered pagan were never respected. The interest of the people was to acquire as much land at the expense of the indigenous people. Eventually due to war and infectious diseases, Indians were reduced to a fraction of their original numbers, which continues to be true even today.

According to studies done by Peter Laslett and others based on the census data of 17th Century England using family-reconstitution technique the nuclear family was the norm rather than the extended family. "According to Laslett, research findings reveal that, except for Japan and possibly Serbia (part of present-day Yugoslavia), household size has not varied to a great extent in the last 300 years. The extended family system is found not to be particularly prevalent" (Mark Hutter, 1988, p. 85).

"In her ground-breaking study of Canadian families, Emily Nett maintains that the historical record available to us, leaves little doubt that regardless of geographical location or urban or rural setting, most Canadians lived in nuclear simple family households" (Karen L. Anderson, 1988, p. 27).

Family and Marriage continued to feel the influence of the Christian churches in Canada till recent times. "The Roman Catholic Church in New France, and the Anglican and Protestant Churches (primarily Presbyterian and Methodist) in the Maritimes and Upper Canada played an important role in early Canadian Life" (Emily Nett, 1988, p. 111). However, the influence of church suffered a rapid decline in Post Second World War days with a decline in church attendance especially among Anglicans and Roman Catholics. This definitely has an impact on family life with increasing tolerance of premarital and post-marital sexual permissiveness.

In a society in rapid transition, it becomes increasingly difficult to give an appropriate definition for marriage. From the traditional institutional perspective, the functional aspects are given primary emphasis. These may include sexual rights leading to reproduction and other obligations of spouses. Probably the most crucial role in married life is the rearing of children, meaning the learning process from early childhood through the years in school, leading them into socially responsible adults. Finally, marriage includes inheritance rights and the responsibility of caring for the old. Family ties preserve and interpret the values of society in general. For the individual, "a sense of self-worth may be generated and nourished through the mutual love, respect and loyalty of members in two, three or four generations" (C. Crysdale & Beattie, 1977, p. 112).

Legal Aspects of Marriage

From a historical perspective, only by the mid 19th century, were there clearly defined family laws. "Early laws regulating family relations were embedded in a variety of property laws, devolution of estate statutes, illegitimacy and guardianship acts" (Jane Ursel, 1986, p. 174).

However, the family law was never properly regulated. It seems the first significant act reducing patriarchal authority was the Married Women's Property Act of 1872. Before this, the husband had complete control of his wife's property. To emphasize the male responsibility to the family, the husband was obliged to support wives and children if marriage broke down. An interesting aspect of the legal position of the husband was that "he never lost access to his wife's sexuality through legal separation, he never lost control in law over that aspect of the woman's reproductive capacity" (Jane Ursel, 1986, p. 176). A further development was Social Welfare legislation to care for dependents who had no means of sustenance.

Legislation recognizing equality is only meaningful if women have equal opportunities, especially eliminating discrimination of women in the labour market. "The assumption of primary responsibility for childrearing and homemaking carries with it a unilateral risk of economic deprivation which is inconsistent with the concept of marriage as a partnership of legal equals" (McCall (Marnie) M. L., Joseph P. Hornick and Jean E. Wallace, 1988, p. 40).

Getting married is a legal contract between a man and woman. A number of conditions are expected in marriage. The parties must be male and female, as there are not yet provisions for homosexual marriages. At the time of the marriage, the parties must be single, emphasizing monogamous union. One is not allowed to marry within prohibited degrees of consanguinity and affinity to prevent incestuous unions. Both parties must have reached the marriageable age. This varies from province to province with a minimum age of fourteen. "Having recommended eighteen as the appropriate minimum age for marriage in the case of both males and females, the Royal Commission on the status of women saw no further role for the notion of parental consent and advocated its abolition as a legal requirement" (Iwan Saunders, 1975, p. 47). In addition to formal marriages, there are informal alliances like common-law relationships which in effect have legal validity.

The State is concerned about the welfare of the children and peaceful resolution of property rights according to Emily Nett. "Generally speaking, spouses have the right of sexual access to their partners, to respect and kindness and to fidelity or the sexual exclusiveness of their partners" (Emily Nett, 1988, p. 213). However, the rights and duties are difficult to enforce. One of the essential aspects of obligation in marriage is financial responsibility. Women are no longer expected to submit to sex and childbearing today compared to what existed in 19th century laws. Laws regarding property also have variations in Provincial laws. A study by the Canadian Research Institute for Law and the Family has mentioned some important points. Historically, at the time of marriage the husband had exclusive rights of property including inherited property. By the turn of the twentieth century, women earned the right to own property. "In Canada, legislation permitting married women to own property in their own right was enacted primarily in the 1920s. In Quebec, however, women did not acquire these rights until 1969" (M. L. (Marnie) McCall, Joseph P. Hornick and Jean E. Wallace, 1988, p. 18). As long as the marriage remained stable, disputes regarding property ownership was not a serious concern.

The Married Women's Property Act moved towards the concept of partnership of spouses. This was precipitated due to the cases where wives were denied their rights even though they had made major contributions to the material success of their spouses. There are some basic features in the present matrimonial property laws. These include assumption of marital partnership with regard to share of assets and their definition and expectation that these will be shared. However, an equitable division can only be accomplished in some cases by disposing of business which in effect undermines the source of income.

Looking at the development of law, alimony or maintenance was awarded to an innocent wife, which means misconduct of a wife makes her ineligible for claim of support. Some provinces recognized the concept. "Under the present Canadian divorce legislation, fault is not considered" (M. L. (Marnie) McCall, Joseph P. Hornick and Jean E. Wallace, 1988, p. 24).

Sexual Relations in Transition

The post Second World War period heralded the stage of permissiveness with affection in sex life. This was followed by sexual permissiveness even without affection by the later part of this century. With the availability of contraception, a major shift in sexual freedom developed as premarital pregnancy fear receded to a great extent.

According to Professor Charles Hobart, the emerging new "Double Standard" specified generally that a higher degree of emotional involvement is expected for premarital sex to be acceptable in the case of women, than in the case of men. "For example, this standard would specify that premarital sex is acceptable for women if they are in love with their partner, whereas it is acceptable for men irrespective of relationship considerations. The second possible standard, the Engagement Standard, is a more stringent version of the Love Standard, specifying that premarital sex is acceptable for those who are engaged to their partners, but not otherwise. The occasion for increased support for such a standard could be a growing discovery of what an elusive, transitory, self-delusive, and binding emotion some versions of 'love' (sex attraction, pity for the other, needing the other, etc.) may be in the absence of specific and mutually binding commitment" (Charles Hobart, 1984, pp. 231–255).

In one of the most significant studies on teenage pregnancy in industrialized countries, the comments on Canada are worth mentioning especially in view of the greater use of contraceptives compared to the United States. "It seems probable that there is less sexual activity among younger Canadian teenagers than elsewhere and that reduced exposure might be partly responsible for keeping the pregnancy rates of young teenagers low in that country" (Elize F. Jones, 1986, p. 213)

With the increasing and alarming increase of AIDS (Stephen Genius, 1991), virginity is re-emerging as a socially responsible value. "Moreover, since AIDS is an "equal opportunity disease," virginity may come to be considered as important for males as for females" (Jean Veevers, 1990, p. 8).

In spite of the availability of sex education and contraception, teenage pregnancy has shown significant increase in Canada according to Statistics Canada Report. Calgary seems to have shown a decrease since 1992.

According to Dr. Brent Friesen, Calgary Medical Officer of Health, "Since the late 1980s we have made a concerted effort to increase sexuality education in schools, and improve and expand our family planning services. It has been a real priority for us simply because teen mothers' opportunities for the future and in life are restricted. Their children are placed into higher-risk settings and there's significant social costs as a result." Dr. Friesen also emphasised for every dollar invested in preventing pregnancy up to $10 is saved in related Provincial Social Services, education and justice department costs. In 1987, 26.3 per 1000 women aged 15 to 19 became pregnant in Calgary, well below the national figure of 41.1 in the same year. Since 1987, the national figures have been rising steadily, peaking at 47.4 in 1994, while Calgary rates reflect a decline, dropping to 25.6 in 1995, and plummeting to 21.3 in 1996.

Teen pregnancies had been declining through most of 1970s and 1980s and the reasons for the upturn are not clear. "There has been no good research on this across the country" said Bonnie Johnson, Executive Director of Planned Parenthood of Canada (Eva Ferguson, 1998, January 17).

The following are some of the findings of the study of attitudes towards cohabitation and marriage in Canada. Some of the forces which affect the norms towards marriage and the family are industrialization, urbanization, higher education, decline in religiosity, increase in female labour force participation, changes in ethnic and language composition, etc. It is hardly surprising that currently married women have a positive attitude towards marriage. Those with positive attitudes are more likely to get married. Besides, those who are married are unlikely to express a negative attitude towards marriage unless they are particularly unhappy with their marriage. In contrast, the women who are never married, separated, divorced or are currently cohabiting are apt to take a liberal attitude towards cohabitation. Women who are residing in rural areas tend to show a more conservative attitude towards cohabitation than women in small towns and cities. These findings support the idea that an urban environment promotes liberal attitudes. Working women are forced to retain more liberal attitudes towards cohabitation than non-working women.

One important finding of this study is the regional effect, namely being a resident of Quebec or residing outside of the province. Quebec residents are more positive towards cohabitation and less so with marriage, a pattern that persists almost unchanged even when other factors are controlled.

Apart from their religious affiliation, the respondents religiosity is found to be associated with the attitudes as well. As hypothesized, the women who attend church more frequently tend to be more conservative in their attitudes. Finally, a desired number of children shows a clear pattern of both marriage and cohabitation scales. The women who desire no children have the highest deviation score on cohabitation and lowest score on marriage (Zheng Wu & T. R. Balakrishnan, 1992). "According to the census results 487,000 couples (or 974,000) individuals) were living in common-law partnerships in 1986, 37% gain over 1981, far outpacing the 2.7% rise in the number of married couples. Consequently, common-law unions accounted for 8% of all couples in 1986, up from 6% in 1981" (Pierre Turcotte, 1990, p. 148).

The expectations in all societies, including Canada, are that all adults will eventually get married and have a family. However, the fact is that an increasing and significant minority choose not to get married and are quite content with a single lifestyle. "An analysis completed in 1985 suggested that, at that time, 17% of men and 14% of women would never marry" (Adams, 1990, p. 143).

"In all age groups except the elderly (65 and over), the proportion of people who were married dropped between 1981 and 1986" (Mary Sue Devareaux, 1990, p. 140). Remarriage rates also show a downward trend especially for the older women. Generally Canadians are delaying their marriage which also affect the reproduction rates. "After reaching a record low of 24.4 years for females in 1968, the mean age of marriage rebounded to 27.7 in 1986. The 1986 census results have reinforced the belief that an increasing number of Canadians have recently been delaying getting married (Bali Ram, 1990, pp. 18–19).

According to Statistics Canada report published in 1997, common-law unions and single parent families in Canada continue to rise while Calgary and Province of Alberta does not keep up with this trend.

The number of common-law families from 1991–1996 show an increase of 28% percent, while Calgary only has a rise of 19.3 percent, which is about 19 percent of the families. There is continuous increase through generations, and young people are now less likely to get married. "We may even see more common-law unions in future" according to Bob Glossup, Executive Director for the Vanier Institute of the Family.

According to the census, common-law unions are increasing at all ages according to Doug Morris, Director of Statistics Canada's Housing, Family and Social Statistics Division. In Alberta 12.9 percent of families are single parent families, the lowest in Canada. "Alberta is not a pleasant place for single parent familes to be," according to Gayle Gilchrist James of the Faculty of Social Work, at the University of Calgary. Shortages and cuts to social programmes have left Alberta mothers in poverty compared to other provinces (Sharon Adams and Shelley Knapp, 1993, October 15).

Churches are at a loss how to deal with premarital cohabitation. "When Reverend Joe Christenson was ordained as a Roman Catholic priest 27 years ago, presiding at weddings was his favourite duty. He used to collect photos of the happy couples. Today, he says, like many priests, he'd rather bury people than marry them." The tension arises from the growing number of couples requesting the Sacrament of Marriage who are already living together. The priests are torn between showing compassion for them or condemning them for living in sin; between the need to keep people in the church and their own deeply held beliefs about the sanctity of marriage. Christenson tackled the issue with a national survey of his colleagues. His report is called The Reality of Common-law Marriage and Its Effect on the Life of the Church.

Christenson found plenty of colleagues who are equally distressed "Out of love and compassion, I will work with a couple, but it is hypocritical of me and other priests who do so," said one Alberta priest. In Nova Scotia, one priest said 75 percent of the marriages he performs are for common-law couples; a Northwest Territories priest put the figure at 100 percent. The national average, Christenson estimates, is 60 percent.

Statistics Canada says that in 1996, one Canadian couple in seven was living in common-law, compared with about one in nine in 1991. In Quebec, one couple in four did without the marriage certificate in 1996 (Joe-Ann Macdonald, 1998, April 23).

Intermarriage

The issue of intermarriage is now significant in Canada due to increasing numbers of immigrants from various cultures who are interacting with each other. The increase of immigration in 1960s based on the point system rather than national origins have brought to Canada families of professionals who are urban oriented. These people are tolerant towards intermarriage compared to the less educated working class people. The favourable attitude towards intermarriages have become more acceptable in the last 15 years compared to earlier periods. The 1981 census of Canada for the first time acknowledged the growing number of ethnic intermarriages by allowing individuals to specify more than one ethnic origin, and nearly one Canadian in ten indicated multiple origins (Statistics Canada, 1983).

"In popular usage, intermarriage represents at the minimum, the linkage of two people with different cultural and behavioral norms and backgrounds grounded or based on religious, racial or ethnic differences. Intermarriage has implications not only for the couple themselves but also impacts on the linkages of larger family and lineage groups. The consequences of the marriage affects future generations as well as present and past generations. The understanding of the nature and dynamics of intermarriage provides insights into the understanding of religion, and ethnic group relationships as they separate both within and between societies" (Mark Hutter, 1990, pp. 143–144).

How far ethnic identity can be maintained is a concern in intermarriages for the couples and the children who are the product of the mixed cultures. In a study done in Winnipeg, "the impact of intermarriage on ethnic identity of the adult offspring of such marriages has furnished evidence consistent with the proposition that mixed parentage tends to be associated with lower levels of both internal and external dimensions of ethnic identity" (Jay Goldstein and Alexander Segall, 1985, pp. 60–71).

According to the interesting analysis of intermarriage by Cerroni-Long, "People can only be tempted to intermarry if potential partners from different religions, racial and ethnic groups are available. But what do we really mean by 'available'? Evidently this is a crucial point and a complex one. Generally speaking we can distinguish three kinds of availability: physical, actual and psychological. Physical availability refers to the sex ratio and numerical size of groups. Actual availability refers to the fact that for people to become potential marital partners they have to be in situations that allow or favour this potentiality. Finally, psychological availability, refers to the fact that intermarriage between two members of endogamous groups is directly proportional to the ratio of 'compatibility' between the groups."

The most obvious rationalization is, of course, provided by real exceptional circumstances. Among these the most typical is created by residence abroad in situations in which the only potential marital partners available are to be found outside one's immediate group and the ties with this group are themselves felt to be looser than normal. The whole "war brides" phenomenon is created by a situation of this kind; and of course, this can also be the case when the sex ratio of an immigrant group is totally imbalanced.

One more situation in which the prescriptive value of the endogamous norm is downplayed or even outright disregarded can happen when an individual willingly rescinds or alternates the ties with his/her primary group of affiliation. This most typically takes place when, because of conversion or loss of faith, a person parts with his/her original religious community. It can also be observed when a minority group is in an advanced stage of acculturation and assimilation. At this stage the group as a whole still maintains its endogamous norm but some individuals, in increasingly identifying with the majority group and in accepting their values, end up considering intermarriage as a most desirable strategy leading to quicker integration. Of course, as said before, if the process of assimilation of the group as a whole proceeds successfully it could well happen that in the long run the endogamous norm is abandoned in *toto*" (E. L. Cerroni-Long, 1985, pp. 25–46).

According to a fairly recent study in Canada, the interreligious marriage pattern was similar for most of the groups. In most cases, the highest proportion of those who outmarried tended to marry into the largest religious groups: Anglicans, Roman Catholics, and the United Church. Religious intermarriage continues to be the highest (60+ percent) among Jews, followed in rank order by non-Christians, Pentecostals and Mennonites (Larsen & Munro, 1990, pp. 239–250).

One of the communities most concerned about intermarriages are people of the Jewish faith. An observer at the Canadian Jewish Congress in 1989 expressed his concern "citing an intermarriage rate of 40 percent, he believes that assimilation of Jews in Canada is a more pressing concern than the situation in Israel or the State of Soviet Jewry" (John Allemang, 1989). In the United States, "Virtually none of the immigrant generation intermarried, but 10 percent of their children did, and so did almost 18 percent of their grandchildren. Exposure to higher education pushed rates up even more: 37 percent of college graduates in that third generation intermarried. These findings, coming at a time when other data indicated a falling Jewish birthrate, evoked great concern among Jewish leaders" (The William Petschek National Jewish Family Center, 1986).

In a recent study of Jewish intermarriage in the Denver area some interesting conclusions emerged. "The intermarriage rate here may not be the highest among World Jewry but in an estimated one- to two-thirds of all marriages involving an American Jew the partner is a non-Jew. Modern Jewish women are more likely to intermarry than their mothers were but they are nearly as likely to raise their children Jewish.

It may be that due to the increased Jewish educational opportunities available to women, they are now better prepared to raise Jewish children although the father is not a Jew. Intermarriage appears to be a function of the changing role of Jews in the American social structure. Despite barriers erected by the parts of the Jewish community designed to exclude non-Jewish spouses from participating in religious and communal activities, there is outreach to the mixed married and many are responding. The traditional Jewish community fears that actions taken to ease the entrance of mixed married into the community will only serve to encourage more intermarriage. Most Jews will continue to consider intermarriage an option as long as ethnic tensions are at a tolerable level and it remains acceptable to identify with one's ethnic heritage. While intermarriage does not necessarily lead to assimilation, assimilation can lead to intermarriage" (Eleanore Parelman Judd, 1990, pp. 251–265).

Intermarriage has lasting implications for the immigrants in Canada from non-European cultures. In spite of the fear of loss of ethnic and cultural identity changes are inevitable. Immigrants who came in 1960s onwards are educated as the point system favour them. Most of them are already exposed to urban oriented lifestyles prior to immigrating to Canada. Therefore, they are well disposed to accepting changes. Now, there is already a generation of youth born and brought up here and their heterosexual interactions are with people of all types of cultural backgrounds outside their own communities. While parents would like to get involved in marital choice decisions, they are at a disadvantage in a society with relatively free premarital heterosexual relations.

The parents who came as immigrants in the early sixties are faced with the reality of dealing with twenty year old sons and daughters who want to associate freely with the opposite sex. For example, for South Asians, there are not sufficient numbers of people in their communities to develop heterosexual friendships. It is inevitable that quite a few of them have friends from other ethnic groups and some of them wish to get married. Some of the parents are accepting the seriousness of these relationships leading to inter-ethnic marriages. Those parents who are keen to get their children to marry within the communities try to place advertisements in matrimonial columns in ethnic newspapers. On the whole, time is not on the side of these reluctant parents.

In a thought-provoking and well written article, the conflicts between immigrants and their children were discussed. "Most parents try to provide an antidote by forcing their kids to adopt what they consider 'Indian' culture. The children are torn between their parents and their friends, and since the desire for peer approval is so strong, they rebel when forced to adopt values they hold in scorn" (Badrinath Krishna Rao, 1991, May 7, p. A17).

Sometimes one finds rather strong reactions among the South Asian youth in Canada regarding the question of arranged marriage. A rebellious young Canadian born girl, who married a non-Indian despite her parents' objections, remarked that, "By the time my sister and I were ready to go out we would never have permitted our parents to arrange a marriage. My brother let himself be bribed into an arranged marriage. He is dumb enough for that" (Joy Inglis & Michael M. Ames, 1967).

The present author made an interesting observation regarding South Asian immigrant families in Australia. Among the number of families familiar to the author all their grown up children married non-South Asians who are of European descent. Most of them are their classmates. This seems to be partly as a result of a lack of available partners in their own community which encourage the South Asian youth to interact frequently with non-South Asians. To a lesser extent, this is true in Canada as well.

In a major study undertaken in Great Britain of 5140 married couples, 1% were intermarried. The female spouses in most intermarriages were white (62%). There was a tendency for intermarried couples to be living in urban areas, to be younger, to be more recently married and to have achieved a higher level of education than their intra ethnically married counterparts (Gary A. Cretser, 1990, pp. 227–238). It is likely that intermarriages in Canada will follow a similar pattern.

Marital Expectations

The expectations in marriage can vary depending on the attitudes of individuals who enter into marital relationship. In a society like Canada where free choice is the norm for most people, the level of expectations in marriage determine the success of the marriage. If a person has high unrealistic expectations and if these don't work out, he or she is not satisfied with the relationship. On the other hand those with low expectations have greater possibility of satisfaction. In most successful marriages, people have realistic expectations based on experience of interacting with many individuals which help them to develop certain level of maturity.

One way of looking at expectations in marriage is to compare modern marriages to traditional arranged marriages which has meaning for many of immigrants in Canada who are from non-western societies. A question that is often asked by people who have accepted self-choice as the normal form of mate selection is about the adjustment process in arranged marriages, since the couple are in a sense strangers compared to modern urban couples. The assumption is that if a young man and woman know each other in a dating situation for at least one year, the adjustment is easy. However, in actual practice, when the two meet each other for several hours a day, they are primarily concerned about close emotional ties. Even for those who tried living together before marriage, the emotional aspect of their relationship became dominant. However, once they formalize their relationship in marriage, and live in the same residence, life moves gradually away from the early romantic situation. One has to face many practical aspects of life like reasonable efficiency of household management with the limited financial resources and allied responsibilities.

The difference between self-choice marriages and arranged marriages is the relative emphasis of expectations in marriage. In self-choice marriages, however much one might claim that love that precedes marriage in modern urban industrial society is not abstract love but is influenced by practical considerations of compatibility, the young couple do tend to idealize each other to a great extent. This is very important to maintain their emotional ties. Therefore, when they get married, they have very high expectations of each other. But when they start living together facing the many issues of daily life in a family, problems might arise. These problems can precipitate some amount of disillusionment which is inevitable because both have the maximum of expectations of each other, which are unlikely to be realized in daily life. The majority of the couples are able to overcome the transition from the ideal to the practical without much strain because they have adequate, mature personalities enabling them to make adjustments in the early stages of married life. On the other hand, there are many who are not able to make proper adjustments. This is the beginning of serious strain in their relationships. At times, the strain builds up and reaches a point at which it is impossible to make adequate adjustments.

During these periods of strain, the young couples themselves are primarily responsible for making adjustments without seeking advice from parents, kin and friends. The very nature of self-choice implies a high value on individuality in which the relationship between the parents, siblings, and friends is one of mutual respect for each others' individuality. It is not easy to accept advice at the first sign of trouble, and also it is difficult for others to initiate help without being accused of some kind of interference. In addition to these problems, the survival of self-choice marriages depends to a most significant degree on the continuation of love and common interests. Once these conditions are weakened, the couple will seriously consider the possibility of separation or divorce. This follows the logic of structural-functionalists.

249

In modern urban industrial society like Canada in which marriage is more a civil contract than a sacrament, divorce is accepted as an alternative to unhappy marriages. Therefore, the social stigma against divorce is less and less relevant, especially in view of the tendency toward liberalizing divorce laws. Religion in western societies is fighting a losing battle against liberalizing of divorce laws.

In arranged marriages, the young men and women are married only after the parents and close relatives have made adequate enquiries about their compatibility of each other and also in relation to the two families. In the absence of emotional commitments, it is possible for the parents and close kin to make an objective appraisal of the qualities of the young men and women and they are informed of each others' qualities. At the time of marriage, they have only the minimum of expectation but it is no exaggeration to claim that in arranged marriages most of the couples get much more than the minimum from the marriage. One also has to consider the fact that these young people do not meet a number of people before getting married. They, therefore, become less critical of each other. In modern self-choice marriages the fact that young people have had the opportunity to meet many of the opposite sex has not necessarily made these marriages more successful. The saying that in self-choice marriages you fall in love and then get married while in arranged marriages you get married and then fall in love, seems significant. In arranged marriages the strengthening of the relationships between the couples with love, in addition to the objective criteria of compatibility, contributes to maximum possible adjustments.

In addition, the sacramental nature of marriage is still dominant in cultures in which the arranged marriage continues to exist. This means that marriage is viewed as a permanent tie, and very little consideration is given to the possibility of separation. Therefore, the couple develops a greater sense of tolerance with give-and-take. After all, no two people can be ideally compatible and, therefore, the greater one's willingness to see the other person's point of view, the more chance there will be significant chance of success of such a marriage. If there are serious problems in a marriage, other family members will do all they can to help solve them. This is not considered interference because the good relationship between the two families is most important, and, therefore, those people who have taken an interest in arranging the marriage are willing to help the couple in their emotional and financial difficulties. This discussion about the adjustment in arranged marriages is not an attempt to claim that all such marriages are successful. In the past, when family interests were more important than those of the individuals who were getting married, it was difficult to assess the success of such marriages. However, in modern arranged marriages, the increasing possibility of expressing individual wishes has weakened the extreme authoritarianism of the families. On the other hand, the role of the family members in providing advice and help continues to be highly valued. This type of arranged marriage definitely contributes a lot to marital happiness and stability (G. Kurian, 1975, pp. 71–75).

"Attendance at religious services can influence attitudes, which in turn have an impact on behaviour. Weekly attenders tend to be more forgiving of marital problems and less likely to cite these problems as a valid reason for ending a relationship. Religious people also hold more traditional family values, placing greater importance on children and the family and on the nurturing role of women within the family. In addition, religious people

250

tend to support having happier, less stressful lives and happier relationships, with their partners" (Warren Clark, 1998).

Marital Roles and Conjugal Power

In the Canadian society, one expects that men and women enter into the role of spouses with some knowledge of marital roles. Sometimes, it is surprising to find that people have no clear idea of their roles in a culture moving away from tradition to modernity. The spouses need to have some basic understanding between marital role expectations and personality needs. As experience in marriage increases, role adjustment changes depending on the circumstances of reactions between them and in relation to others. For example, the initial excitement of managing the household for the wife, might turn out to be routine and not all that interesting. Socialization process in the family can influence the future marital roles.

"An important quality of role playing is the ability to take the role of the other so as to understand and predict the other's behaviour and to relate it to one's own behaviour — in short, having one's behaviour influenced in part by the desires of the significant other" (Bell, 1979, p. 233). Some frustration is inevitable in trying to reach the role expectations which can be a likely experience in a great number of individuals. However, this does not necessarily mean that such marriages are unsatisfactory. Robert Bell has suggested some general theoretical criteria of successful marriages:

1. Satisfaction is achieved in one's marriage role and that of the mate.
2. Each partner in the marriage has some opportunity to express his own personality.
3. Each marriage partner is an important focus of affection for the other.
4. Each partner derives some pleasures and satisfactions from the marriage role relationship. While these may not be universal, these patterns can be considered ingredients for successful marriage (Robert Bell, 1979, pp. 234–238).

The roles can be traditional at one extreme and fully egalitarian at the other end. Most of the traditional roles involve inflexible division of labour based on sex differences with the man as the bread earner and playing only a minimal role in household management and the woman shouldering most household chores and childrearing responsibilities. Ideally speaking, egalitarianism is based on sex-role equality. Canada has no typical family form, but have variations in ethnic, religious and regional differences. "Most attitudinal sex-role studies demonstrate a clear trend toward more equalitarian perception of gender roles" (Nancy Mandell, 1989, pp. 239–243).

One of the most important conditions for successful marital adjustment is the exercise of conjugal power. This subject has interested many scholars. One of the significant contributors to the study of marital power is the Canadian Sociologist, Hyman Rodman. The following are some aspects of his ideas. A finding that is common to many studies of marital power is that the husband's status is positively associated with the husband's power. Several studies have examined marital power in relation to the wife's working status. The findings in most of these studies indicate that working wives have more marital power than non-working wives. When wives work, their husbands are more likely to do more of the housework; although this may be by and large true, some men are still not willing to help in the house. One interesting finding with regard to change of conjugal power is a study done in Greece and Yugoslavia. Although most of the data show a positive correlation between the husband's status and the husband's power, the data for Greece and Yugoslavia show a negative correlation. From the perspective of the developed societies education, income, and occupational status are resources, and the comparative amount of such resources possessed by husband and wife are important in determining the distribution of power. But the reversal of the relationships for the Greek and Yugoslavian data forces one to reconsider the view of education, income and occupation. This is particularly true of education. The more highly educated the Greek man, the likelier he is to hold attitudes that would lead to a more egalitarian status for his wife (Saffilios-Rothschild, 1967).

Interestingly, it is equally true of many immigrants in Canada from traditional cultures. To the extent that it operates to place the man in a patriarchal society in closer touch with equalitarian norms, it decreases his marital power (Hyman, Rodman, 1972, pp. 50–69).

It is of special significance to look at the husband's participation in the household duties. In all traditional cultures there is a clear division of labour of men and women. Men are not expected to participate in household duties and even women are quite willing to support this role. One might hope that in economically developed countries where egalitarian ideology is well entrenched, men will do their equal share of household chores. Not much changes have taken place. "Men are claiming credits for more housework than their mates say they actually do," says *Homemaker's Magazine* editor Jane Gale. According to research conducted for her magazine, Gale said "men report greater participation in household tasks than women attribute to them" (Bob Bragg, 1984).

A study in Calgary of 562 dual earning and dual career couples found that irrespective of wives working outside the home, and even if they had children, the men's contribution to housework does not differ significantly. Further, as expected, the father's proportionate share is consistently less than the mother's in both comparison groups. "This pattern persists on weekends: though fathers increase their help with housework, mothers increase their share of housework even more" (Eugen Lupri, 1988, p. 288). The same pattern of unfairness is reported in American studies. Arlie Hochschild a sociologist at the University of California, Berkeley found that wives typically come home from work to another shift doing 75% of the household tasks. "Men are trying to have it both ways" she claims. "They're trying to have their wives' salaries and still have the traditional roles at home" (Claudia, Wallis, 1989). In a report released called Women and the Labour Force, Stats Canada reported that "In addition to their work in the labour force, married women continue to be responsible for child care and household work," said the report's authors, Patricia Connelly and Martha MacDonald of St. Mary's University in Halifax (Vivian Smith, 1990).

The conflicting arguments about the role within the family and outside in the society continues without clear answers. Women spend most of their time in upaid work at home while men only play a minimal role. "Using Statistics Canada's 30-hour definition for full-time work, most Canadian women work part-time in the labour force and full-time unpaid. There is little status and less security in homemaking, and what security there is from the Canada pension plan and old-age security is shrinking fast. The more time women spend at home, the more likely they will end their lives in poverty" (Paula Brook, 1997).

Canadians are deeply split about whether women should be staying at home or working outside the home, according to Statistics Canada Survey. "On the one hand, the notion appears to embrace the idea that women have a rightful place in the work force. A commanding majority of Canadians even believe that women have a duty to contribute to the household income. The results of the survey are so ambivalent that they suggest Canadians no longer know what the social norms are, even as a majority of women take part in the paid workforce," said Kerry Daly, a Sociologist who is acting Chairman of the Department of Family Studies at the University of Guelph in Ontario.

The Statistics Canada Survey was based on interviews with 11,000 Canadians in 1995 making it a most comprehensive study. The survey found that 68 percent of men and 73 percent of women agreed or strongly agreed that both men and women ought to contribute household income.

Another scholar who has made comments about the survey is Ellen Gee, Sociologist at Simon Fraser University in Burnaby, B.C. The results paint the picture of a nation caught in denial and even fear. "It isn't even ambivalence, it's stronger," she said. "It's uncertainty about women's roles and to some degree men's roles. We really don't know what we're doing" (Alanna Mitchell, 1998, September 17).

Communication

Successful marriages and good communication go hand in hand. Many scholars agree on the special significance of effective communication in marriage. This is something which has to develop before marriage in the dating period. Premarital courses now put emphasis on the development of communication skills. One of the most successful organizations providing premarital counselling is the Pastoral Institute in Calgary. This is an interdenominational organization started by United Church in 1962. Dr. Rev. Ed Mullen was instrumental in the establishment of the Institute. They have individual as well as group sessions. The real test of their counselling is the success of the marriage of people who received counselling. Dr. Mullen has some convincing arguments that the tests conducted by the Institute can find people suitable partners. "I guess we have married about 800 people" estimates Mullen, "and I suppose we have introduced about 6000." Not only that, "but the solid figures we have are that one in 22 marriages divorce," says Mullen, "compared to a one-in-2.7 norm for Alberta" (Barton Jacques, 1985).

After marriage, good communication plays a crucial role in success of marriage. There are two aspects of communication which are verbal and non-verbal. It is interesting to note that there is no clear agreement by scholars about the impact of verbal communication on marital quality. However, "research into the non-verbal behaviour of married partners suggests that non-verbal behavior may be more important in predicting marital distress than is verbal behaviour. One interpretation of this research is that non-verbal communication tends to carry more emotional content than does verbal communication" (James White, 1989, p. 205).

The most frustrating thing is wanting to discuss something important, only to find that your mate refuses your point of view. Most important, keep in mind that it is unrealistic to expect either partner to change his or her habits completely to suit the other. "Whatever you do, don't forget to maintain a good sense of humor" (Amy H. Bergen, 1989).

An essential aspect of good communication is honesty. This helps to clarify feelings, avoid misunderstandings, and resentments. Another aspect of marital communication is sexual communication. "Some couples, who report they communicate well in other areas of their lives, may find talking about sex troublesome" (Laswell, 1991, p. 204). There is also no such thing as conflict-free marriage and if anyone claims otherwise, they are either lying or do not really have any individuality. Fortunately, most people can resolve problems in a mature manner of give and take. Another important aspect which can be part of effective communication is insight which helps to smooth out the relationship. "By anticipating more quickly and more accurately, he or she may be able to influence the partner. That power may be used to help both partners and the relationship or it may be used to profit the one partner at the expense of the other" (Leslie & Korman, 1989, pp. 406–407). Finally, "people who marry for the right reasons combine romantic love, attraction and emotional maturity in their relationships" (Barbara Somerville, 1987).

Marital Satisfaction

Marital satisfaction is a combination of many factors. Some of them are already discussed in marital expectations, marital roles, conjugal power and communication. However, there are still other factors as well.

One of the problems influencing marital satisfaction is the problem of shift work. When both spouses are working, they have very little time to relax. Sometimes they are in different shifts and so hardly ever meet each other leisurely. The evenings at home are demanding with cooking, cleaning and care of the children, which is taken for granted as the female's duties.

In a major study in the United States involving 1668 married women it was found that shift work affects marital quality negatively. "Most notably, shift work is associated with significantly lower marital happiness. One reason shift work reduces marital happiness is because it is less satisfying." The study found that while the negative effect of shift work is small, "The negative effects of shift work are real rather than a sampling artifact" (Lynn White & Bruce Keith, 1990, pp. 453–462).

If both spouses have identical interests, especially when they are both educated, there is a mutual understanding of each other. This is generally true about those who are in professions like teaching, medicine, business partnerships, etc. However, if a woman has no direct economic contribution outside the family, she is frustrated when she is educated. A less educated wife in comparison to the husband becomes alienated and has to put up with the husband's impatience.

In the case of South Asian immigrants, the opposite situation occurs when professionally qualified women marry men with inferior qualifications, which are usually arranged by parents in India. The classical example is provided by persons of the medical profession such as laboratory technicians, nurses and doctors. While in India many of them marry men of well known families such as businessmen and land holders. These husbands have no technical education and are incapable of getting a job of comparable status to that of their wives. Some of these men end up in jobs of sales attendants in a store or even as unskilled workers in a factory.

The conflict arises because he asserts himself as the manager of his wife's earnings and tries to be the lord of the household while not sharing her after-job household chores. The woman gradually realizes that she is the real bread winner and she has higher status than her husband. So she begins to assert her strength and freedom. After a period of intensive conflict either the husband yields to his wife, or as in a few cases, both break up the relationship. Another problem is stress caused by long distance travel in traffic to places of work. When mothers come home they are busy with household work and care of children leaving little time for leisure (A.K.B. Pilai, 1984).

One of the ingredients of successful adjustment is proper management of finances, sharing expenses, keeping records and communicating with each other about proper use of resources. "As with sexual adjustment, the causes of conflict over finances are often inseparable from the effects. As well, effective communication is very important in dealing with such conflict" (Emily M. Nett, 1988, p. 242).

In a Canadian study, it was indicated that men and women assess their marriages differently "Regardless of family life-cycle stage, women tend to be more satisfied with the extent to which their sexual needs are met, while there is greater male satisfaction with spouse's help at home, spouse's time with the children and friendship" (Darla Rhyne, 1982, p. 953). In a recent study it was noted that, "both men and women with larger families report higher levels of distress. Moreover, men indicate experiencing greater role conflict and time pressure, parental stress, marital stress, and physical distress associated with parenting more children" (Maureen G. Guelzow, Gloria W. Bird and Elizabeth H. Koball, 1991, pp. 151–164). "Although many men are more involved in child rearing than fathers were in the past, we are a long way from a situation where shared family and domestic responsibilities is the norm" (S. J. Wilson, 1991, p. 61).

According to a Calgary study of marital satisfaction in the life cycle, it was found that satisfaction declines from the beginning of the marriage until the grown up children leave the parents and interestingly, there is a significant increase in marital satisfaction to the point of contributing to considerable improvement in the marital relationship (E. Lupri & J. Frideres, 1981, pp. 283–306).

One of the interesting aspects of modern marriages is the influence of premarital cohabitation on marital stability. The general impression is that premarital cohabitation does not contribute to the quality of marriage. One of the Canadian studies indicates some positive effects of premarital cohabitation on marital stability. In a study of 10,472 married Canadians, positive effects are discussed by James M. White. His study indicated premarital cohabitation with the spouse prior to marriage has a significant positive effect even though difference between co-habitors and non-cohabitors is only 6%. With regard to marital stability the possibility of continuing marriage favours the cohabitants. He also suggests as cohabitation is increasingly accepted in society the factors that contribute to marital disruption could disappear. Finally he observes that it is difficult to make generalization based on U.S. population for the Canadian society. However, "premarital cohabitation appears to be positively associated with marital stability even when the effects of length of marriage and age at marriage have been controlled. The odds for staying married are much better for co-habitors than non-cohabitors" (James M. White, 1987, pp. 641–647).

Children

The care of Children in a modern urban family is cause of great concern. Women choose to work outside home for professional and personal satisfaction as well as men, women have to work to supplement the family income to maintain a reasonable standard of living. A number of studies in Canada as well as the United States show that over dependence of day care affects the quality of socialization of the children.

"For instance, the National Foundation for Family Research and Education (NFFRE) recently conducted a meta-analysis (the Statistical integration of large volumes of research) of 100 scientific studies examining more than 25,000 children who attended day care. The foundation found that children who attend day care for 20 or more hours per week seem at greater risk for emotional, behavioral and parental attachment problems, when compared with non-day care peers. Based on all the data, it was calculated that day-care children have an increased risk, between 16 and 20 percent, for developing such problems as anxiety disorders, aggressiveness, hyperactivity and attention deficit disorder. Based on this meta-analysis and others it seems that day care, irrespective of quality, is not an adequate substitute for full-time, or close to full-time parental care" (Adrienne Snow, 1998, August 24).

A new study of the effect of working mothers on their children has challenged the prevalent view based on various studies about the negative consequences of children spending considerable time in day care centers.

According to the results of a study of more than 6000 youngsters by Elizabeth Harvey, a psychologist at the University of Massachusetts, "I found that there was no difference between children whose mothers were not employed during the first three years. Being employed is not going to harm the children."

The work examined the children at a later age, 12 years old. This study agrees with an earlier study by David Eggebeen of Pennsylvania State University where problems of children three to four years old of working mothers have gone away by the time children were 12.

"Harvey's study suggests that the number of hours spent away from home is not as important as the quality of parenting," said Lindsay Chase-Lansdale, an associate professor of Lumar development at the University of Chicago.

There were more than 6000 children of alls in Harvey's study, most were evaluated more than once between 1986 to 1994. The youngest child was three and the oldest twelve. In comparison with children of non-working mothers, she found no statistically significant difference (Paul Recer, 1998, March 1).

Children's lives are affected by unstable family relationships. Canadians growing abandonment of marriage is such that more than a quarter of small children do not live with parents who are married, according to Statistics Canada's 1996 census. The census figures published show that 28.7 percent of children under the age of six live either with single parents or with those in common-law union.

In Quebec, where the trend toward common-law is the strongest of any province, the figure is about 45 percent. "It says something about how the institution of marriage may be in crisis, even if the institution of family is not," said Sociologist Robert Glossop of the Vanier Institute of the Family in Ottawa.

In 1996, nearly half of common-law families—47.2 percent—had children at home, up from about 41 percent in 1991. "The old pattern of common-law being the lower-middle-class, lumpen proletariat, is simply wrong," said Susan McDaniel, a Sociologist at the University of Alberta.

The number of children with single parents is nearly 1.8 million. According to Statistics Canada, a large proportion of the parents have never married, although some have been in common-law unions, which are about one fourth of the total (Alanna Mitchell, 1997, October 15).

Not all news is an indication of doom and gloom. The Province of Quebec is an exception. At a time when the Federal Government has abandoned its promise of a national child-care program and provinces are cutting subsidies to day-care centres, the Quebec government is launching a European-style social program that rewards parents handsomely for taking leaves to care for their babies and putting in place the closest thing to universal child care.

Not only is the Quebec government taking a stab at reversing the fortunes of children growing up poor, but in a rare twist in this era of fiscal prudence, it is leaving money in the pockets of middle-class parents who are struggling to balance work and family. "We are investing more money in young children because we know if we have success in reducing poverty, we will have students with better results at school, and we will have citizens who are more responsible," said Pauline Marois, the popular Education Minister (Margaret Philip, 1997, June 17).

Normal assumption in society is that parents have long-term effect on the personality and mental health of children. This age-long idea was challenged by Canadian author Judith Harris. According to her, "I have looked long and hard at the evidence, and the conclusion I came to is that parents have no long-term effects on the personality or intelligence or mental health of their children," Harris told her audience, assaulting a nearly universally held belief about families and human development. She went on to explain her theory that the greatest influence on kids aside from the often-underestimated contribution of heredity, is their peer groups—an idea elaborated on in her jarring new book, *The Nature Assumption: Why Children Turn Out the Way They Do* (Paula Span, 1998, November 25).

According to a report by Statistics Canada, the father's type of income, more than the dollar amount, had a major influence on the incomes children eventually earned as young adults. "In general, sons raised by low-income fathers are less likely to move into the upper half of the income distribution, more likely to remain in the bottom half, and most likely to occupy the same positions as their fathers," the study concludes. Daughters, it says, are

257

also most likely to remain in the low income group, and less likely to reach the top 20 percent. Other findings include: the type of neighbourhood children live in and its median income affect future earnings (Gary Abbate, 1998, November 6).

"Parents looking forward to the tranquillity of an empty nest may have to wait longer than they expected, because more young adults are delaying the move from home or returning after a brief flight," Statistics Canada says.

Monica Boyd, co-author of the report, said that young people are finding the transition to work from school difficult. She said that the living arrangement often is untroubled, but can present problems when parents attempt to impose strict rules or when sons or daughters abuse their parents' generosity.

Young people are also marrying and setting up their own households at a later age. The average age of a woman marrying for the first time was 27 in 1996, up from 24 in 1981, while the average age of a male marrying for the first time rose to 29 from 26.

Adult children, among some of the immigrant population, tend to stay at home. While North American and Northern European young adults leave home early, in other cultures unmarried young adults, especially women, stay in the family home.

Ms. Boyd found in another study that in 1991, 88.5 percent of unmarried women of Greek origin between 20 and 34 lived with their parents. Italians, Portuguese, South Asians, and Chinese all tended to live at the family home, while people of British and French extraction were less likely to do so (Shawn McCarty, 1999, March 12).

Another important concern with regard to children is the adoption of aboriginal children by white families. In most cases, this has not worked out well for the children in spite of the best intentions of those who adopted them.

Many provinces have thrown legal and bureaucratic hurdles in the path of couples wanting to adopt children outside their culture. Driving the change is the fact that so many children raised in white homes run into serious problems. Despite being loved and well-cared for, they have what appears to be a cultural identity crisis when they reach their teens. They turn to alcohol, drugs and crime, rejecting their bewildered adoptive parents—including the adopted son, Michel, of Prime Minister Jean Chertian and his wife Aline, who, in spite of all the advantages, was in and out of prison on assault convictions.

The native children feel that they are not given equal treatment compared to white children, according to comments from them in various studies. In an important study in 1993, conducted by Christopher Bagley, former Professor of Social Work at the University of Calgary, he found that "native child adoptions are significantly more likely than any other parenting situation to involve problems and difficulties." Nearly half of these adopted children leave the parents by age 17.

These children also have poor self-esteem and among them are reported many acts of self-harm including attempted suicides. The report concluded that, "non-adopted native adolescents had adjustment profiles that were not significantly different from those of non-adopted whites" (Margaret Philip, 1999, February 23).

Crisis in the Family

Everyone expects some amount of tension in family life. However, it is important to know about the high level of violence that is part of a significant number of families. Violence in the family is not something new. In almost all societies, male dominance in economic and physical spheres encourages intolerance. In many cases, it may be only at verbal level, but in a large number of cases it is physical. Wife and children are not in a position to prevent it due to their total dependence.

The discussion about family violence was not considered important in family sociology till recent times. For example, the *Journal of Marriage and the Family* the most important publication in family sociology only published articles in the early 1970s. Now there are a number of well known sociologists actively involved in the study of family violence. Some of them are Richard J. Gelles, Murray Strauss and Suzanne Steinmetz. The respect for privacy of the family and also assumption that family is a safe haven have all contributed to the lack of interest in the study of family violence.

Family violence affects every member in the family, and includes wife assault, elderly abuse and sexual abuse of children. Violence is not limited to one social class. "When surveyed under circumstances guaranteeing anonymity, Canadian men aged 18 and over reported that they had committed significant amounts of violence against their partners. While abuse of a female partner was reported by men in all income groups, it was more common among those with low incomes" (Eugen Lupri, 1990, Pp. 170–172).

Wife assault is more than an isolated event. "Half the incidents involved women who were assaulted more than once. The risk of assault was highest for women who were separated" (Holly Johnson, 1990, Pp. 173–176). The violence almost always happens at home. "Women are hit in the head and the face, assaulted with weapons such as stove burner coils, broken bottles, knives and guns. Assaults result in bruises, broken bones, internal injuries and even death" (Janice Drakich and Connie Guberman, 1988, P. 207).

Immigrant wives who are not familiar with North American culture are abused by their husbands who exploit them and use their economic power. For example, Naomi came to Canada from Portugal 10 years ago with her husband and two children. They came to build a better life, but almost immediately her husband began to beat her. Naomi is not alone. She is just one of the hundreds of thousands of women who are victims of violence. According to a 1993 Statistics Canada study, one of four women in Canada is assaulted by a spouse or partner. Every year in Canada, about 78 women are killed by abusive husbands or lovers.

For immigrant or refugee women, the trauma of such violence is exacerbated by language barriers, isolation, lack of knowledge about their legal rights, or lack of information about where to seek help. There is a deep fear of being sent away from Canada, says Rita Mclean, a counsellor at the Jamican Canadian Association which runs a support group for battered women. "They are told by the men they can be deported. The man, of course, has no right to send them home, but some of the women don't know better," she said. What's more, many of these women are wrestling with cultural attitudes about abuse that are intrinsic to their homeland, Mclean says.

In the South Asian community, financial constraints keep many abused women from leaving, says Giselle De Souza, a social worker who counsels battered women at a centre in Toronto. They are dependent on their husbands and they are worried because they don't have work skills or Canadian experience (Debra Black, 1998, December 26).

Physical and sexual abuse of children is far more common than one expects. "The violence of incestuous assault can no longer be viewed as a problem that involves only a few particularly disturbed offenders. It reveals an immense trouble in the contemporary family" (Janice Drakich and Connie Guberman, 1988, P. 213). There is so much media reporting of sexual violence making Canadians aware of the serious problem. In addition to family related sexual abuse, there are numerous reports of teachers accused of sexual abuse. A number of them including some religious leaders were charged in court and some were punished in 1991.

Another problem with which Canadians are increasingly concerned is elderly abuse. "More than 100,000 elderly people, many of them women over 75, are subjected to physical, psychological and financial abuse each year in Canada. And those to blame are not necessarily employees of homes for the aged, but frequently the children of those abused" (Zuhair Kashmeri, 1986, March 23).

There are various types of elderly abuse. "It may include financial exploitation, where pension cheques or other monies are taken; physical injury including beatings or restraints; threats, ridicule, insults, humiliation, and imposed isolation (both physical and social); or a forced change in living arrangements" (Janice Drakich and Connie Guberman, 1988, P. 215).

At present, the law enforcement officials are expected to take action in the cases of all types of family violence, which hopefully may be a deterrent reducing the incidence of the serious problems facing many people.

Another issue which threatens family stability is marriage breakdown. There is a decline in the number of marriages and an increase in divorces. The average proportion of life spent married differs for men and women. Men expect to be married close to half (48%) of their lives, compared with 43% for women (Owen Adams and Dhruva Nagnur, 1990, p. 144). This discrepancy is largely due to the fact that women tend to outlive men.

The Divorce Act of Canada of 1968 granted divorce for marital offense or marriage breakdown. The concept of "no-fault" divorce gradually emerged since marriage breakdown was recognized. "The most recent legislation, the Divorce Act of 1985, was followed by a sharp increase in the divorce rate, which reversed a three-year downward trend" (Owen Adams, 1990, p. 146).

"The Divorce Act of 1985 is a social and legal response to changing trends in Canadian Society. It shows a secularized interpretation of marriage and divorce, conscious of individual and human rights" (John F. Peters, 1988, p. 153). "The number of divorces in Newfoundland, Manitoba and Prince Edward Island rose substantially between 1986 and 1987, Statistics Canada reported yesterday. Alberta was the only province that saw a decrease" (Canadian Press, 1989, Oct. 7).

According to Professor T. R. Balakrishnan a well known Sociologist and Demographer at the University of Western Ontario, marriage breakdown by itself is not necessarily a bad thing. He said, "In one sense it may be good. People are not prepared to stay in a marriage that's not so good...what is now happening is that the good marriages stay intact" (Deborah Wilson, 1986, July 21). One also should consider the fact many of the divorced also remarry. "Although divorce is more frequent than in the past, many divorced people remarry. In 1985, for example, at least one partner in 27% of all marriages was divorced" (Owen Adams and Dhruva Nagnur, 1990, P. 144). Most people are pessimistic about the success of remarriages. "However, the many people who remarry is evidence that they are not against the institution of marriage, but rather than their first was not a good match" (John F. Peters, 1988, P. 160).

Changing Patterns in Canadian Family

Already there are enough signs of the decline in legal marriages with common-law relationships and also the preference to stay single. Due to the desire to succeed in their chosen careers, many postpone their marriages which also encourages non-marital cohabitation. "As the forces of modernization and post industrialization intensify, individualism continues to remain a dominant value in our culture. Thus, further gains in alternative sexual unions and other lifestyles incompatible with long-term commitments to married life will likely continue in the future" (Frank Travato, 1988, pp. 507–521).

Canadian families are also shrinking in size. "In 1986, 84% of Canadians lived in families, this was down from 85% in 1981. Over the 1981–1986 period, the number of lone-parent and common-law unions increased much faster than traditional husband-wife families. The average size of Canadian families is falling. In 1986, there were an average of 3.1 people in each family, down from 3.3 in 1981." (Mary Sue Devereaux, 1990, pp. 135–137).

Canadians also tend to marry late. "In 1986, the average age of first marriage was 28 years for men and 26 years for women. In addition, a growing proportion of Canadians never marry. Overall, the annual number of marriages fell from 200,000 in 1972 to 176,000 in 1986" (Owen Adams & Dhruva Nagnur, 1990, pp. 142–145).

In addition to the fact that Canadians marry late, many women bear their first child later in life. "Almost 25 percent of Canadian babies born in 1982 to women over 30 were first born children,—making this the highest rate of older new parents Canada has ever had," a Statistics Canada Study says. Large families have almost disappeared, and most couples are limiting their families to two children" (Dorothy Lipevenko, 1984, July 12). Along with these bleak statistics, there is increasing unwillingness of Canadians to have large families. "Most Canadians believe there aren't enough people in the country but few are willing to have more children—even if they are paid to do so, a national poll says" (Joan Bryden, 1988, June 4).

Another factor which has direct impact on Canadian families is that "about three-quarter of lone parents in Canada in 1984 were female, according to a new Statistics Canada survey" (Southam News, 1986, Dec. 5).

Some interesting figures regarding economic well being of Canadian families are also important. "The top one percent of Canadian families had an average income of $143,061 in 1980 or $212,000 in today's dollars, five times the national average, according to a

Statistics Canada study conducted last year. And while nearly 50 percent of the income of the country's 63,250 highest-income families came from self-employment and investment, a third of the families would not have been in the highest income bracket had the wife not worked" (Canadian Press, 1986, July 9).

Families continue to improve their standard of living according to Statistics Canada. "Average family incomes in Canada exceeded $50,000 for the first time ever in 1989 as families continued to make up ground lost in the early 1980s (Alan Freeman, 1990, Nov. 30).

On the other hand, most Canadians are not able to keep up with inflation. According to Terrance Hunsley, Executive Director of the Canadian Council of Social Development. "If we were to rank all Canadian families by income and then divide them into five equal layers, we would find most families—80 percent, in fact—did not keep up with inflation between 1981 and 1985" (Thomas M. Hunsley, 1987, Feb. 6). This problem continues even in later years. According to Alan Mirabelli, Director of Administration and Communication for the Vanier Institute, who expressed some of his concerns, "Canadian families are earning more than they did 20 years ago, but it's now taking two parents to do so—and after taxes and inflation there's been almost no real income gain in 10 years. In a study released this month, the Institute shows that the average family income has risen to almost $50,000 from $16,000 in 1971. So the issue of women working isn't a moral issue, it's an economic issue, said Mirabelli" (Joanne Ramondt, 1991, June 5).

In view of the very high probability of instability in marriages many couples contemplate, as well as take, concrete steps to have prenuptial contracts. Later age marriages mean the potential couples individually must have accumulated considerable wealth. Some of them are entering second marriages and that also provides good reason to protect their wealth. "Although exact figures are not available, lawyers involved in the family and estate fields say that the number of couples entering into prenuptial agreements is up sharply" (March Schagol, 1986). Parents also encourage children to draw up prenuptial agreements so that spouses do not make claim on the assets. Marriage contracts make good sense to those whose previous marriage ended in divorce with attendant financial commitments. "It isn't a romantic notion, but it is a realistic one for those people" says Paul Daltrop, a Vancouver family lawyer. "It is a logical step for them." Typically, the gist of most prenuptial contracts is simple: essentially, the parties keep everything they owned before the marriage, but share everything they acquire as a couple" (*Calgary Herald*, 1990, May 17). According to Toronto lawyer Lorne Wolfson, "a majority of people sign these contracts without making a fuss," but warn that discussing the divorce before the ring slides on the finger can destroy the romance. "I'd say that 50% sign the marriage contracts and get married, 25% decide not to sign and get married anyway, while the other 25% break-up" (Michael Salter, 1988).

Another aspect of major change is the fact that for every two Canadian weddings one couple who is already married break-up their marriage per year. This is a dramatic increase and according to Statistics Canada, "in fact, the divorce level in Canada has nearly reached the U.S. level, which 20 years ago was more than twice as high as the Canadian level and 10 years ago was 50 percent higher, the federal agency said" (Sean Fine, 1990, Nov. 16).

Thus, the emerging marriage and family patterns have to make adequate adjustments for changing values and lifestyles.

It is not necessarily that more people are breaking up. Statistics Canada reports that the number of divorces, after peaking at 96,200 in 1987, fell abruptly in 1988, and has leveled off around 78,000 annually. Rather, it's that divorce has indirectly jump-started many sideline businesses in addition to the core need for lawyers.

Mediation is growing. Family Mediation Canada, which was founded in 1985, now has 12 provincial and territorial affiliates across the country. And a January article in the *Boston Globe* cited that a statewide Massachusetts organization for mediators, founded in 1982, now has 165 members (Ka-Ching, 1999, January 28, page A 19).

Unfortunately, children are paying the high price for family instability. Almost 10 years after Judith Wallerstein and Sandra Blakeslee published their research—called Second Chances: Men, Women and Children a Decade after Divorce—their findings were supported by larger studies in the United Nations.

Some of the findings are that divorce can cause serious emotional difficulties for babies and younger children. Even in so-called friendly divorces, children can experience deep insecurity about their attachment to their parents. Most children suffer significant decline in economic circumstances along with feelings of abandonment by parents. Some suffer behavioural problems in school, with depression, poor performance and low self-esteem. When they are grown up, problems continue with depression, low life satisfaction, unhappy marriages, less education and alcoholism.

On this context it is important to note the significance of the Parliamentary Report on custody and access to children after divorce. This includes rewriting the Divorce Act to replace the term "Joint Custody" with "Shared Parenting," and is designed to reduce conflict by requiring parents to detail how they will jointly bring up the children in separate households. Giving children better rights by judges empowered to appoint a legal counsel for a child. Mandatory education for parents who can't agree on a custody arrangement which would cover co-operative parenting after divorce (Anne Mcilroy, 1998, December 9). Thus, the emerging marriage and family patterns have to make adequate adjustments for changing values and lifestyles.

References

Abbate Gay
1998   "How rich will your kids be? That depends on you—Statscan says children's future income is linked to the way parents earn money." *The Globe and Mail*, November 6, p. A-1.

Adams, Owen
1990   "Divorce Rates in Canada," *Canadian Social Trends*, Edited by Craig Mckie and Keith Thompson, Thompson Educational Publishing, Inc., Toronto, p. 146.

Adams, Owen and Dhruva Nagnar
1990   "Marrying and Divorcing: A Status Report for Canada," in *Canadian Social Trends*, Edited by Craig McKie and Kieth Thompson, Toronto, Thompson Educational Publishing, Inc., pp. 142–147.

Adams, Sharon
1999   "Twists on living common-law," *Calgary Herald*, January 6, p. C8.

Adams, Sharon and Shelley Knapp
1997   "Family Structure, Calgary, Alberta Lag Common-law Trend," *The Calgary Herald*, October 15, p. B 3.

Allemang, John
1989   "Intermarriage Directions Judaism in Canada, CJC Delegate State," Toronto, *The Globe and Mail*, May 9.

Anderson, Karen L.
1988   "Historical Perspectives on the Family," in *Family Matters* edited by Karen L. Anderson and others, Scarborough, Ontario, Nelson Canada, p. 27.

Bell, Robert R.
1979   "Marriage and Family Interaction," Fifth Edition, Homewood, Illinois Dorey Press.

Berger, Amy H.
1989   "Fatal Detraction—How a Single Flaw Can Kill A Lovely Relationship," *Calgary Herald*, Calgary, July 15.

Black, Debra
1989   "Abusive Husands trap immigrant women," *Calgary Herald*, Dec. 26, p. F98.

Bragg, Bob
1984   *Calgary Herald*, Calgary, Nov. 23.

Brook, Paula
1997   "Every mother is a working mother," *The Globe and Mail*, Oct. 25, p. D-1.

Bryden, Joan
1988   "Children Not Priority, Polls Shows," *Calgary Herald*, Calgary, June 4.

Calgary Herald
1990   Calgary, May 17.

Canadian Press
1989   "Number of Divorces in Canada Rises 11 Percent," *The Globe and Mail*, Toronto, Oct. 7.

1986   "Working Wives Are Key to High Income Families," *The Globe and Mail*, July 9.

Cerroni-Long, E. L.
1985   "Marrying Out: Socio-Cultural and Psychological Implications of Intermarriage." *Journal of Comparative Family Studies*, Spring, Vol. XVI, No. 1, pp. 25–46.

Clark, Warren
1998   Religious Observance—Marriage and Family, Statistics Canada—Catalogue
            11–008–XPE, *Canadian Social Trends—Autumn, p.7.*

Crester, Gary A.
1990   "Intermarriage between 'White' Britons and Immigrants from the New Com-
            monwealth and Pakistan," *Journal of Comparative Family Studies*, Special Is-
            sue, "Intermarriage," Summer Vol. XXI, No. 2, pp. 227–238.

Crysdale, Stewart and Christopher Beattie
1977   *Sociology Canada — An Introduction Text,* Toronto, Butterworths and Co (Can-
            ada) Ltd., Toronto, p. 112.

Devereaux, Mary Sue
1990   "Marital Status," in *Canadian Social Trends*, Edited by Craig McKie and Kieth
            Thompson, Toronto, Thompson Educational Publishing, Inc., pp. 138–141.

1990   "Changes in Living Arrangements," *Canadian Social Trends*, Edited by Craig
            Mckie and Keith Thompson, Thompson Educational Publishing, Inc., Toronto,
            pp. 135–137.

Downey, Donn
1990   "More Migrating South Than North," *The Globe and Mail*, Toronto, Sept. 20.

Drakich, Janice & Connie Guberman
1988   "Violence in the Family," *Family Matters*, Edited by Karen L. Anderson &
            Others, Butterworths Canada, Toronto, P. 207.

Ferguson, Eva
1998   "Sex Education, Teen Pregnancies," *Calgary Herald*, January 17, p. B6.

Fine, Sean
1990   "Divorce level increases dramatically, Figures approximate U.S. situation, Sta-
            tistics Canada indicates," Toronto, *The Globe and Mail*, Nov. 16.

Freeman, Alan
1990   "Family Incomes Clear $50,000," *The Globe and Mail*, Nov. 30.

Genius, Stephen,
1991   "Risky Sex," Edmonton, KEG Publishing, Box 32025, Edmonton, Alberta,
            Canada.

Goldstein, Jay and Alexander Segall
1985   *Canadian Ethnic Studies*, Vol. 17, pp. 60–71.

Guelzow Maureen, G., Gloria W. Bird and Elizabeth H. Koball
1991   "An Exploratory Path analysis of the stress process for dual-career men and
            women," *Journal of Marriage and the Family*, Feb., Vol. 53, pp. 151–164.

Hobart, Charles W.
1984   "Changing Profession and Practice of Sexual Standards: A Study of Young An-
            glophone and Francophone Canadians," *Journal of Comparative Family Studies*,
            Vol. XV, No. 2, pp. 231-255.

Hunsley, Thomas M.
1987   "Rich Get Rich and the Poor Get Poorer," *Calgary Herald*, Calgary, Feb. 6.

Hutter, Mark
1988   *The Changing Family, Comparative Perspectives,*: 2nd edition, New York, Macmillan Publishing Co.

1990   Introduction, Special Issue on Intermarriage, *Journal of Comparative Family Studies*, Summer, Vol. XXI, No. 2.

Hyman, Rodman
1972   "Marital Power and the Theory of Resources in Cultural Context," *Journal of Comparative Family Studies,* Special Issue. "Comparative Perspectives on Marriage and the Family," Edited by Eugen Lupri and Günther Lüschen, Spring, Vol. III, No. 1, pp. 50–69.

Inglis, Joy and Michael M. Ames
1967   "Conflict and Change in British Columbia Sikhs, Ideal of Family Life," Unpublished manuscript. Canadian Sociology and Anthropology Association, Ottawa, June 10–11, p. 42.

Jacques, Barton
1985   *Calgary Herald*, Calgary, June 7, P.B. 6.

Johnson, Holly
        "Wife Abuse," *Canadian Social Trends*, Edited by Craig Mckie and Keith Thompson, Thompson Educational Publishing Inc., Toronto, Pp. 173–176.

Jones, Elize F.
1986   "Teenage Pregnancy in Industrialized Countries," A study sponsored by the Allan Guttmacher Institute, New Haven & London, Yale University Press.

Judd, Eleanore Parelman
1990   "Intermarriage and the Maintenance of Religio-Ethnic Identity A Case Study: The Denver Jewish Community." *Journal of Comparative Family Studies,* Summer Special Issue, "Intermarriage," Vol. XXI, NO. 2, pp. 251–268.

Ka-Ching
1999   "The Divorce Shakedown," *The Globe and Mail,* January 28, p. A 19.

Kashmeri, Zuhair
1986   "100,000 Elderly Canadians abused a year, Panel says," *The Globe and Mail*, Toronto, March 23.

Kurian, George
1975   "Structural Changes in the Family in Kerala, India," in *Socialization and Communication in Primary Groups*, World Anthropology Series, Edited by Thomas R. Williams, The Hague, Paris, Mouton Publishers, pp. 59–79.

Larson, Lyle E. and Brenda Munro
1990   "Religious Intermarriage in Canada in the 1980s," *Journal of Comparative Family Studies*, Summer, Special Issue, "Intermarriage," Vol. XXI, No. 2, pp. 238–250.

Laswell, Marcia & Thomas Laswell
1991   *Marriage and the Family*, 3rd Edition, Wadsworth Publishing Co., Belmont, California, pp. 193–208.

Leslie, G. R. & Sheila K. Korman
1989   *Family in Social Context*, 7th Edition, New York, Oxford University Press.

Lipevenko, Dorothy
1984   "First Time Mothers Getting Older," *The Globe and Mail*, July 12.

Lupri, Eugen
1990   "Male Violence in the Home," *Canadian Social Trends*, Edited by Craig Mckie & Keith Thompson, Thompson Educational Publishing, Inc., Toronto, pp. 170–172.

1988   "Fathers in Transition," Zeitsukrift für Sozialistions Forschung und Erziehungs-Soziologie, Vol. 8, p. 288.

Lupri, Eugen & J. Frideres
1981   "The Quality of Marriage and the Passage of Time; Marital Satisfaction over the Family Cycle," *Canadian Journal of Sociology*, Vol. 6, pp. 283–306.

Macdonald, Joe-Ann
1998   "Living Together—Priests feel 'hypocritical' marrying many couples," *Calgary Herald*, April 23, p. WB8.

Mandell, Nancy
1989   "Marital Roles in Transition," *Family and Marriage, Cross-Cultural Perspectives*. Edited by K. Ishwaran, Toronto, Thompson Education Publishing Co. Toronto, pp. 239–243.

McCall, (Marnie) M. L., Joseph P. Hornick and Jean E. Wallace
1988   "The Process and Economic Consequences of Marriage Breakdown," Calgary, Canadian Research Institute for Law and the Family, July.

McCarthy, Shawn
1999   "Young Adults flock back to nest in record numbers," in *The Globe and Mail*, March 12, p. A3.

Mitchell, Alanna
1998   "Women's evolving role confuses Canadians—Results of survey suggest uncertainty over Social norms." *The Globe and Mail*, Sept. 17, pages A-1 and A-10.

Murstein, Bernard I.
1974   *Love, Sex and Marriage Through the Ages*, New York, Springer Publishing Co., p. 145.

Nett, Emily M.
1988   "Canadian Families—Past and Present," Toronto, Butterworths Canada Ltd.

Peters, John F.
1988   "Changing Perspective on Divorce," *Family Matters*, Edited by Karen L. Anderson & Others, Butterworths Canada, Toronto, p. 153.

Pillai, A. K. B.
1984   "Asian Indian Family—Psychological and Cultural Adaptation," in Conference of Family-Bicultural Socialization, Edited by B. N. Varma and Jagat-Motwani, National Federation of Asian Indian Organization in America, Washington, D.C., May.

Ram, Bali
1990   "Current Demographic Analysis, New Trends in the Family," Minister of Supplies and Services, Ottawa, Canada.

Ramondt, Joanne
1991   "Two incomes not a 'luxury,'" *Calgary Herald*, Calgary, June 5.

Rao, Badrinath Krishna Rao
1991   "The Agony When East Meets West," *The Globe and Mail*. May 7, p. A17.

Recer, Paul
1999   "Children of working moms well adjusted, study find," *Calgary Herald*, March 1, p. A-3.

Rhyne, Darla
1981   "Bases of Marital Satisfaction Among Men and Women," *Journal of Marriage and the Family*, Nov., pp. 941–955.

Saffilios-Rothschild, Constantina
1967   "A Comparison of Power Structure and Marital Satisfction in Urban Greek and French Families," *Journal of Marriage and the Family*, May, Vol. 29, pp. 345–352.

Salter, Michael
1988   "The High Cost of Leaving," Report on Business, Toronto, *The Globe and Mail*, Oct., pp. 113–119.

Saunders, Iwan
1975   "Canadian Law and Marriage," in *Marriage, Family and Society, Canadian Perspectives*. Toronto, Butterworths Canada, Ltd., p. 47.

Schogol, Marc
1986   "Marriage Contracts Fast Becoming Fact of Life," *Calgary Herald*, Calgary June 7.

Smith, Vivian
1990   "Woman's Occupations still lowest paying, Statistics Canada Study Says," Toronto, *The Globe and Mail*, March 10.

Snow, Adrienne
1998   "Finally, stay-at-home parenting being discussed," *Calgary Herald*, Aug. 24, p. A10.

Somerville, Barbara
1987   *Calgary Herald*, Calgary, May 7.

Southam News
1986   "Single Mothers Top Survey," *Calgary Herald*, Calgary, Dec. 5.

Span, Paula

1998   "Children's Development Nature Versus Nurture—Brash author earns beefs, bouquets for discounting roles of parents." *The Globe and Mail,* Nov. 25, p. G4.

Statistics Canada

1983   Update from 1981 Census: Highlight Information on Ethnicity, Language, etc. Ottawa, Supply and Services, Canada.

The William Petschek National Jewish Family Center of the American Jewish Committee,

1986   New York, Spring, Vol. 6, No.1.

Travato, Frank

1988   "A Macro-Sociological Analysis of Change in the Marriage Rate: Canadian Women, 1921–25 to 1981–85," *Journal of Marriage and the Family*, May, Vol. 50, No. 2, pp. 507–521.

Turcotte, Pierre

1991   "Common-law Unions—Nearly Half a Million in 1986," in *Canadian Social Trends*, Edited by Craig McKie and Kieth Thompson, Toronto, Thompson Education Publishing Inc., pp. 148–152.

Ursel, Jane

1986   "The State and the Maintenance of Patriarchy: A Case Study of Family, Labour and Welfare Legislation in Canada," Garamond Press, pp. 150–191.

Veevers, Jean E.

1990   "Continuity and Change in Marriage and Family," Toronto, Holt, Rinehart & Winston of Canada, Ltd.

Wallis, Claudia

1989   "Onward Women," *Time*, Dec. 4, 1960.

Weinfeld, Morton

1987   "Immigrants are key to the Future," *The Globe and Mail*, Toronto, June 19.

White, James M.

1989   "Marriage A Developing Process in Family and Marriage: Cross-Cultural Perspectives," Edited by K. Oshwaran, Toronto, Thompson Education Publishing Inc., p. 205.

1987   "Premarital Cohabitation and Marital Stability in Canada," *Journal of Marriage and the Family*, Aug., Vol. 44, No. 3, pp. 641–647.

White, Lynn & Bruce Keith

1990   "The Effect of Shift Work on the Quality and Stability of Marital Relations." *Journal of Marriage and the Family*, May, Vol. 52, No. 2, pp. 453–462.

White, Pamela M.

1990   "Ethnic Origins of the Canadian Population," *Canadian Social Trends*, Edited by Craig Mckie and Keith Thompson, Thompson Educational Publishing, Inc., Toronto, pp. 3–6.

Wilson, Deborah

1986 "Family Life in 'Crisis' State, Study Finds," *The Globe and Mail*, Toronto, July 21.

Wilson, S. J.

1991 *Women, Families and Work*, Toronto, McGraw-Hill Ryerson Ltd., p. 6.

Wu, Theng and T. R. Balakrishan

1992 "Attitudes Towards Cohabitation and Marriage in Canada," *Journal of Comparative Family Studies*, Vol. XXIII, No. 1.

11

Health and Health Care in Canada

Harley D. Dickinson

Introduction

Medical sociology has two main branches; the sociology of health and illness, and the sociology of medicine and health care. The focus of the sociology of health and illness is the relationship between the nature of society and the distribution of health, illness, injury and death among different groups within society. The sociology of medicine and health care includes the study of social definitions of, and institutional responses to, illness and injury.

This chapter outlines selected topics within the sociology of health and illness and the sociology of medicine and health care in Canada. It is divided into two main sections. In the first, selected aspects of the differential distribution of mortality (death) are presented. The second consists of a brief overview of the Canadian health care system. It includes a discussion of current reform strategies and some of their consequences.

Sociology of Health and Illness

The nature of society is related to illness and disease in at least four ways: (1) social conditions may cause illness or disease, (2) they may create predispositions among particular groups of individuals for certain diseases, (3) they may facilitate the transmission of the causes of diseases, and (4) they may influence the course and outcome of diseases (Rosen,1963:44).

The inverse of these relationships also is true, that is, the achievement and preservation of health is causally related to the nature and organization of societies (Northcott, 1991). Various social groups are differentially integrated into structured social relations that either impede or facilitate the attainment and preservation of health. One would expect, therefore, a differential distribution of health and illness between groups and over time. That is precisely what is found.

Table 11.1. Average Life Expectancy at Birth, Canada, by Sex, Selected Years, 1931–1997

Year	Female	Gain	Male	Gain	Female-male difference in life expectancy
1931	62.1	–	60.0	–	2.1
1941	66.3	4.2	63.0	2.3	3.3
1951	70.8	4.5	66.3	3.3	4.5
1961	74.2	1.3	68.3	0.7	5.9
1971	76.4	1.2	69.3	0.6	7.1
1981	79.0	1.5	71.9	1.7	7.1
1992	81.2	2.2	74.9	3.0	6.3
1997	81.4	0.8	75.8	1.4	5.6

Source: Statistics Canada, 1976. Deaths. Vital Statistics, Vol. III; Statistics Canada, 1983. Mortality—Summary List of Causes. Vital Statistics, Vol. III, 1981; Statistics Canada, 1988. Mortality—Summary List of Causes, 1993; Star Phoenix, 1999.

Canada, like other advanced capitalist societies during the past several decades, has experienced increased life expectancies at birth and increased average age at death. These general trends hold for both males and females. A traditional female advantage in terms of life expectancy persists, despite a closing of the gap in recent years. Table 11.1 shows the average life expectancy for females at birth in Canada in 1931 was 62.1 years, for males it was 60.0 years, for a difference, at birth, of 2.1 additional years of life for women compared to males. By 1997 the average life expectancy for females had increased to 81.4 years. For males it had increased to 75.8 years. This represented a difference of 5.6 additional years of life expected for females compared to males. The gap between females and males has been declining since 1978 when it reached a high of 7.5 additional years of life (Star Phoenix, 1999). Since that time, although both females and males have continued to achieve gains in life expectancy the gains for males have exceeded those for females.

Part of the reason for the increased life expectancy at birth is the dramatic decline in infant mortality rates. The greatest decline in infant mortality, for both males and females, occurred between 1931 and 1951. The main reason for the decline was decreased mortality from infectious diseases such as whooping cough, influenza, bronchitis, pneumonia, enteritis and diarrhoea (Dominion Bureau of Statistics, 1967: 9). In 1995, about 72% of all deaths for infants under one year were caused by congenital anomalies and other causes specific to the perinatal period.

The infant mortality rate has declined steadily since 1951. Recently, however, the rate of decrease has slowed as a result of the above mentioned shift in the primary causes of death among that age group. Even so, the infant mortality rate per 1,000 live births decreased to 6.1 in 1995 from about 42 in 1950 (Statistics Canada, 1988 a:9, Figure III; Statistics Canada, 1997).

The percentage of all deaths accounted for by those under one year of age and those 65 years and older has changed dramatically, as can be seen in Table 11.2. Deaths in the under one year age group dropped from 11.7 percent of all deaths in Canada in 1951 to 1.1 percent in 1995. Though not as dramatic, there has been a general downward trend for all age groups except those 65 years and older. For that age group, the percentage of all deaths increased from 53.6 to 75.7 between 1951 and 1995. The increased proportion of deaths among those aged 65 years and over is a result a number of factors, including the decrease in mortality in all other age groups and the fact that the Canadian population is getting older.

Table 11.2. Percentage of All Deaths by Age Groups, Both Sexes, Canada, Selected Years, 1951–1995

	1951	1961	1971	1981	1991	1995
Under 1 Year	11.7	9.2	4.0	2.1	1.3	1.1
1 – 24 years	5.7	4.5	4.9	3.8	2.1	1.8
25 – 44 years	7.0	5.8	5.8	5.5	5.5	5.4
45 – 64 years	22.0	21.4	23.0	21.6	17.2	16.1
65 years and older	53.6	53.6	62.3	67.0	73.9	75.7
Total deaths (000s)	125.8	141.0	157.3	171.0	195.6	210.7

Source: Statistics Canada, 1976. General Mortality, 1960 to 1972; Statistics Canada, 1982. Causes of Death, 1981; Statistics Canada, 1997. Mortality—Summary List of Causes, 1995.

Part of the reason for this demographic shift is the reduction of infectious diseases as causes of death. Consequently, individuals generally live longer. Various chronic diseases have become the leading causes of morbidity and death in Canada. Since at least 1950, for example, the leading causes of death have been diseases of the circulatory system, cancer, accidents and respiratory diseases.

Circulatory disease, both heart diseases and stroke, were the leading cause of death for both males and females over the period 1950 to 1995. Despite this, there have been substantial decreases in both male and female age-standardized mortality rates (ASMRs) for circulatory diseases as shown in Table 11.3. Explanations of the observed decline identify the following factors: reductions in risk producing behaviors and characteristics, such as cigarette smoking, obesity, high cholesterol diets, and high blood pressure; increased preventative behaviors, such as higher levels of physical activity; reduced severity of diseases; and improved treatments (Statistics Canada, 1988a:9).

Table 11.3. Age-Standardized Mortality Rates (ASMR) for Leading Causes of Death, Canada, 1950–1993

Causes of Death 1950–1993	ASMR per 100,000		Male excess	ASMR per 100,000		Male excess	% change in ASMR	
	Males	Females	%	Males	Females	%	Males	Females
Circulatory diseases	708	567	25	340	204	67	−52	−64
Cancer	179	165	8	241	154	56	+35	− 7
Respiratory diseases	84	62	35	88	43	105	+ 5	−31
External causes	104	46	126	67	27	148	−36	−41
All other causes	294	244	20	154	106	45	−48	−57

Source: Wilkins, 1995.

The second leading cause of death, for both men and women, is cancer. Table 11.3 shows that the cancer related age-standardized mortality rate (ASMR) for men incresed by 35% between 1950 and 1993. For females, the ASMR for cancer decreased by 7% over that time period.

Among males, lung cancer death rates leveled off after 1984 following decades of increases. Among women, lung cancer death rates are still rising, particularly for those over 65 years of age. Increased female death rates from lung cancer follow increased cigarette smoking, after a lag of at least twenty years (Statistics Canada, 1988b:10). Reduced lung cancer death rates among men in Canada, as well as in a number of other countries, is related to decreased cigarette smoking among men. There is also some evidence that filter and lower tar cigarettes may contribute to reduced risk of lung cancer (Statistics Canada, 1988b:1).

In 1995, respiratory diseases accounted for 9.2 and 8.7 percent of male and female deaths respectively. Between 1991 and 1995 age-standardized mortality rates per 100,000 population rose by a total of 143 percent; 150 percent for males and 131 percent for females (Statistics Canada, 1994: Table 3; Statistics Canada, 1997: Table 4).

Death by accident, which includes all external causes of injury and poisoning, was the fourth leading cause of death both for males and females in 1995, accounting for 8.3 and 4.4 percent respectively of all deaths. In the case of accident related deaths there has been a decrease in the age adjusted rates since the mid-1970s, with a leveling off in the mid-1980s. Motor vehicle death rates continued a steady downward trend that has been attributed to reduced speed limits established in 1976–77, and the introduction of mandatory seat belt use in most provinces between 1976 and 1986.

Although these figures on rates and causes of death reveal important information, they also obscure some significant facts concerning age specific death rates and causes of death. We have already seen that among Canadian infants less than one year old the two leading causes of death are diseases specific to the perinatal period and congenital anomalies.

Table 11.4. Leading Causes of Death, Various Age Groups, Canada, 1995

Causes of Death	Male Number	%	Female Number	%	Total Number	%
Under 1 year old						
certain perinatal causes (excluding still births)	566	43.4	424	41.6	990	42.6
congenital anomilies	372	28.5	312	30.6	684	29.5
respiratory diseases	35	2.7	18	1.8	53	2.3
diseases of the nervous system and sense organs	23	1.8	28	2.8	51	2.2
all other causes	307	23.6	236	23.2	543	23.4
All causes	**1,303**	**100.0**	**1,018**	**100.0**	**2,321**	**100.0**
Ages 1 to 24 years						
accidents and adverse effects	1,778	69.8	593	51.0	2,371	63.9
maligant neoplasms	177	6.9	144	12.4	321	8.7
diseases of the nervous system and sense organs	102	4.0	61	5.3	163	4.4
all other causes	491	19.3	364	31.3	855	23.0
All causes	**2,548**	**100.0**	**1,162**	**100.0**	**3,710**	**100.0**
Ages 25 to 44 years						
accidents and adverse effects	3,517	44.8	951	27.3	4,468	39.5
infectious & parasitic diseases	1,226	15.6	121	3.5	1,347	11.9
malignant neoplasms	945	12.1	1,267	36.4	2,212	19.5
diseases of circulatory system	933	11.9	382	11.0	1,315	11.6
all other causes	1,221	15.6	760	21.8	1,981	17.5
All causes	**7,842**	**100.0**	**3,481**	**100.0**	**11,323**	**100.0**
Ages 45 to 64 years						
malignant neoplasms	8,037	37.9	6,722	53.1	14,759	43.5
diseases of circulatory system	6,671	31.4	2,602	20.5	9,273	27.4
accidents and adverse effects	1,933	9.1	703	5.6	2,636	7.8
all other causes	4,577	21.6	2,629	20.8	7,206	21.3
All causes	**21,218**	**100.0**	**12,656**	**100.0**	**33,874**	**100.0**
Ages 65 years and over						
diseases of circulatory system	32,387	41.3	35,964	44.4	68,351	42.9
malignant neoplasms	22,168	28.3	18,340	22.6	40,508	25.4
respiratory diseases	9,208	11.7	7,930	9.8	17,138	10.7
all other causes	14,705	18.7	18,776	23.2	33,481	21.0
All causes	**78,468**	**100.0**	**81,016**	**100.0**	**159,478**	**100.0**
All ages						
diseases of circulatory system	40,091	36.0	39,025	39.3	79,116	37.5
malignant neoplasms	31,332	28.1	26,478	26.7	57,810	27.4
respiratory diseases	10,210	9.2	8,678	8.7	18,888	9.0
all other causes	29,763	26.7	25,156	25.3	54,919	26.1
All causes	**111,396**	**100.0**	**99,337**	**100.0**	**210,733**	**100.0**

Source: Statistics Canada, 1995. Mortality. Summary List of Causes of Death. Vital Statistics, vol. III

Table 11.4 shows that for those aged 1 to 24 years the two leading causes of death for both males and females were accidents and cancer. For males, accidents accounted for almost 70 percent of all deaths, while cancer, the second leading cause, represented 7 percent of male deaths. For females, 51 percent of all deaths were caused by accidents and 12.4 percent by cancers.

A similar pattern exists among 25 to 44 year olds. In 1995, 44.8 percent of deaths among males were the result of accidents. Interestingly, the second leading cause of death for men in this age group was infectious and parasitic diseases, accounting for 15.6 percent of all male deaths. Nearly 12 percent of all male deaths were caused by diseases of the circulatory system, and 12.1 percent were the result of cancers. For females in the 25 to 44 year age group, 27.3 percent of deaths were the result of accidents and adverse effects; 36.4 percent were caused by cancers, and 11 percent were the result of diseases of the circulatory system.

The pattern remains the same for the next age group. For those between the ages of 45 and 64 years the three leading causes of death were cancer, diseases of the circulatory system, and accidents corresponding to 43.5, 27.4 and 7.8 percent respectively of all deaths regardless of gender. There were also significant gender differences in that age group. The leading cause of death for males was cancer at 37.9 per cent, followed by diseases of the circulatory system at 31.4 per cent, with accidents coming third at 9.1 percent of all male deaths in 1995. The leading cause of death for females was cancers, which accounted for 53.1 percent of all deaths, diseases of the circulatory system was the second leading cause of death at 20.7 percent.

The three leading causes of death for those in the 65 years and older age group for both males and females were diseases of the circulatory system, cancers and respiratory diseases. Diseases of the circulatory system accounted for 41.3 and 44.4 percent of male and female deaths respectively in the 65 years and older age group, 28.3 percent of male deaths and 22.6 percent of female deaths were caused by cancers, while 11.7 and 9.8 percent of male and female deaths respectively were the result of respiratory diseases.

Age and gender are not the only sources of variation in morbidity and mortality rates. Indeed, it is probably the case that observed age and gender differences in mortality rates and causes of death, in many instances, are influenced by the different socio-economic statuses and social positions of men and women, the young and the old. Support for this notion is provided when one examines the distribution of morbidity and mortality by income. Table 11.5 shows that in the late 1970s men in the first quintile of income earners, that is, men in the lowest 20 percent of income earners in Canada, at birth could expect 9.5 fewer years of life compared to women in the same income bracket.

Table 11.5. Income Level by Quintiles, and Life Expectancy at Birth, by Sex, Canada, Late 1970s

Income quintiles	Life expectancy at birth Female	Male
First	76.6	67.1
Second	77.6	70.1
Third	78.5	70.9
Fourth	79.0	72.0
Fifth	79.4	73.4
Total	78.3	70.8

Source: Hay (1988) adapted fom Wilkins and Adams (1983: 1078, Table 3).

Comparing high income earning men to low income earning men reveals a similar pattern (Wolfson, Rowe and Gentleman, 1990). Men in the top 20 percent of income earners, in the late 1970s, could expect 73.4 years of life at birth compared to the 67.1 years expected for men among the lowest 20 percent of income earners. Thus, high income earning men could expect an additional 6.3 years of life compared to low income earning men. In addition to greater life expectancy, high income earning men could expect about 14 more years of disability free life compared to men with low incomes. For women the difference is eight years (Epp, 1986:4)

Income level is also directly related to life expectancy at birth for women, although, as shown in Table 11.5, differences between low income women and high income women are not as great as for men. High income women could expect 79.4 years of life at birth compared to 73.4 years for men for a difference of six additional years of life for high income earning women compared to high income earning men. The difference in life expectancy at birth for high income earning women compared to low income men is the most dramatic amounting to 12.3 additional years of life.

We have observed increased life expectancy at birth for both males and females over the course of most of this century. Associated with that is an increased average age at death, and a transition in the major causes of mortality away from infectious diseases towards chronic and degenerative diseases. Although the major sources of morbidity are not exactly congruent with major sources of mortality, there is substantial overlap (Blishen, 1991).

A good indicator of the main sources of morbidity is reason for hospitalization. The main reasons for hospitalizations generally correspond to the main causes of death discussed above (Blishen, 1991:38). Blishen does not include in his list of the main reasons for hospitalization the rate of patient days for cancers which, as we have seen, is a leading cause of death. According to Blishen's data, the leading causes of hospitalization in Canada in 1969, expressed as age-standardized rates of in-patient days per 1,000 population were heart diseases (181.76), other cerebrovascular diseases (104.92), accidents (152.84), respiratory diseases (129.01), and mental disorders (102.50). By 1982, although the leading causes of hospitalization remained the same, the rank order had changed: mental disorders had become the leading cause of hospitalization at 157.33 age-standardized in-patient days per 1,000 population, followed by heart diseases at 146.77, cerebrovascular diseases at 137.94, accidents at 123.68, and respiratory diseases at 115.57 (Blishen, 1991:37).

An exception to the observation that the leading causes of death and hospitalization correspond, is mental disorders. Mental disorders in themselves are not causes of death. Following the invention and introduction of psychotropic drugs in the early 1950s, and especially since the introduction of hospitalization and medical care insurance in the 1950s and 1960s respectively, the old mental hospital system of treatment has declined and most in-patient treatment has been shifted to general hospitals (Dickinson, 1989). Given the current crisis in health care costs in general and acute care hospitals in particular, one might anticipate renewed efforts to find less expensive alternatives to general hospital in-patient treatment and care for those diagnosed with mental disorders or illnesses.

Reduced reliance on mental hospitals for treating the mentally ill in the 1970s had two consequences; increased treatment in psychiatric wards and even general wards of general hospitals, and the development of community mental health services (Dickinson, 1989). Since then, especially during the late 1980s and1990s with the downsizing of the welfare state, community mental health care has increasingly transformed into homelessness and reincarceration (Scull, 1984; Dear and Wolch, 1987). Given this experience there is reason to be concerned that the current enthusiasm for community based treatment and care of the ill and the injured may be a harbinger of a similar process of abandonment. The fact that in many cases community based care and treatment services are not covered by Medicare amplifies these concerns.

It is interesting to note in light of various cost containment strategies and efforts to reduce utilization rates of health care services discussed below, that there has been a decline in hospitalizations measured as age-standardized rates of in-patient days per 1,000 population for all causes since mid-1970s (Blishen, 1991:37).

Despite variations in the main causes of both morbidity and mortality along gender, age and income lines, it is widely expected that observed trends will continue, perhaps even at an accelerated rate, because of the demographic shift in the nature and composition of the Canadian population. This will continue to have an effect on the level and nature of health care needs, service utilization patterns, and costs.

Anticipation of increased need, utilization, and costs of health care has contributed to the perception of a growing cost crisis in health care (Blomqvist, 1979; Weller and Manga, 1983; Evans, 1984; York, 1987; Brown, 1987; Dickinson and Hay, 1988). Much effort is currently being directed to the analysis of the existing health care system to determine if it provides the most effective and efficient response to current health care needs. It is to an exploration of these issues that we turn in the following section.

Sociology of Medicine and Health Care

The present health care system in Canada, both in terms of its prevention activities and its treatment responses, developed largely as a solution to the problems of infectious diseases and acute injuries. Despite its effectiveness in contributing to the cure and control of certain types of illnesses and injuries, the dominant bio-medical model has been widely criticized.

Most commonly, critics point out the tendency for those employing the bio-medical model, founded as it is on the twin pillars of "germ theory" and the insights of pathology (Shorter, 1985), to individualize the explanation and treatment of illness and injury and, consequently, to fail adequately to recognize the social, economic, political and cultural determinants of health and illness (Illich, 1976; Navarro, 1976; Powles, 1973; Bolaria, 1983; Foss and Rothenberg, 1987; Hewa and Hetherington, 1990b).

This criticism has gained increasing strength in recent years as the major sources of illness and death have shifted from those caused by a single biological organism to those thought to be the result of complex interactions between genetic, psychological, social and other environmental factors and processes. The application of the bio-medical model to explanations and treatments of mental disorders, heart diseases, cancers and accidents, for example, is inappropriate. These, however, are the health problems to which the health care system must now respond. The dominant bio-medical model and related forms of health care are the wrong tools for the main job at hand (Foss and Rothenberg, 1987).

This does not mean that the maintenance of an effective and efficient prevention and treatment system for infectious diseases is unnecessary. Although most diseases of that sort have been controlled within the context of advanced industrial countries, changing economic conditions, alterations in international population movements, variations in the virulence of illness producing organisms and changes in host resistance, require continual vigilance in the areas of prevention and treatment of these diseases (Gellert, Neumann and Gordon, 1989). Resurgences in polio, cholera and malaria in recent years are examples. In addition, new infectious diseases emerge as the nature of social and individual behavior changes in the context of structural transformations of society. The most well known contemporary example is the HIV virus and AIDS. Thus, changes in the nature of the primary health problems facing Canadian society cannot be solved simply by transferring resources from one set of health problems to another. The system must both expand and change. This has implications for the level and allocation of health resources.

Financing and Cost Containment in the Health Care Sector

Under the Canadian constitution health care is a provincial responsibility. Thus, one cannot speak of a national health care system in Canada until after the Second World War. Even then, however, the role of the federal government was, and is, restricted to setting standards and contributing money to, or withholding money from, provincial and territorial governments as an incentive to adopt, or as a sanction for not adopting, federal standards. This jurisdictional situation has resulted in protracted negotiations aimed at establishing mutually agreeable funding arrangements. As a consequence, the development of a national health care system has proceeded slowly and in stages. Indeed, in many respects it can be argued that a national health care system does not exist at all, but rather, there are several more or less congruent provincial and territorial systems that, taken together, constitute the national health care system.

The first federal government financial contribution to the creation of a national health care system was the 1948 hospital construction grants. This was followed with the 1958

Hospital Insurance and Diagnostic Services Act which established a national system of hospitalization insurance cost-shared between the federal and provincial/territorial governments. The most dramatic and contentious step, however, was the introduction of the 1968 Medical Care Services Act.

The 1968 Medical Care Services Act established a national medical care insurance plan, Medicare, on a cost-shared basis. Under its terms provinces and territories were eligible for federal funds to pay for physician services if the following principles were adopted: (1) universality, virtually all Canadian citizens are covered, (2) comprehensiveness, all necessary medical services are included, (3) accessibility, no financial or other barriers to treatment are imposed, (4) portability, eligible residents temporarily absent from their province of residence are covered, and (5) public administration on a non-profit basis.

By 1972 all provinces and territories had adopted these principles and joined Medicare. Opposition to Medicare continued and pressures to move to a more market-based system of health care and health care insurance remained strong. These pressures increased throughout the 1980s when a near political consensus on the need to manage the debt and deficit crisis resulted in massive federal government cutbacks. The cutbacks in federal transfer payments to the provinces in turn resulted in some of the provinces looking to user fees and other service charges as a way to generate lost revenue. In 1984 the federal government responded to these privatization initiatives with the passage of the Canada Health Act. That Act reaffirmed the founding principles of Medicare and imposed a dollar for dollar penalty on provinces that allowed extra-billing.

Table 11.6. Total Health Expenditures in Millions of Dollars, by Category, Canada, 1975, 1985 and 1996

Category	1975	1985	1996
Total Health Expenditures	12,260.9	40,058.1	75,224.7
Personal Health Care	10,503.3	33,680.5	61,551.0
Institutions	6,518.7	5,396.8	1,121.9
hospitals	20,023.2	15,957.9	4,065.3
other institutions	33,218.5	25,714.6	7,503.9
Professional Services	2,737.5	1,838.1	899.4
physicians	9,356.4	6,040.7	3,315.7
other professionals	17,487.2	10,867.5	6,619.7
Drugs	1,247.1	4,300.9	10,856.0
Other Health Care Costs	1,757.6	536.9	468.5
capital	752.2	6,377.6	1,839.0
public health	1,708.4	2,830.2	13,673.7
other expenditures	1,850.1	3,798.6	8,025.1

Source: Health Canada, 1994; Health Canada, 1997.

Table 11.6 provides a breakdown of national health care expenditures over time. There have been dramatic increases in all categories of expenditure over the time period shown despite various cost control efforts. Since the introduction of Medicare, three interrelated strategies have been used to control health care costs: (1) reductions in the episodes of illness requiring medical or hospital care; (2) reductions in the frequency and duration of care required for any episode of illness; and (3) reductions in the cost per contact (Task Force, 1970). Recently a fourth strategy, which consists of reducing the amount budgeted for health care, has been adopted. Selected aspects of these strategies are examined below.

Reductions in Episodes of Illness

Reducing the episodes of illness requiring medical or hospital treatment can be achieved in two ways; first, by improving the health of the population, that is, by reducing the amount of illness and injury in society, and second, by modifying help seeking behaviors so that individuals seek less medical assistance and provide more self-care. In this section attention is focused on aspects of the first strategy. Attempts to alter help seeking behaviors are looked at in the next section.

The health status of the population can be improved by preventing illness and promoting healthy lifestyles. Illness prevention techniques are determined by a number of factors, including the causes of illness and injury. It is generally thought that the main health problems facing Canadians are caused by a number of interacting factors, including, biological/genetic, psychological/behavioral, social and environmental. Effective prevention, therefore, requires interventions and modifications in all four causal factors.

Current medical research suggests that for many contemporary illnesses genetic predispositions play a large role. Drawing upon the art and the science of animal husbandry it has long been known that selective breeding and natural selection increase or decrease a species' resistance to certain illnesses. Historically, the eugenics movement has advocated selective human breeding as a means to control the intergenerational transmission of physical and mental characteristics associated with various diseases thought to be hereditable. The main strategies adopted in the name of the genetic improvement of a race or nation have been controlled immigration, and controlled reproduction of those considered unfit. Controlled reproduction has included compulsory sterilization, restricted marriage of the "unfit" through a system of marriage licences, and the encouragement of fertility among those deemed to have desirable traits (McLaren, 1990).

The eugenical improvement of the stock of the nation was actively encouraged in the name of preventive medicine and mental hygiene by certain sectors of the medical profession, and other emerging "helping professions," in Canada throughout most of the first half of this century, and particularly during the interwar years. The eugenics movement was not restricted to Canada. It was an international movement most fully developed and institutionalized in Nazi Germany. The brutal genocidal policies of the Nazis, carried out in the name of racial and ethnic purity, and legitimated as medical science, led to the collapse of the movement by the end of the Second World War.

281

McLaren (1990: 170) points out, however, that after World War II, "just as the crude social engineering policies campaigned for by the traditional eugenicists were being consigned to the dustbin of history, geneticists were making important breakthroughs that established the basis for a 'new eugenics.'" These breakthroughs made it possible, for the first time, to know the genetic make up of an individual before birth. The expansion of genetics screening techniques and fetal diagnostic technologies, have resulted in greatly increased capacity to diagnose disorders, defects and disabilities such as Downs Syndrome, spina bifida and others. Combined with genetic counselling services, these screening and diagnostic services have enabled the prevention of much illness and misery through therapeutic abortions.

This has helped entrench individual level strategies of prevention based upon genetic intervention. Combined with an increasing consensus that more resources must be devoted to prevention efforts, it seems likely that as a society we will increasingly be faced with the questions who is to live, who is to die, and who is to decide? Current debates over the human genome project, reproductive rights and technologies, euthanasia, and quality of life concerns, are harbingers of social and cultural changes. As the history of the eugenics movement has shown, the application of individual level solutions to social problems, regardless of intentions and motives, can lead us down undesirable paths to equally undesirable destinations.

Strategies and practices for the prevention of illness and the promotion of health must recognize that health and illness are related not only to what we "are" genetically, but also to what we "do" and how we do it, individually and socially. Consequently, substantial effort is directed towards the encouragement and enforcement of health producing and illness preventing behaviors of individuals.

There is a relationship between health and illness status and individual lifestyles. What is often obscured by this self-evident truth is the less evident, but no less truthful fact, that individual lifestyles are themselves largely influenced by the structured social relationships, within which, and through which, we live our lives. Thus, attempts to modify individual behaviors must be based on an adequate understanding of the nature of the social, economic, political and cultural structures within which individuals live. Indeed, health promotion and illness prevention and treatment practices are part of those structured social relations.

Illness preventing and health promoting behaviors exist on a continuum between voluntary and compulsory compliance. Different approaches are taken with respect to different health problems and in different contexts. For example, we all more or less accept the requirement of compulsory vaccination against contagious diseases. It is interesting to point out, however, that acceptance of vaccination has not always existed (Bator, 1983). Its continued acceptance requires constant reproduction both through public health education campaigns and vigilant enforcement of existing legislation.

Other examples of legislated illness and injury prevention behaviors include mandatory seat belt use in motor vehicles, the requirement for motor cyclists to wear safety helmets, motor vehicle speed limits, and the criminalization of impaired driving, as well as a number of other road safety laws and regulations. Usually the legislation of behavior is accompanied by public health education campaigns intended to encourage people to do on a voluntary basis what is legally required. Examples are educational campaigns to encourage people not to smoke, to exercise more, to adopt good nutritional habits, to abstain from drug use, to encourage "responsible" alcohol use, and, to engage in "safe" sex, to name a few.

The government also claims that it attempts to encourage people to give up health damaging behaviors such as tobacco smoking and alcohol abuse through the imposition of heavy consumption taxes on those products. For profit insurance companies use both positive and negative financial sanctions in the form of differential premiums to achieve the same end. Smokers, for example, often pay higher premiums than do non-smokers.

Health promotion and illness prevention initiatives play an important role in a comprehensive health policy. Critics argue, however, that too much effort is directed towards individual behavior modification strategies and too little towards altering the social, economic, and political structures that impede the choice of healthy lifestyles. Policy makers, of course, are aware of the fact that policy decisions in a large number of areas have health consequences. There is also an awareness of the fact that the health dimension of various policy decisions often does not have top priority (Epp, 1986:10).

This is an important insight. To suggest, however, that the problem can be solved by making "health matters attractive to other sectors on much the same way that we try to make healthy choices attractive to people" (Epp, 1986:10), appears to reduce the problem, and the solution, to the individual level. Presented in this way, the problem appears to be a lack of understanding or inappropriate attitudes, that can be corrected by providing more information to individuals. Such an approach, although undoubtedly appropriate in some respects, fails to recognize that various structured impediments and interests may prevent the realization of health priorities even if they are attractive to individuals who recognize their importance.

Sociological research shows that individuals' interests, goals, motives and capacities to achieve them are influenced by the nature of the social system. We have already seen, for example, how social characteristics are related to health and illness patterns among individuals who belong to various social categories and whose lives reflect the different social relationships related to age, gender and income. In particular, the structured inequalities of age, gender, race and class repeatedly have been linked to differential morbidity and mortality patterns. It is also important to point out that in societies where individuals are characterized by structurally determined and differentiated interests, and structurally and individually differentiated capacities to realize those interests, it may not be easy, or even possible, for individuals, acting as an individual, to fundamentally change their lifestyles.

It has been argued, for example, that in capitalist societies irresolvable contradictions exist between the need for profits and the goal of healthy workplaces and safe consumer products. The structurally determined imperative of economic growth and expanded profits impedes the capacity of both government and business to adopt policies and practices that give priority to health (Renaud, 1977). This is true whether or not any individual business person or policy-maker would prefer to put health before profits.

The health promotion efforts discussed above have in common the goal of improving health and reducing the level of injury and illness. It is reasoned that improved health status will reduce the need for, and hence, utilization of, health care services. Reduced utilization will reduce health care costs. Two other methods for reducing utilization and costs, which do not require reductions in need levels, exist. These are reductions in the range and number of services provided, and modifications to help-seeking behaviors intended to reduce utilization rates without necessarily reducing the incidence of illness and injury.

Reducing Contacts with the Health Care System

Conceptually sick role behavior must be distinguished from illness. Illness refers to a physiological condition or state of the individual. Sick role behavior refers to the actions taken by individuals when they are ill, or when they consider themselves to be ill. Sick role behavior is learned. Thus, it is historically and culturally specific and, therefore, subject to change. Related to the concept of sick role behavior is the concept of care giver behavior, or more specifically physician behavior. Alterations in both sick role behavior and care giver behavior are important ways to reduce the number of contacts with the health care system, and thereby, to reduce costs.

Changing Sick Role Behaviors

Containing health care costs by reducing service utilization may be in contradiction with well established health promotion principles and treatment practices. In particular, regular check-ups and screening programs intended to enable early diagnosis and treatment, in some cases, may be ineffective and inefficient uses of health care resources. Thus, individual health care consumers receive conflicting messages concerning appropriate health promotion behavior. Within the modern health promotion framework, self-care and mutual aid are advocated as preferred forms of behavior (Epp, 1986).

Self-care refers to actions taken by individuals to achieve and protect their health. "Simply put," the Epp (1986:7) report states, "encouraging self-care means encouraging healthy choice." Closely related to self-care is the notion of mutual aid, or self-help. Self-help differs from self-care. It refers to a pooling and sharing of resources and information to create socially supportive relations that will foster increased capacity for independent, community-based living. That is, it refers to positive attempts to reduce utilization of the formal health care system.

The goal of reduced service utilization is sensitive because access to necessary medical and hospital services has been a right of Canadian citizenship since the introduction of Medicare (Taylor, 1978; York, 1987; Begin, 1988). Consequently, few politicians, even if they were so inclined, have been willing to suggest that Canadians be denied access to necessary medical or hospital services. Those who do suggest this usually propose an alternative such as home care, or justify restricted access as fair because of some characteristic of the service users themselves. In terms of this second situation, the strategy adopted has been to attack alleged abusers of health care services.

Historically, those who have claimed that overutilization of medical and hospital services was a major factor contributing to the crisis of rising costs, have proposed or imposed various forms or "deterrent," or user, fees. These take the form of direct, out-of-pocket payments by service users for physician or hospital services. User fees, in their several manifestations, however, are charged to all service users. They are not targeted at the alleged service abusers. Such fees, therefore, have the effect of deterring both alleged abusers and legitimate users, particularly low income users (Beck, 1973). By creating a financial barrier to low income Canadians, deterrent fees undermine one of the foundations of Medicare, the principle to equality of access (Grant, 1988).

Proponents of user pay schemes point out that low income users could be identified through a means test and exempted from payment of user fees on that basis. Means testing would lead to the development of a two-tier health care system, one for the rich and one for the poor. If individuals must be officially designated as paupers to receive health care services, they may delay or avoid seeking those services. This is because, in societies like ours, where individual self-sufficiency and independence are highly valued, receiving charity is a degrading and humiliating experience. The humiliation and degradation of means testing can be as real a barrier to health services as lack of money. As we have seen previously, the poor have higher mortality and morbidity rates, therefore, they presumably have the greatest need for health care services. If, as stated in the Epp report, a goal of health policy is to eliminate health status inequities from Canadian society, then deterrent fees or user charges, which create barriers to accessibility, are counterproductive.

The cost of administering means tests also would probably exceed intended savings. Canada-US comparisons of the proportion of health care dollars devoted to administrative expenses, rather than direct service provision, support this claim. In the US, state health insurance is limited to the elderly and the poor, rather than being universally accessible as in Canada. In 1983 US administrative costs were estimated to be sixty percent higher than in Canada (Woolhandler and Himmelstein, 1991). These data certainly lead one to question the widespread belief that the private sector is always more efficient than the public sector.

Another reason altering illness behaviors and reducing utilization rates among certain categories of the population through user fees is unlikely to be effective in reducing costs is because, given the fee-for-service system of remuneration, physicians are able to offset service utilization reductions among one group by generating higher levels of utilization among others. Doctors' diagnostic and treatment practices largely determine service utilization patterns and costs. Physicians directly account for just less than 15 percent of total health care costs. About 80 percent of total health care costs, however, are the result of physicians' decisions (Chappel, Strain, and Blandford, 1986).

Doctors are reluctant to acknowledge that the crisis in Medicare may be largely a result of a system from which they benefit. They are more likely to see "unrealistic public expectations" as the main problem. If unrealistic expectations exist it is partly because of the accomplishments and promises of the medical profession itself (Illich, 1976; Dubos, 1979). Defining the problem this way leads to the solution of better educating the public on when, how or if, to use physician's services (Webb, 1991; Barale, 1991). Resolution of the health care crisis, however, requires changing both patient behaviour and the practice patterns of physicians.

While it may be true that high expectations are producing a crisis of overutilization, those same expectations, coupled with the fact that the bio-medical model has proven to be ineffective in curing the principal diseases of modern life, have contributed to a growing legitimation crisis for the medical profession. A growing number of people are unwilling to assume that "doctor knows best," and they are seeking assisstance from a variety of non-medical sources. This process is referred to as demedicalization.

Several reasons for this change in the nature of the doctor-patient relationship have been suggested, including a reduction in the education gap between doctors and patients, the growth of individual and civil rights consciousness, the challenges of other health care occupations to medical dominance, the growth of medical technology (Blishen, 1991) and, as we have seen, the relative ineffectiveness of medicine to cure the maladies of the age.

The changing distribution of knowledge and hence power, between doctors and patients, is related to the fact that for many of the chronic and degenerative diseases "patients," or other non-medical health care providers, probably know as much about the nature of the problem, and more about the long-term management of it, than do physicians. This shift in knowledge and power towards the "patient" contributes to the transformation of the doctor-patient relationship into one that is more similar to a producer-consumer relationship (Frankel, 1994). In the ideal typical producer-consumer market relationship the consumer is "always right." This is the antithesis of the traditional doctor-patient relationship wherein the doctor "knows best."

These types of relationships can be considered poles on a continuum. The shift in knowledge and power towards the patient-consumer, although by no means absolute, contributes to the growing legitimation crisis of medicine and contributes to the displacement of the medical profession from a position of dominance with the health care system. Certain statutory rights and privileges historically granted to the organized medical profession presently prevent the complete marginalization of medicine, or demedicalization of health care. It must be remembered though that these rights and privileges are not absolute. They were legislatively established and they can be eliminated in the same way.

It seems reasonable to argue that certain aspects of the health care system stand as obstacles to the establishment and institutionalization of new forms of help seeking behavior and health care delivery. These include, but are not restricted to, various legislatively provided rights and privileges of doctors. Thus, only limited changes to illness behaviors and health care service utilization patterns can be achieved by "educating" individuals. The crisis of health care in Canada is not primarily a problem of individual ignorance and, therefore, it cannot be resolved at that level. This is equally true of efforts to understand and change physician behavior and practice patterns. Any efforts to contain health care costs must adequately understand the nature and organization of medical practice and its relationship to patterns of service utilization and costs.

Changing Physician Behavior

Several factors determine physician patterns of practice, including, the nature of health problems they must manage, the form and content of medical education, licencing laws, the system of remuneration, and the practices of others with vested interests in the health care system. Below I examine the nature and effects of the fee-for-service remuneration system and the interests and activities of the pharmaceutical industry. Included is a brief discussion of selected forms of resistance to cost containment efforts aimed at altering physician behavior.

The majority of physicians in Canada derive their incomes from fee-for-service practices (Naylor, 1986). Within a fee-for-service system incomes depend upon at least two factors: (1) the level of fees, and (2) the number of services provided. Cost containment strategies, given this system of remuneration, include attempts to "cap" fees, that is, set upper limits on the dollar amount paid for each type of service provided, attempts to limit the number of services provided or reimbursed, and attempts to limit the number of doctors. Less directly, there are also efforts to alter the form and content of medical education so as to create new expectations among future generations of doctors concerning appropriate forms of medical practice in relation to both patients and other health care occupations.

The fee-for-service remuneration system has a built-in incentive for doctors to maximize the number of services they provide. This is because every billable service provided contributes directly to physician earnings. Thus, there are no financial incentives for doctors to reduce the number of patients they treat or to reduce the number of services they provide to any given patient. Altered practice patterns, therefore, are more likely to be externally initiated. Placing an upper limit on the total amount of money available for medical services, or capping fees paid for each type of medical service provided, are obvious ways to contain rising medical care costs. Given the fact that the containment of health care costs potentially has negative consequences for incomes of individual physicians it is not surprising that doctors have sought ways to resist fee capping. Specialization is one such strategy.

Under the existing remuneration systems specialist fees are higher than General Practitioner (GP) fees, therefore, incomes of individual specialists are higher than incomes of GPs at a given intensity of work. Although the decision to specialize is undoubtedly rational from the perspective of the individual physician, it may be irrational from the societal perspective, at least insofar as it contributes to the maldistribution of medical resources and the perpetuation of inequities of access.

Maldistribution of resources and resultant inequities of access are unintended consequences of the nature, organization and spatial dimensions of specialist medical practice. Most medical specialties are hospital-based and dependent for patients upon referrals from other physicians, consequently, they are concentrated in larger urban centers. This urban concentration results in rural and remote areas of the country being underserved relative to urban areas, and in this way specialization contributes to continued inequities of access to medical services among certain segments of the population.

Another strategy adopted by physicians to offset fees considered to be too low is extra-billing (Northcott, 1988). This is the practice of directly charging patients a fee for services rendered that is additional to that paid to the physician by Medicare. The "right" to extra-bill was one of the concessions the government made to the medical profession in order to quiet their opposition to Medicare (Badgely and Wolfe, 1967; Blishen, 1970). By re-introducing a direct charge to patients, however, extra-billing created an obstacle to access to necessary medical services, particularly for the poor.

Concern about the negative effects of extra-billing increased throughout the 1970s and early 1980s. In 1984 the Federal government passed the Canada Health Act which, among other things, banned extra-billing. This was achieved by instating a dollar-for-dollar reduction in Federal cash transfers to the provinces for every dollar they allowed doctors to extra-bill. Many doctors were vigorously opposed to the ban on extra-billing, claiming it was an illegitimate infringement of medical prerogative and a violation of the sanctity of the doctor-patient relationship.

In Ontario, medical opposition to the ban culminated in a 25 day doctor's strike in 1986. This was the longest strike by doctors in Canadian history. Support for the strike, even among doctors, however, was not complete, and it dwindled as the strike went on. By the date set by the Canada Health Act extra-billing had been eliminated.

As suggested above, medical practice patterns are influenced by the activities of other interested actors in the health care sector, including the pharmaceutical industry. The nature and consequences of the for-profit pharmaceutical industry on physician drug prescription practices has been of concern for some time (May, 1961; Lexchin, 1984, 1994; Kleinman and Cohen, 1991).

The pharmaceutical industry exists to make a profit. This is not to say that it has not contributed to improved health care and health. One would be hard pressed to imagine life without the products of the modern pharmaceutical industry. Having said that, however, one must not be blinded to the fact that the primary goal of capitalist businesses is the maximization of profits, not the creation of health. If both can be achieved concurrently then everyone is happy, if not, evidence suggests priority is given to profits, not health (Lexchin, 1984; 1994). In the pursuit of profits the drug companies are in perpetual competition with each other for increased market shares. This is especially true with reference to patent protected, brand name drugs with high profit margins.

In order to expand the number of high profit drugs the industry is perpetually involved in "Research and Development." This "R and D" often results in minor changes in the qualities of existing drugs (May, 1961). These "new and improved" drugs are often patented and renamed with a view towards maintaining or expanding market share.

The number of insignificant changes is so great that it is impossible for practicing physicians to be adequately informed concerning which drugs are actually new and which are retreads. Into this gap step the drug company "detail" persons. These are drug company employees whose primary mission is to "educate" physicians concerning their company's products in order to persuade them to prescribe their high priced, patent protected, profit generating brand name drugs over those of competitors.

To the extent that the detail persons are successful they contribute to increased costs of health care and they have the effect of influencing physician prescribing behaviors to such an extent that doctors have been described as "pushers" of unnecessarily expensive and, perhaps, even harmful drugs (Lexchin, 1984). This close association of physicians with the drug companies also contributes to the legitimation crisis of medicine insofar as it can be suggested that an overly heavy reliance on drug companies for information about drugs and their use casts doubt on the objectivity of doctors' judgments and prescribing patterns. The crisis of professional credibility is exacerbated by critiques of other aspects of medical practice and malpractice. Included here are revelations about simple medical incompetence as well as accounts of sexual abuse of patients.

Physicians have also been criticized for the inappropriate medicalization of various "problems with living." That is treating psycho-social difficulties as medical problems, and prescribing drugs, often mood modifying drugs, as the treatment (Harding, 1987; Cooperstock and Lennard, 1987). In many cases, critics point out, the medicalization of life's problems and discontents has the undesirable effect of perpetuating unhealthy and oppressive social relationships that are at the root of what appear as personal health problems (Cloward and Piven, 1979). Furthermore, the drugs themselves often have serious side effects that may be as bad as, or worse than, the conditions they were prescribed to treat. At the social level this imputed pattern of inappropriate medical diagnosis and treatment contributes to deteriorating health and the rising costs of health care.

Although modern medicine has been unsuccessful in curing many chronic and degenerative diseases, it has been remarkably successful in prolonging life. We saw earlier that life expectancy and average age at death have been increasing throughout this century. Part of the success in extending the average age at death may be related to the development and application of new medical diagnostic and treatment technologies in the hospital setting.

The development and application of life prolonging medical technologies has a number of far reaching consequences, some of which are forcing re-evaluation of fundamental societal values and creating new problems for medical ethics (Roy, 1988). In many cases individuals who previously would have died now can be kept alive because of new medical technologies. Of course, sustaining life through various heroic medical interventions is an expensive proposition that has prompted some to ask "Is it worth it?" Should the decision to prolong life be taken independently of considerations of the quality of life being prolonged? If the answer to these questions is "no," then who should have the right and duty to decide whose life will be prolonged and who will be allowed, or assisted, to die? If the answer is "yes, all life should be prolonged at all costs," then who should be required to pay, the individuals and their families, or the state? It is in answers to questions like these that the morality and economics of health care converge. Any attempt to deal with these questions in a one dimensional way is inadequate.

Reducing the Cost per Service

The third cost containment strategy includes various efforts directed towards reducing the costs per service provided. This strategy, although applicable in any sector of the health care system, is most apparent in hospital settings. As is evident in Table 11.5 hospitals account for the greatest proportion of health care expenditures. Therefore, any efforts to contain health care costs must focus on hospitals. Within hospitals the greatest proportion of costs are accounted for by wages. Attempts to contain hospital costs, therefore, have focused on workers and wages.

Wages can be reduced absolutely or relatively. Absolute reductions in wage bills can also be achieved in two ways. The first is to pay those who provide the services less. The second is to reduce the number of workers, or the number of hours worked by workers, without reducing the number of services provided. Both strategies are used by employers to achieve absolute reductions in wage bills. Relative reductions are achieved by increasing the productivity of service providers at a rate greater than the rate of increase of wages. This entails having workers provide more services per time period for the same amount or less money. This is accomplished through organizational means, often in the form of extensions to the occupational division of labor, or technical means, which involves development and application of productivity enhancing labor replacing technologies (Braverman, 1974). Again, both strategies have been, and are being, used.

The capacity of employers to reduce the wages is limited by various labor market considerations, including the supply of, and demand for, individuals with requisite skills and credentials. Generally, when demand is high and supply is low, wage reductions are difficult, if not impossible, to achieve. Indeed, under such conditions the norm is rising wages. This is because the relative scarcity of workers to fill available positions is manifest as increased bargaining power for workers, and a relative decrease in power for employers who must offer wage and other incentives to recruit and retain needed workers.

Throughout the post-World War II period until the mid-to-late 1970s, this was generally the situation that existed in Canada, and other nations in the advanced capitalist world, so that real incomes increased. It is interesting to note that despite income gains for nurses during that time period they were never able to raise incomes to the level of the average industrial wage in Canada (Wotherspoon, 1988).

The imposition of wage controls in the mid-1970s had the effect of creating a real wage reduction for nurses and other hospital workers (White, 1990). In fact, government policy since that time has resulted in a real reduction of incomes for many categories of workers in both the public and private sectors (Myles, Picot and Wannell, 1988).

In addition to reducing wages, absolute reductions in the cost per health care service provided have been achieved by transforming the nature and conditions of work. A major element in this strategy involves the replacement of full-time with part-time workers. Part-time workers are less expensive than full-time workers for a number of reasons. First, because they generally are not unionized they tend to be paid less per hour than full-time, unionized workers. A second cost reduction effect of the shift towards part-time workers is derived from the fact that part-time workers are not covered by many of the workplace plans and programs to which employers are required by law to make contributions. This fact alone results in a lowered wage bill, even if part-time workers are paid at the same hourly rate as full-time workers, which, of course, they are not. Savings to employers from this source alone can be as high as 10 to 12 percent. Third, part-time workers are called in to work only at times of peak demand. This enables employers to ensure that they are working at peak intensity the whole time they are at work. In this way "dead time" is reduced. That is, employers are not paying workers for that time when there is little or no work to do (Dickinson, 1991).

Relative reductions in the cost per health care service can be achieved, as indicated above, by having workers produce more in a given time period. This usually takes the form of increasing the intensity of work (Dickinson and Brady, 1984). There are a number of ways in which work is intensified. The two most common are extensions to the occupational division of labor and the application of labor saving technologies.

Labor saving technologies or, what might more accurately be termed, productivity enhancing or labor replacing technologies, tend to be developed to replace workers who perform routine, standardized and repetitive functions. In the hospital setting, although still quite rare because of the generally low wages, it is not unheard of to have robots perform certain functions. It has been reported, for example, that in the US, where hospitals are more often run for profit, robots are being tested to perform tasks such as "the pickup and delivery of medical supplies, lab specimens, meals and linens." The same sources also reported that Toronto's Hospital for Sick Children had acquired a robot for lab specimen preparation (Robertson, 1985).

From the point of view of nurses, and many other waged hospital workers, such strategies result in a deterioration of their working conditions and a reduction in their capacity to provide the personal care that is generally thought to be the hallmark of good quality nursing (Warburton and Carroll, 1988). From the patient's perspective the rationalization of nursing work in the unrelenting pursuit of efficiency is often experienced as a lack of caring, compassion and understanding. There is agreement that currently these conditions constitute a crisis in nursing (Hewa and Hetherington, 1990a). This crisis manifests itself in numerous ways, including, difficulty in recruiting and retaining nurses because of job dissatisfaction, job created stress, and frustration and disappointment which results from a disjuncture between expectations created in the professional socialization process and the realities of the alienating, oppressive and exploitative conditions with which they work (Stroud, 1983; Armstrong, 1988; Campbell, 1994).

Strikes in and of themselves are unlikely to be an adequate solution to the problems confronting the health care system. Nurses' strikes, however, sensitize the general public to the crisis in health care and the need for changes. Recent nurses' strikes have generated substantial public support. Doctors' strikes, particularly the 1986 Ontario strike, on the other hand, may well have contributed to a declining social support and respect for doctors who seemed only to be concerned with protecting their right to extra-bill patients. During that strike doctors were unsuccessful in linking their narrow professional interests with broader public interests. Nurses on the other hand have been much more successful in making such a linkage by emphasizing their goal of putting the "care" back in health care.

Reducing Health Care Budgets

The cost containment strategies we have looked at so far are all based on the assumption that a universal, comprehensive, accessible, portable and state administered health care insurance program exists, and currently, of course, it does. There is no reason to assume, however, that it will continue to exist, at least in its present form. There are several contemporary developments which suggest that profound changes are imminent.

The most obvious of these is changes to the system of federal government financing of health care services. Many feel that past and present reductions in federal funds foretell the erosion of Medicare as we know it. Before we briefly examine possible consequences of current and proposed changes let us look at the nature of the funding changes that already have taken place.

The original federal-provincial cost sharing arrangements entered into with the introduction of hospital insurance and medical care insurance tied federal contributions directly to provincial government expenditures. The federal government had no control over its own health spending because it was determined by what each province spent. From the federal government's point of view this was an undesirable situation. From the perspective of the provinces the original cost sharing arrangements was too inflexible. In order to be eligible for federal funds the provinces were required to spend their health care dollars on medical care (doctors') services and hospital services.

Initiatives in cost containment and the development of alternative forms of health care were discouraged by that arrangement. Every reduction in the cost of hospital services made by the provinces resulted in reductions of federal government money transferred to them. Thus, the cost sharing arrangement discouraged the provinces from attempting to make hospital services more efficient. Similarly, because of the fact that only hospital and physician services were eligible for federal cost sharing the provinces had little incentive to pursue other avenues of health expenditures such as health promotion or non-hospital forms of institutional treatment and care. Thus, both federal and provincial governments were interested in changing the structure of the cost sharing arrangement (Soderstrom, 1978).

This was done in 1977 with passage of the Established Programs Financing Act (EPF). The arrangement negotiated at that time reduced federal contributions to health care from approximately 50 percent to 25 percent, uncoupled them from provincial expenditures, and limited future direct federal increases to growth in the Gross National Product (GNP). In order to make this change attractive to the provinces the federal government reduced its level of income taxation and transferred "tax points" to the provinces so that they could increase their tax rates to make up for the reduced direct federal cash transfers.

Under the terms of the 1977 arrangement any provincial health care expenditures that exceeded the rate of increase of GNP were met entirely out of provincial government revenues; increased health care expenditures over that amount did not result in increased federal cash transfers. Clearly this arrangement gave the provinces increased incentive to contain costs in the medical care and hospital sectors (Vayda, Evans and Mindell, 1979).

In 1986 the federal government further limited its financial contributions to the provinces for health care by limiting annual transfers to a rate 2 percent below the rate of increase in the GNP. Amendments to the federal-provincial cost sharing arrangements, in the form of Bills C-20 and C-69, further reduced federal government cash transfers to the provinces for health care, post-secondary education and other social programs. The formula established held federal transfers to the provinces for health care and post-secondary education in 1990–91 and 1991–92 to 1989–90 levels. In 1992–93 federal transfers were allowed to increase at the rate of GNP growth less 3 percent. Over the next few years federal transfers to the provonces for health care declined by about $6.5 billion.

Mounting public opposition to continued cuts and restructuring of the health care system, combined with increasing worker militancy, especially among nurses, has encouraged the federal government to reinvest some funds back into the health care system. In the 1999 federal budget, for example, it was announced that $11.5 billion federal dollars will be put back into the health care system over the next five years through the Canada Health and Social Transfer (CHST).

The main concerns these new funds are intended to address are waiting lists, crowded emergency rooms and diagnostic services. A new framework for federal-provincial relations in the areas of health and social services, called the Social Union Agreement was also signed by the federal government and all the provincial premiers except the Quebec premier. Among other things, the Social Union Agreement stipulates that the new federal transfers for health care would in fact be used for health care, and that this would be done within the context of the September 1998 agreement reached at the meeting of the federal/provincuial/ territorial meeting of the ministers of health.

The reduction of federal cash transfers to the provinces for health care and other social services in the 1990s initiated a series of provincial health care reforms. The main manifestation of these reforms and, at the same time, the main means for their accomplishment, has been the regionalization of health care decision-making and service delivery.

Regional health boards can be understood as policy instruments intended to realize one or more of a number of reform objectives, such as, controlling costs, linking policy-making and service delivery to the needs of local residents, increasing public participation in health care decision-making and service delivery, facilitating the integration and coordination of health care services, and improving health outcomes.

Currently all provinces, except Ontario, have some form of regionalized health care. There is wide variation, however, between the provinces relative to the structure, function, and powers of regional health authorities. What is common, however, is that they are a manifestation of both devolution and centralization of powers. The scope of authority has ranged widely from limited authority over hospitals in New Brunswick to extensive control over integrated health, welfare and social services in Prince Edward Island. The scope of authority is, however, evolving; expanding in some jurisdictions and contracting in others.

The composition of regional health boards also varies. In most jurisdictions board members are appointed, in Saskatchewan, however, boards are composed of both appointed and elected members. Saskatchewan currently is the only province with elected board members. Several other provinces have stated the intention of having regional health board elections, but recently they have all backed away from that commitment. A number of provinces also have excluded health care providers from serving on regional health boards. Some are worried that individuals with vested interests might push particular agendas inimical to the objectives of reformers.

The various forms and functions of regionalized health care systems in Canada accentuates the fact that Canada does not have a singular, unified health care system. The diversity of forms of regionalization is indicative of different policy priorties and objectives in the different provinces. In some provinces, for example, the main objective may be cost control, while in another it may be service coordination and integration.

The diversity in forms of regionalization is positive insofar as it indicates that the goal of making the health care system flexible and responsive to local needs is being met. There is, however, always the concern that diverse regional health boards, under the banners of flexibility, responding to local needs, and enhanced community participation in health care decision-making may abandon the founding principles of Medicare. Although the 1984 Canada Health Act is intended to preserve the foundation of Medicare, historically there have been forces opposed to it (Badgley and Wolfe, 1967), and, according to some, this continues to be the case. Fuller (1998), for example, argues that an alliance of the organized medical profession, private for-profit insurance companies, the pharmaceutical industry and other health care goods and services corporations is vigorously working to "privatize" Canada's health care system.

The fact that an increasing proportion of health care spending in Canada is being privatized is cited as support for this argument. Fuller (1998:282) points out that private spending on health care has increased from about 24% of total spending in the mid-1970s to over 32% currently. She also notes that "private spending on health care now exceeds total federal government spending" (p. 282).

Cutback the Number/Type of Services Provided

This response to reduced revenues for health care is simply a more direct way of scaling down the scope of state health care insurance. A common response to cutbacks in federal government transfer payments to the provinces has been to deinsure or delist previously covered services. Persons who desire or require uninsured diagnostic or therapeutic services must either pay directly out of pocket or purchase private health insurance. This leads to a two tiered health care system where those who can afford it can get the required services and those who cannot afford can't.

Others argue for a two-tiered system of health care on moral grounds. Some have proposed, for example, that smokers, drug addicts and alcoholics should be treated last. The rationale being that because these people have engaged in behaviors which put them at risk for developing certain health problems, they are individually responsible for their illnesses and injuries and, therefore, they should be punished by limiting or barring their access to publicly financed health care services (Saskatoon Star Phoenix, 1989b).

The reasoning behind such suggestions is deceptively persuasive. It can also be extended to expanded categories of individuals; those who have sexually transmitted diseases because they did not practice safe sex, those who are injured in accidents while under the influence of alcohol, those who suffer from cardiovascular diseases because they have not exercised sufficiently and/or because they consume too much high fat food. The list could go on, but the point is clear. Given the fact that some lifestyle factors might be implicated in many, if not most, forms of injury and illness where does one stop blaming the victims of ill health and injury?

The logical fallacy underpinning the suggestion that those who are responsible for their own health problems because of lifestyles that include known or suspected risk factors is based upon a confusion of risk factors and causes. Risk factors are not causes. Risk factors are simply factors that are correlated with the risk of developing certain illnesses. They do not by themselves cause the illnesses, and in many cases the relationship between the risky behavior and the illness is non-existent (Marantz, 1990).

The possibility exists, within this line of thought, to establish two categories of people; the deserving sick and the undeserving sick. The deserving sick will be eligible for publicly funded health care services, the undeserving sick will not be eligible, or will have limited entitlement. For many, this creation of a human hierarchy, where some peoples lives are considered more valuable than others, is unacceptable. Proponents of this, and some other forms of rationing, retort that making decisions concerning the most effective and efficient allocation of scarce health care resources is not only rational but essential (Mickleburgh, 1991). Not to do so, they maintain, threatens the viability of the entire health care system.

At a more general level, this same argument is used to critique the principle of universality, not only with regard to health care services but also in reference to the whole array of social, and possibly educational, services. From one perspective, universality is seen as a non-affordable relic of the past, a crushing monument to an archaic idealism that has long since become unsupportable. Critics of universality argue, again in a deceptively convincing way, that not only is universal access to comprehensive, publicly financed health care services too expensive to sustain, but maintenance of such a system is irrational and renders the health care system ineffective and inefficient. Some health care services, both preventative and treatment services, it can be argued, are simply not necessary or efficiently applied to all individuals or categories of individuals.

An apparent case in point is mammogram screening of women for breast cancer. Recent evidence suggests that early detection of breast cancers among women who are less than fifty years of age does little or nothing in terms of increasing survival rates and saving lives. The situation is different, however, with respect to women over the age of fifty. For that category of women there is evidence to show that survival rates and longevity can be significantly increased by mammogram screening and early detection.

Some have suggested on the basis of this evidence that screening be made available only to those women in the age group where there is a demonstrated statistically significant chance of a positive outcome. Younger women should not have free access to mammogram screening for breast cancer. Others, particularly those who have a vested interest in the production and marketing of the equipment required for mammography, or who have an interest in providing the services for their own financial gain, or who have an interest in fanning the cancer hysteria for fund raising purposes, argue that all women regardless of age should be regularly screened through the mammogram technique.

Other examples can be provided. Some argue that AIDS education efforts should not be aimed at the whole population. Such efforts should be targeted to those groups of individuals most at risk, particularly homosexual males, prostitutes and IV drug users. As we have seen above, others take the position that individuals who engage in lifestyle behaviors known or thought to be risk factors in the contraction of certain diseases should be exempted from, or restricted in terms of their access to, health care services.

Despite these debates over service rationing and cutbacks, the most obvious area of straight forward cutbacks in the health care system is currently occurring in the hospital sector. Virtually every province has cutback the number of acute care hospital beds available by 25 percent of more. This action has been accompanied by others, including a reduction in the number of physicians and caps on the amount of money available for physician and hospital services. The money which is expected to be saved by cutting back on expenditures for hospital and doctors' services is to be used to further develop alternative forms of health care services.

Change the Types of Services Provided

It has been agreed for some time that the future of health care lies in a more co-ordinated approach between acute care hospital and physician services and other kinds of institutional and community-based types of care. The growth of various kinds of Home-Care programs and special care institutions is indicated by increased expenditures for such purposes in recent years. Planners and policy makers agree that further moves in that direction are required. This is not to say that physician and acute care hospital services will be replaced altogether, obviously that is both undesirable and impossible. Rather, the intention is to better co-ordinate social and health care services within a health promotion framework to ensure that institutionalization does not occur when more appropriate, less expensive and independence sustaining alternatives are available. The challenge is to create the conditions whereby it is possible to make the innovations considered necessary to meet the changing health care and social support needs of a changing population.

One widely cited example of such an undertaking is the Extra-Mural Hospital of New Brunswick (Adams, 1987; Ferguson, 1987). It is not possible to provide a detailed description of this innovation in health care here. Suffice it to note that the Extra-Mural Hospital provides a wide range of health care services to patients in their homes who otherwise would be required to stay in more expensive acute care hospital beds as they recuperate or to be admitted to those beds in the first place because previously that was the only place to receive the services now provided by the staff of the Extra-Mural Hospital. According to the director of the hospital about half the patients are early discharges from acute care hospitals and about half are admitted directly from the community thus delaying or preventing their admission to acute care hospital beds.

Although the budget of the Extra-Mural Hospital in New Brunswick is in addition to the budgets of the existing acute care hospitals, so that in the short run no immediate savings are realized, it is thought that in the long run and within the framework of a more co-ordinated health and social services system that such a facility will result in a more effective and efficient use of health care and social service dollars. Indeed, it is thought that the Extra-Mural Hospital will itself be the master institution from which a more integrated and co-ordinated system will develop (Ferguson, 1987).

The shift away from hospital based to community based services is also associated with increased privatization of the health care system (Fuller, 1998). This is because many community-based rehabilitative and long term care services are privately owned and operated. As a result, even if services are covered by Medicare, public sector funds are being channeled into the private sector. Increasingly this means they are being channeled into large multinational health care corporations.

Conclusions

It seems clear that in the current situation of changing health care needs and scarcity of health care resources, whether real or fabricated, the allocation and utilization of health care resources becomes highly politicized. Given the magnitude of resources involved much is at stake and this ensures the existence of powerful actors intent on protecting and enhancing their self-interests. Within this political and economic arena possibly the weakest contenders are individuals, particularly the young, the elderly, the poor, and members of other marginalized groups, who are not well organized politically and who, therefore, may not be able to protect their interests, or even have them clearly elucidated.

On the other hand changed circumstances bring about new conditions, including new political alliances and forms of organization that may contribute to the further empowerment of otherwise marginalized categories of individuals. This, however, just won't happen.

It will take considerable political will and organizational effort to ensure that one's interests are considered in the allocation and distribution of health care resources. The burgeoning of various self-help and advocacy groups in and around the health care sector testifies to the fact that many are actively engaged in attempts to protect and achieve their interests in this and other areas of social life.

References

Adams, O.
1987   Hospital without walls: Is New Brunswick's Extra-Mural Hospital the way of the future? Interview with Gordon Ferguson." *Canadian Medical Association Journal* 136 (April 15): 861–864.

Armstrong, P.
1988   "Where have all the nurses gone?" *Healthsharing* (Summer): 17–19.

Badgely, R.F. and S. Wolfe
1967   *Doctors' strike: medical care and conflict in Saskatchewan.* Toronto: McMillan.

Barale, A.E.
1991   "Patients have unrealistic expectations of system." *Saskatoon Star Phoenix* 16 September: A5.

Bator, P.A.
1983   "The health reformers versus the common Canadian: The controversy over compulsory vaccination against small-pox in Toronto and Ontario, 1900–1920." *Ontario History* 75: 348–373.

Beck, R.G.
1973   "Economic class and access to physician services under public medical care insurance." *International Journal of Health Services* 3: 341–55.

Begin, M.
1988   *Mecicare: Canada's right to health.* Montreal: Optimum Publishing International.

Blishen, B.R.
1991   *Doctors in Canada: the changing world of medical practice.* Toronto: Statistics Canada in association with the University of Toronto Press.

———
1970   "Social Change and Institutional Resistance: The Case of Medicare." In *Social and Cultural Change in Canada, Volume II.* (Edited by W.E. Mann). Vancouver Toronto Montreal: Copp Clark: 223–29.

Blomquist A.
1979   *The health care business: international evidence on private versus public health care systems..* Vancouver: The Fraser Institute.

Bolaria, B. Singh and T. Wotherspoon
1991   "Income Inequality, poverty and hunger." In *Social Issues and Contradictions in Canadian Society*. (Edited by B. Singh Bolaria) Toronto: Harcourt Brace Jovanovich: 464–80.

_____
1988   "Sociology, Medicine, Health, and Illness." In *Sociology of Health and Health Care in Canada*. (Edited by B. Singh Bolaria and Harley D. Dickinson) Toronto: Harcourt Brace Jovanovich: 1–14.

Braverman, H.
1974   *Labor and monopoly capital: the degradation of work in the twentieth century.* New York: Monthly Review Press.

Brown, M. C.
1987   *Caring for Profit: Economic Dimensions of Canada's Health Industry*. Vancouver: The Fraser Institute.

Brym. R. with B. Fox
1989   From Culture to Power: The Sociology of English Canada. Toronto: Oxford University Press.

Campbell, M. L.
1994   "The structure of stress in nurses' work." In *Health, Illness and Health care in Canada, Second Edition* (Edited by B. Singh Bolaria and Harley D. Dickinson) Toronto: Harcourt Brace: 592–608.

Chappell, N. L., L. A. Strain, and A. A. Blandford
1986   *Aging and health care: a social perspective.* Toronto: Holt, Rinehart and Winston.

Cloward, R.A. and R. F. Piven
1979   "Hidden protest: the channeling of female innovation and protest." *Signs* 4.

Cooperstock, R. and H. L. Lennard
1987   "Role strains and tranquilizer use." In *Health and Canadian Society: Sociological perspectives, second edition*. (Edited by D. Coburn, C. D'Arcy, G. Torrance and P. New). Toronto: Fitzhenry and Whiteside: 314–32.

Dear, Michael and Jennifer Wolch
1987   *Landscapes of despair: from deinstitutionalization to homelessness.* Princeton: Princeton University Press.

Dickinson, H. D.
            "The Domain of Sociology." In *Sociology*. (Edited by Peter S. Li and B. Singh Bolaria). Toronto: Copp Clark Pittman, forthcoming.

_____
1991   "Work and unemployment as social issues." In *Social Issues and Contradictions in Canadian Society*. (Edited by B. Singh Bolaria) Toronto: Harcourt Brace Jovanovich: 278–99.

1989   *The Two Pschiatries: The Transformation of Psychiatric Work In Saskatchewan,*
        1905–1984. Regina: Canadian Plains Research Center.

_____ and D. Hay
1988   "The Structure and cost of health care in Canada." In *Sociology of Health and*
        Health Care in Canada. (Edited by B. Singh Boliaria and Harley D. Dickinson)
        Toronto: Harcourt Brace Jovanovich: 51–73.

_____ and P.D. Brady
1984   "The labour process and the transformation of health care delivery." In *Contra-*
        dictions in Canadian Society: Readings in Introductory Sociology.. (Edited by
        John A Fry). Toronto: John Wiley and Sons: 194–206.

Dominion Bureau of Statistics
1967   *Life expectancy trends 1930–1932 to 1960–1962.* Ottawa: Minister of Trade and
        Commerce.

Dubos, R.
1979   *Mirage of health: utopias, progress, and biological change.* New York: Harper
        Colophon Books: [1953].

Epp, J.
1986   *Achieving health for all: a framework for health promotion.* Ottawa: Health and
        Welfare Canada.

Evans, R.G.
1984   *Strained mercy: the economics of Canadian health care.* Toronto: Butterworths.

Ferguson, G.
1987   "The New Brunswick Extra-Mural Hospital: A Canadian Hospital-at-Home."
        Journal of Public Health Policy 8(4):561–70.

Frankel, B. G.
1994   "Patient-physician relationships: changing modes of interaction." In *Health,*
        Illness and Health Care in Canada, Second Editrion. (Edited by B. Singh Bolaria
        and Harley D. Dickinson) Toronto: Harcourt Brace Jovanovich: 183–198.

Foss, L. and K. Rothenberg
1987   *The second medical revolution: from biomedicine to infomedicine.* ed Boston:
        Shambhala Publications.

Gellert, G. A., A. K. Neumann, and R. S. Gordon
1989   "The obsolescence of distinct domestic and international health sectors." *Jour-*
        nal of Public Health Policy 10: 421–24.

Grant, K. R.
1988   "The 'inverse care law' in Canada: differential access under universal free health
        insurance." In *Sociology of Health and Health Care in Canada.* (Edited by B. Singh
        Bolaria and Harley D. Dickinson) Toronto: Harcourt Brace Jovanovich: 118–34.

Greensields, V.
1989   "Don't rely on gambling funds: NDP." *Saskatoon Star Phoenix* 23 February: B11.

Harding, J.

1987   "The pharmaceutical industry as a public health hazard and as an institution of social control." In *Health and Canadian Society: Sociological perspectives*, second edition. (Edited by D. Coburn, C. D'arcy, G. Torrance and P. New). Toronto: Fitzhenry and Whiteside: 545–64.

Hay, D. A.

1988   "Mortality and health status trends in Canada." In *Sociology of Health and Health Care in Canada*. (Edited by B. Singh Bolaria and Harley D. Dickinson) Toronto: Harcourt Brace Jovanovich: 18–37.

Health Canada

1994   *National health expenditures in Canada, 1975–1993*. Ottawa: Health Canada, Policy and Consultation Branch.

_____

1997   Fact Sheets. Ottawa: Health Canada, Policy and Consultation Branch.

Hewa, S. and R.W. Hetherington

1990a   "Specialists without spirit: crisis in the nursing profession." *Journal of Medical Ethics* 16:179–84.

_____

1990b   "Specialists without spirit: Limitation of the mechanistic biomedical model." Paper presented at the 25th Annual Meetings of the Canadian Sociology and Anthropology Association, Victoria, BC.

Illick, I.

1976   *Limits to medicine, medical nemesis: the expropriation of health*. London: McClelland and Stewart in association with Marion Boyars.

Kleinman, D. L. and L. J. Cohen

1991   "The decontextualization of mental illness: the portrayal of work in psychiatric drug advertisements." *Social Science and Medicine* 32 (8): 867–74.

Lexchin, J.

1994   "Profits first: the pharmaceutical industry in Canada." In *Health, Illness and Health Care in Canada, Second Edition*. (Edited by B. Singh Bolaria and Harley D. Dickinson) Toronto: Harcourt Brace Canada:700–720.

_____

1984   *The real pushers: a critical analysis of the Canadian drug industry*. Vancouver: New Star Books.

Marantz, P. R.

1990   "Blaming the victim: the negative consequences of preventive medicine." *American Journal of Public Health* 80 (10): 1186–87.

May, C. D.

1961   "Selling drugs by 'educating' physicians." *The Journal of Medical Education* 36 (1): 1–23.

McLaren, A.
1990   *Our own master race: eugenics in Canada, 1885–1945.* Toronto: McClelland and Stewart.

Mickleburgh, R.
1991   "Plan ranks illness on basis of priority." The Globe and Mail 12 June: A5

Myles, J., G. Picot and T. Wannell
1988   "The changing wages distribution of jobs, 1981–1986." *The Labour Force,* October 1988. Ottawa: Supply and Services Canada: 85–129.

Navarro, V.
1976   *Medicine under capitalism.* New York: Prodist.

Naylor, D. C.
1986   *Private Practice, Public Payment: Canadian Medicine and the Politics of Health Insurance, 1911–1966.* Kingston Montreal: McGill-Queen's University Press.

Northcott, H.C.
1991   "Health status and health care in Canada: contemporary issues." In *Social Issues and Contradictions in Canadian Society.* (Edited by B. Singh Bolaria) Toronto: Harcourt Brace Jovanovich: 178–95.

_____
1988   "Health care resources and extra-billing: financing, allocation, and utilization." In *Sociology of Health and Health Care in Canada.* (Edited by B. Singh Bolaria and Harley D. Dickinson). Toronto: Harcourt Brace Jovanovich: 38–50.

Powles, J.
1973   " On the limitation of modern medicine. *"Science, Medicine and Man* 1 (1): 1–30.

Renaud, M.
1977   "On the structural constraints to state intervention in health." In *Health and Medical Care in the U.S.: A Critical Analysis.* (Edited by V. Navarro). Farmingdale, NY: Baywood Publishing Company: 135–146.

Robertson, S.
1985   "Check-up." *Saskatoon Star Phoenix* 25 November: A11.

Rosen, G.
1963   "The evolution of social medicine." In *Handbook of medical sociology.* (Edited by H.E. Freeman, S. Levine and L. G. Reeder). Englewood Cliffs, NJ: Prentice Hall: 17–61.

Roy, D. J.
1988   "Decisions and dying: questions of clinical ethics." In *Sociology of Health and Health Care in Canada. (* Edited by B. Singh Bolaria and Harley D. Dickinson) Toronto: Harcourt Brace Jovanovich: 527–36.

Saskatoon Star Phoenix
1989a   "Time to rethink medicare: CMA." *Saskatoon Star Phoenix* 9 March: A1.

301

1989b   "Smokers, addicts should be treated last: prof." *Saskatoon Star Phoenix*. 26 October: D10

Scull, Andrew
1984   *Decarceration: community treatment and the deviant—a radical view. Second edition*. Englewood Cliffs: Prentice-Hall.

Seguin, R.
1991b   "Quebec Liberals call for tax on health care." *The Globe and Mail* 31 October: A1.

Shorter, E.
1985   Bedside manners: the troubled history of doctors and patients. New York: Simon and Schuster.

Soderstrom, L.
1978   *The Canadian Health System*. London: Croom Helm.

Statistics Canada
1976   *General mortality 1950 to 1970*. Ottawa: Minister of Supply and Services.

1978   Death, vital statistics, volume III, 1976. Ottawa: Minister of Supply and Services Canada.

1982   Causes of death, vital statistics, volume IV, 1981. Ottawa: Minister of Supply and Services Canada.

1983   *Mortality—summary list of causes, vital statistics, volume III, 1981*. Ottawa: Minister of Supply and Services.

1986   *Provincial government finance, revenue, and expenditure, 1983 (Fiscal year ended 31 March 1984)*. Ottawa: Minister of Supply and Services.

1987   *Federal government finance*. Ottawa: Minister of Supply and Services.

1988a   *Mortality—summary list of causes, vital statistics, volume III, 1986*. Ottawa: Minister of Supply and Services.

1988b   *Causes of death, vital statistics, volume IV, 1986*. Ottawa: Minister of Supply and Services Canada.

1994   *Mortality—summary list of causes, 1991*. Ottawa: Minister Responsible for Statistics Canada.

1995   *Mortality—summary list of causes of death. vital statistics, vol. III*. Ottawa: Minister Responsible for Statistics Canada.

1996   *Mortality—summary list of causes, 1993*. Ottawa: Minister Responsible for Statistics Canada.

1997   *Mortality—summary list of causes, 1995*. Ottawa: Minister Responsible for Statistics Canada.

Shroud, C.
1983   "Silent Nightingales." *Quest* (March) 62–8.

Task Force on the Cost of Health Services in Canada.
1970   Volumes 1–3. Ottawa: Information Canada.

Taylor, M. G.
1978   *Health insurance and Canadian public policy: the seven decisions that created the Canadian health insurance system*. Montreal: McGill-Queen's University Press.

Waitzkin, H.
1983   *The second sickness*. New York: The Free Press.

Walker, R.
1991   "Medicare abuse targeted." *Calgary Herald* 14 June: A1.

Warburton, R. and W. Carroll
1988   "Class and gender in nursing." In *Health, Illness and Health Care in Canada, Second Edition*. (Edited by B. Singh Bolaria and Harley D. Dickinson). Toronto: Harcourt Brace: 556–569.

Webb, J.
1991   "Education, not political interference will fix medicare." *Saskatoon Star Phoenix* 6 September: A5.

Weller, G. R. and P. Manga
1983   "The push for re-privatization of health care services in Canada, Britain, and the United States." *Journal of Health Politics and Law* 8(3): 495–518.

White, J.P.
1990   *Hospital strike: women, unions and public sector conflict*. Toronto: Thompson Educational Publishing.

Wilkins, Kathryn
1995   "Causes of death: how the sexes differ." Health Reports Vol. 7 No. 2: 33–43.

Wilkins, R. and O. B. Adams
1983   "Health expectancy in Canada, late 1970s: demographic, regional, and social dimensions." *American Journal of Public Health* 73 (98): 1073–80.

Wolfson, M., G. Rowe and J.F. Gentleman
1990   "Earnings and death effects over a quarter century." Research Papers Series, No. 30, Social and Economic Studies Division, Analytical Studies Branch. Ottawa: Statistics Canada.

Woolhandler, S. and D. Himmelstein
1991   "The deteriorating administrative efficiency of the U.S. health care system."
        New England Journal of Medicine 324 (18): 1253–58.

Wotherspoon, T.
1988   "Training and containing nurses: the development of nursing education in Canada." In *Sociology of Health and Health Care in Canada.* (Edited by B. Singh Bolaria and Harley D. Dickinson) Toronto: Harcourt Brace Jovanovich: 178–95375–92.

Vayda, E., R. G. Evans and W.R. Mindell
1979   "Universal health insurance in Canada: history, problems, trends." *Journal of Community Health* 4 (3): 217–31.

York, G.
1987   *The high price of health: a patient's guide to the hazards of medical politics.* Toronto: James Lorimer and Company, 1987.

Note

1. This information provided through the cooperation of Statistics Canada. Leaders wishing further information may obtain copies of related publications by mail from Publications Sales, Statistics Canada, Ottawa, Ontario KIA 0T6 or by phone at 1-613-951-7277 or national toll free 1-800-267-6677. You may also facsimile your order by dialing 1-613-951-1584.

The Organization of Work

Paul P. Divers

This chapter continues our series of readings to introduce sociology to students. The two primary organizing concepts that are emphasized in this chapter are social structure and social history.

Of all social structures that frame our lives the most, the places where we work are of the most critical. From the time we enter grade school as children, we are being socialized to be competent, compliant, and faithful people who, it is hoped, will be involved in some way in the economy of Canada. Then after many years of education (averaging now about sixteen years), we are expected to be, again, competent, compliant and faithful workers. In this way, work, as outlined in the introduction, structures our personal identity in major ways. And when we look at the research on the experience of unemployment, we find that it is devastating to our identity as Canadians.

In a word, then, our places of work frame our lives in very real ways. Here, we will find that this framing takes on the face of being industrialized workers, post-industrial employees, and proletarians who constantly need to be aware of what kinds of work are expanding and which ones are declining.

The other central concept that is salient in this chapter is that of history. We will see how our species has adapted to centuries of changes in the way we work from hunting and gathering societies through to post-industrial ones. This historical perspective is important because it enables us to see ourselves in the larger picture and expands our horizons.

Introduction

As long as I kept finding I could do something, I still felt I was able to feel I was in control. The worst times are when you realize that you're done, or you feel that there isn't one more thing you can possibly do. You have made all the phone calls, you've written all

The author would like to express his appreciation to Elaine Grandin and Bradley Zipursky for their editorial comments on earlier draft of this chapter.

the letters, you've sent all the resumes and done absolutely everything: that's when the feeling of hopelessness sets in. Helplessness, too.

So long as I can find even one more thing to do, to help get me out of this situation, I'll do it. It gives me a little more incentive. To go on the next day and not give up.

—an unemployed worker
—(Burman, 1988:16)

You only need to listen to a person who is looking for a job to realize the importance of work in our society. The majority of us throughout our adult lives will work. Work will consume the best part of our days. In general, **work** is often defined as "continuous employment, in the production of goods and services, for remuneration" (Chen and Regan, 1985:5). Or, to put it simply: work refers to paid employment (Jenkins and Sherman, 1979). Yet, work is much more than these definitions suggest. Work remains a critical factor in defining our social existence; including, who we are, how we think, and what we hope to become. Bryant (1972) argues:

> One's standard of living, style of life, political ideology, basic value orientations, choice of friends and spouse, health, daily routine, mode of child rearing, and general satisfaction with life, to name a few considerations, may well be the indirect, if not direct, result of one's work. We are shaped, molded, regulated, even assimilated by our work. Work is our behavioral product, but so, too, are we in many ways the product of our work. (p. xvii)

Once students realize work is more than just earning an income, they are naturally interested in the world of work, how it is changing, and the implications of those changes for themselves and their families.

In this chapter we will explore the world of work, with specific emphasis on Canada. Specifically, we will discuss work in three different, yet intricately related ways: (i) the historical development of industrialization and how it changed the way in which we work today; (ii) the social organization of work in Canada which is commonly known as the societal level *(or structural level)* of analysis since it primarily focuses on large-scale change, trends, and the structuring of work in a society; and, (iii) organizational life or, as it is mainly referred to, the micro-level of analysis since it deals primarily with occupational careers, occupational choices, socialization practice, and so on.

After you have read this chapter, you should have a general understanding of the following key terms and concepts:

Industrialization	**Secondary sector**	**Deprofessionalization**
Social organization	**Tertiary sector**	**Occupational segregation**
Division of labour	**Labour Force**	**Work satisfaction**
Technology	**Labour markets**	**Deskilling**
Unemployment rate	**Occupational choice**	**Skill disruption**
Primary sector	**Profession**	

The Emergence of Industrialization

The Social Transformation of Work in World History

Since the beginning of time human beings have engaged in work activities to meet their survival needs. To meet these needs, human beings developed and were shaped by the technology and social organization of the society. **Social organization** refers to the relations among those involved in work. For example, is their a division of labour or do people perform all the tasks necessary to meet their subsistence needs? **Technology**, on the other hand, refers to the tools and skills used in the process of work. The technology and social organization at a given stage of history determined the nature of that society, including its degree of social inequality; which set the stage for the next level of development (Marx, 1967 [1887]; Lenski, 1966).

The social organization of work as we know it today, is a relatively recent phenomenon in world history. In fact, the present stage of social organization represents less than one percent of known human existence on this planet. To better understand the present form of social organization, we need to understand the evolution of work throughout history. Figure 12:1 highlights the historical progression of work; we will discuss each stage in turn.

Nomadic Hunting and Gathering Societies

By about 300,000 B.C. the human species, *Homo sapiens,* had evolved to its present form. Human beings lived as nomadic hunters and gatherers, moving from one place to the next as food resources were depleted in an area. Human beings lived as nomadic hunters and gatherers until about 8,000 B.C., accounting for about 97 percent of the history of our species! (Hodson and Sullivan, 1990). Hunting and gathering people did not perceive of "work" as a separate sphere of life. Those activities needed to secure sustenance took place on a daily basis. People did not expend energy collecting a surplus of game, berries, and edible roots because they could not store food nor transport it for future usage.

Figure 12:1. Timeline of the Social Organization of Work

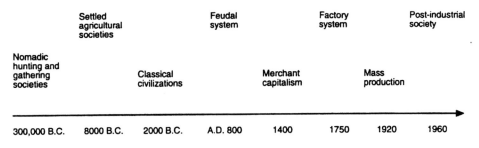

Source: Hodson, R. and Sullivan, T. *The Social Organization of Work.* Belmont, Calif.: Wadsworth Publishing Company, 1990.

Technology was very simple. Most work-related skills were shared in common, so that any single member could do all or most of the tasks required by the group as a whole. There did exist, however, primitive forms of a division of labour based on gender and age. Initially, the division of labour based on gender resulted from biological differences between men and women. However, this division of labour was not strictly based on strength differences nor socially-constructed inequalities. Most women spent much of their adult life, which was short, either pregnant or nursing children. Their primary duties were to pick berries, hunt for small animals, attend to the fire, cook meals, and sew furs together to make clothes for the band. Men, on the other hand, were responsible for hunting big-game, assessing the amount of resources available in an area, and making tools and weapons (i.e., stone cutters and wooden spears). Lee (1981) points out that there is considerable evidence available to suggest that women's small-game hunting and gathering activities were more productive than were men's big-game hunting activities, in both quantity and regularity of contribution.

Settled Agricultural Societies

Early agricultural societies developed independently in several places around the world (including Southeast Asia, the Persian Gulf, and Mesoamerica) from 9,000 B.C. to 3,000 B.C. The major differences between settled and nomadic societies includes (i) settled societies could accumulate a surplus supply of food and other goods since they lived in one area; (ii) technology was more sophisticated in settled societies but still extremely primitive according to our standards; and, (iii) a division of labour became more prominent, but was not restricted to, gender and age based differences.

As these societies matured, improvements in agricultural technology gradually allowed more people to leave agricultural work. These improvements included terracing and irrigation, the increased use of animal and human fertilizers, and advances in metallurgy that led to the proliferation of metal tools (Lenski, 1966). In addition, during the later stages of this societal form, the emergence of political officials, military leaders, artisans and craft specialists were emerging as the economic activity and settled areas expanded.

Classical Civilizations

Large agricultural societies gradually replaced small agricultural societies through military exploitation and subjugation by 2,000 B.C. leading to immense classical empires. For instance, historians estimate that the Inca Empire included about four million people at the time of the Spanish arrival (Lenski, 1966). Other examples of these civilizations include the Mayans and the Aztecs of Central America, the Azande of East Africa, the Phoenicians and the Egyptians of the Mediterranean, and the Imperial Chinese (Lenski, 1966:149). In these cities, several thousand people lived off the agricultural surplus of the subjugated areas. New craft skills were developed in the cities to produce more refined products for the rising tastes of the empires' rulers, officials, and attendants (Hodson and Sullivan, 1990:11).

In the centuries preceding the birth of Christ craftsman formed guilds to regulate standards and to limit the number of skilled craftsman. Membership was restricted almost exclusively to men. Most guild members were the sons of craftsman; rarely did someone gain entry unless they were related by blood to a guild member. Few technological advances occurred in classical civilizations because of the availability of slave labour. Membership in a guild was usually social in nature.

Feudal System

The feudal system was really an extension of simple agricultural societies. The major difference was that peasants in simple agricultural societies only turned over a portion of their crops to support rulers, priests, warriors, and civic officials. In feudal society, however, landlords extracted surplus crops from the peasants, known as *serfs,* to pay for Church taxes, military protection, and for their own personal use. The expropriation of surplus crops forced *serfs* to work continually to meet their sustenance needs. This period of time is probably considered to be one of the most extreme periods of inequality of human history.

Several significant developments occurred in feudal society. Artisans, specialized guilds based on new technologies, and merchants became organized in a more structured manner. The new guilds that were formed controlled not only standards for its members, but also hours of work, and the regulation of prices. These medieval guilds were similar to the guilds of the classical civilizations but they played a much more significant role in organizing the economic and political life of the growing medieval cities.

Many changes led to the passing of feudal society and the transition to modem industrial society. This transition has provided a focus for much of the social history written since that time (Hodson and Sullivan, 1990). This period in the social organization of work was also a central concern of the forerunners of modern sociological thought such as Karl Marx, Max Weber, and Emile Durkheim. In brief, the transition from feudal society to industrial society was brought about by an expansion in trade, markets, and the population base of cities, and the emergence of a factory system of production.

Merchant Capitalism

The period between feudal society and industrial society was one in which increased trade provided the impetus for changes in the social organization of work. This period lasted from the fourteenth century to the advent of the first modern factory in England in the mid-eighteenth century. Merchant capitalism existed not as a way to organize production, but as a means, to organize trade. Prior to this period, craftsmen were responsible for obtaining their own raw materials before they transformed them into finished goods. Under merchant capitalism, merchants took on these roles. Merchants gradually became more powerful since they controlled trade in the market. Eventually craftsmen were required to work for merchants since they had the capital and contacts to obtain the raw products necessary for the craftsmen to perform their trade. These merchants also utilized unskilled non-guild workers to perform simple tasks required for the craftsman to produce his finished product. Essentially, these simple tasks were traditionally performed by the craftsman, but merchants realized if they hired unskilled non-guild workers to perform some of the preparatory and rudimentary tasks for the craftsman, the craftsman would have more time to concentrate on the quality and quantity of finished products. It was under merchant capitalism that we began to see an early form of the division of labour generally associated with industrial society.

Factory System

As the industrial revolution began in 1750, the social organization of work underwent a rapid transformation. A factory system of production emerged with many employees working under one roof for specified periods of time each day. This system of production emerged first in England. The Industrial Revolution in England had begun in the wool industry. The focus shifted quickly, however, as the New World grew and markets for British textiles expanded to Asia and North America. Numerous technological inventions facilitated the rapid growth of the textile industry, including the flying shuttle (1733), the spinning jenny (1767), the water frame (1769), the spinning mule (1779), the power loom (1787), and the cotton gin (1792) (Faunce, 1981:14). The rapid growth of the textile industry quickly spread to other industries since many of the technological inventions in the textile industry required coal to provide steam to operate much of its technology.

These developments not only had a major impact on the economy of England, but also on the social organization of work. Employers began to realize that if they divided all the tasks to manufacture a product into more refined tasks and had certain workers attend to each task separately, they could increase daily production. Adam Smith in 1776 in his book *The Wealth of Nations* (1937), described the advantages of the new division of labour in the manufacturing of pins for the textile industry:

> One man draws out the wire; another straightens it; a third cuts it; a fourth points it; a fifth grinds it at the top for receiving the head; to make the head requires two or three distinct operations; to put it on is a peculiar business; to whiten the pin is another; it is even a trade by itself to put them into the paper; and the important business of making a pin is in the manner divided into about 18 distinct operations, which in some manufactories are all performed by distinct hands, though in others the same man will sometimes perform two or three of them.... Ten persons, therefore, could make among them upwards of 48,000 pins in one day. (p. 4–5)

Prior to this elaborate division of labour, ten men could only produce 20 pins each per day for a total of 200 pins.

Mass Production

The factory system of production continued through to the twentieth century. By 1920, a new system of production emerged . . . mass production. Five characteristics differentiate this system of production from the early factory system of production: (i) scale of industry increased; (ii) ownership of factories fell into the hands of the few; (iii) a bureaucratic structure to organize all facets of production and to control workers emerged; (iv) an assembly-line system of production was instituted; and, (v) shift work over 24 hours periods, seven days a week became the norm of operation (Hodson and Sullivan, 1990). These social inventions changed the way people worked by organizing all work-related activities according to scientific procedures. This new approach became known as *scientific management* and is most often identified with the work of Frederick Winslow Taylor, an American industrial engineer who felt that thinking should be removed from the realm of the worker. Scientific management, or *Taylorism* as it came to be known, involved a detailed study of industrial processes in order to break them down into simple operations that could be precisely timed and organized. Taylor actively studied the work done by workers on shop floors and assembly-lines before redesigning those jobs to increase maximum efficiency for maximum productivity. Taylor's approach was actively resisted by workers because it made them feel like automatons instead of human beings. Nevertheless, controlled output and worker performance strategies were to become commonplace.

Post-Industrial Society

Since 1960 we have seen an increase in technology and a growing service sector (i.e., finance, insurance, and transportation industries, as well as professional and business services). This new trend has brought about a number of occupations that did not exist or employed very few people. We will not describe this stage in the social organization of work at this time since we will return to it in greater detail later in the chapter. Instead, we now turn to how industrialization emerged in the context of Canada.

Industrialization in Canada

The term **industrialization** basically refers to the replacement of human skills in the production of goods and services with machines and the replacement of human or animal energy with inanimate sources of power (Smucker, 1980:1). The course of industrialization in a society is usually unique to that society. In other words, the course of industrialization in Canada has been different from that of England, Germany, Japan and the United States. This may not seem obvious to you until you recognize that the time period of industrialization, the social milieu, and the early manufacturing organizations of each country have been different which inevitably resulted in various courses of development. The historical development of industrialization in each country mentioned above is beyond the scope of this chapter. Instead, we will provide an overview of industrialization in Canada which will allow you to understand the next section on occupational structure.

The economic development of Canada as a colony first of France and later of England was built up around the exploitation and export of natural resources (Rinehart, 1987:25). This economic emphasis persisted well into the nineteenth century. By the mid to late nineteenth century, Canada was primarily known for its trade in furs, timber, and grains. This time period in the development of industrialization can best be considered a pre-industrial period in the Canadian economy since most work done was labour intensive (not aided by machinery) and most exports were not in the form of finished goods. The vast majority of trade was with England and it was there where furs, timber, and grains, were transformed into finished, usable goods.

At the time of Confederation (1867), Canada remained a basically rural nation with 50 percent of the nations labour force employed in agricultural pursuits. Although there were manufacturing in Montreal, steel and railroad car production in Hamilton, and numerous other manufacturing pursuits evident in Toronto, Canada had not yet entered a period of industrialization. Between 1870 and 1890 Canada began to emerge as an industrialized nation stimulated by a protective tariff. Investment in machinery became prevalent resulting in more and larger factories. By 1890 Canada had 70,000 manufacturing firms producing a variety of semi-finished and finished goods; but, by 1920 this number dwindled to 22,000 manufacturing firms (Rinehart, 1987:45). The reduction in the number of manufacturing firms was not a sign of a weakened industrialized nation. On the contrary, it was a sign of a strengthened industrialized nation since one of the signs that Marx so vividly pointed to was a concentration of capital in the hands of the few. In other words, multinational corporations were emerging resulting in greater concentration, centralization, and bureaucratization of production. This process has continued to the present day.

Today, Canada as a society is generally perceived to have the characteristics basic to a member of the fortunate group of advanced industrial nations (Craib, 1986). It has superior levels of modern technological activity in many parts of the country and in some sectors of the economy. The standard of living in Canada is relatively high and most Canadians are able to find work, buy a home, own a car, and periodically take vacations. Canada rates as one of the leading nations in per capita gross national product (GNP). The GNP is the total value of goods and services produced in a country plus the monies earned from foreign investment divided by the number of persons in the country. In 1988, Canada had a GNP per capita of $14,120 U.S., which placed it as the 4th largest in the world behind Norway (3rd), United States (2nd), and Switzerland (1st) (World Bank, *World Development Report,* 1988). The goods produced in this country, however, tend to be based on our natural resources (i.e., oil and natural gas), agricultural products (i.e., wheat and barley), and semi-finished products such as lumber. Our reliance on the exportation of our natural resources, as well as foreign investment in the country, has given rise to two main issues: (i) dependence on foreign trade and (ii) the effects of foreign investors buying Canadian companies and taking the profit out of the country. Presently, close to 50 percent of the mining, petroleum, timber, and manufacturing industries are foreign owned and controlled mostly by American, then German and Japanese investors (Royal Commission on the Economic Union, 1985). The problem with extensive foreign investment, such as that seen in Canada, is that we are unable to be self-sufficient nor are we in a position to reap the profits from our own resources. In addition, economic decisions made within the country and abroad can lead to plant closures outside the control of the workers.

The United States is unquestionably our principal trading partner. Approximately three-quarters of both Canadian exports and imports are with the United States (Royal Commission on the Economic Union, 1985). This trading relationship is expected to strengthen as a result of the Free Trade Agreement between Canada and the United States signed on January 2, 1988 by Prime Minister Brian Mulroney and former President Ronald Reagan. For the Progressive Conservative government, the free-trade agreement represents the centerpiece of its economic strategy for Canada. The agreement is intended to enhance Canada's competitive position, using the American market as a springboard for reaching other international markets. The government argues that Canadian industry needs tariff-free access (that is, the elimination of duties on certain kinds of imports and exports) to the North American market with its 250 million consumers. For the U.S., the economic impact of the pact is small, but not insignificant. A report prepared for the U.S. Trade Representative by the American International Trade Commission showed U.S. industry had little to gain, or lose, from tariff reductions, but the free-trade agreement is still important to Americans. It offers the U.S. nondiscriminatory access to

Canadian natural resources, a significant long-term advantage (Cameron, 1988). At a time when the U.S. is running short of key raw materials, including petroleum, Canada has agreed not to favour Canadian resource users over American users.

The long-term impact of the free-trade agreement has been, and will continue to be, debated for some time. The effects that the pact will have on the Canadian economy and its market, remain unclear. We can only hope as Canadians that the pact will in fact bolster our industries and ensure the economic viability of our markets in the years to come.

In this section we briefly described the emergence of industrialization in Canada. In addition, we explored Canada's economic position vis-a-vis its trading partners. The next section will closely examine Canada's changing occupational structure and the implications of that structure for working Canadians.

Occupational Structure in Canada

Canada's Industrial and Labour Structure

There are several ways in which we can conceptualize the work done in the labour force. One way is to categorize labour force participants by the *industry* in which they work. By convention, there are three major sectors within the labour force: primary, secondary, and tertiary.

1. **Primary sector**—consists of labour force participants who work in agriculture, fishing, logging, hunting, trapping, or mining; with the vast majority working in the farming industry.

2. **Secondary sector**—consists of labour force participants who work in construction and manufacturing.

3. **Tertiary sector**—consists of labour force participants who work in transportation, communications, commerce, finance, health, education, and so on (Hedley, 1988:498).

The occupational categories within the primary sector involves some kind of extraction or harvesting. Generally, there is no transformation of raw products into finished products for consumption. The occupational categories within the secondary sector, by contrast, typically involve manufacturing finished or semi-finished products. Some industries, however, do include both sectors (Hedley, 1988). For example, occupational categories in the fisheries industry includes primary and secondary sector occupations. Individuals who catch the fish are considered to have primary sector occupations since the product is still in its natural state (i.e., a tuna fish). On the other hand, individuals who are employed in fish canning factories are considered to have secondary sector occupations since they transform the raw product into a manufactured good (i.e., canned tuna). According to Daniel Bell in his much acclaimed book, *The Coming of Post-Industrial Society* (1967), when at least half of the labour force works in the *secondary sector* (i.e., a

313

canning factory, an automobile assembly plant, a steel company, etc.), we live in an **industrial society.**

Bell also suggested that when at least half of the labour force works in the *tertiary sector* (i.e., services, communications, health, education, etc.) we live in a **post-industrial society.** Labour Force participation statistics for Canada show that seventy-two percent of the labour force is presently employed in the *tertiary sector,* while six percent are employed in the *primary sector,* and twenty-two percent are employed in the *secondary sector (Statistics Canada, 1990).* This clearly places Canada as a post-industrial society. However, the number of labour force participants in each sector is not necessarily consistent across the provinces. Table 12:1 reveals the percent of labour force participants in each industry by province. For example, we can see that Saskatchewan has a much larger agricultural industry (primary sector) but a much smaller manufacturing based economy (secondary sector) compared to the other provinces in the country. Similarly, in the Maritimes, few labour force participants are involved in agriculture but more are involved in public administration work compared to the other provinces. It is evident, however, that the number of service jobs is most consistently the predominant type of employment for labour force participants.

Recent projections of the occupations expected to contribute most to employment growth in Canada are overwhelmingly *tertiary sector* occupations. Table 12:2 highlights

Table 12:1
Labour Force by Industry and Province, Canada, 1990

Industry	B.C.	Alta.	Sask.	Man.	Ont.	Que.	Maritimes	Total
				Percent				
Agriculture	2.0	6.5	16.5	7.1	2.2	1.9	0.2	3.2
Other primary	3.3	5.5	3.3	1.7	0.9	1.5	4.8	2.2
Manufacturing	11.5	7.9	5.9	11.8	19.2	18.9	10.7	15.7
Construction	7.4	7.1	4.9	4.5	6.8	5.9	6.9	6.5
Transportation/ communication	8.2	7.3	7.0	8.6	6.5	7.8	8.8	7.4
Trade	18.9	18.8	17.4	18.2	17.8	18.5	19.7	18.3
Finance/insurance/ real estate	6.5	5.4	4.7	5.5	6.8	5.5	3.5	5.4
Service	36.4	35.6	33.5	35.7	33.4	32.7	34.2	34.5
Public administration	5.5	5.7	6.6	6.6	6.0	6.5	8.1	6.4
Unclassified[1]	0.3	.2			0.4	0.8		0.2
Total (%)	100.0	99.8	99.5	99.7	100.0	100.0	97.0	100.0
N, 1000s)	(1,597)	(1,321)	(471)	(532)	(5,227)	(3,328)	(1,033)	(13,509)

1. This category consists of unemployed persons who have never worked for pay and those who have not worked in the last five years.
2. Statistics Canada does not provide provincial estimates of less than 4,000. These omissions lead to total percentages of less than 100 percent.
Source: Calculations based on Statistics Canada, *The Labour Force* (December 1990, #71-001, Table 11), p. B-24.

these occupation categories for the years 1986 to 1995. Most evident from these projections is that most of the occupations expected to contribute to growth tend to be of the low wage, service variety. We will expand this point later in this chapter.

The classification of the labour force by *industry, or what is being produced,* is not the only way that we can come to understand the Canadian labour force. Often, the labour force is categorized by *occupation,* or the *kind of work* that is being performed. Often we differentiate the kind of work that individuals do according to whether they are *white collar* or *blue-collar* occupations. The term **white collar** occupation typically is applied to the work of managers, nurses, lawyers, teachers, salespersons, and office workers. Phrases such as *intellectual* and *mental tasks, working with people,* or *ideas or information* (rather than things) are commonly encountered. In contrast, **blue-collar** occupation typically is applied to work roles involved in manufacturing: the creation of products. It is sometimes presumed to require only manual or labour intensive tasks, usually summarized as "working with the hands." Electricians, carpenters, truck drivers, machine operators, and labourers are considered to have blue-collar occupations. Blue-collar work is often subdivided into two categories: **skilled crafts** and **unskilled work.** *Skilled crafts* are those in which the work requires some degree of manual dexterity combined with a broad

Table 12:2

Occupations Expected to Contribute Most to Employment Growth in Canada, 1986–1995

Occupational Title	New Growth in Employment
Salesperson, commodities	91,000
Food Service	80,000
Bookkeepers	56,000
Secretaries and stenographers	54,000
Chefs and cooks	47,000
Cashiers and Tellers	47,000
Janitors and cleaners	40,000
Truck drivers	33,000
Sales management	26,000
Barbers and hairdressers	26,000
Motor vehicle mechanics	25,000
Nurses	24,000
Financial officers	22,000
Supervisors; food and beverage preparation	19,000
General office clerks	18,000
Labourers, services	17,000
Services management	16,000
Receptionists and information clerks	15,000
Carpenters	15,000

Source: Krahn, J. H. and Lowe, G. S. *Work Industry and Canadian Society.* Scarborough: Nelson Canada, 1988:62
Original Source: Employment and Immigration Canada; based on *COPS 1986 Reference Scenario.*

knowledge of tools, materials, and processes. All craft work combines formal training and certification as well as some experiential knowledge. Skilled crafts include such blue-collar occupations as electricians, plumbers, welders, and masons. *Unskilled work* are those occupations that require no formal training nor certification primarily because the skill level required to perform the task is considered to be minimal. These jobs virtually always consist of routine tasks, require very little training, and are often considered to include tasks that anyone "off the street" can perform. Examples of such jobs include dishwashing, stocking shelves, garbage collection, cleaning offices, and waitressing.

The classification of the labour force by occupation is somewhat misleading since not all white collar jobs are necessarily high paying, provide promotion opportunities, nor are prestigious; conversely, not all blue-collar jobs are low paying, offer few career advancement opportunities, nor have little occupational prestige in the eyes of the general public. For example, selling vacuum cleaners door-to-door is considered to be a white-collar occupation but usually is not well paid and has low occupational prestige. On the other hand, a blue-collar occupation such as being an electrician may include wage benefits that far surpass many white-collar occupations and provides greater occupational prestige; which is often the result of unionization in Canada. These categories, therefore, are only convenient social constructions to classify the kind of work that people perform in the labour force.

As we approach the twenty-first century, it is abundantly clear that the trend toward an ever-increasing *tertiary sector* complemented by a continued growth in *white-collar* occupations is likely to continue for some time. The distribution of males to females in each occupation is still not reflective of the number of females now participating in the labour force (see Table 12:3).

Table 12:3
Labour Force Participation by Sex, Canada, 1901-1990 (Selected Years)

Year	Female	Male	Both Sexes
1901	16.1%	87.8%	53.0%
1911	18.6	90.6	57.4
1921	19.9	89.8	56.2
1931	21.8	87.2	55.9
1941	22.9	85.6	55.2
1951	24.2	84.1	54.3
1961	29.1	80.8	55.1
1971	39.9	75.4	58.0
1976	45.0	75.5	58.0
1981	51.8	78.3	64.8
1986	55.1	76.7	65.7
1990	57.6	74.1	65.7

Note: "Both sexes" category represents the total labour force participation rate for all adults working in each respective year.
Sources: 1901–1981 from Chen, M. and Regan, T. *Work in the Changing Canadian Context.* Toronto: Butterworths, 1985:135; Krahn, J. H. and Lowe, G. S. *Work Industry and Canadian Society.* Scarborough: Nelson Canada, 1988:40; 1990 from Statistics Canada, *The Labour Force* (December 1990, #71-001, Table 1), p. B-5,

As we can see in Table 12:4, in 1990 males were dispersed over a variety of occupations whereas females tended to be more concentrated in lower paying, lower status white-collar occupations. In particular, 29.6 percent of all females in thelabour force were employed in clerical (i.e., secretarial and receptionist jobs), while an additional 16.2 percent were employed in service occupations (i.e., waiting tables and hairdressing). Most of the work that many women do in the labour force is simply an extension of what they have traditionally done in the home (Armstrong and Armstrong, 1984). Hedley (1988) suggests that secretarial and clerical work, cooking, waiting tables, hosting, teaching small children, nursing, cleaning, and sewing are all chores that women have done since time immemorial. The only difference between what most are doing now and what they traditionally did is that they are being paid directly for their labour. Women today, however, are beginning to find entry into traditionally male dominated occupations. This has been a long struggle for women since socialization practices, occupational sex segregation and unequal treatment in the work place has contributed toward female underrepre-

Table 12:4
Labour Force Employment by Occupation and Sex, Canada, 1990

Occupation	Number (1000s)			Percent[1]		
	Total	Female	Male	Total	Female	Male
Managerial/administrative	1,653	661	992	13.5	11.9	14.8
Natural sciences	481	89	392	3.9	1.6	5.9
Social sciences	259	154	104	2.1	2.8	1.6
Religion	33	7	26	0.3	0.1	0.4
Teaching	557	355	203	4.6	6.4	3.0
Medicine and health	655	538	117	5.4	9.7	1.7
Artistic, literary and recreational	230	100	130	1.9	1.8	1.9
Clerical	2,041	1,644	397	16.7	29.6	5.9
Sales	1,259	575	684	10.3	10.3	10.2
Service	1,551	901	650	12.7	16.2	9.7
Farming/horticultural	406	106	299	3.3	1.9	4.5
fishing/hunting/trapping	33	–[2]	31	0.3	–	0.5
Forestry and logging	44	–	43	0.4	–	0.6
Mining and quarrying	57	–	56	0.5	–	0.8
Processing	349	85	264	2.9	1.5	3.9
Machining	209	10	200	1.6	0.2	3.0
Fabricating/assembling/repairing	934	188	746	7.6	3.4	11.4
Construction	651	15	636	5.3	0.3	9.5
Transportation	456	46	410	3.7	0.4	6.1
Materials handling	249	50	199	2.0	0.9	3.0
Other crafts/equipment operating	142	32	110	1.2	0.6	1.6
Total	12,248	5,560	6,688	100.0	99.5	100.0

1. Percentages are calculated by sex, based on the raw numbers in each occupation row divided by the total number employed for each sex.
2. Statistics Canada does not report estimates of less than 4,000 because of concerns about the reliability of small estimates of sample data.
Source: Statistics Canada, *The Labour Force* (December 1990, #71-001. Table 14), p. B-27.

sentation in many higher paying, higher status occupations. We will return to these issues on several occasions in sections dealing with the impact of technology, the barriers to primary labour market entry, and occupational choice.

The degree of inequality can be partly understood by investigating labour market segmentation in Canada. Let us turn to bow labour is segmented in an attempt to explain inequality among the work force.

Labour Market Segmentation in Canada

Labour markets are the structural emphasis that sociologists place on the positions and places where people work. They are, in general, "the economic arenas in which employers seek to purchase labour from potentially qualified employees who themselves are seeking employment suitable to their present education, experience, and preferences" (Krahn and Lowe, 1989:62). What a person dictates as a "good job" or a "bad job" and what an employer dictates as a "good employee" or "bad employee is determined by the rewards and benefits that each exchange for the output that is necessary for the task at hand. Often the two are not commensurate for the jobs and the skills available in the labour market at any give time period. That is, often there are more skilled, experienced, and highly educated people than the number of jobs available to accommodate them. Conversely, those jobs that require fewer skills, education, and experience tend to have a lot of people seeking opportunities for employment. Nevertheless, labour market theories emphasize that it is important to know where individuals and their occupations are located in the labour market if we are to understand career development.

The chief spokesperson for the labour market approach to understanding the types of jobs that people perform, Piore (1969, 1970, 1975), divides the labour market into two sectors: **primary** and **secondary**. The primary labour market is subdivided into upper and lower tiers with the professional (i.e., doctors and lawyers) and technical (i.e., computer programmers) as well as the managerial and administrative groups belonging to the upper tier, and sales (retail outlet employees), clerical, and skilled crafts (i.e., licensed mechanics) comprising the lower tiers. The secondary labour market consists of semi-skilled (i.e., a telephone repairmen) and unskilled nonfarm labourers (i.e., carpenters helpers) and service workers (i.e., gas station attendants). According to Piore (1975):

> The former [primary sector] offers jobs with relatively high wages, good working conditions, chances of advancement, equity and due process in the administration of work rules, and above all, employment stability. Jobs in the secondary sector, by contrast, tend to be low paying, with poorer working conditions and little chance for advancement; to a highly personalized relationship between workers and supervisors which leaves wide latitude for favouritism and is conducive to harsh and impulsive work discipline; and to be characterized by considerable instability in jobs and a high turnover among the labour force. (p. 126)

Jobs that tend to have little remuneration and benefits (the secondary labour market) tend to be occupied primarily by lower educated, female, and visible minority groups. Those jobs with higher pay and benefits (usually in the primary labour market) tend to be occupied by those individuals with higher education, more experience, and skill; typically, but not exclusively, white males. In general, because of low employer investment in

318

updating worker skills and knowledge, the occupations in the secondary market offer little opportunity for career development. Finally, because of the differences in skills and knowledge required by the occupations in the various markets, little mobility occurs between the secondary and primary labour markets. Consequently, an individual who works in the secondary labour market tends to remain in that market throughout their work lives unless they upgrade their skills and knowledge.

Barriers to primary labour market entry are numerous. These include gender discrimination, age discrimination, "contacts" (or the so-called *old "boys" network*), and racial and ethnic discrimination. In most cases, *gender discrimination* as a barrier to primary labour market entry is based on managers and corporations discriminating against women. For years, women have been denied the opportunity to either enter the primary sector or once they move into primary sectors they are denied upward mobility. In a recent study conducted in Calgary, Alberta, Cahoun found that of the private and public sector organizations, surveyed, females represented 47.9 percent of the labour force. Yet, only 13.6 percent were executives, 22.3 percent were middle managers, and 37.4 percent were front-line supervisors (Calgary Herald, January 19, 1991:F1). In another Canadian study conducted by the Canadian Bankers' Association, women were found in 90.7 percent of all the bank teller and clerking positions, while only 5.7 percent were bank executives (Calgary Herald, February 16, 1991:F1). Although, women are gaining greater entry into the upper levels of the primary labour market, they still are significantly underrepresented. Women are often perceived as less competent than males even though many have similar credentials (i.e., degrees and experience). In addition, many organizations are still hesitant about spending time and money training women for fear that they are not serious about their careers and will leave them for traditional female roles (i.e., childrearing).

Age discrimination has also been considered a barrier to primary labour market entry. Young adults are often discriminated against because they lack the experience and maturity to work in "good jobs." How many times have you thought or said to an employer "how can I get the experience if no one gives me a job?" More recently, age discrimination has worked against middle-aged workers who have lost their jobs. Employers have begun to discriminate against middle-aged people partially because they may expect higher salaries than a younger adult, and partially because they often lack the qualifications that so many younger people who are entering the work force have today. The combination of these two factors detracts from middle-aged workers' ability to effectively compete with the surplus of higher educated younger workers in today's labour market.

Barriers to primary labour market entry also takes the form of job vacancy knowledge. Often, public and private organizations have internal competitions (that is, seeking to fill the vacancy from within the organization) that excludes applications from outside the system. Labour unions also practice this same strategy as a way to provide security and incentives for card carrying members. Research has shown that one-half of all jobholders in this country have found their positions through personal contacts (Anderson and Calzavara, 1986). These findings demonstrate that access to information can act as a barrier to primary labour market access.

Finally, racial and ethnic discrimination can act as a barrier to primary labour market entry. Discrimination of this kind is similar to gender and age discrimination since it is based on physical or socially undesirable characteristics of the individual. The barriers to primary labour market entry discussed here do not entirely account for the difficulties that some groups of individuals face in the labour market today. However, they do provide us with part of the explanation for why some people have "good" jobs and others have "bad" jobs. It should be clear that the structure of our society can have as much influence in this process as individuals themselves do. As these barriers become more pronounced and more people are denied entry into the labour market, unemployment in Canada is likely to rise.

Unemployment

Work is often considered to be a major part of a person's sense of self-identity. The importance of having a job to a strong self-identity is exemplified when you meet a new person in a social encounter where the first question they ask you or you ask them is "What do you do for a living." Most people are able to identify one job or another. What is it like to be without a job? How does it feel to admit being unemployed? How do people react to joblessness? These are important questions in our present society since people are subject to layoffs as a consequence of an unstable economy.

Unemployment Rates

In Canada, an **unemployment rate** is calculated by dividing the number of individuals out of work and who are actively seeking work by the total number of labour force participants (including the unemployed). These rates, however, are only crude estimates since not all people seeking work are known nor do they include those individuals who are **underemployed**—individuals who are presently working in jobs that require less skill than their experience and education would suggest but do so in order to make a living. Unemployment rates vary over time, across regions, and industry in this country.

In Canada, regional differences in unemployment is considerable. These differences are often directly linked to the economic base of the various regions. In particular, provinces with a diverse economic base (economies with primary, secondary, and tertiary sector industries) tend to fare better than others. Table 12.5 breaks down the unemployment rate by province since 1982. As can be seen, the Maritime provinces consistently show the highest rate of unemployment in the country. The unemployment rate of the Maritimes is almost double that of Ontario and the Prairie provinces for any given year.

Unemployment realities in Canada are also differentially distributed across age and sex (see Table 12.6). The percentage of persons, ages 25–44 years, overwhelmingly constitute the bulk of the unemployed in the country. This is alarming since this is the time period in which people begin to develop their careers and have the greatest financial obligations (i.e., childrearing and mortgage payments). Prolonged unemployment has the potential to create irreversible economic hardships and diminish career advancement opportunities. We now turn to the subjective experiences of the unemployed.

320

Table 12.5
Unemployment Rate by Province, Canada, 1982–1990

					Percent					
Year	NFLD	PEI	NS	NB	QUE	ONT	MAN	SASK	ALTA	B.C.
1982	16.5	12.9	11.9	14.0	12.2	8.5	7.6	5.8	5.6	9.8
1983	19.5	16.7	15.8	16.2	15.3	12.7	10.9	8.9	11.6	16.1
1984	20.5	12.8	13.1	14.9	12.8	9.1	8.3	8.0	11.2	14.7
1985	26.2	16.5	15.3	16.7	13.0	9.9	9.5	9.7	11.9	16.4
1986	21.9	16.3	14.3	16.8	12.3	8.2	8.9	9.1	9.2	14.0
1987	21.4	17.8	15.8	15.0	11.7	7.4	9.0	8.5	11.5	15.3
1988	20.6	17.9	11.7	13.7	10.0	5.0	8.7	8.1	8.3	10.8
1989	16.3	16.4	10.4	13.5	9.7	5.8	8,7	9.1	8.0	10.8
1990	18.5	20.5	12.3	13.2	11.2	6.5	7.5	8.9	7.5	8.5

Source: Statistics Canada, *The Labour Force*, #71-001 (1982, Table 29, p.79; 1983, Table 56, p. 79; 1984, Table 109, p. 145; 1985, Table 54, pp. 94–95; 1986, Table 54, pp. 81–82; 1987, Table 54, pp. 81–82; 1988. Table 54, pp. 81–82; 1989, Table 37. p. B50; 1990, Table 37, p. B53).

Table 12.6
Unemployment Distribution by Age and Sex, Canada, 1990

Age	Male	Female	Total
15–24 years	28.9%	25.2%	27.3%
25–44 years	52.2	55.6	53.7
45–and over	18.9	19.2	19.0
Total	100.0%	100.0%	100.0%

Note: Statistics Canada reports data using the actual (or estimated) numbers of individuals in each category. The data in this table have been converted into percentages. For example, 52.2% of all unemployed males are between the ages of 25–44.
Source: Statistics Canada, *The Labour Force* (December 1990, #71-001, Table 29), p. B-42.

Subjective Experiences of Unemployment

In 1988, *Killing Time, Losing Ground: Experiences of Unemployment* by Patrick Burman was published. The book was based on a study of the unemployed in London, Ontario. Burman showed that the subjective experience of being unemployed was one of fear, insecurity, anger, helplessness, and dismay. Although most of the participants in the research became unemployed involuntarily (i.e., layoffs and plant closures) many believed there was something wrong with them because they could not find immediate employment. Burman's analysis not only provides insight into how individuals feel bout being unemployed, it also shows how the macroinstitutional sphere (i.e., the Unemployment Insurance Commission, Welfare Departments, and Canada Manpower) provide little solace for the circumstances of the jobless. Although these institutions are established to provide a necessary service, they are often seen by their clients as sources of frustration and degradation. The subjective experiences of several respondents are reflected in the following excerpts:

> They really make you feel like you're begging. Their whole attitude is, "You don't deserve this but, out of the goodness of our heart, we're going to give it to you." (p. 69)
>
> They have a real looking-down-on-you attitude, and my back just gets right up. I don't find them very pleasant people. I keep thinking how people less assertive than me deal with that. I bet there's a lot of people that cry. Because they're so negative to you. There's no understanding. It's like, "you quit your job, and you did this just so you could do nothing." (p. 85–86)
>
> There is some sort of thing where you punch in your interests and your education and it comes up with a job or an area that you are suited for.... Well, I went to this and punched in all the stuff and it turned out that I wasn't suited for anything. (p. 72)

According to Burman, the bureaucratic structure of these organizations strips away individuality and the uniqueness of the jobless. Moreover, the longer an individual is unemployed the less assistance these institutions are able to provide which leads to a sense of being trapped in a maze in which the exit seems more and more remote. The interplay among, bureaucratic assistance, loss of occupation, weakening social networks and family hardships, tends to lead to a change in self-identity and individual worth.

From Burman's study of unemployment we can learn so much about employment in our society. By understanding the experiences of the unemployed we are able to comprehend why people often "consent" to *exploitative* and *alienated labour* and why individuals become attached to and express "satisfaction" with jobs that lack intrinsic gratifications. Rinehart (1988) suggests that financial independence, self-respect, and the opportunity to socialize are job-linked elements that are extrinsic to the content of work, but stabilize and give meaning to our lives. Employment insulates us from the abyss of joblessness: a job, any job, is preferable to no job at all.

More recently, researchers have become concerned about the effects of new technologies and their implications for tomorrow's labour force. Will new technologies lead to more unemployment or will they create more job opportunities? And, will technology of the future lead to a more skilled or less skilled work force? It is these questions that we will address in the next section.

Work and Technology

Technology and Its Impact on Skill

The impact of technological change on skill requirements for work is one of the most debated subjects in the study of work and occupations (Form, 1987). This debate has reached new heights with the rapid introduction of microcomputer technology (often referred to as *microelectronic technology*) in the workplace; and is further fueled by the known and unknown potential of future technologies. **Skill level**, can be defined simply as "a complex organization of behaviour (physical or verbal) developed through learning and directed toward a particular goal or centered on a specific activity." Wallace (1989) suggests there are three perspectives on the impact of skill level currently dominating the field: *the upgrading thesis, the downgrading thesis,* and the *mixed effects thesis.*

1. Proponents of the *upgrading thesis* argue that "advanced technologies require that workers take on more responsibility, use more judgment and discretion, and have a broader understanding of the total production process" (Blauner, 1964). This argument is supported by the belief that microelectronic technology will require initial learning and subsequent relearning to keep pace with the advances made in the technology in the future.

2. Proponents of the *downgrading thesis,* however, agree that initially technological change may create a temporary increase in skill requirements for some workers or even that a few workers may experience permanent increase in skill (Bright, 1966). Nevertheless, they argue that the prevailing outcome of technological change for most workers is one of de-skilling, routinization, and closer supervision. This argument was most notably advanced by the neo-marxist Harry Braverman (1974) in his seminal book *Labor and Monopoly Capital: The Degradation of Skill in the Twentieth Century.*

3. The third perspective is the *mixed effects thesis.* Proponents of this perspective argue that both upgrading and downgrading of skill level will result from technological change, but in the long run they tend to balance out resulting in no net change in the skill distribution in the workforce (Wallace, 1989:364–366).

Empirical evidence can be found for each of the perspectives discussed. Blauner (1964) in his work *Alienation and Freedom* provided historical evidence to support the

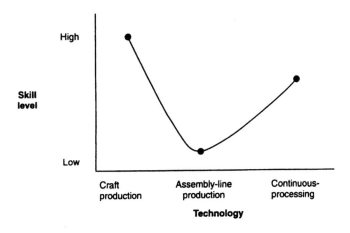

323

upgrading thesis by showing that industrial societies moved through several stages of development—craft production, assembly-line production, and continuous processing (automation). According to Blauner, skill level was at its highest level during the early years of industrialization, at its lowest during the assembly-line stage, and increases once again due to automation associated with the modern technology available today in corporations and industries (see Figure 12:2). Specifically, long-term occupational trends reveal that industrialization has increased skills by reducing unskilled work and increasing semi-skilled, skilled, clerical, technical, professional, and administrative work. Empirical studies tending to support the upgrading perspective rely primarily on self-reports by workers. For example, Wallace (1988) suggested that the "subjective experiences of workers" is typically one of skill upgrading, since they feel that they are constantly learning new things and tend to disregard the fact that skills previously acquired have fallen into disuse. For example, clerical workers today primarily do most of their daily work on microcomputers. However, most do not recognize that previous skills such as shorthand dictation, filing, and so on are seldom required to the same extent and have been replaced by microcomputers and dictaphones. Today these technological innovations are the new skills of the workplace.

Support for the *downgrading thesis* can be seen in the work of Glenn and Feldberg *Degraded and Deskilled: The Proletarianization of Clerical Work* (1977). Their analysis was based on observations in organizations, discussions with managers and intensive interviews with 30 clerical workers. Glenn and Feldberg concluded that automation of office work was routinized, required fewer skills than were previously needed, and reduced the clerks' control over their job activities because the computer silently monitors every action and has the implicit pressure for greater output. Similarly, Phillip Kraft (1979) in his historical analysis of the changing technology in the computer programming industry suggested that a once highly skilled field has fallen to increasing fragmentation and routinization of the tasks involved in present day software programming. Kraft argues that the skill level of programmers has decreased because once initial programming has been developed, all other software packages can be developed with minor modifications. Kraft concludes that, "programmings transformation into software production shows that even the most complex work can be trivialized, and underscores the self-development in general—that improved machines automatically mean better jobs."

As suggested earlier, proponents of the *mixed effects thesis* note that the distribution of skilled, semi-skilled, and unskilled occupations has remained relatively stable for several decades, despite changes in the particular mix of occupations. Some mixed effect proponents find different effects of technological change of specific workers in an industry. For instance, Baran and Teegarden (1984) found that automation in the insurance industry led to the displacement of many professional occupations, a shift in the burden of work to low-paid clerical workers, and an increase in the supervisory workers, resulting in a net increase in the average skill of the remaining workers. Similarly, Calhoun and Copp (1988) found that computerization of legal work had mixed effects in that the position of elite segments of the law profession (i.e., constitutional and corporate law) was strengthened at the expense of non-elite segments (i.e., wills and trusts and family law), thus reinforcing trends which were already underway.

324

Irrespective of the position one takes on this debate, it is reasonable to conclude that technological change in the form of microelectronics will at minimum lead to **skill disruption**, whereby a portion of the acquired skills are rendered obsolete and the worker must acquire some new skills to function within the environment created by the new technology. Hodson (1988) argues that the degree of skill disruption will be contingent on the pace of technological change, which is likely to be substantial, the compatibility between old skills and new skills, and the availability of retraining programs to ease the transition from the old technology to the new. As new technology is introduced into most occupations the form of the work force is likely to be rapidly altered. This is the subject of our next section.

Telecommuting Technology and Its Impact on the Workforce

The emphasis on computers and work was fueled in part by Alvin Toffler's notion of the "electronic cottage," presented in his book *The Third Wave*. Toffler argued that as the structure of our economy changed from industrial to information-based, the computer would offer more freedom on the job, including the freedom to take work home to the "electronic cottage." Shortly thereafter, another futurist, Jack Nilles, coined the word "telecommuting" (Christensen, 1988).

The basic idea behind telecommuting is that employees and/or contracted individuals can work at home for an employer via a computer networking system. Several models are compatible with the telecommuting concept, including: full-time telecommuting from home offices, split work weeks, and split work days. Moreover, the potential for telecommuting has also seen the rise of "home entrepreneurs"; persons who use computers to develop their own businesses, which are frequently spin-offs of businesses in which they were previously employed. Telecommuting using personal computers offers benefits for both workers and employers, but it also holds great potential for increasing the exploitation of workers. On the positive side, Christensen (1988) suggests that groups such as the elderly, the handicapped, and working mothers can be employed gainfully in jobs that fit their schedules. Flexibility and autonomy are benefits that are typically mentioned for home workers. Employers argue that working mothers can save on child care by tending children while they work, but others contend that workers who try and tend children while they work cannot do justice to either job. Wallace (1989) points out other drawbacks of this technology:

> Recent experience with some types of "high-tech homework," such as clerical workers who process insurance forms, shows that employers often pay substandard wages and benefits, and do not allow paid vacations, health benefits, workmen's compensation, or unemployment compensation. (p. 380)

Hence, one has to look closely at specific cases to weigh the advantages and disadvantages of working in the home that advanced technology allows.

Educational and Retraining Requirements for New Technologies

In 1981, a report commissioned by the Federal Government of Canada entitled, *"The Task Force Report on Labour Market Development in the 1980s,"* recommended that resources be modestly re-allocated from education, general arts and sciences and social work to engineering, business, economics and technology. The report essentially emphasized that the labour market needs in Canada required a computer literate and technically trained labour force that could lead the country into the twenty-first century.

The recommendations of the Task Force Report are consistent with the pervasiveness and rapidity of technological change in North America. Several studies (Menzies, 1981; Groff, 1983; Abeshouse, 1987) all reach variations of the same conclusion that the de-skilling of jobs in some sectors will be offset by the upgrading of jobs in other sectors, leaving a labour force that, on average, requires the same amount of education and skills. However, whereas workers a generation ago could expect to change jobs two or three times before they retired, today's workers will change jobs six to seven times (Abeshouse, 1987). Consequently, rather than being a straight climb as we have become accustomed to, work careers are likely to entail several detours involving a substantial retooling of job skills.

The disruptive nature of career paths and the de-skilling of many jobs will require further training and retraining of workers throughout their lives. Choate (in Abeshouse, 1987) has suggested that workers will require "regular booster shots of education and training" to keep up with changes in technology.

The basic requirement of a university degree or college diploma will continue to be a prerequisite for most "good jobs" in the workplace, if only because such a degree serves a credentialing function in the job market (Collins, 1979). Nevertheless, it would appear that the content of a post-secondary school education will probably change as suggested by the Task Force Report in 1981. Microelectronic technology will not only be reserved for the technically trained, but also for those seeking liberal arts education. Wallace (1989) clearly identifies this as a necessity:

> People who do not educate themselves—and keep educating themselves—to participate in the new knowledge environment will be the peasants of the *information society.* (p. 381)

Technology and Occupational and Class Structures

Hodson and Parker (1988) found that occupations with projected growth rates of over 50 percent for the decade of the 1990s include data processing mechanics, office machine servicers, and computer operators, analysts, and programmers. However, among similar lists of the fastest-growing occupations in *absolute numbers,* most are "low-tech" jobs that comprise the lower echelon of the white-collar and service sectors. Many of these are relegated to what has come to be known as the "pink-collar ghetto": low-paying, dead-end jobs occupied predominantly by females (e.g., secretaries, cashiers, fast-food workers, and so on). These jobs, naturally will offer little solace or real opportunity to the middle-aged, displaced steel workers whose standard of living is based on an income nearly twice as high. Hodson and Parker (1988) conclude:

The overall effect of advanced technology appears to be to increase the prevalence of upper-level professional jobs and lower-level operative and service jobs. The demand for middle-range jobs, particularly clerical jobs, will in all likelihood be reduced by high technology developments. The impact of these changes on the distribution of differentially rewarded positions in the economy will be to *increase inequality* [our emphasis] between the top and the bottom of the occupational distribution and to reduce the proportions of middle-range positions. (p. 17)

At the societal level, technological displacement of relatively high-paying jobs in manufacturing and other fields will lead to a phenomenon known as the "declining middle" (Kuttner, 1983). This trend has been occurring during the 1980s and will likely be commonplace in the years to come. Rosenthal (1983) found that between 1978 and 1983, 23.6 percent of households formerly classified as "middle-class" moved out of the middle. Of those displaced from the middle-class, about one-fourth advanced into a higher position, but three-fourths declined. Rosenthal explains this phenomenon by pointing to: (i) the sharp decline in the number of relatively well-paid (often unionized) manufacturing jobs; (ii) accompanied by a rise in low-paid retail and service jobs; and, (iii) the rise of a relatively small layer of well-paid professional and technical jobs. Observations such as these have fueled fears of a two-tiered society in which there are sharper social and political divisions between the "haves" and the "have nots" (see Kuttner, 1983).

Whether or not we believe in the extent of this foreseeable impact at the societal level, it should be recognized that further technological change will have some effect on the socioeconomic status of many individuals; given education, income, and occupational status will likely alter with technological advancement.

Career and Occupational Choice

A basic interest in the study of work is the question of why and how people first enter specific occupations, or types of work. In sociology, we categorize these questions in a broad category, commonly known as *occupational choice*. The term occupational choice has different meanings to different researchers (Chen and Regan, 1985; Ginzberg et al., 1951; Rothman, 1990). The discrepancy of the use of the terminology is based on the fact that the process leading up to entry into the labour force is imperfect. In addition, the term "choice" implies a conscious, logical, rational, decision-making approach to careers. The problem with this implication is that although people do believe that they do make choices, often the choices made are shaped and limited by events and forces that the individual has little, if any, ability to control. It is important to recognize that choices occur in a social context. Often occupational choice begins at an early age but changes as we grow older. You probably remember as a youngster that you wanted to be an astronaut, a doctor, a nurse, a teacher, or an athlete when you grew up. But a combination of factors (i.e., ability, motivation, changing interests, and access to opportunity) made some of your early career choices unattainable.

Numerous theories have been put forth by both sociologists and psychologists for examining the decisions surrounding why and how people make specific occupational choices in their lives. Developmental psychologists, for instance, have concentrated on the *individual-ambition model*, while sociologists have concentrated on the *structure-opportunity model* (Speakman, 1980). A brief discussion of each model should provide you with a general understanding of the approaches taken by the theorists in each discipline.

The Individual-Ambition Model

The developmental theories first appeared during the 1950s in psychology. These theories attempt to explain human behaviour and attitudes in terms of maturation of the individual's innate capacities. Most notably, the work of Eli Ginzberg (1951) represents this model which emphasized viewing a person's occupational choice as a maturational and cumulative process whereby choices change over time and are influenced by previous experiences.

Ginzberg's approach is based on viewing the developmental process of occupational choice as a series of compromises between a person's interests, capacities, opportunities and values. At an early age (six to eleven years of age), children are able to express very specific occupational roles that they identify with through media coverage (i.e., athletes, firefighters, nurses, and cowboys), parents, and people in their immediate environment who are role models. Ginzberg calls this the *fantasy phase* since the occupational choices made by a child is uninformed and not based on a realistic appraisal of their own abilities, the requirements of the work, or the social constraints which will later effectively limit their occupational attainment (Rothman, 1990). The next stage of development, according to Ginzberg, occurs between eleven and seventeen years of age, known as the *tentative choice phase* and can be subdivided into four stages: the interest, capacity, value and transition stages. Basically, this phase typifies the gradual maturation of the self-concept and the growing awareness of the internal and external factors that can influence the choice of a career. During the tentative choice phase adolescents begin to reach an understanding of their interests which is limited by their perceived abilities. This appraisal leads to an evaluation of the possible occupations available to them. The transition stage is usually reached during the last years of high school or the first few years of college when the individual begins to face the constraining effects of external factors that influence their occupational choice (i.e., cost of schooling and the competitiveness of entry into an occupation). The third, and final stage is known as the *realistic choice phase* occurring around age eighteen. This phase is characterized by a realistic appraisal and decision based on a compromise between interests, abilities, and the opportunities available.

Ginzberg's theory has been criticized on several grounds. First, many young adults today do not make occupational choices until after they have finished some post-secondary schooling, while others take a job or travel until they have decided what they would like to do for a career. Today, career choices and decisions are often delayed by young adults compared to young adults of fifty years ago when occupational decisions were forced by educational systems. Secondly, some adolescents leave school at an early age and take a job even before they have moved through the last phase. In particular, Ginzberg has been criticized for not taking into account differences among socioeconomic background, gender, and ethnicity as intervening factors in choosing a career. Finally, occupational choice decisions do not necessarily begin or end during early adulthood. Today, more adults are returning to school at a later age and/or changing occupations throughout their working lives. Ginzberg's theory does not take into account both developmental decisions later in adulthood nor situational and contextual factors (i.e., unemployment and new opportunities to acquire education) that may lead to decisions about career choices.

The Structure-Opportunity Model

The structure-opportunity model has been the focus taken by sociologists to understanding individual decisions about occupational choice. In contrast to the individual ambition model which focuses on the individual's processes of psychological development, the structure-opportunity model stresses the effects of the individual's structural content in influencing occupational choices (Chen and Regan, 1985). In this sociological perspective, the social characteristics of the individual are viewed as "external influences over which the individual has little or no control. In this way they set limits upon and constrain the kinds of occupational choices and decisions that individuals make" (Pavalko, 1971:51). Simply put, sociologists emphasize the social characteristics such as gender, ethnicity, and parental socio-economic status which can have a profound effect on socialization to particular kinds of occupations, access to opportunity, and subsequent decisions about career choices.

Socio-Economic Background

In Canada and the United States, parental socio-economic origin (measured by educational and occupational attainment) is one of the most powerful and pervasive factors in occupational choice. Research over the past 25 years has shown a direct relationship between social origins and educational aspirations. However, even controlling for levels of ability and aspirations, children of higher status parents tend to achieve higher levels of education. In addition, children from higher socio-economic background tend to attain better jobs than children from lower status backgrounds with equivalent levels of education. Rothman (1990) suggests that the continuing impact of socio-economic status reflects the interaction of a combination of factors including the advantage of economic resources, and differential values and orientations, and subsequent experiences in the school system (p. 292). These differences seem to provide part of the answer for determining how and why many individuals make decisions about occupational choices available to them.

Gender

Even from an early age men and women are socialized differently. You will recall the discussion in the chapter on Socialization that whether consciously or not, parents tend to assign household tasks according to the gender of their children. By the time children reach school age they have come to identify with **occupational sex-typing**, that is, a societal view that certain occupations are more appropriate work for one sex than the other. Through an allocative process sex-typing has the effect of limiting perceived occupational choices which channels males and females in different directions. For example, occupational choices among males and females have been influenced by such traditional views as men are doctors and women are nurses; men are managers and women are secretaries. These views have been reinforced through various mass mediums, including television shows, advertising, commercials, and children's storybooks. As we saw earlier in this chapter, women tend to occupy those occupations located in the tertiary sector but of the low pay, low status variety (i.e., clerical and sales). It is true that more women today are entering the traditional male-dominated occupations, but, this trend is not significant enough to suggest that the perceived occupational choices available to women has increased substantially over the last twenty years.

Ethnicity

As suggested in the chapter on Culture, Canada is considered to be a multicultural society. Recent immigration by Asian and Caribbean peoples has reinforced the ethnic diversity in our country. Yet, at the same time, occupations available to many immigrants tend to be those occupations that are less desirable to white Canadians. You only need to walk through a college campus at night time and see who is cleaning offices. Naturally, occupational choice for new immigrants in particular can be limited because of language barriers and education. We must be careful not to suggest that these are the only factors that contribute to the type of work that they perform. Discrimination and prejudice also has contributed to **occupational segregation**, the concentration of members of one sex or ethnic group in relatively few occupations compared to the opposite sex or ethnic groupings. These trends will hopefully change as the second generation gains access to education and fair treatment.

Research in the area of occupational choice and social inequality has contributed to recent legislation at the federal and provincial levels of government, as well as at corporate levels across the country. Recent legislation (i.e., the Canadian Constitution) has encouraged employment equity programs (also known as *affirmative action programs*) designed to increase the number of persons who are not well represented in the professions, management and other upper tertiary sector careers. The groups recognized as under-represented in these occupational groups, include: (i) visible minorities; (ii) aboriginal peoples; (iii) persons with disabilities; and, (iv) women. Once members of these groups gain access to these higher status occupations, it is likely that more members from these groups will have greater occupational choices in the future.

The structure-opportunity model shows that career decisions are sometimes hindered by social characteristics that are beyond the control of the individual. Although this is the view adopted by most sociologists working in this area, it is probably true that the individual developmental model also has an effect on actual occupational choices. Occupational choice, then, is likely based on a constellation of factors that cannot be separated out by theoretical argumentation. Further empirical work still needs to be conducted in this area.

In our next section we will discuss the present state of the professions in our society.

Professions and Professionalization

The use of the term *professional* has several meanings in our society. The term includes those who work for monetary compensation for an activity, differentiating them from those that do not. For example, a professional hockey player versus an amateur hockey player, a professional figure skater with the Ice Capades versus an Olympic figure skater. The term *professional* is also used to identify those individuals with specialized knowledge, talents and/or skills. Examples of this category include doctors, lawyers and professors. Finally, many occupational groups utilize the term *professional* as a form of self-identification to create a positive public image. This category includes occupational groups such as human resource managers, realtors, police, and automobile mechanics.

Sociologists use the term still another way to identify occupations enjoying, or seeking to enjoy, a unique position in the labour force. The use of the term *professional* in this context is reserved for those occupations which have exclusive jurisdiction over certain kinds of services, are able to negotiate freedom from external intervention and have control over the content of their work activities in the delivery of services. In this section, we will emphasize: (i) the identifiable characteristics of a profession; (ii) the debate about whether or not the professions are becoming deprofessionalized or proletarianized; and finally, (iii) the future of the professions.

Characteristics of a Profession

A **profession,** according to Ritzer (1986), can be defined simply as:

> An occupation that has had the power to have undergone a developmental process enabling it to acquire, or convince significant others (for example, clients, the law) that it has acquired a constellation of characteristics we have come to accept as denoting a profession. (p. 62)

This definition alone does not tell us any more about what a profession is unless we identify what are the salient characteristics of a profession. You should be aware before we proceed that the literature on professions and professionalization is voluminous in scope. Obviously, what is presented here is narrow in scope. To begin with, sociologists have suggested that for an occupation to reach the status of a profession, the following characteristics must be met:

1. creation of a full-time occupation;
2. establishment of a training school;
3. establishment of a national governing association;
4. efforts to win legal support; and,
5. establishment of a legal code.

These characteristics were first identified by Wilensky (1964) in his classic article *"The Professionalization of Everyone?"* Numerous authors over the years have identified the same characteristics using different terminology. Wilensky's characteristics however, really have stood the test of time.

Most of you will undoubtedly say that you can identify numerous occupations that meet these criteria. What you must keep in mind, however, is that most occupations lack one, two, or three key criteria. In addition, most occupations lack the autonomy (*or self-regulation*) that most professions have. For example, a complaint against the competency of a medical practitioner is usually dealt with by the provincial medical association. Seldom are external authorities able to determine whether or not the medical treatment provided by the medical practitioner is of the nature that would question their competency. Occupations that are designated as professions usually have a specialized and theoretically-based knowledge beyond a layperson's general understanding. It should be clear to you from this discussion that those occupational groups that proclaim themselves to be *professionals* (i.e., taxi drivers, bartenders, etc.) are using the term inappropriately.

Ritzer and Walzcak (1986) have identified a classification continuum for occupations that either are, or aspire to be, a profession. Accordingly, the continuum is based on how well occupations meet the identified characteristics of a profession. The continuum consists of the following:

1. *Old Established Professions*: occupations in this category on the continuum consist of those professions that are well-established and have control over their knowledge. These include, physicians, lawyers, and university professors.

2. *New Professions*: occupations here include the natural and social scientists with Ph.D's.

3. *Semi-Professions*: although they are professionalized to some degree and have made great effort to make it to the professional end of the continuum, this group of occupations has lacked the power to win widespread recognition as professions. Included in the semi-professions are school teachers, nurses, social workers, and librarians.

4. *Would-be Professions:* these are occupations that have sought or are actively aspiring to professional status, but which, for a variety of reasons, have had even less power than the semi-professions and have had less success in convincing the relevant audiences that they have acquired the needed characteristics. Examples include personnel managers and funeral directors.

5. *Marginal Professions:* included here are a variety of occupations that work 'hand in hand' with the professions, perform many of the same functions, but lack the capacity to acquire professional status in their own right, partly because they very often labour in the shadow of the established professions. Occupations in this category include laboratory and scientific technicians as well as various paraprofessionals. (p. 63)

Although many occupations attempt to seek the status of the professions, many do not. More recently, some sociologists have expressed that we are now moving into a period of deprofessionalization, while others argue that the professions are becoming proletarianized. Let us briefly turn to the arguments supporting these views.

Deprofessionalization or the Proletarianization of the Professions

The process of **deprofessionalization** may be described as the erosion of autonomy and monopolistic privileges of the professions. Figure 12.3 shows that occupations must move from left-to-right along the continuum in order to reach professional status. Movement right-to-left toward the status of most occupations would be suggestive of the deprofessionalization process.

This perspective on the professions is based on the notion that clients are revolting against the authority and decision making powers of the professional. Sociologists (Haug, 1975; Toren, 1975) have argued that the general public is much more educated today than they were 30 years ago and are now in a position to question the judgment of professionals. Deprofessionalization in this form, according to Hodson and Sullivan (1990), is a result of *demystifying the esoteric knowledge* of the professions and *empowering the consumer* (p. 276). You only need to think about all the "do-it-yourself" kits for legal matters, home medical screening kits, and the wealth of information disseminated in the popular press. Much of the knowledge in the public domain today was once exclusive to and protected by many of the professions. Secondly, professionals are now working in large bureaucratic organizations (i.e., universities, hospitals, and corporations) which have financial bottom lines that they must meet. Bureaucratic organizations require professionals to conduct themselves in a certain way which weakens their professional sovereignty. Thirdly, allied professionals are able to do many of the tasks that were traditionally reserved for the professional. In the legal field, for instance, paralegals are filing claims, presenting cases in court, and assisting clients with court documents. Similarly, dentists are no longer cleaning teeth nor taking x-rays, instead a dental hygienist or dental assistant performs these tasks. Finally, recent concerns over professional abuses has diminished the credibility of many professional groups. For example, extra billing, cases of fee-splitting and other complaints about the performance of medical practitioners are rarely made available to the general public by provincial medical associations.

A second perspective on the professions is known as the **proletarianization** of the professions. This perspective differs from the deprofessionalization thesis because it argues that the professions are losing total control over the conditions of work and are

Figure 12.3. A Schematic Diagram of Professionalization and Deprofessionalization

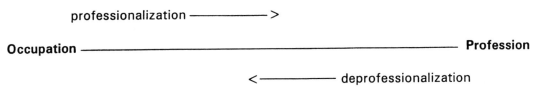

experiencing a serious reduction in compensation. The proletarianization perspective is based on a Marxist orientation (Derber, 1982; Oppenheimer, 1973). Basically, sociologists working with this perspective suggest that white-collar bureaucrats have control over the professional and dictate the nature of the workplace and how professional technology will be used. In addition, the division of labour (*or specializations*) in the professions results in an ever-narrower range of tasks in the delivery of services. The evidence provided for this perspective includes: (i) today hospitals are administered by managers not medical practitioners which diminishes their self-regulation and control over medical practices; (ii) task specialization implies that the medical practitioner is not responsible for the complete treatment nor recovery of the patient; and, (iii) hospital administrators determine what medical technology will be purchased and which drugs will be made available for their patients.

The two views discussed in this section both suggest that the professions are losing ground in maintaining their status and control over their work. The difference between the two is that the deprofessionalization view foresees a modest decline in the status of the professions, while the proletarianization view suggests that the professions will continue to decline and lose most of the control and autonomy that they now have. Whether or not either view is correct is difficult to determine at this time. Further studies will be required to follow the changes, if any, in the professions.

The Future of the Professions

The professions have become significant models for other occupations, because they have achieved so much autonomy, authority, and status. Membership in a profession confers considerable prestige and usually higher income. Today, many of these individuals are considered members of the "new middle-class," which achieves its position based on knowledge and achievement. The future of the professions may take several forms. The positive outlook for the professions is based on the notion that as knowledge expands, specialization within the professions multiplies, and as the economy is transformed by knowledge and service sector industries, the collective prestige of the professions is likely to grow.

The dimmer view stresses the two perspectives described in the last section: deprofessionalization and the proletarianization of the professions. These processes not only threaten the professions but also those occupations that strive to emulate them. It is likely that many professions will lose some authority and control over their practices in the future since many professionals work in large-scale bureaucratic organizations. Whether or not the professions lose the amount of autonomy and control over their activities to the extent suggested by the deprofessionalization and the proletarianization perspectives is really dependent on how fast their knowledge base and specializations grow relative to the empowerment of the consumer. It is likely that the professions will need to be more responsive to consumer needs. Conversely, the consumer of professional services will need to recognize that knowledge is power and they will be unable to keep pace with the knowledge explosion of the future.

Work Satisfaction

One of the most researched areas in the study of work since the 1940s is that of work satisfaction. **Work satisfaction** (*or job satisfaction*) typically refers to a summary attitude of favourable or unfavourable feelings that people experience about their work. Hodson and Sullivan (1990) suggest that work satisfaction is "the result of job tasks, characteristics of the organization in which people work, and the individual differences in needs and values" (p. 97). When workers join an organization, they bring with them a set of wants, needs, desires, and past experiences that combine to form work expectations. Work satisfaction expresses the amount of agreement between one's emerging expectations and the rewards that the work provides.

Organizations have been concerned with work satisfaction because they assume that productivity is affected when workers are dissatisfied. In most studies, the general question that is asked of people is "In general, are you satisfied with your job?" Research has shown that individuals with high occupational levels compared to those from low occupational levels, report higher levels of satisfaction. The result is that professionals and upper-tier administrators usually are more satisfied than skilled workers, who tend to be more satisfied than semi-skilled and unskilled workers. In addition, as workers grow older, they tend to be slightly more satisfied with their work. There are a number of reasons, such as lowered expectations and better adjustment to their work situation because of greater work experience. Younger workers, on the other hand, tend to be less satisfied because of higher expectations, lower adjustment, and other factors (see Figure 12.4). Gender differences, however, are infrequently found in work satisfaction surveys (Northcott and Lowe, 1987).

Early studies on work satisfaction tended to concentrate on interpersonal relationships and the work environment. Over time the research has clearly shown that the sources of

Figure 12:4. The Relationship of Work Satisfaction to Age and Occupational Level

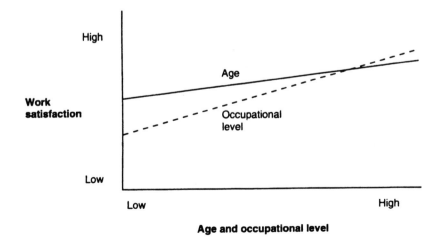

335

work satisfaction lie beyond positive interpersonal relationships on the job but include the structural components of work itself. Specifically, surveys show that higher satisfaction tends to be associated with such factors as intrinsic interest in the work (it is interesting and meaningful), level of control (the ability to make decisions), level of pay and economic security, and opportunities for social interaction (Scott, 1989). These factors seem to be predominant and consistent across all occupational and professional groups today.

In surveys that address the satisfaction level of employees, however, satisfaction rates among workers tend to be fairly high (approximately 80%). However, researchers have come to realize that at the best of times work satisfaction surveys are suspect. The reason for this is that the response rates of surveys (that is, the number of individuals who complete the questionnaire and return it) tends to be between 35 and 50 percent. The question we should ask ourselves as sociologists is: Are those who do not return the questionnaire satisfied or are they so dissatisfied that they refuse to complete the questionnaire? This is difficult to determine since the anonymity guaranteed to respondents prevents researchers from contacting those individuals who do not complete the questionnaire. Work satisfaction surveys are also subject to criticism because work satisfaction is closely linked to *life satisfaction*. The nature of an individual's environment off the job is bound to influence their feelings on the job. Similarly, since work is an important part of life, work satisfaction influences an individual's general life satisfaction. The result is that there is a spillover effect that occurs in both directions between work and life satisfaction. Consequently, in order to address work satisfaction in a comprehensive way we need to study the overall life satisfaction of workers.

Summary

In this chapter, we introduced the world of work with a specific emphasis on work in the Canadian context As stated in our introduction, work is more than earning an income since it permeates all other aspects of our social existence. After reading this chapter you should make sure that you have an understanding of the following points discussed:

1. Since the beginning of time human beings have engaged in work activities to meet their survival needs. To meet these needs, human beings developed and were shaped by the technology and social organization of the society. **Social organization** refers to the relations among those involved in work. **Technology**, on the other hand, refers to the tools and skills used in the process of production. The social organization of work as we know it today (i.e., advanced industrial society), constitutes less than one percent of known human existence on this planet.

2. **Industrialization** refers to the replacement of labour-intensive skills in the production of goods and services with capital-intensive technology (i.e., machinery and computers), accompanied with an elaboration of the **division of labour** (a functionally integrated system of occupational roles or specializations within a society). Early signs of the growth of industrialization in

Canada did not emerge until 1870–1890. Today, Canada is perceived to have the characteristics basic to a member of the fortunate group of advanced industrial nations (Craib, 1986). In 1988, Canada had a Gross National Product per capita of $14,120 U.S., which placed it as the 4th largest in the world behind Norway (3rd), United States (2nd), and Switzerland (1st). The goods produced in the country, however, tend to be based on our natural resources (i.e., oil and gas).

3. Presently, close to 50 percent of the mining, petroleum, timber, and manufacturing industries are foreign owned and controlled mostly by American multinational corporations. Approximately, three-quarters of both Canadian exports and imports are with the Untied States. The free trade agreement between Canada and the U.S. signed on January 2, 1988 was intended to provide a tariff-free North American trading partnership. The long term effects of this arrangement on our own markets and industries will not be known for some time.

4. The labour force structure in Canada can be categorized by the *industry* in which participants work. By convention, there are three major sectors within the labour force: **primary**, **secondary**, and **tertiary**. At the turn of the century, most Canadians worked in the *primary sector* (i.e., agriculture). By 1920, most Canadians were working in the *secondary sector* (i.e., manufacturing). Presently, labour force participation statistics for Canada show that 72 percent of the labour force is employed in the *tertiary sector* (mostly service industries), while 6 percent are employed in the *primary sector,* and 22 percent in the *secondary sector.* For this reason, Canada is known as a *post-industrial society.*

5. A second way in which the labour force structure in Canada can be categorized is by *occupation,* or the kind of work that is being performed. Often we differentiate the kind of work that individuals do according to whether they are **white-collar** or **blue-collar** occupations. The term *white-collar* typically is applied to the work of managers, nurses, teachers, salespersons, and office workers since these occupations involve working with people and ideas. The term *blue-collar* typically is applied to work roles involved in manufacturing. *Blue-collar* work is often subdivided into two categories: **skilled crafts** and **unskilled work**. *Skilled crafts* are those in which the work requires some degree of manual dexterity combined with a broad knowledge of tools, materials, and processes (i.e., welders and plumbers). *Unskilled work* includes those occupations that require no formal training nor certification primarily because the skill required to perform the task is considered to be minimal (i.e., waitressing and dishwashing).

6. **Labour markets** are the economic arenas in which employers seek to purchase labour from potentially qualified individuals who themselves are seeking employment suitable to their present education, experience, and preferences. (Krahn and Lowe, 1989). Labour markets are often divided into

two sectors: **primary labour markets** and **secondary labour markets**. The *primary labour* market usually offers jobs with relatively high wages, good working conditions, chance of advancement, and employment stability. Jobs that are in the *secondary labour market,* by contrast, tend to be low paying, with poorer working conditions and little chance of advancement. Studies have shown that barriers to *primary labour market* entry include gender discrimination, age discrimination, "contacts" (or the so-called *old "boys" network),* and racial and ethnic discrimination.

7. Unemployment in Canada varies by region, type of industry, age, and gender. **Unemployment rates** are calculated by dividing the number of individuals out of work and who are actively seeking work by the total number in the labour force (including the unemployed). In 1990, the percentage of persons, ages 25–44 years, overwhelmingly constituted the bulk of the unemployed in the country. The subjective experiences of those who are unemployed are ones of fear, insecurity, anger, helplessness, and dismay. Often they feel that the various governmental institutions are not helping them and appear to blame them for their circumstances.

8. The impact of technological change on skill requirements for work is one of the most debated subjects in the study of work and occupations. There are currently three general perspectives on the impact of skill currently dominating the field: *the upgrading thesis, the downgrading thesis,* and *the mixed effects thesis.* The impact of microelectronic technology seems to have fueled this debate.

9. A basic interest in the study of work is the question of why and how people first enter specific occupations, or types of work. In sociology, we categorize these questions in a broad category, commonly known as *occupational choice.* Two models on how individuals make particular career choices were discussed. The **individual-ambition model** viewed occupational choice as a developmental process that culminated in a series of compromises between an individual's interests, capacities, opportunities and values. In contrast, the **structure-opportunity model** stressed the individual's structural content in influencing occupational choices. The structural content of an individual includes such factors as their parental socio-economic status, gender, and ethnicity which purportedly has a profound effect on socialization to particular occupations, access to opportunity, and subsequent decisions about career choices.

10. The term professions to denote certain occupations is used in a very specific way by sociologists. It is reserved for those occupations which have exclusive jurisdiction over certain kinds of services, are able to negotiate freedom from external intervention and have control over the content of their work activities in the delivery of services. For an occupation to be deemed a profession, it must meet certain characteristics. Many occupations meet several of the identifiable characteristics of a profession but they do not meet all. Sociologists

have developed an occupational continuum to identify how well occupations meet the identified characteristics of a profession. The continuum includes: old established professions, new professions, semi-professions, would-be professions, and marginal professions. Recently, some sociologists have argued that the professions are experiencing an erosion of their autonomy and monopolistic privileges. These arguments range from a **deprofessionalization** of the professions to a **proletarianization** of the professions.

11. **Work satisfaction** typically refers to a summary attitude of favourable or unfavourable feelings that people experience about their work. Overall, work satisfaction tends to be positively correlated with age and occupational status. Recent research on work satisfaction shows that higher satisfaction levels also tend to be associated with such factors as intrinsic interest in the work, level of control, level of pay and economic security, and opportunities for social interaction (Scott, 1989). Work satisfaction surveys, however, tend to be criticized because response rates are low and it is usually closely linked to life satisfaction.

References

Abeshouse, R. P.
1987   *Lifelong Learning Part One: Education for a Competitive Economy.* Washington, D.C.: Roosevelt Centre for American Policy Studies.

Anderson, Grace M. and Liviana M. Calzavara
1986   "Networks, Education and Occupational Success," in Lundy, K. L. P. Lundy and Warme B. eds. *Work in the Canadian Context: Continuity Despite Change,* Second edition. Toronto: Butterworths.

Armstrong, Pat and Hugh Armstrong
1984   *The Double Ghetto: Canadian Women and Their Segregated Work.* Toronto: McClelland and Stewart Limited.

Baran, Barbara and S. Teegarden
1984   "Women's Labor in the Office of the Future," in Kraft, Phillip, *A Review of Empirical Studies of the Consequences of Technological Change on the Work and Workers in the United States.* New York: Monthly Review, pp. 125–153.

Bell, Daniel
1976   *The Coming of Post-Industrial Society.* New York: Basic Books.

Blauner, Robert
1964   *Alienation and Freedom.* Chicago: University of Chicago Press.

Braverman, Harry
1974   *Labor and Monopoly Capital: The Degradation of Work in the Twentieth Century.* New York: Monthly Review Press.

Bryant, Clifton D.
1972   *The Social Dimensions of Work.* Englewood Cliffs: Prentice Hall.

Burman, Patrick
1988   *Killing Time, Losing Ground: Experiences of Unemployment.* Toronto: Wall and Thompson, Inc.

Calhoun, C. and M. Copp
1988   "Computerization in Legal Work: How Much Does New Technology Change Professional Practice?" in Simpson, R. and Simpson, I. eds. *Research in the Sociology of Work,* 4: pp. 233–259.

Cameron, Duncan
1988   *The Free Trade Deal.* Toronto: James Lorimer and Company.

Chen, Mervin Y. T. and Thomas G. Regan
1985   *Work in the Changing Canadian Society.* Toronto: Butterworths.

Christensen, Kathleen
1987   "A Hard Days Work in the Electronic Cottage." *Across the Board,* 23 (April), pp. 17–21.

Collins, Randall
1979   *The Credential Society.* New York: Academic Press.

Craib, Prudence W.
1986   "Canadian-based Research and Development: Why So Little?" in Lundy, Katherina and Warme, Barbara. *Work in the Canadian Context: Continuity Despite Change,* Second edition. Toronto: Butterworths, pp. 6–22.

Derber, Charles
1982   *Professionals as Workers: Mental Labor in Advanced Capitalism.* Boston: G. K. Hall and Company.

Faunce, William A.
1981   *Problems of an Industrial Society.* New York: McGraw-Hill.

Federal Government of Canada
1981   *The Task Force Report on Labour Market Development in the 1980s.* Ottawa: Minister of Supply and Services.

Form, William
1987   "On the Degradation of Skill." *Annual Review of Sociology,* 13, pp. 29–47.

Ginzberg, Eli, S.W. Ginzberg, S. Axelrad, and J.L. Herma
1951   *Occupational Choice: Toward a General Theory.* New York: Columbia University Press.

Glenn, Evelyn N. and Roslyn L. Feldberg
1977   "Degraded and Deskilled: The Proletarianization of Clerical work." *Social Problems,* 25: pp. 52–64.

Groff, W.
1983   "Impacts of High Technologies on Vocational and Education." *Annals of the American Academy of Political and Social Sciences,* 470, pp. 81–94.

Haug, Maria
1973   "Deprofessionalization: An Alternative Hypothesis for the Future," in Halmos, Paul ed. *Professionalization and Social Change*. Staffordshire: The University of Keele, pp. 195–211.

Hedley, R. Alan
1988   "Industrialization and Work," in Robert Hagedorn ed. *Sociology,* Fourth edition. Toronto: Holt, Rinehart and Winston of Canada, Limited.

Hodson, Randy
1988   "Work in High-Tech Settings: A Review of the Empirical Literature," in Simpson, R. and Simpson, I. eds. *Research in the Sociology of Work,* v. 4, pp. 1–29.

Hodson, Randy and R. Parker
1988   "Good Jobs and Bad Management: How New Problems Evoke Old Solutions in High-Tech Settings. In England P. and Farcas eds. *Industries, Farms and Jobs: Sociological and Economic Approaches.* New York: Plenum Limited, pp. 247–279.

Hodson, Randy and Teresa A. Sullivan
1990   *The Social Organization of Work.* Belmont, Calif: Wadsworth Publishing Company.

Jenkins, Clive and B. Sherman
1979   *The Collapse of Work.* London: Eyre Metheun.

Kraft, Philip
1979   "The Industrialization of Computer Programming: From Programming to Software," in Zimbalist, A. ed. *Case Studies in the Labor Process.* New York: Monthly Review Press, pp. 1–17.

Krahn, Harvey J. and Graham S. Lowe
1988   *Work Industry and Canadian Society.* Scarborough: Nelson Canada.

Kuttner, B.
1983   "The Declining Middle." *Atlantic*, July, pp. 60–72.

Lee, Richard B.
1981   "politics, Sexual And Nonsexual, In An equalitarian society," in Berreman, General D. ed. *Social Inequality: Comparative and Developmental Approaches.* New York: Academic Press, pp. 83–102.

Lenski, Gerhard
1966   *Power and Privilege: A Theory of Social Stratification.* New York: McGraw-Hill.

Marx, Karl
1967   *Capital, Volume One [1887].* New York: International Publishers.

Menzies, Heather
1981   *Women and the Chip: Case Studies of the effects of Information on Employment in Canada.* Montreal: The Institute for Research for Public Policy.

Northcott, Herbert C. and Graham, S. Lowe
1987   "Job and Gender Influences in the Subjective Experience of Work." *Canadian Review of Sociology and Anthropology,* 24, pp. 117–131.

Oppenheimer, Martin
1973   "The Proletarianization of the Professional," in Halmos, Paul ed. *Professionalization and Social Change.* Staffordshire: The University of Keele, pp. 212–224.

Pavalko, Ronald M.
1971   *Sociology of Occupations and Professions.* Itasco, Ill.: F. E. Peacock.

Piore, M.
1969   "On the Job Training in the Dual Labor Market," in A.R. Weber, F. Cassell, and W. L. Ginsberg eds. *Public-Private Manpower Policies.* Wisconsin: University of Wisconsin, pp. 101–132.

1970   "Jobs and Training." In S. H. Beer and R. H. Barringer eds. *The State and the Poor.* Wisconsin: University of Wisconsin, p. 53–83.

1975   "Notes for a Theory of Labor Market Stratification," in R. Edwards, M. Reich, and D. Gordon eds. *Labor Market Segmentation.* Lexington, Mass.: D.C. Health, pp. 125–150.

Rinehart, James
1988   "Forward," in Burman, Patrick. *Killing Time, Losing Ground: Experiences of Unemployment.* Toronto: Wall and Thompson, Inc.

1987   *The Tyranny of Work: Alienation and the Labour Process,* Second edition. Toronto: Harcourt Brace Jovanovich.

Ritzer, George and David Walczak
1986   *Working: Conflict and Change.* Englewood Cliffs, New Jersey: Prentice-Hall.

Rosenthal, Neal
1985   "The Shrinking Middle Class: Myth or Reality?" *Monthly Labor Review, 108* (March): pp. 3–10.

Rosenthal, Robert A.
1987   *Working: Sociological Perspectives.* Englewood Cliffs, New Jersey: Prentice-Hall, Inc.

Royal Commission on the Economic Union and Development Prospects for Canada
1985   *Report One.* Ottawa: Minister of Supply and Services.

Scott, W. Richard
1989 *Organizations: Rational, Natural, and Open Systems,* Second edition. Englewood Cliffs: Prentice-Hall.

Smith, Adam
1937   *The Wealth of Nations [1776].* New York: Random House.

Smucker, Joseph
1980   *Industrialization in Canada.* Scarborough: Prentice-Hall of Canada.

Speakman, Mary Anne
1980   "Occupational Choice and Placement," in Esland, G. and Salaman, G. eds. *The Politics of Work and Occupations.* Toronto: The University of Toronto Press.

Toffier, Alvin
1980   *The Third Wave.* New York: Bantam.

Toren, Nina
1975   "Deprofessionalization and Its Sources: A Preliminary Analysis." *Sociology of Work and Occupations,* 2, pp. 323–337.

Wallace, Michael
1989   "Brave New Workplace: Technology and Work in the New Economy." *Work and Occupations,* 16 (4), pp. 363–392.

Wilensky, Harold
1964   "The professionalization of everyone?," *American Sociological Review,* 70, pp. 137–158.

World Bank
1988   *World Development Report.* London: Oxford University Press.

The Sociology of Religion
An Introduction

Don Swenson, PhD

Orientation

This is the final chapter of the text that introduces us into a fourth institution, religion. Again, the central concepts in sociology are revealed here as well. Religion should be seen as an aspect of culture for its focus is upon world views and the living out of these world views. Its link to social action is through the first kind of social action as outlined in the first chapter, affective social action. It is affective in that, as we shall see, the genesis of religion is in the experience of the sacred which is an affective kind of a relationship. The structural dimensions of religion emerge when one looks at the construction of religious organizations.

I shall begin with outlining a definition of religion that will also frame the chapter. This chapter is a part of a larger work by the author (Swenson, 1999) which is a social scientific study of the sacred, spirituality, religion, and society. Emerging from the definition of religion presented in that work, we will look at it from the inside. Topics to be covered here include: experience of the sacred, world views known as myths or, more commonly, belief systems, ritual, ethos (morality), and organizations. Another way to look at religion is to link it to other social institutions like politics, economy, family, and culture. Although this is important, at this introductory level this would make this chapter too complex.

I begin by presenting a definition: "religion is the individual and social experience of the sacred expressed in myths, rituals, ethos, and integrated into a social collective or institution" (Swenson, 1999:66). This definition is a synthesis of a number of definitions from a wide variety of sources from sociological and anthropological studies. As each of these elements constitute the contents of this chapter, I shall refrain from explaining their meaning now.

This definition comprises what has been defined by sociologists as having substantive or functional interpretations. A substantive definition of religion focuses on the essence or nature of religion. Berger (1974) notes that it is seen in terms of the meaning of the contents of the phenomenon. The substantive approach comes from historians of religion like Rudolf Otto and Mircea Eliade. We shall meet these authors later in the chapter.

Functional definitions emphasize the effects of religion on people and on the social order. They may define religion in positive functional terms with religion providing meaning, social legitimation, social cohesion, integration, and a source of morality. Functional definitions see religion as being a product of human activity, which in turn acts back on members of a society in ways that contribute to the maintenance of the social order. It is religion that is regarded as an important agent of socialization and a guardian of societal values. This approach has been codified by Emile Durkheim, Bronislaw Maninowski, and Karl Marx. For Marx, however, religion is seen to have a negative effect on people causing alienation and control.

As will be argued in the next section, the heart of religion is the *sacred*. Social scientifically, this can be further subdivided into the *sacred within,* the *sacred between,* and the *sacred among*. The sacred within refers to the internal, individual aspects of religion such as beliefs, attitudes, values and spirituality. The social behavioural discipline that focuses on this is psychology. The sacred between is that part of the sacred that exists between social actors. The work of social psychologists (whose mother disciplines represent psychology, sociology, and anthropology) focuses on the process through which religious reality is socially constructed. These scholars seek to understand the two-way link between the individual and religious institutions. Some social psychologists emphasize the role that social actors play in creating the religious order; others take a somewhat broader perspective to study the impact the institutionalized product has upon individuals.

The dialectical relationship between the individual and society may be best described by the phenomenological sociologist Peter Berger (1963). He sums it up in three succinct statements: society is a human product; society is an objective reality; and human beings are social products. In other words, men and women throughout time have created the social world in which they live. I would suggest further that religious reality has come about, at least in part, as a result of encounters of human beings with the sacred. Such encounters or religious experiences are an important part of any study of religion. Religious experiences are the catalysts that have led to the development of dogma, ritual, and religious institutions that are part of the real social world. Institutional religion, in turn, acts back on people to socialize them into its norms and values.

The proper domain of sociology is the sacred among. Here the sociologist accents the study of culture (myths and world views), religious institutions, and the relationship between a society and religion. We begin with looking at individual and the social experience of the sacred.

Individual and Social Experience of the Sacred

From an historian of religion (Otto, 1958), I commence the investigation of the meaning of religion by outlining what the sacred or the holy (in Latin, *numen*) is. Durkheim (1965) aids us in a preliminary definition: "things separate and set apart." He interprets this to mean that the sacred is distinctly different from the profane or the ordinary. The contrast is between mundane or everyday life or other worldly or eternal life. Weber added that the sacred as being.... "uniquely unalterable" (1978: 406). More recently, the British sociologist Nottingham (1971) acknowledged that the sacred should be at the center of a sociological study of religion. This is further professed by Bailey (1998), who considers it to be the key concept in the study of religion.

Otto (1958) expands on this. As depicted by Table 13.1, there are two dimensions: *mysterium tremendum* and *fascinadus*. As a believer approaches the sacred, two kinds of experiences are elicited. The first one is awe and distance. The religious person is in touch with a power, a force that is illustrated by terms like: august, a shuddering, dread, fear, being overpowered, a sense of being a creature and of relating to the sacred as being wholly other.

Table 13.1. *Numen* or the Idea of the Holy

Mysterium Tremendum	Fascinadus
Awe	Wonderfulness
Distance	Rapture
August	Becoming One with the *Numen*
A Shuddering	Desire
Dread	Blissful Excitement
Fear	Exaltation
Overpowering	Over Abundance and Plenty
Creature Fleeing	Love
Plenitude of Being	Mercy
Energy	Compassion
Wholly Other	Kindness
	Understanding

In contrast, the believer is fascinated by the sacred and is mysteriously drawn towards it. Feelings such as wonderfulness, rapture, desire, excitement, exultation, plentitude, love, mercy, compassion, kindness and understanding emerge.

Thus, a dilemma confronts the religionist: a drawing close to but, in the opposite, a pushing away. This forms the most fundamental dilemma of religion that is reflected in much of the research on religion.

Religious experience, then, is to be understood by a unique kind of human experience—the experience of the sacred. I shall briefly outline some of the philosophical and social scientific studies on religious experience to link this kind of experience to the lives of people.

In the late 17th century, Friedreich Schleiermacher (1799) attempted to justify Christianity against Enlightenment rationality that threatened its credibility by arguing that religion is best grounded in sentiments, not in ideas. People have experiences that cannot be comprehended within the bounds of the everyday world. As they reflect on such experiences, they come to conceptualize God in certain ways. According to Schleiermacher, science and philosophy may attack religious conceptualizations or ideas but they cannot undercut the experiences themselves (Proudfoot, 1985).

Those who follow Schleiermacher accept religious experience at face value. For them, religion cannot be destroyed by rational critique for it is grounded in the experience of believers. It was Schleiermacher who influenced some early social scientists who wrote about religious experiences, including social psychologist William James (1842–1910).

James considered experience to be the genesis of religion, arguing that the founders of every religion had some sort of direct, personal communication with the divine. The "divine," according to James, is "primal reality" that the "individual feels impelled to respond to solemnly and gravely" (James, 1902:38). It is the foundation of religious experience, which according to James are

> the feelings, acts, and experiences of individual men in their solitude, so far as they apprehend themselves to stand in relation to whatever they may consider divine (James, 1902:31).

James envisioned religious experience as something that exists *sui generis*—as something that is really real. Conventional religion was but a pale reflection of the energizing experience that propelled the saints and prophets. As James describes it

> It would profit us little to study this second-hand religious life. We must make search rather for the original experiences which were the pattern-setters to all this mass of suggested feeling and imitated conduct. These experiences we can only find in individuals for whom religion exists not as a dull habit, but as an acute fever rather (1902:24–25).

One approach to the study of religion has been to follow William James in taking experience as the core of religion. Although this tradition has been criticized for being too individualistic and subjectivistic, it has provided an important foundation from which to explore the origins and renewed fervor of religious groups.

As referred to in the definition of religion, it is presented as the "individual and social experience of the social." I refer to Weber's work to help us to understand the individual experience and Durkheim for the social experience.

Although Weber focuses on the individual person, he links religious experience of the individual to the social. His focus is on relationship between charisma, the affective action of religious leaders, and social organization. Weber's *charisma* appears to be similar to what Durkheim and Otto call the sacred. As Weber states:

> [Not] every person has the capacity to achieve the ecstatic states which are viewed...as the preconditions for producing certain effects in meteorology, healing, divination, and telepathy. It is primarily....these extraordinary powers that have been designated by such special terms as "mana," "orenda," and the Iranian "maga" (the term from which our word "magic" is derived). We shall henceforth employ the term "charisma" for such extraordinary powers. (1947:400)

Weber terms the individual bearer of charisma a "prophet," citing such religious figures as Zoroaster, Jesus, Muhammad, and the Buddha (Weber 1947:339–40). According to him, charisma cannot remain in its pure form, but becomes routinized or institutionalized.

This is another important dilemma in religious experience: from beginning with charisma and to ending in a routinized form of it. This insight helps us a lot to understand why religion can be a source of social change and vivacity or an inhibition to change and become "dead weight."

In somewhat of a contrast to Weber and to what the psychologists of religion say, Durkheim (1965:417) argues that religious experience is more of a collective one and less an individual one. For example, in his work on aboriginal peoples of Australia and North America, it is when believers in hunting and gathering societies gather together in a ritual, a religious ceremony, that they are carried beyond themselves into another world. It is in this group ritual that they experience ecstasy, enthusiasm, effervescence, joy, interior peace, serenity and a sense of being "transported into another world."

In summary, Durkheim is saying that because of the group experience (not possible as an individual) in the celebration of ritual, the believers adhere to a conviction that the deity, filled with energy and power, is real and present to him or her.

Myths

The second element of religion is the belief system or, the term that I am using, myth. It is important to emphasize that when using the term "myth," it is not to imply that such beliefs are false or fictitious. Nor is myth intended as a synonym for fairy tales or folk narratives (Roberts, 1990:77). Myths are accounts or stories that undergird different religious world views. Their truth or falsity is not the concern of social science. All are essentially treated as being "true" in a sense because they are defined as being so by believers. Even false definitions of a situation have psychological as well as social implications. The social scientist's task is to determine the effects of myth on believers and their society. I shall discuss substantive and functional definitions of myth and conclude this section with research on changes in myths with the growth of modernity both in select Muslim countries and in Canada.

Substantive Definition of Myth

Religious myths once provided *the* paramount definition of reality for people in pre-modern societies. Although different cultures may have had very divergent ideas about the non-empirical world of their mythic figures, all shared the conviction that the spirits had an impact on life.

As with religion, the study of religious myths, as seen through the eyes of the scholar of mythology, Joseph Campbell (1964), may be approached using two perspectives: substantive and functional. The *substantive approach* attempts to define the essence of a myth. It seeks to clarify and illuminate, much as we have been doing in our present discussion of myth in this chapter. The *functional approach*, on the other hand, seeks to determine what effects myths have in the lives of people and the larger society. In other words, an important task of the functional perspective is to determine the purpose myth serves in maintaining the social order. While these two approaches may appear to be distinct, in actuality there is overlap. What may begin as a substantive approach may end in a discussion of the functions of myth; what is intended to be a discussion of the functions of myth may produce a tentative definition. Despite the fact that these two approaches are not mutually exclusive, discussing them separately does enable us to provide a comprehensive discussion of the nature and purpose of myth.

Mircea Eliade, an anthropologist who wrote extensively about religion of hunting-gathering and agricultural-pastoral societies, has provided us with a concise description of the substantive nature of myth:

> In short, myths describe breakthroughs of the sacred (or the supernatural) into the world. It is this sudden breakthrough of the sacred that really *establishes* (italics in the original) the world and makes it what it is today. Furthermore, it is a result of the intervention of supernatural beings that man himself is what he is today, a mortal, sexed, and cultural being (Eliade 1973:70).

Eliade contends that myth presents a sacred history, a story of what took place in primordial time. It informs the believer of how, through the deeds of supernatural beings, the cosmos came into being. It represents a breakthrough, or more accurately, a "break into" the mundane world of the common place by non-terrestrial beings. In constructing his theory of myths, Eliade built on the work of Otto (1958), referred to above.

Functional Definition of Myth

Campbell (1964) explains the functional definition of myth. He divides these functions into three: cosmological, sociological, and psychological. The first one, cosmological, presents people with an account of the origins of the universe or of "making sense" of the cosmos. The prophet or seer has received some illumination, but the understanding of the seer must be translated into cultural images, symbols, rites and texts for it to become viable. Unless this is done, the vision will die with the visionary. There is a tension, however, between making the mystery available to the culture while at the same time retaining the awe of the mystery. This tension may be briefly demonstrated by what happened over time to the accounts of creation presented in Genesis. Most religions, including the Judeo-Christian tradition, have cosmological accounts of creation that attempt to capture its mystery. The stories are intended to help "make sense" of the origins of the world. At the same time they must capture the sense of mystery and awe reflected by the rhythm of life's polarities and paradox that includes birth and death, light and darkness, sowing and reaping, peace and war. When a creation story is twisted into the mold of history and science (as the book of Genesis has been countless times), a sense of mystery and awe is often lost. Paradoxically when the myth becomes rigid doctrine, its power to serve as an effective source of cosmology is weakened.

A second purpose of myth identified by Campbell is sociological that includes social control, social support, and socialization. Myth functions as an agent of social control in that it reinforces the existing social order. The ten commandments given to Moses on Mount Sinai warn people against such socially divisive practices as lying, stealing, and murder. Although generally functional for society in their power to bind people together, myths may also become dysfunctional (i.e., work against the good of the social system). Myth has been used to uphold anti-social practices, including slavery, the burning of women thought to be witches, spouse and child abuse, and unfair labor practices. Myth may function to support legitimate order in society, and it may be used to bolster illegitimate power. Emile Durkheim, a founding father of sociology, tended to emphasize the positive functions of myth for upholding the social order. Durkheim (Bellah, 1973) believed that religion had provided an essential moral base for all societies....

The sociological function of myth is built into a classic definition of religion advanced by Emile Durkheim. Durkheim (1965: 62) defined *religion* as "a unified system of beliefs and practices relative to sacred things, that is to say, things set apart and forbidden—beliefs and practices that unite into a single moral community called a Church, all those who adhere to them." In this definition we see that religion includes both myth and the rituals that reflect mythical beliefs. These beliefs and corresponding rituals are of a particular kind that pertain to the sacred (not the mundane or the secular). They function to unite believers into a single moral community; in other words, into a socially cohesive group. This community is both a source of support and an agent of control.

Karl Marx, another important early social theorist, stressed the negative functions of religion in general and myth in particular. For Marx, religion was a form of "false consciousness" which had been used throughout history to keep men and women in bondage (Marx and Engels, 1964).

Some more recent research gives credibility to the thesis that mythologies do have an impact on social actors. One way to operationalize myth is to look at who religious actors imagine God to be. Swenson (1989), in a dissertation on linking family and religion from an American data base of Roman Catholic believers, found that those who viewed God as a judge were more likely to have traditional familial attitudes than those who did not have that view. In another study using divine images, Piazza and Glock (1979), in a sample of people in San Francisco, discovered that those who saw God as influential in their own lives are consistently the most likely to accept traditional religious beliefs, to engage in traditional religious practices, to be pro-feminist, and to possess liberal racial attitudes. In addition, those who saw God as "in charge of the social order" (a Durkheimian theme) were likely to be politically conservative. In a study of Canadian evangelical ministers, Swenson (1997) saw links between divine images and marital quality. He found that ministers who viewed God in intimate terms had higher levels of marital quality than did those who did not.

Myth not only functions on the social level; it also functions on the individual level. Campbell (1964) terms this the "psychological function" of myth. Myth may initiate the individual into the reality of his or her own psyche, guiding a person toward spiritual enrichment. Campbell asserts that in primitive and traditional forms of myth, the principle of personal development was often downplayed or even suppressed. In the modern world with its emphasis on individuality, myths are more likely to accent the development of full personal potential (Campbell 1968).

An example of this function emerges from the mythology of the New Age Movement. New Age adherents report a sense of self-affirmation, a release from guilt, and an acceptance of life as it is. Evil is described as linked to ignorance and as a lack of enlightenment.

A tenet of the mythology is transformation. Transformation consists of the movement from ignorance to enlightenment. This transformation is all inclusive: personal, social, societal, and cosmological. It, however, begins with the personal and the power to bring about this transformation is through taping into a universal energy (Newport, 1998).

Changes in Myth

In a sociological study of Islam in Pakistan, Malaya, Turkey, Iran (before the revolution of 1979), Tunisia and Morocco, Kanwar (1974) found that modernization and secularization had taken their toll on the mythology and practice of Islam. These changes reflect new values, a changing concept of the state, ways of living, family life and education. It should be added, however, that since Kanwar wrote this text, there have been many changes in the countries he researched, particularly Pakistan and Iran, where there is a strong movement back to traditional Islam where the state and religion were much more linked.

Research in Canada by the sociologist of religion, Reginald Bibby (1987) also reveals a shift in myth. In previous times, according to Bibby and Durkheim, believers tended to accept the whole mythology of a particular religion. With the rise of modernity, however, they tend to become somewhat sophisticated and are more likely to select what is more suited to their own circumstances. Bibby uses the term "fragmented gods" to describe this phenomenon. He garnishes evidence from a number of Canadian national surveys.

Contrasts in Kinds of Myths

An additional dichotomy will assist us in understanding various mythologies. One set of myths is called "human ascent and divine response," in contrast to "divine descent and human response".

"Human ascent and divine response" refers to a myth which presents a sacred world view that sees the human condition as one of struggle and hard work or of the human quest as being one of ascending to the divine realm by one's own efforts (be they good works, proper sacrifices, well performed rituals, or moral codes). The hope is that the divine figure would look with kindness on these efforts and reward the seeker with eternal life, riches, blessings, and good things. The human subject may be called the "seeker." Empirical credibility to this kind of myth is given to us from Weber's summary of Asiatic religion (Hinduism, Buddhism, Confucianism and Taoism). He argues that all the philosophies and soteriologies of Asia had a common presupposition which was that knowledge, *gnosis* (having the right knowledge), was the absolute path to holiness (1958b:330).

Two images capture this kind of myth: a seeker on the bottom of a mountain begins a long ascent to the top where the sacred dwells. The hope is that once the top is reached, justice and rewards will be forthcoming. Another image comes from a common theme in myths: light and darkness. Most myths see people living in darkness and groping for the light. However, there is, typically, a large chasm that separates the two eternal regions and the seeker needs to build a bridge to cross over through his or her own effort.

The second set of myths, "divine descent and human response," refers to the divine descending down to the human condition and inviting a response from the human subject (here called the "one who trusts"). In the mountain image, the sacred, manifested as a conscious person, descends down from the mountain and offers to take the one who trusts up to the top. All the human subject has to do is to respond in trust (expressed also in behaviours that reflect the sacred) and be carried. In the second image of darkness and light, the divine constructs a bridge from the realm of light, walks across it to the region of darkness, and carries the one who trusts back to the light.

All mythologies that express the first option, are the mythologies of the East, folk societies, and Islam.[1] Only Judaism and Christianity reflect the second option. The divine descent myth is at the core of Judaism in that the deity loves people and creates a group so that salvation can be given to all humankind.

Several texts from the Hebrew bible illustrate this kind of mythology. The God of Israel is described as one who is "a God of tenderness and compassion, slow to anger, rich in graciousness, relenting from evil" (Jonah 4:2). This deity was seen to act on behalf of the people that is illustrated in a dialogue between Yahweh and Moses, the deliverer and law giver: "I have seen the miserable state of my people in Egypt, I have heard their appeal to be free of their slave drivers. Yes, I am well aware of their sufferings. I mean to deliver them out of the hands of the Egyptians and bring them up out of that land to a land rich and broad, a land where milk and honey flow" (Exodus 3:8). Another text explicates the sacred descent: "He let you hear his voice out of heaven for your instruction; on earth he let you see his great fire, and from the heart of the fire you heard his word. Because he loved your fathers and chose their descendants after them, he brought you out of Egypt, openly showing his presence and his great power. . . and brought you into their land to give it to you for your heritage (Deuteronomy 4:35-38). After the rescue, the people were required to be obedient to a covenant established by God in the Sinai desert (Exodus 20) and thus continue to experience this intimate care.

Christianity goes a step further in its mythology that the sacred actually becomes human in the person of Jesus and bids people to come to him and thus enter into a divine life. It is in this latter mythology that God is defined as love and is intimately involved in the human condition. An early Christian writer says it in this way:

> Out of his loving-kindness for us he came to us, and we see this in the way he revealed himself openly to us. Taking pity on mankind's weakness, and moved by our corruption, he could not stand aside and see death have the mastery over us; he did not want creation to perish and his Father's work in fashioning man to be in vain. He therefore took to himself a body, no different from our own, for he did not wish simply to be in a body or only to be seen. . . In death the Word made a spotless sacrifice and oblation of the body he had taken. By dying for others, he immediately banished death for all mankind (St. Athanasius 1976: 1808).

However, the response was not only trust but also to take on the character of Jesus, who forgave those who hurt him, loved the marginalized, and showed mercy to the forsaken. Morality becomes a goal not of reaching the sacred but living out the myth in everyday life (see section on ethos).

Ritual

Consistent with the approach began in the discussion on the substantive and functional definitions of religion and myth, I continue to look at ritual in a similar way. In addition, this is to be seen as an example of the sacred between—the presence of the sacred in ritual interaction.

The elaboration of a substantive definition of ritual emerges from the works of anthropologists, religious studies scholars and sociologists. From several sources, a comprehensive description of a substantive understanding of ritual will be presented.

From the work of Geertz (1966), Davis (1948–1949), Hargrove (1989), Durkheim (1989) and Smith (1956), I present a substantive definition of ritual as:

> Repeated consecrated (sacred) behaviour that is a symbolic expression of the moods and motivations of religious participants and unseen powers. Ritual forms a bond of friendship, community and unity with the believer and her/his god. Finally, ritual transports the participant into another world (the world above) wherein there is peace and harmony.

To illustrate this definition, I will use Watts' (1954) study of myth and ritual within pre-Vatican II Catholicism.[2] In this religion, the historical myth-event of Christ takes on an eternal dimension that is not restricted to two thousand years ago but is something perennial, both in all time and beyond all time. This church follows an annual cycle called "the Church Calender" which begins with Advent, a period of preparation for Christmas, symbolizing one's personal death and the permanent coming of Christ's kingdom, and continues with Lent which prepares the participants for the death/resurrection myth of the Christ. The third period is the post-Easter period wherein the church members are reminded of the "mysteries" which they just experienced ritually. The final period is a post Pentecost time wherein the participant reflects upon the long period of history when the church exists in this "world" under the "power of the Holy Spirit." The cycle begins again to repeat the previous periods.

Just as there is a functional definition of religion and myth so also is there a functional definition of ritual. It accents what ritual does—its function both for the individual and for the social group or society. Eight functions of ritual can be identified from the literature (again, from a wide variety of anthropologists, religious studies scholars and sociologists):

1. remembering
2. social bonding
3. regulating the moral behaviour of members
4. socialization and changes in social statuses
5. psychological development
6. bonding to nature (the ecological function)
7. being empowered
8. evoking the nefarious.

Remembering

The remembering function recalls to the believer that which he/she tends easily to forget: the mythologies of the past. One example from the anthropological literature will illustrate this function. Geertz (1966) outlines an example of a collective ritual from Bali (an Indonesian island east of Java which has been Hindu since the 7th century A.D.). Two key actors represent Rangda (a satanic figure) and Barong (a comic figure). The contest continues over a long time with one figure gaining the upper hand at one time and the other at another time. Most of the tribal members participate actively and are "drawn near" to the two main figures. As they participate, they move into a mass trance and enter "into the world of Rangda and Barong." The ritual functions to have the participants "remember" the original conflict between these two figures and to be present with them in that conflict. Rangda reflects the cultural trait of fear whereas Barong represents playfulness, exhibitionism, and extravagance: both realities close to the life experience of the people.

Social Bonding

Social bonding occurs because as one is bonded to her/his god so also is she/he bonded to other members of the social group or the society. Two examples from native American religions will aid us in understanding this function. Research on the Mohegan Indians of New England by Kertzer (1988:20–21) is a case in point. These people had been struggling to find an identity ever since their tribe was outlawed by the state legislature in 1880. By 1930 they had lost much of their identity and bonding through intermarriage, language loss, and cultural demise. The Monhegans solved this crisis by stressing rites and symbols that identify themselves as Indians and Monhegans. The central rite is the annual powwow wherein native dances are performed, local crafts are displayed, and native clothes are worn. These repeated rites, then, functioned to create unity and bonding among members.

Another example from American Indians peoples is the rite of the Sacred Pipe. Paper (1989) gathered together evidence that the most central and most universal rite of the North American Indians is the smoking of the Sacred Pipe. The rite has many elements that do not vary substantially from tribe to tribe and from region to region. At an appropriate time (for example in council), the Sacred Pipe is ceremoniously filled with tobacco and the shaman lights it from a fire. Then, he raises the pipe up to the zenith and down to the nadir as well as pointing it to the east, west, north and south. Thereafter, he passes it to all who are present and each smokes. The significance of the various gestures is in raising up to the zenith which symbolizes an offering to the deities and a resultant communion with them. The pointing to the earth signifies a unity with the earth whereas the circle pointing is a sign of unity with the whole of the universe. The sharing of the pipe is the sharing of lives: therein is the source of bonding and unity among the participants. Paper (1989:36) writes: "Basic to the ceremonial use of the Sacred Pipe is that it is passed among the participants: it creates social communion; it joins all into a sacred circle."

Canadian survey data from the General Social Survey (GSS) of 1995 gives evidence for this function of ritual from Clark (1998) who found that Canadians who were weekly church attenders were 1.5* as likely as nonattenders to be bonded to their spouses.

Regulation of Behavior

Another function is one of regulation of behaviour. For social life to be possible, it has been long understood by both anthropologists and sociologists that there needs to be some sort of common base, some sort of common value or moral foundation that integrates individual persons together. Wuthnow (1987), a sociologist of religion, sees that the central function of ritual is moral. In a simple word, ritual is that which maintains moral order or (1987:107) "Ritual regulates and defines social relations" and (1987:109) ritual is ...."a symbolic expressive aspect of behaviour that communicates something about social relations, often in a dramatic or formal manner." In the tradition of Durkheim, then, the moral function of ritual is to put order into human relationships, to provide a code whereby men and women can live by and interact together.

Evidence for this function of ritual is provided from the same GSS survey of 1995, when Clark (1998), found that Canadians who were weekly church attenders had reduced divorce rates, less likely to be delinquent, and less likely to abuse drugs and alcohol.

Socialization

Another sociological function of ritual is present when individuals are in the process of being socialized into being active members of a society. The literature on ritual terms these "rites of passage" and include such rituals that surround birth, puberty, marriage and death. An example of this is provided from a case study by Kligman (1988) who studied the marriage rites of a people called the "Ieud Maramures" of northern Romania. She analyses the ritual according to the three phases of separation, transition, and incorporation. The separation stage consists of the marriage preparation, the "dance of the groom's flag" and of the "dance of the bride's crown," a symbolic ritual of bride bargaining, the dressing of the bride and the mutual asking forgiveness of the parents both of the bride and the groom. The dance of the groom's flag consists of the friends of the groom gathering to sew together a flag the evening before the wedding. This flag is symbol of colourful vitality and power between men and women. It is patriarchal in nature and is the dominant marriage symbol. It is carried by a flag bearer who leads the groom and together they go to the home of the bride on the day of the ceremony and lead the bridal entourage into the church.

It is in the home of the bride that the "dance of the crown" ritual is celebrated. Here the bride's maid, with another woman, hold the crown (made of flowers) and lead a dance of both men and women. The crown is a symbol of the bride's virginity and is shown to friends and the future husband.

The transitional stage consists of the actual church ceremony, post-ceremonial meals, gift exchanges between wife-givers and wife-takers, and rituals of asking for the bride and the "song of the hen." After the church ceremony, the bride returns to her parents home. It is late in the night that the groom comes to the house and asks the father for his bride. Through many tries, the father "gives" over the bride to her new husband. After this, a meal is shared. Here the families are gathered and a roast chicken is prepared for food. All but the bride eat for the passing and the eating of the chicken symbolizes the virginity of the bride.

Now that the transfer from the family of the bride to the family of the groom has taken place, she is now brought to the groom's house where she is symbolically undressed. This is the new status and the woman now moves from a status of freedom and carefreeness to that of being a child-bearer and one having full adult responsibilities. The husband, now, is also no longer free and is also a full adult.

Psychological Development

Ritual also serves the individual to develop psychologically. In one way, it may help to elicit as well as to control emotions and, in another way, contribute to individual well-being. O'Dea and O'Dea (1983) provide us with an interpretation of religion being a response to people's experiences of "limit situations" or feelings of contingency, powerlessness and scarcity. Ritual practices can, as noted by Smith (1956), Kluckhohn (1968) and Hargrove (1989), reduce the anxiety produced by these feelings. Kluckhohn argues that rites remind believers of how the ancients did it. These ancients (he uses the example of the Navaho people) meet similar "limit situations" and conquered them. If the rites are performed properly, the participants can also reduce anxiety and be at peace.

Data from the same GSS survey of 1995 provides evidence for this function of ritual when Clark (1998) found that Canadians who were weekly church attenders had reduced levels of stress and were 1.7* as happy as those who did not attend church on a weekly basis.

Ecological

The ecological function of ritual is not common. What is understood by this is that for some religious participants, rituals put them in touch with nature, with the natural ecology. They function to form some kind of communion with the earth, the fields, waters etc. This function will be illustrated with an investigation of native American religion. As is well known from native studies, the aboriginal peoples of America and Canada have a profound respect for the natural environment. Paper (1989) describes the ecological and cosmological meaning of the Sacred Pipe. The bowl of the pipe (made of stone) is a miniature cosmos that is female. The tobacco is put into the bowl in minute pieces that symbolizes bringing the entire cosmos into the bowl itself. The stem (made of wood) of the pipe is male in nature and is symbolic of the trees, and the sky.

When the Sacred Pipe is smoked in a formal ceremony, there is signified a connection of the self (the participant) with the world of social relations (fellow participants, family, clan, and nation), to that of animals who are extensions of social relations (nature is depicted in personal, familial terms), to the earth, to the sky and to the whole of the cosmos. This ritual, in effect, then, is understood to integrate people with nature for all things are "relatives."

Empowerment

The seventh function is empowerment. The argument here is that when participants gather together they experience something they do not when they are alone: empowerment and a sense of having received a supernatural power. Two studies on the charismatic movement

357

will illustrate this function. In her work on Catholic Pentecostals, McGuire (1982:7) identifies four characteristics of power among participants within a prayer group ritual: that the power of God is given directly to ordinary human beings (you need not be a professional cleric); that individuals have power to see the relevance of religion in their ordinary lives; that this power has a strong experiential component; and that all these beliefs (and rituals) compel members to seek out a community of fellow believers.

Swenson (1990) argued that through the central rituals of a small, evangelical/charismatic church, individuals gave witness to being empowered. The four key rituals were:

1. holy communion
2. the Sunday worship service
3. adult baptism
4. membership ceremonies

The Sunday worship service is the rallying point, the core ritual that focuses within a few hours the drama of the people's Christian myth, the charismatic heritage, and empowerment for service. There are two pulpits in this ritual service: the "Word Podium" and the "Music Podium." "The Word Podium" symbolizes the importance of the literal word as found in the Christian scriptures. It is in this setting that the senior pastor spends about one-half an hour in teaching, exhortation, and preaching. This "Podium" is a focus of faith, of life, of empowerment and of action. The sermon is understood as having practical effects like touching people's hurts, and being a balm to soothe the brokenness experienced by members throughout the previous week.

Not as important, but still central, is the "Music Podium." Nearly equal time is given to worship songs. These have an effect of "clothing" participants with praise, wherein something happens in the spiritual realm and the worshipper communicates with the divine.

Evidence is that these rituals are vehicles of empowerment: assisting the participants in feeling stronger, less alienated, and more ready to serve others. It should be accented that in both cases, empowerment, although is personal, it is directed to the social group wherein the whole group (or church) becomes empowered as well.

Nefarious

The last function is negative and is the invocation of the nefarious. As religion can be dysfunctional both for individuals and societies, so also can ritual. This function will be illustrated from some studies of witch hunting rituals of early America. In Salem New England about 1650, a ritual of hunting for witches occurred. Weisman (1984), an historian, noticed a common characteristic of most of the women accused of witchcraft: they were older, single or widowed, and poor. The ritual process began with an accusation of one person against a particular woman who had a rupture of normal relationships with the community. The accusation was countered by the accused which, sometimes, took on the form of curses, threats, and being outspoken in public. These actions of the accused brought upon herself more accusations from the larger community. She began to be labelled a "witch" not only by the one accuser but also by the community. Weisman interprets this level of accusation in terms of a symbol of conflicts within the community itself: of those who had means of living and those who had not. The woman began to be a "scapegoat" to fears and conflicts of the village.

The next stage evoked the judicial system of the colony. Courts were set up and witnesses for and against the accused were heard. If the evidence gathered confirms the accusation, she would either be imprisoned or executed—depending on the severity of the "witchcraft."

Rituals like this provide evidence that religion, in some circumstances, is harmful to persons. In this case, it is marginalised women who become victims.

Ethos

As myths and rituals are extensions of religious experiences so is ethos. The term comes from the anthropologist of religion, Geertz (1973). One may see this as a cluster of behavioural codes including values, norms, morals, and laws. Anthropologists and cultural sociologists have referred to values as providing a general orientation to life while norms as outlining more specific kinds of behaviour. Another way we may look at norms is to consider them as "the rules or standards that govern interaction" (Moot,1965:24). A particular species of a norm is what a founder of American sociology, Sumner (1906), terms the *more* that has the authority of facts (1906:80). Mores, or moral codes, carry more weight and channel human behaviour according to effects: rewards for conformity and punishments for disobedience. Laws are specific norms and mores are codified by some state or societal authority.

The cultural analyst Robert Wuthnow (1987) adds another important element to an understanding of morality: the provision for social order in a society. This recalls Durkheim who also saw morality as a basis of social solidarity.

In religious circles, these mores have even more of an impact because they carry with them some sort of divine approbation and legitimacy. A popular term to describe them as an *ethic* and a collection of ethics would be called an *ethical system*. For example, as in the case of the ten commandments of Judaism, conformity means long life and prosperity and disobedience connotes suffering, a shortened life and poverty (see Deuteronomy 28 in the Jewish or Christian Bible).

There appears to be a general consensus among anthropologists and sociologists of religion that the moral or ethical dimension is central to the understanding of religion. However, some dissenting voices include the 19th century anthropologist, Edward Tyler (1929) and the functionalist anthropologist, Bronislaw Malinowski (1932).

Inspired by Yinger's (1959) outline of the connection between religion and morality, the Rice University anthropologist Edward Norbeck (1961), saw some basis for Tyler's and Malinowski's position. For example, he found that, among the Inuit, morality is relatively removed from religious myths and to break a moral code is not to entail after-life punishment. However, in contrast to Tyler and Malinowski, Norbeck discovers that for the Manus peoples of Melanesia, morality is intricately tied to religion. Strict moral codes govern sexuality. To illustrate, one is guilty of sexual transgression even if s/he sees the private parts of the opposite sex by accident. Laziness, theft, and disobedience of elders incur illness as a punishment from the ancestral spirit. He writes (1961:184): "Any moral transgression is thus the concern of everyone and the compulsion to follow the code is strong. Public accusations of guilt, confession, and expiation also bring shame and loss of social prestige and serve to strengthen the supernatural sanctions."

The bulk of the evidence does reveal that there is a substantial inter-connection between myth, ritual and morality in religion. Inspired by Geertz (1973), Figure 13.1 illustrates this connection:

> We begin with the heart of religion, the sacred that is interactively linked to myth, ritual and ethos. Geertz (1973:126ff) explains the connection of myth, ritual and ethos in the following way. Religion consists of a myth, ritual and a code. Myths provide believers with what "is," the factual, a view of reality and the ethos is the "ought" that flows from the myth.

These world views, however, are not merely in the idea realm. They are represented in symbols such as a Buffalo totem of the Sioux peoples of the American Great Plains, the cross of Western Christianity, the icon of Eastern Christianity, the serene Buddha statue in Burma or the crescent of Islam of Saudi Arabia. As we saw in the last section, rituals dramatize and make present the myth. This is to enable the practitioners to have a religious experience. Thus, the connection between myth, ritual and the ethos is profound. In other words, myth makes meaning of the cosmos, ritual enacts the myth, and ethos provides the quotidian channel to live out the myth. Again, we come full circle. Ideally, if believers know the myth in an experiential way, enact it through ceremonies and live it out in daily life, they increasingly come in contact with the sacred.

Figure 13.1. The Sacred: Myth, Ritual and Ethos

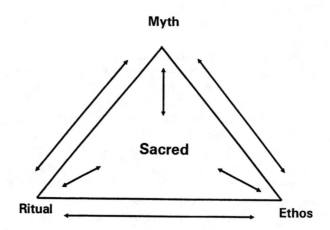

Linkage between Myth, Ritual and Ethos

What I propose to do in this section is to provide empirical evidence for these connections. The thesis is that myth and ethos mutually reinforce one another and ritual reinforces ethos. I shall provide evidence on the link between myth, ritual and ethos from recent surveys in North America.

Survey research documents a reasonably long tradition of linking myth, ritual and morality. Gerhard Lenski (1963), in the late 1950s in Detroit, conducted research of 656 Roman Catholics, Protestants and Jews. He found that devotionalism (as measured by personal communication to God through prayer and meditation) was associated with an ethic of helping or humanitarianism. Allport (1966), in his study of religion and prejudice, found that even though religious affiliates were more prejudiced than non-affiliates, members who were most active in their churches were least prejudiced.

Later research is consistent with these studies of the 1960s. In a 1973 survey of San Francisco Bay area residents, Piazza and Glock (1979) found linkages between myth, measured by images of the divine, ritual, church attendance and daily prayer, and morality, willingness to perform compassionate acts. Those who had what the researchers called a "personal view of God" or a belief that God was active in their lives were more likely to attend church and pray and more likely to loan money to a co-worker without interest and give money to a stranger for bus fare. Morgan (1983) adds further credibility to the linkage between ritual and morality from data of a national representative sample (N=1,467). His findings reveal that those who pray frequently or those who have integrated prayer into their day-to-day lives are more likely to "stop and comfort a crying child," be a "good listener," "get along with loud and obnoxious people," and "turn the other cheek," than those who do not.

Lastly, another national study conducted by the Gallup organization (Poloma and Gallup, 1991), reveals similar results. Poloma and Gallup extend the measure of prayer beyond mere frequency to types of prayer: ritual prayer, reading from a prayer book or reciting memorized prayers, and conversational prayer, talking to God in one's own words. Two other types include petitionary prayer, asking God for favours, and meditative prayer, illustrated by those who spend time thinking about God, feel a divine presence, worship God, and try to listen to God speaking. A bivariate analysis[3] reveals that those who pray meditatively are more likely to forgive others who have hurt them and are less likely to nurture resentments than are those who use the other forms of prayer.

Substantive and Functional Ethos

In the first and second parts of the text, we have given both substantive and functional definitions of religion, myth and ritual. In a typology of morality, we also discover both substantive and functional elements. A substantive understanding of morality is a precept or moral code that is proximate to the sacred. The example given is from Goode (1951) who uses Durkheim's distinction between the sacred and the profane which is at the core of our text. Almost universally among primitive peoples, Durkheim (1965) and Goode (1951) observe that the profane must not intrude into the sacred. One might construct a

361

moral code that would reflect the reality: *"You shall not let the profane intrude into the sacred."*[4]

Functional morality is what morality is to do. Within functional morality, seven different forms appear: empowerment, bonding, ecology, social integration, worldly success, social control and alienation. An explanation will be given with empirical examples to illustrate each type.

The Function of Empowerment

The focus on morality in Durkheim's work is on social control. Not only do moral codes come from the gods to induce conformity, they also empower the conformists. To be an effective member of a society, Durkheim (1965) argues that one must not only conform externally but also internally. In the process of internal conformity or socialization, one becomes elevated and magnified. In addition, these moral codes become "moral powers" within us and we develop a moral conscience. By conforming to the codes, one senses a protection from the deities and one has confidence to meet the challenges of the everyday life.[5]

A case study of American Pentecostals further illustrates this function. In a non-representative sample of Pentecostals, Gerlach and Hine (1970) gathered data from 230 respondents, all of whom acknowledged being empowered with "the Holy Spirit." This empowerment is believed to enable the Pentecostals to commit themselves to each other, who, in turn, add more of a "pool of power" to the church.

The Function of Social Bonding

The example of this function comes from Goode's (1951) analysis of the Murngin of Australia. These people consist of a large clan of about 40 to 50 thousand members who live in a geographical region comprising 360 square miles. The religious and social centre of the clan is a large water hole which is believed to house the unborn children. It is necessary that parents obey the codes of their clan in order to free the spirits of the children to become incarnated. After birth, a child must follow the age graded codes of his or her gender. In doing so, the child becomes bonded to his or her group. As an adult, a man grows into spiritual manhood and in so doing, increasing bonds with his fellows. Thus, by following the moral codes, he builds a bond with the spiritual world and with the world of his clan.

Empirical evidence of this bonding and how it affects morality is given from the Detroit study of Lenski (1963). He found that people who were "communally involved," measured by how many of one's close friends and relatives are members of the same religious group or a measure of social bonding, showed changes in behaviour in their everyday life.

The Ecological and Cosmological Function of Morality

This function of morality connects believers to nature and to the cosmos. Obedience to moral precepts bonds people to brothers and sisters, to the earth, the water, the sky, the animals and to the stars. For example, Eliade (1959) argues that by following the codes of sexual intimacy, one becomes bonded to the heavens, for the heavens are to the earth as the male is to the female. Or, when one lives out a married life, one represents the divine wedding to the whole universe.

The clearest example of this function is from the Amerindian peoples. Before European contact, there were an estimated four to twelve million people in North America who spoke 550 different languages. Even though there was a wide ethnic variation, they all shared some fundamental myths, rituals and ethical codes. The social historian of American religion, Albanese (1981, 1990) describes it in this way. "Nature Religion," the central concept, is a descriptor of a mythology of connectedness: the world and the cosmos is redolent with power, vivacity, unity, and purpose. The view is fundamentally a relational one that connects individuals, societies, nature and the universe into a sacred tapestry. The material world is a sacred world, a safe world, a world "peopled" with mysterious persons.

The fundamental value and explicit moral code for all these people, termed by Albanese (1990: 26), is "the harmony ethic." In pragmatic terms, one is to respect and honour all around you: animals, plants, the earth, water and fellow humans. The well being of all persons depends fundamentally upon how well one lives out this basic precept. Not to honour nature (kill more than one can eat, cut down more trees than necessary, fish beyond the dietary needs of your group) is to cause disharmony with your fellow brothers and sisters. A specific code that is common among the Amerindians is to apologize to an animal if you have to kill it in order to live.

The complimentary ethic to this is what she calls the "ethos of reciprocity" (1990:27). If you follow the harmony ethic, you will, in turn, be treated well by your fellow humans, by nature, indeed, the whole cosmos will smile upon you.

The Function of Social Integration

Another function that removes morality further from delimitation is that of social integration. It is argued that as members of a social group, a tribe, a religious organization honour the moral codes that are common for all the members, then they will integrate more and more into the whole of the community. For the Inuit of the north, it is very important to avoid breaking the religious taboos. If one does, the spirits will be angered and will take their anger out on the members of the group (Norbeck, 1961:177).

Another example of morality influencing social solidarity is among the Kammatic Buddhists of Burma. In what is called a Buddhist lent, people go on a pilgrimage throughout local villages to collect articles and money to give to the monasteries. The manifest function of the practice is to gain merit for one's better-future karma but the latent function (to use Merton's famous term) is the creation of village solidarity. In fact, Spiro (1982) notes that being a Buddhist adds to the solidarity of the whole Burmese society for to be Burmese is to be Buddhist.

The Function of Worldly Success

A further elaboration of morality is reflected in religion's tendency to affect change in peoples' mundane world. Religion is pragmatic and it is effective in providing believers with a better place in life. Weber's (1958a) study of Protestantism is a classic expression

363

of this function. He argues that the Protestant ethic (as represented by the Calvinistic ethic of hard work and diligence that would bring eternal rewards) has a latent function: to empower people to succeed in wealth and status. It is too simplistic to think that if one adheres to this ethic one will prosper financially. However, the ethic becomes a moral force, a power to work hard, to be honest, to save, not to steal. An offshoot of this is success in the world. Weber goes to great lengths to present credible evidence to substantiate the thesis and his work has been replicated in many research projects since his time.

The Function of Social Control

We turn to Durkheim's research to illustrate morality as social control. In fact, as we have seen, it is at the very heart of his theory of religion. Again, society is a moral force coercing members to conform. It is in this conformity that society is made possible.

Norbeck (1961) portrays this function well in his analysis of the Manus people of Melanesia. The Manus, as we saw before in Section 2, are very strict in regard to sexual mores. Again, each family has a guardian spirit who keeps a close eye on the actions of the family members. If members are obedient to the precepts (Norbeck identifies sixteen), they will have wealth and a long life. If they transgress, they will become ill, live a short life and be poor. Nordeck writes of the power of social control among the Manus:

> Any moral transgression is thus the concern of everyone else and the compulsion to follow the code is strong. Public accusation of guilt, confession, and expiation also bring shame and loss of social prestige and serve to strengthen the supernatural sanctions (1961:184).

Most of the research using morality to control people is found in the literature linking religion and politics. The basic thesis is that political regimes use religion as an instrument of power and enforce it through the medium of religious morality (especially those that protect the power of the regime). Yinger (1959) refers to the Russian Orthodox Church of 1915 being used by the aristocracy to control the people. MacIver and Page (1957:318) expand this interpretation: "The religious codes often emerge as powerful engines of control to maintain the interests of the established order against the processes of change, as when the Russian Orthodox Church became a bulwark of the tyranny of the Russian Tzars."

The Moral Function of Alienation

The last function that we identified is really a dysfunction: alienation. Berger (1969) explains that religion (and religious ethics) is a product of social construction that occurs in conversations between persons, groups and institutions. In the process of this construction, some projections can become so reified as to appear objective and not dependent at all on social creation. The actor does not act but is acted upon and is but a passive receptor in the process. If this involves codes of behaviour, these codes become "alien" to the person and are dysfunctional to him or her.

A good historical example is the publication of *Malleus Malificarum*[6] in 1486 by two German medieval theological professors[7] (Buckland, 1993). In this document, the authors outline how to identify and prosecute women who are suspected of witchcraft and sorcery

(Mahoney, 1987). These particular codes illustrate how far removed morality can be from the sacred, and they are used not only to control people but also to imprison them. This is the ultimate extent of the elaboration of ethos.

The Emergence of Formal Religious Organizations

This part of the chapter outlines how sociologists of religion have categorized and specified religious formal organizations. One might argue that religion becomes formalized according to different ways of meeting the need to have an elaboration of roles and institutionalized procedures on one hand and of maintaining the charismatic element on the other hand. The literature provides us with five basic ways in which formal, religious organizations emerge: sect, the church, cult, movement of renewal, and the denomination. These different alternatives will be outlined.

Before I leave the discussion of defining a religious organization, it is important to add that a distinction can also be made between a substantive and a functional definition of a religious organization. A substantive definition consists of a religious organization that facilitates both the individual and collective experience of the sacred while a functional definition embodies a religious organization that serves to provide social solidarity, integration, global well-being, and meaning.

Sect

Using a wide variety of sources (Weber,1946; Troeltsch, 1931; Demerath III, 1965; Coleman, 1968; Wach, 1944; Stark and Bainbridge, 1979), a summary of a definition of the sect seems to encompass three domains: leadership, membership and the relationship to the environment. A sect is:

> A religious organization that includes members who are considered to be converted, who follow stringent rules of behaviour, who form a small, primary and intimate group, who opt for spontaneity rather than for formalized ritual, and form an egalitarian moral community. The leaders of the organization protest against the "over-accommodative" nature of the church type and tend to be lay, charismatic, non-professional and, adhering to clear doctrinal statements. As a whole, the organization stands in a high-tension relationship to the environment and is organizationally precarious in that it endeavours to maintain the pristine message while providing a sense of social order. As an organization, it tends not to accommodate to the external environment and may take a stance of indifference, intolerance or hostility towards that environment.

Table 13:2 illustrates the characteristics of a sect:

Table 13.2. Elements of a Sect

Leadership	Membership	Relationship to the Environment
lay	converted	high tension
charismatic	members follow the leader	non accomodative
non professional	stringent rules	organizatinally precarious
	they form into primary groups	indifference to the outside environment
	spontaneous	

To exemplify the sect type, two cases from Alberta will be presented. Although O'Toole (1996) argues by that the sect is not the predominant form of Christianity in Canada, neither in the past or the present, this does not mean that the sect is without merit as a vital religious form in the nation. The examples presented here include the main features of the sect type as outlined in this definition. Also, the first example of vibrant sects during the years following World War I, the Great Depression, and after World War II, enables us to understand case histories of sects that both protest against the more traditional churches and respond to widespread social unrest. The second example, that of a modern sect in central Alberta, illustrates a protest against a modern church as well as an organization in high-tension with the external environment.

Mann (1955), a former sociologist from the University of Toronto, researched churches, sects, and cults that reveal a somewhat unique feature of religion in North America. In common with most other religious awakening and reform in North America, the Alberta case is not unique. However, its distinctiveness is that from this religious ferment emerged a vibrant political movement called the Social Credit Party that was the government in the province from 1935 until 1971. The political base of the party was predominately evangelical Christianity, and William Aberhart (the founder of the party in Alberta) was also a pastor and radio evangelist.

In 1946, there were an estimated 228,190 members in all Protestant churches in Alberta. Of these, 53,790 or 24 percent were members of evangelical sects (Mann 1955:30–31). These sects were inheritors of the fundamentalist movement of the early part of the century which was unified by a very strident protest against modernity (especially the theory of evolution). They were united doctrinally in that they shared a tight ascetic code of morality and belief in the literal truth of the Bible, in the personal second coming of Christ, the existence of a fire and brimstone hell, and the necessity of a dramatic conversion experience. Other characteristics included hearty congregational singing, enthusiastic preaching, a congregational form of government, a unanimous attack against modernism, and a condemnation of the coldness, formality, and class consciousness often found in the churches (Mann 1955:27–32). A special characteristic is that these sects grew at the expense of the more established churches. These converts, or "switchers," came from such churches as Roman Catholic, Orthodox, Methodist, Baptist, United,[8] Lutheran, Presbyterian, and Anglicans. However, the switching did not tend to occur over a wide range of denominational differences. Frequently, Mann argues, the converts tended to follow ethnic lines such as German Lutherans joining German sects: "In general, shifts in religious conviction followed lines of least ethnic, religious, and social resistance: new Canadians attached themselves to sects composed of their own ethnic group" (Mann 1955:34).

As noted above, the liturgies celebrated by these evangelical sects were lively, enthusiastic and vibrant. Mann (1955:45) observes that the informality and friendliness may have accounted for some of the sects' appeal to farmers as well as to highly mobile urban people. This religious practice offered lonely and marginal people a simple way of certifying their belonging to a tight-knit group.

Another example of a sect is one located in a mid-sized city in Alberta. The sect emerged at a very different time in Alberta than were the ones illustrated above. It was formed from several charismatic prayer groups within the United Church of Canada. For about ten years, members of these prayer groups served in several United Church congregations in the hope of "renewing" the churches. Increasingly, their protest became nullified without any changes happening. Also, the United Church of Canada was going through modernization processes such as questioning the literal meaning of the Bible, speaking of God in inclusive language, and allowing practising homosexual persons to be ordained ministers. Several members of these groups left the denomination and eventually invited a minister of a Pentecostal church (of the *Fellowship of Christian Assemblies*) to pastor the nascent congregation. From a small number (40 members) in the early 1980s, the sect had grown to over 300 members by 1991. Swenson (1991) argues that there is significant evidence that most of these members came from the mainline churches (especially Roman Catholic, United, and Anglican) because they experienced deligitimation[9] from their previous commitments.

Both the Mann and Swenson studies challenge the Bibby and Brinkerhoff (1973, 1983, 1994) thesis of the circulation of the saints.[10] Their research on evangelical churches in Calgary during the 1970s and 1980s reveals that most of the growth of the evangelical congregations came from successful youth socialization and movement from one evangelical church to another. Mann and Swenson's data reveal that membership increase came not from other sects but, rather, main line, church type denominations. I would suggest that the sect in central Alberta drew on people from the mainline churches because many were members within these churches before and had a conversion experience within them but did not receive support from them. They eventually became alienated and left to create and join the sect. The Bibby and Brinkerhoff data reveal people who have always been evangelical and were but "circulating" from one sect to another.

The Church

From the same authors who informed us on what a sect was (with the addition of Clark, 1948) and using the same dimensions as the sect, I define the church as:

The leaders of the church usually are priests or ministers who are professionally trained and hold not a personal charisma but a charisma of office. Authority is "top-down" in a series of hierarchical rankings. There tends to be a liaison between the religious and the secular leaders. The religious leaders seem to be concerned about the welfare of the larger society. These leaders tend to be conservative in doctrine, especially in traditional societies, but move towards liberalism in the modern world.

Members are mostly members from birth and have an ascriptive status. The people appear to be socially controlled by the leaders, large in numbers and there is a relatively high level of organizational stability. Ritual is more important than spontaneity and the fellowships lean toward impersonality and a kind of collectivity. Church members tend to be ascetic in religious practices in traditional societies but are much more relativistic in the modern setting.

The church accommodates itself to the external environment and thus may become overly secularized. It has a level of low tension with this environment and because of its bureaucratic "weight" tends to break down.

Table 13:3 illustrates this definition.

Table 13.3. Elements of a Church

Leadership	Membership	Relationship to the Environment
priest or minister	not converted	low tension
not charismataic	from birth	accomodative
professional	loose rules	tends to be secularized
hierarchical order	control is from the leaders	heavy bureaucracy
liaison with the secular order	ritual is vital	
conservative in traditional times	impersonal social group	
liberal in modern times	aesetic in traditional times	
	relativistic in modern times	

Before an example of the church type with a Canadian illustration is presented, it may be useful to know how important this organizational type has been to the development of Canada as a whole. O'Toole (1996), in an essay on religion in Canada, makes a cogent argument that the evolution of Canadian religion has followed the European model rather than the American one. In the spirit of revolution, the United States has been dominated by the sect as the most common kind of religious organization. In contrast, religion Canadian style has had strong roots in the social establishment common in the church type of organization. It has had, especially historically, strong links to commanding political, business, and cultural elites. This has had a continued impact, O'Toole argues. About two-thirds of Canadians consider themselves to be members of the Roman Catholic, Anglican or United Church. This has not changed even with the introduction of non-Christian religions as well as with the growth of secularization. Citing *Maclean's* (1993), O'Toole notes that 80 percent of Canadians self-describe themselves as Christians. Of them, 20 percent belong to conservative Christian sects while a full 80 percent still adhere to one of the "Big Three": Roman Catholic, Anglican and United.

Yinger (1970:257–258), dissatisfied with the simplicity of the church/sect typology, adds further refinements to the continuum. He distinguishes the church type into *the universal institutionalized church* and *the universal diffused church*. The former has all the major characteristics of the above definition with the additional fact that it is co-extensive with the whole of society, as in Christendom of the middle ages. The second type also has the same characteristics but is only one type of religious organization in a complex, modern society. Within modern Christianity, there are currently no examples of the former type. Within Islam, however, there are contemporary examples in Saudi Arabia and Iran.

Nonetheless, the rural parish church of Quebec of relatively recent past is an example. Miner (1939) presents an ethnographic analysis of this type of religious organization. St. Denis is a rural parish community about eighty miles downstream from Quebec city. Although the history of the community goes back to 1695, it was formally established as a parish in 1833. The economic base was entirely agricultural, with the centre of the social life of the community being the parish itself. Because the civic boundaries of the community are co-extensive with the parish, we can rightly call St. Denis a universal church. The parish is the "first point of reference" of the people into which is enmeshed the family. The family type is primogeniture (inheritance given to the first son). All of the other children (ranging in number from five to seven) were to leave the farm. One was to become a priest, another a nun, and the rest professionals or emigrants to the northeastern part of the United States to work in the textile industry.

When Miner was writing, the role of religion was very powerful. Sacred beliefs supported the time-tested, successful right behaviour. The Sunday ritual, the Mass, was the key ritual attended by virtually every person in the parish. In this setting, the priest (called the *curé*) presented directives for a righteous life. This ritual functioned to create solidarity and cohesiveness within the group of believers. This ritual was augmented by sacred feasts which brought further integration. One such example is a celebration in the autumn called All Souls' Day. In this ritual families were integrated with their ancestors in a series of prayers for the deceased. This kind of religious organization permeates the daily life of its members, is present as a powerful means of social control, and creates social solidarity and cohesiveness among a people. However, it is out of step with modernity, which emphasizes individual choice and personal freedom.[11]

Since the time that Miner completed his work, St. Denis has not changed much but Roman Catholicism beyond the village has changed dramatically. O'Toole (1996) informs us that the church has moved from a triumphalist position to an exile or abdication from the centre of Canadian Francophone life. It has been displaced by the state in education and health care, has experienced a drastic decline in clergy, and is beset with an increasingly large number of members who do not frequent religious services. In addition, these Francophone Catholics dissent from official church teachings on matters of birth control, legalized abortion, and premarital sexual activity.

On the other side, however, a full 86 percent of Quebeckers identify themselves as Roman Catholics. The organization itself has also changed to include liturgical flexibility, ecumenical dialogue, and a compassionate concern for social justice. The more central institution in the lives of Francophobe is the Catholic-parochial school. Even though the adults do not go to church on Sunday, they send their children to the schools still under the directorship of the Church. Citing Lemieux (1990), O'Toole writes:

> Raymond Lemieux suggests that, in contemporary life, it [Quebec Catholicism] has acquired a multi-faceted character. It has become a diffuse, churchless faith which simultaneously supports a vague, almost subliminal civil religion of reassuring familiarity and a privatized popular religiosity whose discrete spiritual quests evoke and involve "religious effervescence, emotional communion, affirmation of universal values and explosion of imaginary" (1996:123).

Before this section is completed, it is worth indicating that the church is best illustrated by a functional definition of the religious organization. This is for two reasons. The church is an example of routinized charisma or the sacred and is defined as that type of religious organization that accommodates itself to the secular environment.

Cult

Becker (1932), Mann (1955), Westley (1983), Stark and Bainbridge (1979 & 1985) and Johnstone (1992) are the authors that I shall call upon to present us with an understanding of what a cult is. From their research, we can identify several elements which converge around three domains of the cult: deviant beliefs, accent on the individual and the relationship with the environment. Table 13.4 and the following definition illustrate these domains:

Table 13.4. Elements of a Cult

Deviant Beliefs	Membership	Relationship to the Environment
deviant from the religious doctrine of the host society	converted	high tension
syncretic	achieved status	accomodative tendency varies with type of group
selection of beliefs from several sources	individual is considered to be divine or sacred	
hierarchical order	loose and informal social group	
	group tends to be informal	

A cult is a belief system which is deviant from the traditional religious doctrines of the host society. Members tend to blend non-traditional with traditional tenets that make it a syncretic. There is a special accent on the individual who becomes almost sacred. This emphasis on the individual leaves the association thus formed in a loose, informal, organizational structure. Finally, the cult stands in a high tension relationship with the external environment.

Before I proceed to discuss examples of cults, a further distinction into types of cults is necessary. Paloutzian (1996) accepts the divisions as presented thus far. He adds another meaning of the term and calls it "a destructive cult." By this he means a cult that seeks to control and radically alter the personalities of their groups. There is much controversy about using the term in this way. To give some credibility to his description, Paloutzian provides evidence from some members who have left the Moonies or the Unification Church. Critics of using the term "cult" in this way would argue that ex-members are not the ones to ask since they may be exaggerating their sense of a loss identity. There does seem to be some evidence, however, to classify some noteworthy cults in this light: the Jonestown cult, the Solar Temple, Heaven's Gate, and the Branch Davidians. In the case of Jonestown, the Solar Temple and the Heaven's Gate groups, members committed suicide—the kind of suicide that Durkheim (1951) would call "altruistic suicide" or a suicide that indicates a willingness to take one's own life for the sake of the group.

Campbell (1998) adds another term that is useful for our understanding of the phenomenon. He uses the term *cultic milieu* to refer to a society's deviant belief systems, rituals, and associated collectivities, institutions, and individuals. Additionally, it is characterized by all the worlds of the occult, magic, spiritualism, psychic phenomena, alien intelligences, lost civilizations, and faith healing or nature cures.

With this background in mind, I will illustrate this ideal type with an empirical case study of new religions in Montreal, Canada. Westley (1983) researched six groups which are categorized as being part of new religions movements:[12] Scientology, Psychosynthesis, Arica, Est, Shakti, and Silva Mind Control. It is beyond the scope of this presentation to detail the unique elements of these religions. I will present the common characteristics such as beliefs and organizational features.

Using several authors (Stone, 1976; Ellwood, 1973; Gaustad, 1974 and Bach, 1973), Westley (1983) presents the following common characteristics of these groups: being drawn from the encounter group/therapy tradition; having the idea of pre- and post-existence in a spiritual state; the idea of a plurality of worlds, each with its own spirits and angels; believing in the Renaissance notion that divine and human consciousness are co-extensive; adhering to the intimate connection between the body and the mind; believing that bodily conditions are a direct reflection of mental states; and being part of the human potential movement which accents individual changes from an intense group encounter. These groups, what Westley calls "the cult of man or the cult of the individual," are:

> ...a mixture of the late stages of the human potential movement, the positive-thought movement, and the occult traditions. The point of agreement of all six of these is that it is the human individual who is seen as sacred, as all powerful. This sacred power is seen as located deep within the individual personality. Actions in the outer world become significant, not in themselves, but only in terms of their impact on this inner self (Westley, 1983:38).

There are several distinguishing organizational features that these six groups share together. To participate in the group activities, fees for services are asked. Rather than have teachings on certain themes common in churches and sects, the fee for service is offered in exchange for a course on a certain topic. Membership transience is another feature of these groups. In fact, as long as the individual grows or develops, the continued presence of the group is not necessary. Partial commitment or involvement is also common. One can come and go at will and one will not be asked "why did you miss the gathering last week?" (Westley, 1983: 39–58).

The mythology corresponds to this informal, loose kind of organization. Faith (as trust in a supernatural power or person) is substituted for learning scientific technology. Rather than accenting healing that would integrate one into a community, it is purification from polluting ideas, especially negative ones, that is important for members of these groups. One may argue that faith (as trust in a person or adherence to basic doctrines) is exchanged for knowledge. In this way, these particular groups are Gnostic[13] in a fundamental manner.

Another example of a cult is The Nation of Islam. It has a similar mythology but a very different kind of organization that is not at all loose but is rather tight, hierarchical, and structured. Before I proceed to discuss the organizational features of the movement, it might be worth commenting the study by Gardell (1996) interpretation of its mythology, for it has relevancy to its organization. He considers it to be fundamentally gnostic with roots in Sufi Islam,[14] Manichaeism, and Druze religion.[15] The Nation's belief system, like Gnosticism, is hidden, esoteric, and veiled. It can be presented but only in symbolic and mystical terms. Evil is a spirit that travels in human bodies and is, especially, manifested in the white person. There is the great cycle of time that looks something like the following. In the first cycle of time, there was paradise and there was an essential unity between God and man, for God created himself in the form of man. The second great cycle began with the creation of the white race (in gnostic terms, the separation of the divine and the human) and the black person lost his or her knowledge of self. The third stage begins with a period of enlightenment when saviours show that the way to unity again is to become aware of one's inherent divinity. This mythology can be interpreted only by messengers who have been appointed to do so. In the case of the Nation, this is Minister Louis Farrakhan, the current leader.

From this belief, the hierarchical nature of the Nation flows. Minister Farrakhan is the primary authority figure who has deputies to carry on specific ministries. There are elected representatives from all the NOI mosques throughout the United States. In the upper regions of the hierarchy, two ministries should be noted: the ministry for women and the one for defence. The former is headed by a woman (called the MGT Caption or national instructress of women). The defence ministry holds a key position—a military male cadre of highly disciplined men who "defend" the Nation. They are not to be aggressors but protect the name, property, and assets of the people. In Farrakhan's words: "we will whip the hell out of any that comes against us, short or tall, armed or unarmed" (Cited in Gardell 1996:142).

Gardell (1996) notes that in the resurrection of the Nation after a decline of the movement during the 1970s, it began in small study groups within members homes, and in rented halls. By the mid 1980s, there was such a boom that mosques were created throughout all of the states in the United States. To become an official member of the Nation, at least 40 people apply to the headquarters and agree to abide by the rules and regulations of Minister

Farrakhan and his chiefs of staff. Each mosque has a leader who is similar to the imam[16] of mainstream Islam.

In concluding this section on the cult, is it to be considered an illustration of the substantive understanding of a religious organization or the functional one? I would say that it can be both. It can be considered to represent the substantive dimension because it does not accommodate itself to the environment. On the other hand, it can be considered to be closer to the functional if it creates a mythology that is focussed on, for example, control of persons as in the case of the Nation of Islam.

Movement of Renewal

The fourth type of religious organization that is reflected in the literature is the movement of renewal. Its central feature is a protest from within an existing church that does not involve any secession or a schism but, rather, a desire and mobilization to change the tone, the emptiness, the routinized charisma of the church through a renewal of a tradition. The renewal movement members strive hard to maintain connections with the authorities of the church. Table 13.5 reflects the characteristics of a Movement of Renewal or MOR.

Table 13.5. Elements of the MOR

Leadership	Membership	Relationship to the Environment
lay	conversion	high tension
charismatic	achieved status	low accomodative
not professional	small primary groups	non schismatic to the church environment
in liaison with the larger church	in liaison with the larger church	

A current example of a MOR is the Catholic Charismatic Movement. Swenson and Thompson (1986) did a content analysis on key texts and magazines of this movement from 1967 to 1976. Using Wach (1944), Hill (1973) and O'Dea and O'Dea (1983) as a theoretical base, they review Catholic Charismatic spokespersons such as Ranaghan and Ranaghan (1969), Ford (1970), O'Connor (1971), Clark (1971), and Byrne (1971) to illustrate that the Catholic Charismatic Movement is a movement of renewal.

All of these spokespersons write of the need for members of the movement to remain loyal to the Roman Catholic Church in its leadership and its core beliefs. In their writings, Swenson and Thompson (1986) also observed that to legitimatize the charismatic dimension of this movement in the eyes both of the followers and the church hierarchy, they take great pain in locating the charismatic dimension in the traditions of the Catholic church. Such "sacred pasts" consist of the New Testament, the early church, the monastic movement and the mystical saints of the medieval period. A recent past was the Vatican II council in the early 1960s. Relying on the documents (Abbot, 1966), these spokespersons make a case that the highest authority in the Catholic Church, the gathering of all the bishops and the Pope, approved of the vitality of the charismatic gifts.

But of the movement of renewal, substantive or functional? I would argue that it approximates the substantive dimension for reasons the same as the sect: the quest for authenticity (for the sacred) and the non-accommodative nature of the religious organization. This completes our investigation into cults and movements of renewal. The last organizational type, common in modern societies, is the denominational one. I will outline its main features and then present a case history of one such denomination: the United Church of Canada.

Denomination

The term denomination was introduced into the sociology of religion by Niebuhr (1957). It is seen as one type of routinisation of charisma that represents an accommodation to the class divisions within a society. He argues that a sect exists only for the period of time of the reformer. Soon after the death of the reformer, the sect begins to accommodate itself to the host society and the denomination emerges. The denomination, then, is a routinized sect that reflects the class, ethnic, and racial divisions in a society.

Martin (1962), a sociologist from England, expands. He notes that sects do not necessarily become a denomination but may continue for many generations as, for example, established sects. What is unique about the denomination is that it has some features that are common to the church and sect type as well as having characteristics unique to itself.

Rather than presenting my usually summary definition of the different types of religious organizations, I choose to select Martin's own definition of the denomination:[17]

> It does not claim that its institutional borders constitute the one ark of salvation, its concept of unity is a unity of experience and its historical sense is likewise a unity of experience rather than an institutional succession. Its attitude to organization and to cultic forms tends to be pragmatic and instrumental, while its sacramental conceptions are subjective. This subjectivity is related to a fundamental individualism. In the field of eschatology its conceptions are traditional and in the field of moral theory its conception of the relation of faith and works is dynamic but balanced (1962:11).

With this definition as a background, we will illustrate this type with a church from Canada: The United Church of Canada. On June 10, 1925, this church became a formal organization of three churches (Presbyterian, Methodist, and Congregational) and one small amalgam, the General Council of Local Union Churches. Grant (1967) argues that the union was not so much a result of ecumenism (it had not yet been born) but, rather, one of exigency and practicality. Canada was still a frontier expanding country at this time. Vast lands with small populations left rural areas with many churches in competition with one another and each with few members. Union, then, made a lot of pragmatic sense.

The *Basis of Union* presents a presbyterian polity wherein each congregation and pastoral charge (there were 4,200 congregations in 1990 and 2,400 pastoral charges or one or more congregations under a minister) has a representation and a voice in a particular presbytery (98). Each presbytery, in turn, has its own elected representatives in the conference (a union of local presbyteries and numbering 13). Finally, each conference has its elected persons to the national church, the General Council, wherein major decisions are made (Morrow, 1923 and Grant, Chambers, Forrest, Greene, Lee and White, 1990). One of the ways the early founders found consensus is that each church would not accent its own "brand" of Christianity. In other words, there were to be no "Wesleyans," or "Calvinists." A consequence of this meant a lessened emphasis on "ours" and "theirs" (Grant, 1967:101).

Morrow (1923) outlines a history of the discussions within each of the churches that eventually led to the union. The *Basis of Union* (Morrow, 1923:322–327) establishes both the doctrinal and political basis of the new church. All representatives agreed that the union was to be based upon the faith given by the apostles and prophets of the New Testament with Jesus Christ as the "corner stone." The Bible is understood to be the primary source and ultimate standard of the faith. In addition, the representatives hold allegiance to the early creeds and the teaching of the reformers. The document goes on to detail the common beliefs regarding God, revelation, the divine purpose, creation, the sin of man, the grace of God, the divine-human nature of Jesus, the Holy Spirit, the need for regeneration, faith, repentance, sanctification and prayer. The doctrines of the law of God, the meaning of the Church, the sacraments, the ministry, fellowship and the teachings of eschatology all follow basic reformation theology.

A significant contrast is found in the (unofficial) currently accepted "doctrines of faith." Grant et al, present a creed in the following words:

> We are not alone, we live in God's world. We believe in God who has created and is creating, who has come in Jesus, the Word made flesh, to reconcile and make new, who works in us and others by the Spirit. We trust in God. We are called to be church: to celebrate God's presence, to love and serve others, to seek justice and resist evil, to proclaim Jesus, crucified and risen, our judge and our hope. In life, in death, in life beyond death, God is with us. We are not alone. Thanks be to God (1990:160).

From this latter creedal document, one is able to see how very concerned the leaders of the United Church take a middle ground approach that is quite indicative of the denominational type. This church sees itself as only one way among many to salvation, being pragmatic, seeing the divine presence in others, accenting personal choice, and combining both faith and works.

O'Toole's (1996) reflections on the United Church add further credence to this interpretation. Even though 11.6 percent of Canadians affiliate with this church, this figure is a decline from 20 percent in previous times. In addition, only 16 percent attend religious services on a regular basis. Mythologically, the church exhibits a moderate progressivism that tries to steer between extreme liberal and conservative belief systems. This has become, indeed, its most crucial challenge. On one hand, conservative members are concerned about the maintenance of orthodox doctrine and sexual morality while the liberals are committed to social justice, equity, and inclusiveness. The importance of inclusiveness brought the church to near crisis in the late 1980s when professed homosexuals were given freedom to be ordained as ministers. Although a full-scale schism did not occur, there continues to be a high level of tension between the conservatives who are becoming more marginalised.

There is recent evidence, however, that the denomination is leaning more to a left position and not a middle one. Rev. Bill Phipps, the current moderator of the denomination, challenges orthodox United Church teachings. In contrast to a New Testament text that says: "In his body [Jesus Christ] lives the fulness of divinity" (Colossians 2:9), Phipps says: "I believe that God is more than Jesus. God is huge, mysterious, wholly beyond our comprehension and beyond our total understanding. Jesus does not represent or embody all of God, but embodies as much of God as can be in a person." The resurrection should not be taken literally but, rather, "it is the belief in transforming energy that calls us into the world to follow Jesus who, we say, gives life over death." And, finally, "heaven and hell are what we create on earth" (MacLeans, 1998:43).

Summary

Concepts which are central to our understanding of these various types are tension, accommodation and protest. One may argue that a religious organization begins from the charismatic moment when the processes of routinization commence. The sect appears to be the closest type to this moment. As the sect accommodates more and more to the cultural environment (in a state of tension), the church type may emerge (as in the case of the post-reformation churches) or a denomination (as in the case of churches during nineteenth century America and documented by Niebuhr).

As the church type moves more to the extreme of accommodation, some members and possibly a prophet protests the accommodation. The kind of response to the tension and accommodation directs the kind of organization into a sect, a movement of renewal or a cult. The denomination is seen as standing midway between the sect and the church: an accommodation that settles on a balance of the polarities as being part of the accommodative process of the church and the non-accommodative process of the sect. In this way, one may consider that the denomination has both a substantive and functional dimension.

Conclusions

It is the hope of the writer that the student of introductory sociology has come to a better appreciation of the contents of the social scientific study of religion. Here, I have outlined an investigation of religion by using a definition and expanded on it from as wide a perspective as possible. There are many things that have not been reviewed, especially the link of religion to the other social institutions.

Notes

1. Weber substantiates this impression in noting "But Islam was never really a religion of salvation; the ethical concept of salvation was actually alien to Islam. The god it taught was a lord of unlimited power, although merciful, the fulfillment of whose commandments was not beyond human power" (1978:625).

2. Vatican II Council happened between 1963–1965 in Rome where all the bishops of the Roman Catholic Church meet to update the teachings, rituals and organization of Catholicism.

3. The type of analysis that investigates to see if there is a significant relationship between two variables.

4. Another example of the substantive meaning of morality is from the Decalogue of Judaism. Of the ten commandments, the first three are ordinances specifically related to honouring Yahweh or the central sacred element of the religion.

5. This is reflected in the sacred text of Christians, the New Testament. It is told that after Jesus rose from the dead, he sent his Holy Spirit to his disciples. If they would obey his precepts, they would be empowered from "on high" to continue his mission upon earth.

6. A detailed legal and theological document regarded as the standard handbook on witchcraft, including its detection and its extirpation, until well into the eighteenth century. Its appearance did much to spur on and sustain some two centuries of witch-hunting hysteria in Europe. The *Malleus* codified the folklore and beliefs of the Alpine peasnats and was dedicated to the implementation of Exodus 22:18: "You shall not permit a sorceress to live."

7. Two Dominicans: Johann Sprenger, dean of the University of Cologne in Germany, and Heinrich (Institoris) Kraemer, professor of theology at the University of Salzburg, Austria, and inquisitor in the Tirol region of Austria.

8. The United Church of Canada was created as a union of Methodist, Presbyterian, and Congregationalist churches in 1925.

9. The term refers to those devotees who have become disillusined from their current religious affiliation and consider that it is no longer a legitimate institution.

10. In their 1994 study, the authors nuance their original thesis. Although the data continues to reinforce the thesis, there have been recent changes in that there has been an increase of nonevangelical community membership.

11. Ten years later, Miner returned to the parish. Already by this time modern values and technology were invading the tight community.

12. Although there is a wide variation of new religious movements, Wilson provides us with a general definition:

> that salvation is gained by becoming acquainted with a special, perhaps secret, knowledge from a mystic source; that ultimate salvation and knowledge comes from the liberation of powers within the self; that real salvation is attained by belonging to a saved community, whose lifestyle and concerns are utterly divergent from those of worldly people (1976:63).

13. The term is from the Greek, *gnosis*, a word that simply means "knowledge." The mythology that extends the meaning of the term is Gnosticism. Its origins go back to Egyptian religion which had a central tenet, "He who knows himself, knows the All." Other important features include the teaching of the Divine Man (a man who was both human and divine); Sophia or the feminine manifestation of the divine essence similar to the Divine Mother; having special knowledge available only to a few; a strong distinction between the

spiritual and the material; and, lastly, a symbolic reading of canonical texts from Judaism, Christianity, and Islam (Eliade 1995).

14. Ascetic, mystical Islam.

15. An independent sect situated mainly in Lebanon, Syria, and Israel, that is an offshoot of Islam.

16. Arabic IMAM ("leader," "pattern"), the head of the Muslim community; the title is used in the Koran several times to refer to leaders and to Abraham.

17. Some later work has been done on developing this type (Berger, 1961; Morioka and Newell, 1968 and McGuire, 1992). However, these more recent references do not add anything substantially different than Niebuhr and Martin.

References

Albanese, Catherine
1981   *American Religion and Religions.* Belmount, CA: Wadsworth.

Albanese, Catherine
1990   *Nature Religion in America: From the Algonkian Indians to the New Age.* Chicago: The University of Chicago Press.

Allport, Gordon
1966   "The Religious Context of Prejudice." *Journal for the Scientific Study of Religion* 5:447–457.

Athanasius, St.
1976   In the Divine Office. *The Liturgy of the Hours. Volume II.* New York: Catholic Book Publishing Co.

Bailey, Edward
1998   "Sacred." In William Swatos, Jr. (ed.). *Encyclopaedia of Religion and Society.* pp. 443–444. Walnut Creek, CA: Altamira Press.

Becker, Howard
1932   *Systematic Sociology on the Basis of the Beziehungslehre and Gebildelehre of Leopold Van Wiese.* New York: Wiley.

Berger, Peter
1961   *The Noise of Solemn Assemblies: Christian Commitment and the Religious Establishment.* Garden City, NY: Doubleday.

Berger, Peter
1963   *Invitation to Sociology: A Humanistic Perspective.* Garden City, NY: Doubleday.

Berger, Peter
1969   *The Sacred Canopy.* New York: Doubleday and Company.

Berger, P.
1974   "Some Second Thoughts on Substantive versus Functional Definitions of Religion." *Journal for the Scientific Study of Religion* 13:125–133.

Bibby, Reginald and Merlin B. Brinkerhoff
1973   "The Circulation of the Saints: A Study of People Who Join Conservative Churches." *Journal for the Scientific Study of Religion* 12:273–83.

Bibby, Reginald, and Merlin B. Brinkerhoff
1983   "Circulation of the Saints Revisited: A Longitudinal Look at the Conservative Church Growth." *Journal for the Scientific Study of Religion* 22:253–62.

Bibby, Reginald, and Merlin B. Brinkerhoff
1994   "Circulation of the Saints 1966–1990: New Data, New Reflections." *Journal for the Scientific Study of Religion* 33:273–280.

Bibby, Reginald
1987   *Fragmented Gods: The Poverty and Potential of Religion in Canada.* Toronto: Irwin Publishing.

Buckland, R.
1993   *Buckland's Complete Book of Witchcraft.* St. Paul, MN: Llewellyn Publications.

Byrne, James
1971   "Charismatic leadership," pp. 187–210. In Kevin and Dorothy Ranaghan eds., *As the Spirit Leads Us.* Paramus, New Jersey: Paulist Press.

Campbell, Joseph
1964   *The Masks of God: Occidental Mythology.* New York: The Viking Press.

Campbell, Joseph
1968   *The Hero With a Thousand Faces.* Princeton, NJ: Princeton University Press.

Campbell, Colin
1998   "Cult." In William Swatos, Jr. (ed.). *Encyclopedia of Religion and Society.* pp. 122–123. Walnut Creek, CA: Altamira Press.

Clark, S.D.
1948   *Church and Sect in Canada.* Toronto: The University of Toronto Press.

Clark, Stephen
1971   "Charismatic Renewal in the Church," in Kevin and Dorothy Ranaghan eds., *As The Spirit Leads Us.* Paramus, New Jersey: Paulist Press. pp. 17–37.

Clark, Warren
1998   *Religious Observance: Marriage and the Family.* Ottawa: Statistics Canada: Catalogue 11–008–XPE.

Coleman, John S.J.
1968   "Church-Sect Typology and Organizational Precariousness." *Sociological Analysis* 29:55–66.

Davis, Kingsley
1948–49 *Human Society.* New York: MacMillan.

Demarath, N.J. III
1965   *Social Class in American Protestantism.* Chicago: Rand McNally.

Durkheim, Emile
1951 [1897] *Suicide: A Study of Sociology*. Glencoe, IL: Free Press.

Durkheim, Emile
1965 [1915] *The Elementary Forms of The Religious Life*. Translated by Joseph Ward Swain. New York: Free Press. Originally published in London: George Allen and Unwin, 1915.

Eliade, Mircea
1959 *The Sacred and the Profane: The Nature of Religion*. New York: Harcourt, Brace & World, Inc.

Eliade, Mircea
1973 "Myth," p. 70–78, in *Readings on the Sociology of Religion*. by Thomas O'Dea and Janet O'Dea eds.. Engewood Cliffs, NJ: Prentice Hall.

Ford, J. Massingberd
1971 "Tongues-Leadership-Women." *Spiritual Life* 17:19–23.

Gardell, Mattias
1996 *In the Name of Elijah Muhammad, Louis Farrakhan and the Nation of Islam*. Durham: Duke University Press.

Geertz, Clifford
1966 "Religion as a Cultural System." p. 1–46 in Michael Banton ed. *Anthropological Approaches to the Study of Religion*. London: Tavistock Publications.

Geertz, Clifford
1973 *The Interpretation of Cultures*. New York: Basic Books.

Gerlach, Luther, and Virginia Hine
1970 *People, Power, Change Movements of Social Transformation*. Indianapolis: The Bobbs-Merril.

Goode, William
1951 *Religion Among the Primitives*. New York: Free Press.

Grant, John W.
1967 *The Canadian Experience of Church Union*. Richmond, Virginia: John Knox Press.

Grant, John W., Steven Chambers, Dianne Forrest, Bonnie Greene, Sang Chul Lee, and Peter G. White
1990 *Voices and Visions: 65 Years of the United Church of Canada*. Toronto: The United Church of Canada Publishing House.

Hargrove, Barbara
1989 *The Sociology of Religion*. Arlington Heights, Ill: Harland Davidson, Inc.

Hill, Martin
1973 *The Religious Order*. London: Heinemann Educational Books.

James, William
1902   *The Varieties of Religious Experience.* New York: Longmans, Green and Company [1920].

Johnstone, Ronald L.
1992   *Religion in Society. A Sociology of Religion.* Fourth Edition. Englewood Cliffs, New Jersey: Prentice Hall.

Kanwar, Mahfooz
1974   *The Sociology of Religion.* Calgary, Alberta: Mount Royal College Press.

Kertzer, David
1988   *Ritual, Politics and Power.* New Haven: Yale University Press.

Kligman, Gail
1988   *The Wedding of the Dead: Ritual, Poetics, and Popular Culture in Transylvania.* Berkeley, CA: University of California Press.

Kluckhohn, Clyde
1968   "Myths and Rituals: A General Theory." p. 137–183, in R. A. George ed. *Studies in Mythology.* Homewood, Ill.: The Dorsey Press.

Lemieux, Raymond
1990   "Le cathololicisme quebecois: une question de culture." *Sociologie et Societes* 22:145–164

Lenski, Gerhard
1963   *The Religious Factor.* Garden City, New York: Doubleday and Company, Inc.

Macleans
1993   "God is Alive: Canada is a Nation of Believers." April 12, pp. 32–42.

Macleans
1998   "Phipps, Word for Word."December 15, p. 43.

MacIver, R.M. and Charles H. Page
1957   In J. Milton Yinger, Ed., pp. 318–329, *Religion, Society and the Individual.* New York: MacMillan Company.

Mahoney, John
1987   *The Making of Moral Theology: A Study of the Roman Catholic Tradition.* Oxford: Claredon Press.

Malinowski, Bronislaw
1954   *Magic, Science, and Religion and Other Essays.* Garden City, New York: Doubleday Anchor Books.

Mann, W. Edward
1955   *Sect, Cult, and Church in Alberta.* Toronto: University of Toronto Press.

Martin, D. A.
1962   "The Denomination." *The British Journal of Sociology* 13:1–14.

Marx, Karl, and Fredrick Engels
1964   *Marx and Engels on Religion.* New York: Schocken Books.

McGuire, Meredith
1982   *Catholic Pentecostals: Power, Charisma, and Order in a Religious Movement.*
         Philadelphia: Temple University Press.

McGuire, Meredith
1992   *Religion: The Social Context.* Belmont, CA: Wadsworth Publishing Company.

Miner, Horace
1939   *St. Denis: A French-Canadian Parish.* Chicago: The University of Chicago
         Press.

Morgan, S. Philip
1983   "A Research Note on Religion and Morality: Are Religious People Nice Peo-
         ple?" *Social Forces* 61:683–693.

Morioka, Kiyomi and William H. Hewell
1968   *The Sociology of Japanese Religion.* International Studies in Sociology and So-
         cial Anthropology 6. Leiden, Netherlands: Brill.

Morrow, E. Lloyd
1923   *Church Union in Canada.* Toronto: Thomas Allen.

Mott, Paul
1965   *The Organization of Society.* Englewood Cliffs, NJ: Prentice-Hall.

Newport, John
1998   *The New Age Movement and the Biblical Worldview.* Grand Rapids, MI: William
         B. Eerdmans Publishing Company.

Niehbur, H. Richard
1957 [1929]   *The Social Sources of Denominationalism.* New York: World Publishing.

Norbeck, Edward
1961   *Religion in Primitive Society.* New York: Harper and Row.

Nottingham, Elizabeth
1971   *Religion: A Sociological View.* New York: Random House.

O'Connor, Edward
1971   *The Pentecostal Movement in the Catholic Church.* Notre Dame: Ave Maria
         Press.

O'Dea, Thomas and Janet O'Dea
1983   *The Sociology of Religion.* 2nd. Ed. Engelwood Cliffs, NJ: Prentice Hall.

O'Toole, Roger
1996   "Religion in Canada: Its Development and Contemporary Situation." *Social
         Compass* 43: 119–134.

Otto, Rudolph
1958   *The Idea of the Holy.* New York: Oxford University Press. [1923].

Paloutzian, Raymond
1996   *Invitation to the Psychology of Religion.* 2nd. Ed. Boston: Allyn and Bacon.

Paper, Jordon
1989   *Offering Smoke: The Sacred Pipe and Native American Religion.* Edmonton, Alberta: University of Alberta Press.

Piazza, Thomas and Charles Glock
1979   "Images of God and Their Social Meanings." pp. 69–91. In Robert Wuthnow ed., *The Religious Dimension:New Directions in Quantitative Reseach.* New York: Academic Press.

Poloma, Margaret and George Gallup, Jr.
1991   *Varieties of Prayer: A Survey Report.* Philadelphia: Trinity Press, International.

Proudfoot, Wayne
1985   "Attribution Theory and the Psychology of Religion." *Journal for the Scientific Study of Religion* 14, 4:317–330.

Ranaghan, Kevin and Dorothy
1969   *Catholic Pentecostals.* Paramus, New Jersey: Paulist Press.

Roberts, Keith
1990   *Religion in Sociological Perspective.* Belmont, CA: Wadsworth Publishing.

Schleiermacher, Friedrich
1799   *On Religion: Speeches to Its Cultured Despisers.* Trans. Richard Crouter. Cambridge University Press: New York. [1988].

Smith, W. Robertson
1956 [1989]   *The Religion of the Semites.* New York: The Meridian Library.

Spiro, Melford
1982   *Buddhism and Society: A Great Tradition and Its Burmese Vicissitudes.* Berkeley: The University of California Press.

Stark, Rodney, and William Bainbridge
1979   "Of Churches, Sects, and Cults: Preliminary Concepts for a Theory of Religious Movements." *Journal for the Scientific Study of Religion* 18:117–131.

Stark, Rodney and William Bainbridge
1985   *The Future of Religion.* Berkeley: University of California Press.

Sumner, W. G.
1906   *Folkways.* New York: Mentor Books.

Swenson, Don
1989   *Cultural and Structural Factors of Family Attitudes in Roman Catholic Parochial Environments.* PhD Dissertation. Notre Dame: The Department of Sociology, Notre Dame University.

Swenson, Don
1990   "A Charismatic Church: A Cultural Analysis." Annual meeting of the Canadian Sociology and Anthropology Association, May, in Victoria, B.C.

Swenson, Don
1995   "The Religious Bases of Marital Quality: A Study of Ministers and their Spouses." Paper presented in the Religion and Family Section at the annual meeting of the National Council of Family Relations, Portland, Oregon, November.

Swenson, Don
1999   *Society, Spirituality, and the Sacred: A Social Scientific Introduction*. Peterborough, ON: Broadview Press.

Swenson, Don and John Thompson
1986   "Locus theologicus and constructing a sacred past: Charismatic Renewal among Catholics as a movement of renewal." Paper presented at the Annual Meeting of the Canadian Association of Sociology and Anthropology, Winnipeg, Manitoba.

Troeltsch, Ernest
1931   *The Social Teachings of the Christian Churches. Vols I and II*. Translated by O. Wyon. New York: Harper and Row.

Tyler, Edward
1929   *Primitive Culture*. New York: Brentano.

Wach, Joachim
1967   *Sociology of Religion*. Chicago: University Press; Phoenix edition. Originally published in 1944.

Watts, Allan W.
1954   *Myth and Ritual in Christianity*. New York: Thomas and Hudson.

Weisman, Richard
1984   *Witchcraft, Magic, and Religion in 17th-Century Massachusetts*. Amherst: The University of Massachusetts Press.

Westley, Frances
1983   *The Complex Forms of The Religious Life:* A Durkheimian View of New Religious Movements. Chico, California: Scholars Press.

Wuthnow, Robert
1987   *Meaning and Moral Order: Explorations in Cultural Analysis*. Berkeley: The University of California Press.

Weber, Max
1946 [1906]   *From Max Weber: Essays in Sociology*. Edited by H. H. Gerth and C. Wright Mills. New York: Oxford University Press.

Weber, Max
1947   *The Theory of Social and Economic Organization*. by Hans Gerth and Don Martindale. New York: Free Press.

Weber, Max
1958a [1904–1905]   *The Protestant Ethic and the Spirit of Capitalism*. New York: Charles Scribners and Sons.

Weber, Max
1958b [1916] *The Religion of India*. New York: Free Press.

Weber, Max
1978 [1894] *Economy and Society*. Berkeley: University of CA Press.

Yinger, J. Milton
1959   *Religion, Society and the Individual*. New York: MacMillan Company.

Yinger, Milton
1970   *The Scientific Study of Religion*. New York: Macmillan.

Glossary

Aboriginal: native, first in the land mass, original as in aboriginal Canadians consisting of Inuit, Indian and Métis peoples.

Achievement: class mobility based upon personal attributes like hard work and education; a cognate term: achieved status.

Anomie: Durkheim's term for a condition of society in which people become detached, cut loose from the norms that usually guide their behavior.

Ascription: a status in society based upon what you are born with: sex, ethnicity, race and religion; a cognate term: ascribed status.

Authourity: legitimated power of a person over another or a group of people over another.

Back stage: Goffman's term to describe our behaviors that are performed outside of the view of others; where people rest from their performances, discuss their presentations, and plan future front stage performances (see front stage).

Blocked socialization: socialization that is substantially thwarted; typical among institutionalized and feral children.

Bourgeoisie: Marx's term to describe the capitalist class who are dependent upon the proletariat but also exploit them.

Bureaucracy: (from Weber) the type of organization that uses legal/rational authourity; organization by a rigid hierarchy of bureaus, administrators, and petty officials; a body of officials and administrators; excessive multiplication of, and concentration of power in, bureaus or administrators.

Charisma: Weber uses this term in the sociology of religion to describe a person who is extraordinarily gifted; one who has a divine or sacred gift; one who attracts followers because of this charisma.

Charismatic authourity: the authourity of a person who has charisma; one who has authourity to inspire others to obey this person

Church: a moral community of believers; a routinized form of religious organization; with formal religious services; adapted to the social environment.

Class: strata in a society based upon income, prestige, education and occupation.

Cognitive culture: mental culture; ideas, mythologies, world views and ideologies.

Cognitive development: socialization seen from how well the human person matures mentally; the rational development of individuals; a theory by Piaget that focuses on the ability of the child to develop logical thinking.

Common law unions: couples who live together and who have an intimate, sexual relationship without being married.

Communication in marriage: Kurian's term to describe how married couples talk to one another, are open to each other and who are willing to lay bare their deepest concerns.

Conflict theory: a theoretical framework in which society is viewed as composed of groups competing for scarce resources.

Consanguineal: bonds between persons normally found in families that reflect generational blood relations.

Construct: used in methodology to describe an abstract idea that can be used to develop theory; refers to the potential of being able to be measured in the empirical world.

Control variables: a variable that is held constant in an attempt to further clarify the relationship between two other variables (independent and dependent).

Correlation: the simultaneous occurrence of two or more variables; two variables which influence each other without knowing which one causes the other.

Counterculture: a group whose values place its members in opposition to the values of the wider culture.

Counterrevolution: the Canadian colonies response to the American and French revolutions by not only apposing these revolutions but of instilling measures in state and economic matters to adhere to the traditional British way of life.

Crime: deviance from the law.

Cult: a belief system which is deviant from the traditional religious doctrines of the host society; members tend to blend non-traditional with traditional tenets that make it a syncretic; there is a special accent on the individual who becomes almost sacred; this emphasis on the individual leaves the association thus formed in a loose, informal, organizational structure; finally, the cult stands in a high tension relationship with the external environment.

Cultural lag: where the rate of technical change surpasses the culture's ability to develop the moral and legal institutions to accommodate and manage the change.

Cultural relativism: understanding a people from the framework of its own culture; all cultural practices should be judged in their terms, not ours.

Cultural transmission: the transformation of one's culture to another.

Culturally competent: describing the need of all adult members of a society to learn the culture of the same society in order to function well; in modern societies, this is the goal of educational institutions.

Culture: the way of life of a group of people, a complex of shared concepts and patterns of learned behaviour that are handed down from one generation to the next through the means of language and imitation; it is learned, shared, transmitted, cumulative, and human.

Culture shock: happens when a person encounters cultural practices that are vastly different from their own and they become disoriented and bewildered.

Counter culture: a sub-culture against the socieita wide culture.

Demography: the social scientific study of a society's people: it includes topics like birth and mortality rates, migration rates, marriage rates, divorce rates.

Denomination: a type of religious organization that is adapted best to a democracy; it accents pragmatism, democracy, freedom of choice.

Deprofessionlization: the erosion of autonomy and monopolistic privileges of the professions.

Deskilling: the process of breaking down a skill into its component parts with the intent of paying a worker less for labour related to that component.

Deviance: variation from a social norm.

Discrimination: action that excludes all members of a group from certain rights, opportunities or privileges; it may involve *ethnopaulisms* that are derogatory terms or slurs such as "honkie," "nigger," or "Injun."

Division of labour: the process in modern societies whereby more and more different kinds of work are required to meet the needs of a complex society.

Divorce: an official declaration by a state that a marriage has dissolved.

Emergent ethnicity: a people who have a recognizable culture, are aware of themselves as a unit, are recognized as a unit by outsiders, interact with other groups members, and feel a sense of obligation to defend and support one another; not perceived as clinging to old loyalties or resisting change but, rather, a product of both the contemporary situation with which the ethnic group must deal and cultural continuity from the past.

Empirical: information garnished from observations of the visible world about us.

English Great Rebellion: the Puritan revolt against the monarchy of England that happened between 1640 and 1650; it introduced more of a parliamentary system with a wider range of representation by the people.

Enlightenment: The dominant philosophy during the 17th and 18th centuries that focused on science, rationalism, secularism, and an optimism of progress.

Ethnicity: a shared cultural heritage.

Ethos: an element of culture; a system of values, attitudes, mores, laws and codes.

Ethnocentrism: the practice of judging another culture by the standards of one's own culture.

Ethnopaulisms: derogatory terms or slurs such as "honkie," "nigger," or "Injun."

Eugenics movement: a movement built on a science concerned with improving a breed or species, especially the human species, by such means as influencing or encouraging reproduction by persons presumed to have desirable genetic traits.

Evolutionary psychology: similar to sociobiology except that the subject matter is the individual person.

Experiment: a research method for investigating cause and effect under highly controlled conditions.

Exploitation: from the sociology of Marx wherein it is argued that the bourgeoisie take from the proletariat a value of their labour that the proletariat should have for themselves.

Expressive abilities: in family and the study of intimate relations that accents nurture, care, emotion, and love.

Family: a group of intimate persons who are bound together by procreative, consanguineal, sexual, emotional and economic ties that, typically, include children who are socialized into being socially competent and who all live in a common residence.

Family violence: a range of negative behaviors including emotional, physical and sexual abuse inflicted on family members.

Fasciandus: from the work of the philosopher of religion who uses it to describe that part of the sacred which reflects the attraction of the believer to the holy.

Feminism: the study of women that includes the advocacy of gender equality between men and women ranging from the most intimate (as in families) to the most public (as in economy and politics).

Fieldwork: the kind of social scientific research which involves the researcher living among a people and observing them in their most natural of settings.

First Nations Movement: A movement among the First Nations peoples towards sovereignty over many of their institutions and ways of life.

Folkways: behavioral codes among a people that are flexible and malleable according to a wide variety of tastes. An example would be dress codes.

French Revolution: The revolution in France that began in 1789 that culminated in the demise of the monarchy, the secularization of the Roman Catholic Church, and the beginnings of democracy in that state.

Front stage: Erving Goffman's term to describe the kind of behavior that we present to others that is governed by the roles we fulfill; where the performances are given in front of others who are considered an audience.

Functional definition of ethos: what religious ethos does or what its social effects are.

Functional definition of myth: what myth does in people's lives and how it affects institutions and whole societies.

Functional definition of religion: what the effects of religion are.

Functional definition of ritual: the effects and consequences of ritual to people and to societies.

Gender: the cultural and social construction of sex.

Generalized other: George Herbert Mead's term to indicate the norms, values, attitudes, and expectations of others "in general." It is an important stage in the development of a child as she or he relates to society as a whole.

Hamlite Rationalization: A misreading of a Jewish biblical text from Genesis (9:22–25) wherein Noah curses one of his sons (Ham) because he saw him naked. This was taken up by some Christians who thought that Ham was the ancestor of the African peoples and were thus cursed.

Hawthorne effect: From the social research tradition wherein the presence of the researcher significantly influences the people he is observing and thus contaminates the results.

Hidden curriculum: the unseen and unwritten codes of schools that socializes children beyond what is explicitly taught.

High culture: culture of the rich and the powerful.

Historical methods: methods in research used by investigators who study historical records like newspapers, church records, letters, diaries, and autobiographies in order to reconstruct the social life of people of previous generations.

Hypothesis: a proposition that is specific enough to be tested with empirical data.

Ideology: in culture a system of ideas; a more specific meaning is the system of ideas that a group of people use to control others.

Individual discrimination: action taken by an individual against a member or members of a group.

Industrial Revolution: a process of economic change that began in England about 1775 that included large factories, steam engine power, wage labour and mass production of commodities.

Industrialization: the results of the industrial revolution.

Institutional racism: overt discrimination that has become legitimized, either as custom or as part of a legal system.

Instrumental abilities: in intimate and familial relationships that accent a bond based on a goal or a purpose.

Intermarriage: marriage between persons of different religions, races or ethnic groups.

Internal colony: A nation state taking part of its territory and designating it as an area wherein people of different racial or ethnic backgrounds are to live; an example is the Aboriginal Peoples' reservation.

Labour force: those persons in a modern society who are currently or potentially working for a salary or a wage.

Labour markets: the economic arenas in which employers seek to purchase labour from potentially qualified employees who themselves are seeking employment, suitable to their present education, experiences, and preferences.

Laws: norms which have been legislated by a state.

Legal/rational authourity: is present when the mechanism of influence is contained in a position or an office; these people with this kind of authourity use legal and rational means to influence others.

Liberal feminism: generally considered to be the more moderate feminism based on the preposition that all peoples are created equal and should not be denied equality of opportunity because of gender.

Life chances: chances that individuals experience in their hopes and dreams for a successful life especially in their career and work aspirations.

Looking-glass self: Charles Cooley's term to describe social action wherein others become mirrors of us so that we learn from them who we are.

Manifest Destiny an ostensibly benevolent or necessary policy of imperialistic expansion.

Marital power: the emotional, physical, financial ability of a married person to influence his or her spouse.

Marital roles: a set of specific rights and obligations that a married person has in relationship to his or her spouse.

Marital satisfaction: a measure of the global well being of married persons that includes sexual, emotional, financial and intimate satisfaction.

Marriage: in most societies as at least one woman and one man who have established an approved relationship and who maintain a common residence.

Material culture: the physical output of human labour and expression.

Medicalization of problems with living: defining social or physical problems as medical problems and thereby including the health care system in order to meet these problems. An example is that in the United States in the 19th century, child birth was defined as a medical issue rather than a normal part of familial life. In effect, this eliminated the need for midwives.

Mercantilism: an economic theory which proposed the following: that the mother country was entitled to accumulate wealth in any form and that it was entitled to exploit its colonies as a source of raw materials and a market for finished products, thereby maintaining a favourable balance of trade for the mother country.

Merchant class: the social class that emerged in Western Europe about the time of the age of discovery and the European exploitation of Africa, the Americas, and Asia; this class functioned as middle men who purchased the products from these lands and, in turn, sold them to Europeans; in doing so they incurred many profits.

Methodology: the whole scientific process of gathering data, analyzing them, and making the results known to the public.

Moral entrepreneur: those who act like economic entrepreneurs and try to "sell" or influence others regarding moral standards; an example would be the Catholic Pope who frequently speaks out on moral issues like abortion, euthanasia or the death penalty; another example would be feminists who appose pornography.

Mores: standards which members of a society consider to be an obligation.

Movement of Renewal: a type of religious organization that is a protest from within an existing church that does not involve a secession or a schism but, rather, a desire and mobilization to change the tone, the emptiness, the routinized charisma of the church through a renewal of a tradition; in it, members strive hard to maintain connections with the authorities of the church; an example would be the monastic movement within Catholicism.

Multiculturalism: social policy planned to create ethnic or cultural heterogeneity.

Mysterium Tremendum: from the work of the philosopher of religion, Otto, who uses it to describe that part of the sacred which reflects awe and distance of the believer to the holy.

Mythology: a system of beliefs; a system of myths that describe breakthroughs of the sacred or the holy into the world; it is this sudden breakthrough of the sacred that really establishes the world and makes it what it is today; it is a result of the intervention of the holy that humans make themselves what they are.

Narrative factors: the way the media presents news

Native: term to describe the indigenous peoples of North America; alternative terms may include: aboriginal, First Nations, Amerindian, Indian (however, there is a strong reaction against using the term "Indian" as it was a term given by Columbus because he thought when he came to the Caribbean islands he thought he had reached India).

New eugenics movement: made possible through screening techniques and fetal diagnostic technologies to determine various kinds of disorders like Downs Syndrome.

Noblesse oblige: the moral obligation of the rich or highborn to display honorable and generous conduct

Non-material culture: a vast array of values, norms, folkways, and mores.

Norm violation: deviance from a norm.

Normative culture: that dimension of culture which includes codes of behaviour like values, attitudes, norms and mores.

Norms: social expectations of others that impact our behaviour.

Occupational segregation: from gender studies that refer to the practice of segregating women into predominantly female places of work (like nursing or elementary teaching) and men into predominately male places of work (like construction and mining).

Operationalization: from social methodology; it is the process of specifying how a construct can be measured.

Patriarchy: from the Latin and Greek words that mean, literally, "the rule by the Father"; in current diction it means an institution, organization or a society in which power is held by and transferred through males.

Pattern variables: from the work of Talcott Parsons and Seymour Lipset which illustrates cultural value patterns in modern societies.

Physical availability: from family studies; the term illustrates the physical availability of persons in intimate relationships.

Political economy: a concept emerging from the work of Karl Marx and conflict theorists; it refers to the union of politics and economics from the capitalistic perspective; it indicates the integral union of the two institutions in modern societies.

Popular culture: culture of the majority of members of a society.

Post-industrial: a modern economy based upon information, service, and knowledge; most advanced capitalist nation states are post-industrial.

Post-positivism: science that focuses upon social models that are not rooted in empirical data sources; an era wherein sociologists use methods other than surveys and censuses to gather their data; close to qualitative research.

Prejudice: based on a fixed mental image of some group or class of people and applied to all individuals of that class without being tested against reality; it involves thoughts, attitudes, beliefs, and emotions but not actions.

Primary sector: in modern economies, the sector that focuses on primary production of commodities like oil, grain, forestry, fish.

Primordial Ethnicity: ties that bind a people together stemming from common blood, religion, language, attachment to a place or customs; an ascribed status.

Principal of deterrence: a practice to encourage conformity to laws by inflicting punishment on the offender.

Profession: being reserved to those occupations which have exclusive jurisdiction over certain kinds of services, are able to negotiate freedom from external intervention and have control over the content of their work.

Proletariat: in Marxist class analysis those people who are wage earners and depend upon the bourgeoisie for employment.

Proletarianization: professions are losing control over the conditions of work and are experiencing a serious reduction in compensation.

Proposition: in sociological theory, a generic statement positing a relationship between two or more constructs.

Protestant Reformation: an important initial process that initiated the early modern period; the reform of Christianity that resulted in a succession from the Roman Catholic Church; the religious change that resulted, according to Weber, in changes in the economic system of Europe from a traditional economy to a capitalist economy.

Psychoanalytic: a systematic structure of theories concerning the relation of conscious and unconscious psychological processes; the origins are in Freud's theories of personality.

Psychological availability: in familial and intimate relationships; the range of availability of a person to another psychologically or emotionally.

Punishment: a penalty inflicted for an offense, fault or a crime committed.

Qualitative research: investigation by which a researcher gathers impressionistic, not numerical data.

Quantitative research: investigation whereby a researcher collects numerical data.

Quiet Revolution: a period during the 1960s in Quebec which was one of rapid change from a traditional, rural, conservative and Catholic society to favor an ethic of Rattrapage, catching up, with social, political, and economic development in the rest of Canada and the Western world.

Race: a classificatory term like kind, type, breed or stock; in Winick (1970), race is given a biological basis with distinctive, hereditary, transmissible physical characteristics as Negroid, Causcasoid and Mongoloid; many anthropologists and sociologists are more prone to dismiss the concept of race as a viable term and replace it with ethnic groups.

Racialism: the ideology of racism.

Racism: a belief that humans are subdivided into distinct hereditary groups that are innately different in social behaviour and mental capacities; that some groups are superior or inferior to others.

Radical feminism: that gender inequality is rooted in all of the social institutions of modern society and that it is patriarchy and not capitalism which is the root of the problem.

Random sample: in sociological research wherein a sample in which everyone in the target population has the same chance of being included in the study.

Regionalism: a concept that describes a people's tendency to identify with their region of residence and with those who live there with them; this identification may in turn lead them to 'think differently' about certain things than residents of other regions; in time, this regionally distinctive set of attitudes and values may lead them to behave differently as well.

Religion: the individual and communal experience of the sacred expressed in myths, rituals, ethos and integrated into a social collective or institution.

Religious organization: a cluster or a complex of ranked roles that are, in turn a cluster or a complex of norms that are routinized elements of charismatic or affective social action that is focussed on creating relationships of an individual to the divine, the cosmos, nature, others and oneself.

Religious experience: the feelings, acts, and experiences of people both privately and socially in so far as they apprehend themselves to stand in relation to whatever they may consider to be sacred.

Research process: a process in sociological methodology which involves the exploration of, description of, and explanation of social data.

Resocialization: radically altering an inmate's personality through deliberate manipulation of the environment.

Ritual: Ritual is repeated consecrated (sacred) behaviour that is a symbolic expression of the moods and motivations of religious participants and unseen powers. Ritual forms a bond of friendship, community and unity with the believer and her/his god. Finally, ritual transports the participant into another world (the world above) wherein there is peace and harmony.

Role-taking: the process of becoming socialized into a social group, a culture, or a society that involves the taking of the role of others.

Routinization of charisma: Weber's term to describe a process that frequently happens within religious organizations; it includes the charisma of the original founder or founders becoming routine, ordinary, even profane.

Sacred: also called the holy; the term from Durkheim and Otto that specifies the religious object as separate from and removed from the profane; see *mysterium tremendum* and *fascinadus*.

Sauvage: uncivilized, unsophisticated, natural and inferior being.

Secondary sector: work in construction and manufacturing.

Sect: a type of religious organization that stands apart from the larger society.

Sex: the biological characteristic of being male or female.

Sexism: the belief that one sex is innately superior to the other.

Significant other: an individual who significantly influences someone else's life.

Social action: human action that assumes that persons are free agents who, in their relationships with others, attach a subjective meaning to their behaviour and take into account the behaviour of others.

Social competency: the ability that a person has to relate well to others.

Social desirability: the tendency in social scientific research for the subject not to be honest with a researcher and to give what she or he would want to hear.

Social structure: every way of acting, fixed or not, capable of exercising on the individual an external constraint; or again, every way of acting which is general throughout a given society, while at the same time existing in its own right independent of its individual manifestations.

Socialist feminism: the understanding that gender inequality is rooted in the patriarchal, capitalistic relationships of power that are firmly held by men.

Socialization: the process by which people learn the characteristics of their group—the attitudes, values, and actions thought appropriate for them.

Sociobiology: a framework of thought that views human social behavior as the result of natural selection and considers biological characteristics to be a cause of this behavior.

Sociological theory: theory designed to offer explanations for social action, group behavior and societies.

Sociological imagination: C. W. Wright's term to describe human social action in terms of individual biography, social structure, culture and history.

Sociology: the science of the social group that ranges from a dyad of two persons to whole societies and accents understanding social action and social structure.

Sociology of medicine and health care: the study of both individual and institutional definitions of, and responses to, illness and injury.

Sociology of health and illness: the study of both individual and institutional definitions of, and responses to, illness and injury.

Statistics: a mathematical method used to analyze social data that is numeric in nature; a statistic refers to a characteristic of a sample of a population.

Status conflict: when one status that you have is in conflict with another that you fill.

Status set: the several statuses that one person fills at any given moment.

Stereotype: a cognitive structure that helps individuals to process information about the environment without reasoning about that information.

Structural functionalism: a framework for creating theory that envisions society as a complex system whose parts work together to promote solidarity and stability.

Structural discrimination: covert, unintentional discrimination that exists because of the structure of society and societal institutions.

Subculture: the values and related social action of a social group that distinguishes its members from the larger culture.

Substantive definition of ethos: what ethos is; the living out in everyday life the experience of the holy or the sacred.

Substantive definition of myth: what myth is; the stories of the sacred being manifested in human conditions and various situations.

Substantive definition of religion: what religion is in itself; the core of religion is the experience of the sacred, both personally and socially.

Substantive definition of ritual: what ritual is; the reliving of the experience of the holy or the sacred.

Survey: the collection of data by having subjects answer a series of questions related to their social lives.

Symbolic interactionism: a theoretical orientation in which society is seen as composed of symbols that individuals use to create meaning, establish their world views, and inter-relate with one another.

Taboos: a norm so strong that it brings with it a revulsion if so disobeyed.

Technology: the tools and skills used in the process of work.

Tertiary sector: work in transportation, communications, commerce, finance, health, and education.

Traditional authourity: is present when an individual is granted influence because of his/her lineage, descent, or what has been "proven" to be good or true from the past.

Unemployment rate: the number of individuals out of work and who are actively seeking work divided by the total number of labour force participants (including the unemployed).

Variable: a construct that is measured numerically; a construct whose value changes from case to case.

White collar crime: crimes like computer illegal access, stock market frauds, real estate fraud, lawyers embezzlement, and medical malpractice.

Work: continuous employment in the production of goods and services for remuneration.

Work satisfaction: the enjoyment or pleasure one receives from labour.

World view: a life orientation; a personal reflection on what a person believes about him or herself, others, society, the world, the cosmos and the sacred.

Index

liberal feminism, 161, 171–172
life chances, 89, 105, 114, 118, 122–123, 175
Lipset, Seymour, 49–54
Lombroso, Cesare, 187
looking-glass self, 69, 71, 77, 96

marital power, 251–252
marital roles, 238, 251, 254
marital satisfaction, 238, 254–255
marriage, 32, 24, 40–43, 84, 237–266, 281
Marx, Karl, ix, x, 3–4, 7–8, 10–15, 17–22, 105, 111–115, 124, 169, 193, 212, 227–228, 307, 309, 312, 346, 351
material culture, 41
Mead, George H., 17, 22, 69, 72, 74, 96
medicalization of problems with living, 288
merchant class, 7, 8
Merton, Robert, 16–18, 21, 29, 190, 210, 227
methodology, 27
Mills, C. W., 25
mores, 41, 43, 359
movement of renewal, 365, 373–374, 376
multiculturalism, ix, 54
mysterium tremendum, 347
mythology, 210, 349, 351–353, 363, 372–373, 385

narrative factors, 45
Native, x, 51–53, 55
Niehbur, H. Richard, 382
Nisbet, Robert, ix, 5, 8,
Noblesse oblige, 50
non-material culture, 41
norm violation, 186, 191
norms, 42, 72–73, 84, 88–90, 97, 165, 185, 190–192

O'Dea, Thomas and Janet O'Dea, 357, 373, 380
occupational segregation, 330
operationalization, 33
Otto, Rudolph, 346–348, 350

Parsons, Talcott, ix, 16–20, 22, 51, 55, 80, 84
patriarchy, 19, 164, 166–167, 173–174
pattern variables, 51–54
physical availability, 246
Piaget, Jean, 64–67, 73–74, 95, 189
political economy, 15–16, 19
popular culture, 42
Porter, John, 21, 30
post-industrial, 9, 22, 261, 314
post-positivism, 9
prejudice, 132–136, 195, 201
primary sector, 313–314, 318–319, 337
principal of deterrence, 211
profession, 94, 196, 254–256, 281, 285–288, 293, 300, 324, 331, 334, 338
proletariat, 8, 11–12, 28–29, 33, 65, 111, 113, 124, 171
proposition, 246
Protestant Reformation, 6, 7, 22
psychoanalytic, 68, 70, 95–96, 188, 189
psychological availability, 246
punishment, 67, 95, 189, 191–192, 198–200, 202, 207, 209–214, 221–223, 225, 228, 230–231

qualitative research, 29, 52–53
quantitative research, 29, 52–53

race, 88, 103, 114, 116, 119, 122–124, 127–135
racism, 127–128, 132–140, 142–145, 149–152, 168
radical feminism, 161, 170, 172–173
random sample, 33
Ravelli, Bruce, 1, 39
regionalism, 1

religion, 5–7, 10, 13–14, 19, 28, 32, 40, 76, 128, 145, 149, 165, 175, 185, 196, 210, 202, 237–238, 246, 250, 345–381

religious experience, 346–349, 359–360, 381

religious organization, 345, 363, 365, 368–370, 373–374, 376

research process, 27

resocialization, 75–76, 210

ritual, 13, 238, 345–346, 349, 351–352, 354–363, 365, 368–369, 371, 377

role-taking, 69

routinization of charisma, 349, 365, 370, 373–374, 376

sacred, 238, 345–357, 360–363, 365, 369–371, 373–374, 377–378, 380

secondary sector, 313–314, 318–319, 337

sect, 365–368, 374, 376, 378–379

sex, 41–42, 91–92, 110, 113, 119–120, 122, 124, 130, 145, 153, 161, 165, 168–169, 172, 201, 214, 216–217, 238, 240–243, 250–251, 254–255, 259–261, 317, 320, 329, 359

sexism, 88

significant other, 70, 72, 92, 251, 331

Skinner, B. F., 189

Smith, Dorothy, 9, 21

social action, 3, 4, 11–12, 48

social desirability, 34

social structure, 3–4, 12–17, 19, 21, 51, 63, 138, 147, 162, 269, 169, 172–173, 185, 209, 226–227, 247, 271, 282–283, 305

socialist feminism, 161, 170

socialization, 1, 16–17, 20, 47, 63–64, 69–70, 72–83, 85–90, 92–97, 165, 168–169, 171, 173, 175–176, 182, 191–192, 198, 237, 251, 256, 291, 317, 329, 338, 346, 350, 354, 356, 362, 367

sociobiology, 46

sociological imagination, 1, 3

sociological theory, 168

sociology, 1–22, 27, 31, 39, 42, 47, 50–51, 55, 69, 89, 113–114, 137, 145, 153, 161, 163–164, 167, 170, 185, 189, 192, 210, 218, 226, 229, 238, 259, 271, 278, 298–303, 305–306, 327, 338–339, 345–346, 351, 359, 374, 376, 378, 380

sociology of health and illness, 271–272

sociology of medicine and health care, 271, 278–279

statistics, 35, 87, 208, 214, 219, 222, 225, 240, 243, 245–246, 252–253, 257–263, 265, 272–275, 297–304, 314, 337

status conflict, 47

status set, 47

stereotypes, 87, 92, 120, 134, 152, 165, 175, 195, 210, 224

structural functionalism, ix, 10, 15–16, 18–19, 21–22, 29, 191

subculture, 43, 86, 88, 93, 95, 97, 192, 227

substantive definition of ethos, 359–361

substantive definition of myth, 349

substantive definition of religion, 364

substantive definition of ritual, 353

survey, 9, 15, 33, 154, 226–227, 245, 253, 259, 261, 319, 336,

Sutherland, Edwin, 192

symbolic interactionism, 15–18, 20–22, 29, 168

taboos, 45, 363

technology, 9, 14, 18, 75, 286, 307–308, 310–311, 318, 322–327, 334, 336, 338, 372, 377

tertiary sector, 314, 316, 319, 330, 337

traditional authourity, 48

unemployment rate, 320

variable, 28–33, 146, 148–149, 152,
185, 224, 227

Weber, Max, ix, 3, 6, 10, 13–15, 19–22,
28, 30, 32, 51–54, 105, 112, 114,
193, 347–349, 352, 363–365,
376–381

White-collar crime, 228, 230
Wilson, Edward, 46
work satisfaction, 335–336, 339
world view, 39, 185, 345–346, 349,
352, 360
Wright, Erik-Olin, 105, 114–115
Wuthnow, Robert, 356, 359